Views Beyond the
Border Country

Critical Social Thought

Series editor: Michael W. Apple
Professor of Curriculum and Instruction and Educational Policy
Studies. University of Wisconsin-Madison

Already published

Views Beyond the Border Country

Raymond Williams and
Cultural Politics

Edited by
DENNIS L. DWORKIN and
LESLIE G. ROMAN

ROUTLEDGE
New York and London

Published in 1993 by

Routledge
An imprint of Routledge, Chapman and Hall, Inc.
29 West 35th Street
New York, NY 10001

Published in Great Britain by

Routledge
11 New Fetter Lane
London EC4P 4EE

Library of Congress Cataloging in Publication Data

Views beyond the border country : Raymond Williams and cultural
    politics / edited by Dennis Dworkin and Leslie G. Roman.
        p.   cm. — (Critical social thought)
    Includes bibliographical references and index.
    ISBN 0-415-90275-4 (HB) — ISBN 0-415-90276-2 (PB)
    1. Williams, Raymond—Political and social views. 2. Williams,
Raymond. Border country. 3. Social problems in literature.
4. Literature and society. 5. Politics and culture. I. Dworkin,
Dennis, 1951–   . II. Roman, Leslie G. III. Series.
PR6073.I4329Z93   1993
828'.91409—dc20   92-11709
                                                      CIP

ISBN 0-415-90275-4 HB
ISBN 0-415-90276-2 PB

Contents

Contents

Series Editor's Introduction

Michael W. Apple

I begin writing my introduction to this volume on Raymond Williams with a desk piled high with his own books and essays. In preparation, I have taken them off of the shelf. It's quite a long shelf. I start to read not in the order in which they were written, but almost at random. Soon I am reading more than my many underlinings and notations in the margins, but reading entire passages, chapters, essays again.

What is remarkable is that while some of his arguments were and are not always totally correct, so much of his corpus continues to have the capacity to illuminate, in striking ways, the cultural, political, and economic relations in which we live. As I reread even his earlier work from the fifties and sixties, the acuteness of his observations, both theoretical and political, is often even more apparent today.

I must continue to speak personally here for a moment. In the mid–1970s, when I was engaged in writing what ultimately became a series of books including *Ideology and Curriculum*, *Education and Power*, and *Teachers and Texts*,[1] I was struggling with a number of issues. Among the most important of them was how to think through the relationship between culture and power. More particularly, how could I understand the complicated connections between what counts as official knowledge in our cultural and educational institutions and those groups who are culturally, economically, and/or politically dominant? Just as critically, how could this be analyzed in a non-reductive way, without sacrificing the "relative autonomy" of culture?

Reading Williams at that time was not simply significant. Indeed, this word doesn't begin to capture the effect his work had not only on me, but on an entire generation of individuals engaged in similar work in so many fields.

It is perhaps important to mention one other rather personal thing. Having grown up in a working-class family in a dying industrial city on the East Coast of the United States, I found in Williams so much more. Even though his work may have had possible flaws and contradictions, what gave his writing much of its power for me was not only the writing itself, but the *life* that stood behind it. This was a life I understood, one that as a writer, political and educational activist, and union leader, I had practiced myself. I am certain that I am not alone in this regard.

In his introduction to a volume of Williams's essays, Robin Blackburn notes that what set Williams apart was "his rare combination of integrity and boldness, originality and scholarship."[2] In his theoretical work, his textual analyses, and his novels, one of the most crucial areas he consistently focused upon was the complex ways culture is produced and reproduced. Notice the two words—*produce* and *reproduce*. For Williams was just as concerned with the historical, current, and future possibilities of a truly democratic set of human arrangements as he was with the ways existing arrangements denied us the values we most prize.

When Raymond Williams died in 1988, he was considered "the most authoritative, consistent and original socialist thinker in the English-speaking world."[3] Blackburn is not overstating when he says that:

> Williams approached literature, cultural studies, communications, and adult education in such radically new ways that he revolutionized their study and practice. While this cultural work was linked to his conception of a democratic "long revolution," its validity and importance were nevertheless recognized by many who had no prior commitment to his anti-capitalist politics. Similarly Williams's drama and novels explore profoundly political themes but, like all his writing, are couched in a language far removed from received political discourse. Part of the value of Williams's work to the Left is that it does not belong to the Left alone.[4]

Yet, the fact that Williams's work "does not belong to the Left alone" does not detract from one's recognition that it was always grounded in a vision of a radically transformed and more democratic social order. He was continually and directly involved in political interventions and those "experiences and commitments helped inform his major critical studies."[5]

In *The German Ideology*, Marx articulates one of his most famous claims. Paraphrased, it reads in essence that "The ruling class will give its ideas the form of universality and represent them as the only rational universally valid one."[6] While there have been interpreters of this point who have chosen to see this process as a conscious conspiracy, for Marx it was considerably more complicated. For him, out of the constitutive power relations, conflicts, and contradictions of capitalism there were specific tendencies generated. Among these tendencies was the "natural" production of principles, ideas, and categories that support the unequal class relations of that social formation. These ideas were under constant threat, however. They needed constant attention because hegemonic control was not guaranteed. Because of the class conflicts also generated out of, and causing, changes in that mode of production, there always existed the possibility of different ideological tendencies that could subvert the dominant ones.

In some accounts, this "subversion" followed naturally. It simply came about in much the same way as the laws of history determined (in the strong sense of that term) the linear progression of development from capitalism to socialism to communism.[7] Culture and ideology are as predictable as the stages of economic organization.

All of this rests on what we might call the "automaticity thesis" within traditional Marxist theory. This assumes that somehow—automatically—as conditions worsen within capitalist economies, the working class will rise. Since they have no vested interests in society as it currently exists, they will see through the veneer of ruling class ideologies and develop a "true understanding" of the exploitative relations in which they are caught. Revolution is inevitable, especially in industrialized nations with large proletarian populations.

Yet these predicted revolutions didn't occur, or at least did not occur how and where they were supposed to. Among the major explanations for these "non-events" are those that see that capitalism is not only an economic system but a cultural system, a "whole way of life," as well. It goes to the very heart of a people's common sense, so that they see the existing world as the world "tout court," the only world. Capitalism becomes hegemonic. It creates what Williams, in essence following Gramsci's lead, called an "effective dominant culture."[8] As Gramsci himself recognized in his arguments against economistic Marxism, winning popular consent is essential under capitalism. This requires dominant groups to attain leadership on a variety of fronts in a social formation. Cultural struggles and conflicts, the battles (if you will forgive the somewhat militaristic and masculinist metaphor) over common sense, are not epiphenomenal, but real and crucial in the maintenance or subversion of hegemony.

The questioning of the automaticity thesis has been profound. It has led to a search for alternative explanations, ones that are less class-reductionist, economistic, and functionalist. Whereas before, nearly everything was explained by the natural working out of the power relations, conflicts, and contradictions at the economic level, it became much clearer that in order to understand the realities of capitalism's continuing power it was essential not only to focus on how economic relations were reproduced. The cultural, ideological, and political took center stage as well.

What institutions, what forms of life, play an important role here? As Marx himself recognized, the family, the state, and cultural institutions, including the press and other mass media, the arts and literature, all need to be examined. The Marxist legacy may often have been relatively reductive in its analyses of these things—with its class and economic determinism, its tragic inability to take patriarchal and racial formations as truly seriously as they deserve, its lack of coherent focus, until relatively recently, on language, popular culture, and the politics of the body and pleasure[9]—but it became all too clear that one had to take relations and resources outside the economy very seriously if one was to understand how domination worked.

Few people have been as important to our understanding of this as Raymond Williams. For him, culture (itself a complex historical concept) can never be epiphenomenal. It has its own materiality, its own history, its own specificities that can never be understood in a reductive manner, though the Marxist and neo-Marxist traditions increasingly for him offered the tools to engage in a more subtle analysis of all this when they were reconstructed.[10] Williams's treatment of hegemonic culture, literature, language, and cultural production in, for example, *Marxism and Literature* demonstrates his major contributions to our thinking about these issues.[11]

As Dworkin and Roman remind us, Williams's starting point in much of his work is simple (not simplistic). "Culture is ordinary. That is the first fact."[12] From these beginnings, a cultural politics is added. "What kind of life can it be, I wonder, to produce this extraordinary fussiness, this extraordinary decision to call certain things culture and then separate them, as with a park wall, from ordinary people and ordinary work?"[13] It is this connection between culture, politics, and "ordinary" life both as possibility and limitation that provides the problematic that guided a good deal of his efforts over the years.

The current importance of his work is nowhere more evident than in the attempts by neoconservatives and the Right to return us to an utterly romanticized version of a "common culture." In opposition to those who—like Allan Bloom and E.D. Hirsch, currently—seek to preordain a common culture that we must all learn if we are to be "culturally literate,"[14] Williams articulates a strikingly different position:

> [A] common culture is not the general extension of what a minority mean and believe, but the creation of a condition in which the people as a whole participate in the articulation of meanings and values, and in the consequent decisions between this meaning and that, this value and that. This would involve, in any real world, the removal of all the material obstacles to just this form of participation.[15]

As the essays in this volume show, Williams's own position on this and on other issues of culture and politics may still be partly insufficient—especially in terms of gender, race, and imperialism—but there can be no doubt that engaging with his writing and arguments is something that can change oneself in important ways on the major issues of cultural politics confronting all of us.

We can best show respect for people upon whose shoulders we stand by taking their work utterly seriously. That is, rather than simply offering an exercise in panegyrics, our task is to rigorously interrogate the work of individuals such as Raymond Williams, refine and extend it, use it, and, if necessary, criticize it for its silences. It is this combination of explanation, refinement, extension, and criticism that this volume takes as its task.

What Dworkin and Roman accomplish is clear in their own words. "We see this volume as a means of making better known the scope of [Williams's] achievements, conveying his political vision and commitments, and exploring the implications of his practice." (p. 1) This is not to be uncritical, however. The entire volume is what might best be called an "appreciative critique." And it is an appreciative critique that enables the reader to come to grips with an individual who justly earned the respect in which he is held.

It would be usual in a Series Editor's Introduction to stop here, but it is wise, I think, to give the last word to Williams himself. Throughout all his theoretical and political labors, Williams was what might be called an optimist without illusions. Yet, for him, one of the most important elements in our struggles against exploitation and domination in all of their many forms was "the difficult business of gaining confidence in *our own* energies and capacities."[16] As he put it:

> It is only in a shared belief and insistence that there are practical alternatives that the balance of forces and chances begins to alter. Once the inevitabilities are challenged, we begin gathering our resources for a journey of hope. If there are no easy answers there are still available and discoverable hard answers, and it is these that we can learn to make and share. This has been, from the beginning, the sense and impulse of the long revolution.[17]

Views Beyond the Border Country makes us more able to use and extend many of the resources that Williams made available to us to continue that long revolution.

Michael W. Apple
The University of Wisconsin, Madison

Introduction:
The Cultural Politics of Location

*Dennis L. Dworkin and Leslie G. Roman**

This book of essays honors the life and thought of Raymond Williams, one of the most important socialist thinkers of the postwar era. The thought of Williams has inspired and stimulated radical intellectuals engaged in cultural politics throughout the world, and has influenced many academic disciplines, including history, literature, cultural studies, mass communications, and education. Equally important, Williams is one of those rare intellectuals who, although committed to radical democratic politics and the building of a socialist culture, has been able to speak to audiences beyond the academy. His writing remains widely accessible, rarely straying far from ordinary speech. Unlike so many radical intellectuals who, regrettably, are content to write for other academics, Williams often wrote for general readers in such publications as *The Guardian*, *The London Review of Books*, *Monthly Review*, *The New Statesman*, *The New York Review of Books*, *The Times Literary Supplement*, and *Tribune*, one of the major voices of the Labor Left.

Though the loss of Williams has been generously acknowledged by the British Left, his thought has been insufficiently examined in the United States, in part because that country has historically lacked an effective socialist tradition.[1] We see this volume as a means of making better known the scope of his achievements, conveying his political vision and commitments, and exploring the implications of his practice.

We did not know Williams personally, but like so many others who

---

*Dworkin and Roman shared equally both the editing of the volume and the writing of the introduction; the order of our names is merely alphabetical.

have read his work over the years, we are deeply moved by the loss of such a powerful and generous spokesperson for new social movements. In his 1989 Raymond Williams Memorial Lecture, Edward Said reminds us that Williams is the twentieth century critic who is the most

> organically grounded . . . in the profound and sustaining rhythms of human life. And as the actual date of his death slowly recedes one finds oneself taking stock of what in the solid foundations of social life his work depends on so finely, so scrupulously, so resolutely. Who more than he rooted his observations and analyses of English literature in the actual lived life not just of poets, novelists and dramatists but of city and country folk, workers, families, peasants, gentry, young people, adventurers, pamphleteers, teachers, children, technicians, policemen [policepeople], and bureaucrats? And who more than Williams nourished his literary work with the generative and regenerative processes by which human life produces itself locally, nationally, regionally?[2]

We live at a time when socialist thought is in crisis. The Left for a variety of reasons seems unable to engage, must less sustain, a popular base. The Right, on the other hand, has understood all too well how to transform the popular sentiment of diverse groups for its own purposes. At this crucial moment, we believe that we can learn from Williams's approach to the dynamic relationship between representations and histories, and his understanding of the cultural and material processes by which representations play a determinate role in people's experiences, subjectivities, and situations—what he describes as an insider-outsider juxtaposition of "their pressing realities."[3] Likewise, we can learn from Williams's critical examination of both traditional Marxist and conservative cultural and social theory.

At the same time, we think that it is important to come to grips with the limits of Williams's practice. For instance, in many respects the thinking of Williams remains tied to the "Great Tradition" of literature championed by critics such as F. R. Leavis. Ironically, although Williams played a pioneering role in providing theoretical resources for the study of cultural forms produced by subordinate groups, he himself devoted most of his life to rereading works in the Western and predominantly English literary canon, and thus unconsciously reproduces the "selective tradition" he so strenuously opposed. Second, we question many of the a priori assumptions that underpin his conception of the "long revolution"—an historical vision, it might be added, that is still held by many on the Left. Williams all too often equates the subjects of emancipatory practice with white male workers. He represents their consciousness not only as inherently progressive and oppositional, but also as free of contradictory interests. His understanding of the "long revolution" is rooted in Eurocentric notions of political and historical change.

Continuing in the critical tradition of Williams himself, we will not eulogize him by romanticizing his work. We shall offer an appreciative critique, one that goes beyond the conceptual and methodological terms provided by Williams, but does not treat [T]heory as an end in itself. The collaborative spirit of our project is captured by Stuart Hall's description of the ongoing role of theory in cultural studies. He speaks of theory as a form of critical pedagogy which is "always self-reflectively deconstructing itself," "always operating on the progressive/ regressive movement of the need to go on theorizing."[4] But equally important, we see our book as sharing the inspiration that motivates Nancy Fraser's recent volume. Fraser sees the relationship between critical theory and political practice as threefold.

> [F]irst, it valorizes historically specific, conjunctural struggles as the agenda setters for critical theory; second, it posits social movements as the subjects of critique; and third, it implies that it is in the crucible of political practice that critical theories meet the ultimate test of viability.[5]

In light of such practical tests, a major impetus for this book comes from the need to redefine the boundaries of Marxist and feminist cultural politics. Our goal is to reflect more properly the movement to decenter both the West and the First World by those who have been informed and transformed by critical Third World and feminist perspectives and politics. What emerges from our rethinking of the work of Williams is not so much a critique of occasional blind spots or silences. Rather, we argue that the theoretical, epistemological, and political frameworks of Western Marxisms and feminisms have themselves been mute to the voices of subordinate or colonized, but nonetheless resistant political subjects, within the shifting borders and margins of international capitalism. Our contributors draw upon contemporary debates in anti-imperialist and feminist struggles to critique Williams's systematic marginalization of the experiences of women and men of subordinate racial groups and non-Western national cultures. Our edited volume addresses Williams within such an international frame by drawing upon contributors who themselves have inhabited multiple and conflicting border countries.

The title of this book suggests multiple and sometimes conflicting meanings, purposes, and audiences. Taken from the title of one of Williams's novels, it signifies his own marginalized and contradictory subjectivity and position as a working-class Welshman who was formally educated and taught at Cambridge University. The title also signifies the recognition that "borders" are historically constituted by economic and cultural relationships of imperialism. Many of our contributors will persistently ask whether Williams himself pays sufficient attention to this issue, whether his work prefigures or provides the basis for such analyses, and discuss ways of going beyond his understanding of the "border country."

Part One: Culture is Ordinary

The first part of *Views Beyond the Border Country*, entitled "Culture is Ordinary," highlights Williams's rich and suggestive contributions to cultural theory developed first in *Culture and Society* (1958) and *The Long Revolution* (1961) and subsequently in texts such as *Marxism and Literature* (1977). Williams expands the idea of culture to include both "high" and "popular" culture—culture as "the whole way of life." He retains the Leavisite sensitivity to cultural practices without mystifying the "Great Tradition." He accepts the Marxist emphasis on class conflict, while rejecting the idea that cultural practices are reducible to the economic base. Williams's ability to negotiate between the cultural radicalism of the Leavisites and the historical materialism of the Marxist tradition opens up a new intellectual and political space, one in which culture is the mediator between individual experience and class relations.

In his later work, Williams expands his idea of culture through a critical adaption of Antonio Gramsci's concept of "hegemony." For Williams, hegemony is a process of cultural domination which is never static or total, but continually "renewed, recreated, defended, and modified."[6] He sees it as being in continuous conflict with oppositional forces: "emergent" and "residual" cultural forms which pose a threat to the dominant order, even if confined and marginalized by hegemonic constraints.

Our contributors address the theoretical and political issues raised by Williams's "cultural materialism," while exploring its resonance for areas that he himself either gestured toward or left unexplored. From different points of view, Laura Di Michele and Dennis L. Dworkin look at Williams as a political and cultural theorist. Di Michele examines Williams's novel *Border Country* as a meeting ground of social theory and autobiographical reflection. In "Autobiography and the 'Structure of Feeling' in *Border Country*," she portrays Williams's first novel as a work of self-exploration, as a representation of the working class movement from a Marxist perspective, as a reexamination of the organicism of the rural community in the tradition of Hardy and Welsh novels, and as "a form of communication which transgresses generic boundaries, containing within itself different ways of writing, autobiography, cultural analysis and theory, political assessment." For Di Michele, the main character Matthew, who, like Williams, crosses back and forth between two cultures, holds a privileged position, enabling him to listen to and record the diverse experience of members of the community, while understanding that their lives are connected by a unified structure of feeling. Matthew, like Williams, is at once "cultural analyst/historian/sociologist who acts as a catalyst for a whole process of structured remembrance."

From Di Michele's point of view, Williams always inhabited the border, in "a sort of metaphorical 'border country' " of his own, enabling him to simultaneously enter into the consciousness of English and Welsh culture. "From privileged 'border country' experience, Williams (and Matthew similarly) could conceive the ideas of a multifaced world-view which let him discover significant relations between people." While Di Michele attributes Williams's understanding of politics and culture to his contradictory position in British culture, Dennis L. Dworkin sees Williams's thought as part of a broader historical and political movement. In "Cultural Studies and the Crisis in British Radical Thought," Dworkin examines Williams's pioneering contribution to cultural studies as part of a wider response to the deepening crisis of the British Left. He discusses the subsequent movement in cultural studies away from Williams's ideas, especially the work of the Centre for Contemporary Cultural Studies at Birmingham University, as part of an ongoing attempt to resolve it.

For Dworkin, Williams's original formulation of cultural studies is rooted in the debates on mass culture and working class affluence of the 1950s. Like Edward Thompson and Richard Hoggart, he rejects the necessary correlation between material hardship and political response. It is not poverty, but the collective aspirations inherent in working-class life that underpin the socialist project. Williams's commitment to the "long revolution" is founded on the belief that the welfare state is one more stage in the long march of the working class. The Birmingham Centre's reformulation of cultural studies, on the other hand, reflects a gloomier political climate, part of the growing crisis of the Left in the 1970s and the 1980s. As a result, Centre researchers are as concerned with the reasons that "the people" accept the hegemony of the dominant classes as they are with political alternatives. Drawing on French structuralism, semiotics, and the writings of Gramsci, they see culture as a field of signification, a site of ideological struggle between dominant and subordinate groups. For Dworkin, the movement of cultural studies in the 1970s away from the thought of Williams is even more pronounced in the 1980s, in large part because "he never came to terms with the great diversity of feminist work on the construction of subjectivity and consciousness." Dworkin believes that Williams's historical approach to understanding signification is still relevant, but he sees his political conception of socialist renewal as already being part of a different age.

Di Michele and Dworkin discuss Williams within the context of intellectual and political history. Loren Kruger and Jon Thompson, on the other hand, investigate cultural practices not necessarily studied by Williams himself, yet in ways that acknowledge their debt to him. They believe that Williams plays a critical role in breaking down the false dichotomy between high and low culture, and is instrumental in defining a new cultural terrain founded on the idea that culture is ordinary. They critique, refine, and expand Williams's notion of culture and cultural processes. While their work represents critical appreciation of Williams's achievement, they also constitute important contributions to cultural theory in their own right.

In "Placing the Occasion: Raymond Williams and Performing Culture," Loren Kruger attempts to redress the neglect by critics and scholars of Williams's lifelong interest in drama and theatre. In her view, Williams's writing on drama consists of more than cultural materialist rereadings of great dramatists. They have important implications for his cultural theory more generally. Williams sees theatre in historically specific terms. The place and occasion of a play's performance, not some intrinsic quality it contains, is responsible for its status as culture, art, or entertainment. Kruger argues that this way of conceiving cultural categories not only challenges canonical literary criticism but the cultural studies tradition itself. Cultural theorists implicitly and explicitly have tended to equate popular culture with the culture of the people, and consequently have too easily categorized contemporary Western theatre as "high culture" simply because it has tended to serve an "elite" audience. Yet Kruger is by no means uncritical of Williams.

She argues that Williams hesitates at the critical border of his own making and thus cannot fully accept his own idea that culture is both art and activity. Confronted with the radical implications of culture being truly ordinary, he "returns to the high ground of aesthetic *value* and the apparently inalienable concept of *art*."

Kruger explores this newly formulated terrain of culture in discussions of the performance and variations of *Antigone* in contemporary South Africa and the practice of the Women's Theatre Group in Britain. Her analysis of the latter makes a significant contribution to a feminist materialist understanding of popular culture. As Kruger points out, what makes the plays of the Women's Theatre Group feminist is not only that they present ordinary culture in the form of pressures and dilemmas that their audiences of young women might face. These plays are also important examples of feminist popular culture, because they challenge their audiences to reevaluate their own contradictory experiences of femininity. Popular culture, she argues, is most vital when it disrupts our daily routines, not so much as to create an escape route, but to make it possible for us to imagine other ways in which culture can be performed.

Like Kruger, Jon Thompson sees Williams as offering a way of going beyond the paralyzing dichotomies of high and low culture which in literature have resulted in the stigmatization of popular cultural forms. In "Realism and Modernisms: Raymond Williams and Popular Fiction," Thompson credits Williams with creating a "shift of attention away from the vexed question of literary *value* to an understanding of the full historical complexity and richness of literary *practices*. . . ."

In Thompson's view, one of the implications of such an approach is that it enables us to reexamine the relations among realism, modernism, and popular culture. Drawing on Williams's distinction between dominant, residual, and emergent forces in cultural formations, he argues that modernism and realism are not necessarily mutually exclusive categories: "residual" relations of realism can exist within institutionally "dominant" modernist practices. This entails theorizing literary modernism as inhabiting a much wider cultural space than avant-garde production. According to Thompson, the American hard-boiled detective novels of Dashiell Hammett illustrate this wider concept of modernist practice. Hammett shares many of the philosophical concerns of writers like Kafka, Joyce, Lawrence, and Woolf, but his language is rooted in the tradition of pulp fiction and represents the culture of the street. His "fiction throws into relief the *conventional* character of high modernism and it suggests the possibility for seeing, and resisting, the ways in which different traditions, whether literary or cultural, organize and interpellate texts—and subjects."

Part Two: Education from Below?

Although Raymond Williams is not an educational theorist per se, his ideas on radical democratic politics, language, and cultural formations have had a considerable influence upon recent debates in the radical sociology of education and the curriculum. In "Education from Below?" Michael W. Apple, Fazal Rizvi, Leslie G. Roman, and Wendy Kohli explore the relevance of Williams's cultural and political theory for contemporary dilemmas faced by the Left in varied national and regional contexts of emergent neoconservatism.

One of the strengths of Williams's effort to define culture is that it is rooted, particularly in his later work influenced by Gramsci, in an understanding of hegemonic struggles. He recognizes both the existence of political conflicts between social classes, and the need for subordinate groups to create institutions and cultural forms which encourage meaningful, effective, and widespread political participation. Yet often Williams underestimates the effect of State politics and the interests of gender, race, and national culture in re-prioritizing class alliances. In this section, our contributors draw upon Williams's critical understanding of the complex workings of hegemonic struggle between subordinate and dominate groups. But they reject his class reductionism and romanticized conception of working-class resistance. And they question whether his emphasis on "cultural politics from below" actually captures the full complexity of asymmetric power relations characterizing cultural struggles over meaning.

A related question our contributors address is whether, and to what extent, Williams's conception of a "common culture" pays sufficient attention to the often "non-synchronous" ways that race, class, and gender produce unlikely alliances.[7] If a more complex and contradictory notion of interest is acknowledged, must the idea of a common culture be abandoned altogether? Alternatively, how might we retheorize cultural and educational practices by better understanding hegemonic processes and struggles in the contexts of shifting power relations among different social formations? These are questions which from a different point of view the contributors to the third section of the book, "Culture's Others: Culture or Cultural Imperialism?," take up as well.

In various ways, the essays of Apple, Rizvi, and Roman examine how neoconservative groups have appropriated and reinscribed the language of the Left in order to roll back recent democratic reforms made in education and elsewhere by new social movements. Apple and Rizvi examine the rearticulation of Left educational reforms and policies in the United States and Britain respectively by Reaganism and Thatcherism. Roman, on the other hand, analyzes the effects of New Right discourses on classroom interactions and their implications for antiracist pedagogy in Louisiana. Regardless of whether they take a macro or micro level approach to analyzing the relationships between State, educational, and cultural politics, they draw our attention to the discursive strategies employed by the Right. They argue that such strategies are often powerful and effective means of managing and transforming popular conceptions of democratic participation, education, equality, racial discrimination, and minority rights.

Michael W. Apple's essay "Rebuilding Hegemony: Education, Equality, and the New Right" has two major aims. On the one hand, he examines the influence of Williams's work on critical educational studies in the United States. Apple argues that Williams's cultural theory was indirectly responsible for freeing educational theorists in the 1970s from dependence on overly psychologistic and economistic approaches to educational practice and schools. On the other hand, Apple draws on many of the concepts of Williams to analyze recent shifts in the meanings of equality, a consequence of the fractures in the post-World War II "largely liberal consensus that guided much of educational and social policy." The United States, Apple observes, is in the most powerful structural crisis since the Great Depression, a crisis which, he believes, created the conditions for Social Darwinist ideologies to fundamentally alter the existing discourses of educational reform. In the process, the Right has redefined which people comprise the subjects of education, that is, who shall be educated, as well as the purposes of education, and the meaning of educational quality.

Extending Stuart Hall's influential analysis of Thatcherism as "authoritarian populism" and Herbert Gintis's important work on the concept of property rights, Apple examines reports and policy statements on educational reforms that have framed the programs of the Reagan and Bush administrations. Certain dominant groups within the State, he argues, are attempting to reconstruct hegemony by eroding the important benefits and civil liberties gained by disenfranchised groups during the 1960s and 1970s. This has been achieved by redefining and equating the meaning of education and equality with individual property and the consumer rights of dominant class and racial groups.

Like Apple, Fazal Rizvi finds the New Right's reformulation of educational choices within the discourses of consumerism and individualism to exemplify conservative attempts to roll back Welfare State gains in Western capitalist democracies. In "Williams on Democracy and the Governance of Education," Rizvi examines the British Educational Reform Act to examine how Thatcher's "vision of a 'popular capitalism' " overturns more collective and locally responsive meanings of democratic participation. Rizvi believes that Williams would consider recent Tory educational reform initiatives as instances of "managed popular participation": a perversion of the original radical democratic impulse underlying his cultural materialism.

Rizvi argues that Williams's understanding of "devolution, self-governance, parent and community participation and school-based decision making" differs significantly from the Right's deployment of them in "instrumentalist and consumerist" discourses of individual choice. He shows how in both *The Long Revolution* and *Towards 2000*, Williams conceives of education as a cultural activity rather than as " 'a fixed abstraction, a settled body of teaching and learning,' to be distributed in institutions over periods."[8] According to Rizvi, Williams's insight anticipates as well as challenges the increasing tendency of representative democracies to acquire more rather than less centralized state power over the lives of people.

Against those critics who might cast Williams as a liberal humanist, Rizvi argues that Williams's analysis of the relationship between the State, its educational institutions, and the wider cultural politics emanates from a critical but nonetheless "realist" tradition. In Rizvi's view, what distinguishes Williams's analysis from neoconservative as well as liberal conceptions of representative democracy is his radical commitment to meaningful and widespread political participation under equality of material conditions. If socialism is to survive in a renewed form, he suggests, its "practical politics" must acknowledge, as Williams begins to in his later work, the importance of the new social movements of peace, ecology, and feminism for radically altering the priorities of class politics.

Leslie G. Roman amplifies Rizvi's observation that Williams's conception of education and cultural politics is founded on an epistemology of critical realism. In " 'On the Ground' with Antiracist Pedagogy and Raymond Williams's Unfinished Project to Articulate a Socially Transformative Critical Realism," Roman examines Williams's often misunderstood and contentious defense of Brechtian critical realism. In her view, Williams's reading of Brecht is part of his "larger provisional project within cultural materialism to formulate a new socially transformative practice of realism" which has implications for critical practice that reach well beyond the popular theatrical stage.

Roman bases her argument upon her recent experience as a university professor in Louisiana at a time when David Duke's rise to national political legitimacy in recent campaigns for State Senator and Governor has been premised upon his appropriations of the language of the Civil Rights movement and the category of racial oppression for ultraconservative purposes. In this urgent context, she explores the ethical and political dilemmas she faced in a racially-mixed graduate seminar where as a white teacher she confronted her white students' "defensive appropriations" of the category of racial oppression. While such defensive appropriations have been increasingly legitimated in recent national politics, Roman argues that they must also be analyzed in light of the specificities of local and regional cultural politics. For Roman, the ethical and moral issues that she faced in this situation were at once practical and theoretical. She distinguishes her own feminist materialist position from the a priori relativism assumed in particular variants of postmodernism and postmodern feminism. In her view, any a priori commitment to relativism would leave feminist and other critical educators without the evaluative resources to make important moral and political distinctions among the conflicting "reality" claims of their students.

Roman argues that Williams's unfinished adaption of Brechtian realism provides the basis to make the evaluative distinctions lacking in particular variants of postmodernism. Yet as a feminist she realizes that Williams's position is limited by masculinist treatments of gender, class essentialism, and Eurocentrism. She also contends that Williams often resorts to organicist and holistic notions of culture when representing several objectively conflicting interests who have stakes in dramatizing "reality" from different points of view. Roman argues, however, that these problems are not intractable, since Williams's conception of realist practice allows, even if ambivalently, for the radical notion of contradictory social subjectivity. Ultimately, she believes that his failures and contradictions can be read as "symptomatic silences" subject to ongoing testing, challenge, and transformation in the actual political practice of teaching critically.

Roman's interest in Williams's ambivalent openness toward a notion of contradictory social subjectivity is extended by Wendy Kohli in "Raymond Williams, Affective Ideology and Counter-Hegemonic Practices." Following a well-established feminist tradition of analyzing the relationship between the so-called personal and public spheres of daily life, Kohli begins her essay by reflecting on her own autobiographical relationship to the work of Williams. For Kohli, Williams opens the "theoretical space" within which she could begin to theorize the contradictions of her own working-class experience—a step she values for its power to foreground the idea that social subjects rarely "create culture and consciousness in a straightforward, rational linear way, proceeding to revolutionary action."

In opposition to the overly rationalistic conception of ideology held by much of the male Left, Kohli focuses on the ways in which educational practice can "interrupt" and transform the processes of "affective ideological internalization" and "incorporation" preventing oppressed groups from resisting their own as well as others' oppression. She draws upon Williams's novels *Border Country* and *Second Generation*, as well as his broader social and cultural theory, to grapple with the "contradictory material realities of working-class people," who like herself, move between the divided worlds of their working-class origins and emergent middle-class positions. While Kohli believes that Williams's novels capture the contradictory interests and dynamism of this process, she does not find that his cultural and social theory exhibits the same theoretical openness in accounting for the effects of gender interests on class consciousness. Like Roman, Kohli argues that Williams pauses just short of fully realizing the significance of a radical notion of contradictory social subjectivity and affective ideology in the construction of class interests—interests which are shaped as much by gender as they are by class. For Kohli, the work of recent feminist social theorists and educators is far more instructive and promising than prolonged interrogations of Williams's silences and blind spots on the interrelatedness of different forms of oppression.

Part Three: Culture's Others: Culture or Cultural Imperialism?

The third and last part of the book looks at the ways in which Williams's ideas about culture are linked to the project of British colonialism and imperialism. While recognizing that Williams himself steadfastly opposed imperialism, the contributors to this section still draw attention to the structural ways in which Williams's discourse on culture is either limited by, or predicated upon, a narrative of colonialism—what may be called "the failed articulation of the texts of community and empire."[9]

In a variety of ways, Fernando Coronil, Forest Pyle, R. Radhakrishnan, Julie Skurski, and Gauri Viswanathan call attention to those aspects of Williams's ideas about culture which reinscribe the narratives of Western colonialism and imperialism. Furthermore, they consider the political usefulness of Anglo- and Eurocentric Marxist work on culture for studies of subaltern cultural formations and their relationships to imperialist centers of domination in colonial and postcolonial periods. Most ask whether Williams's ideas about culture—conceived both within and against English literary culture of Burke, Arnold, and Leavis—can produce a knowledge of England's role in establishing British colonialism or Western imperialism more generally. While the contributors to this part are appreciative of Williams's sustained body of work on culture, they remain critical of his failure to employ poststructuralist, deconstructionist, and other avant-garde approaches to theorize the relationship between colonial and postcolonial cultural formations. They argue that his thought is part of a discourse which fails to systematically acknowledge that the very concept of culture is embedded in relations of economic and cultural imperialism, and must be criticized on these grounds as a precondition to constructing alternative theoretical approaches to understanding the problematic relationship between culture and empire.

In "Raymond Williams and British Colonialism: The Limits of Metropolitan Cultural Theory," Gauri Viswanathan establishes a theoretical paradigm to grasp the relationship between cultural practices and imperialism. She argues that the most pronounced failure of British Left literary and cultural studies has been its "unproblematic conflation of the terms 'national and imperial,' " and she offers a powerful critique of the effects of interchanging them. She finds this conflation to exist even among such contemporary Left critics as Brian Doyle, Alan Sinfeld, and Robert Colls and Phillip Dodd "where the 'naturalness' of English culture is rejected as a false premise obscuring a history of invented discourses and disciplines." Such a conflation permits, in her view, the unfortunate effect of eliminating "important distinctions that would make the equations between class and racial ideologies more difficult, if not impossible." It also makes it more difficult to broaden analyses of English national culture to include the effects of colonizer-colonized relations upon the shaping of English culture and ideologies of national identities in a "cross-referential" way.

Viswanathan considers the work of Raymond Williams as pivotal to a long genealogy of English leftist writers who have persistently and consistently resisted theorizing English culture in relation to the historically specific contingencies of imperialism. Viswanathan's cri-

13

tique is not that Williams is silent on the question of imperialism. Indeed, she praises his attempt to situate the English social formation within the economics of imperialism in *The Country and the City*. Rather, in her view, he fails to produce a relational analysis of England and its colonies, a consequence of "an internal restraint that has complex historical and methodological origins."

To illustrate this failure, Viswanathan analyzes Williams's stated intention of properly acknowledging the colonies' historical role in shaping the internal dynamics of English society. In other words, his understanding of English culture could be extended to "transcultural or cross-referential situations." But, while as a cultural materialist Williams seems well placed to confront "England's colonial adventure," his understanding of it remains implicitly tied to orthodox Marxist approaches. He ignores, among other issues, the functional role of the colonies and the periphery in the shaping of the city/metropolis of English culture, and, as a consequence, ultimately obscures the relation of English culture to imperialism. Viswanathan's understanding of center-periphery relations from the point of view of "cross-referentiality" provides a theoretical foundation whereby postcolonial scholars can empirically explore the constantly transforming political imperatives of empires and the relationships among imperial powers and their colonies.

In many important ways, Julie Skurski and Fernando Coronil's essay, "Country and City in a Postcolonial Landscape: Double Discourse and the Geo-Politics of Truth in Latin America," represents an elaboration of Viswanathan's theoretical project. Coronil and Skurski critique Williams's model of the country and the city which, they contend, is founded on a rigid Enlightenment opposition between imperial and colonial nations. This view erroneously assumes that capitalism disrupts and reorders rural society in vastly differing localities according to a universal logic, creating "essentially similar" historical experiences within and between center and periphery. For Coronil and Skurski, such a model cannot account for the manner in which colonial urban centers in Latin America were both "civilizing outposts" which "linked the spread of Catholicism to the consolidation of a transnational kingdom" and places where "the control of its [their] subjects was a recurrent cultural and political problem." Coronil and Skurski examine the "mutual constitution" of imperial and colonial discourses—what they call the "double discourse of post-coloniality"—in the context of inventing the dominant political knowledge of Venezuela. In their view, Venezuela is a "peripheral nation where both of its terms 'country and city' are located in the 'country'—the hinterland of the metropolitan centers— and are therefore subsumed within an overarching category of backwardness and colored by the hostile meanings associated with the colonized."

Coronil and Skurski raise important issues concerning the maintenance of hegemony within this context of double articulation. They are concerned, for instance, with understanding how colonized dominant sectors claim to rule or represent their authority when they are simultaneously the agents and the subjects of a "doubling of consciousness." To examine such questions, they focus on two instances exemplifying a reordering of a populist nationalist solution: Romulo Gallegos's novel, *Dono Barbara* (1929), and the official representations of the 1988 Amparo massacre. In both these cases, Coronil and Skurski overcome the internal constraints of Williams's model of the "country and the city" by explaining how colonialism and postcolonialism fracture national identities within peripheral countries in ways which make the truth-claims of different forms of media implicated in relations of power that are contested and mediated in a double discourse.

Like Coronil, Skurski, and Viswanathan, Forest Pyle is interested in the double discourse of culture that develops in colonial contexts and its importance for the concept of culture more generally. In "Raymond Williams and the Inhuman Limits of Culture," Pyle pays tribute to Williams's "materialistic deliverance" of culture, characterizing it as a radical rearticulation of the dominant structures of feeling that govern modern thought. Yet, for Pyle, Williams will not be remembered by the achievement of this redemption: his work contains "inevitable" and "compelling" failures which disclose the linguistic, political, and colonial limits of the concept of culture. Pyle's discussion of these limits is twofold. First, he traces them to Williams's ideas about language and community, most apparent in the posthumously published writings on modernism and postmodernism. Pyle argues that Williams regards modernism as being founded on the formal and thematic renunciation of the Victorian concept of community: the displacement of real communities by the "community of the medium." Williams has the false hope that beyond the fragmentary experience of modernity and postmodernity lies the restoration of the concept of community; and he regards the linguistic turn, typical of modern and postmodern practice, as a barrier to the recovery of the alternative traditions of culture. But, as Pyle observes, "the material properties and rhetorical activities of the sign exceed the capacity of the subject to master them; there is an irreducible aspect of language which resists accommodation with the concept of the human." Drawing upon Paul de Man's deconstructionist philosophy, he concludes that Williams's encounter with twentieth-century experience is "in fact predicated on the very denial of materiality" that elsewhere is so critical to this work.

Second, Pyle argues that Williams's aspiration for a common culture that renders community knowable is not only an idealist project: it is ideological as well. For Pyle, a "knowable community" is a fiction that can only be conceived in relationship to the idea of a nation, an idea which in England cannot be disengaged from its empire. Inscribed within the idea of culture, then, is the failed articulation of the texts of community and empire. In this context, Pyle contrasts Williams's thought with that of the poet and literary critic Roberto Fernandez Retamar in his well known "Caliban" essay. Retamar's " 'notes toward a definition of culture' refuse the nostalgia—even in its critical forms—of Williams's invocations of a shared culture or 'knowable' community and thereby discover instead the insistently 'mulattoed' or 'hybrid' nature of any Latin American 'culture.' "

Like Forest Pyle, R. Radhakrishnan's interrogation of Williams's cultural and political theory draws on a combination of elements from avant-garde literary theory and postcolonial perspectives. Yet where Pyle's approach implicitly suggests that the universalist tendencies and silences in Williams's thought are best criticized by combining these two points of view, Radhakrishnan, in his essay "Cultural Theory and the Politics of Location," argues this in a more sustained way. Though he acknowledges the significant differences between the two, Radhakrishnan insists that "the need to find alternative political practices through an epistemological revolution and the desire to embody a historical significance for the language of the 'post-' may be said to have found a concrete set of issues in postcoloniality that both uses and transforms poststructuralism."

The occasion of Radhakrishnan's essay is the recent revolutions in Eastern Europe, which, in his view, provide a suitable vehicle for coming to grips with the thought of Williams. In Radhakrishnan's view, the revolutions at first glance might appear to confirm Williams's vision of a common humanity, but they also raise questions about whether his ideas can be transplanted from the First World to the periphery, especially postcolonial arenas. He argues that, while Williams's enduring faith in human agency is a much needed component of any revolutionary politics, his inability to be self-reflective about his status as a first world intellectual limits the reach of his thought. This is nowhere more apparent than in the posthumously published dialogue with Edward Said, in which Williams asserts that historical methods for understanding the politics of representation can effortlessly move between different political terrains.

16

Radhakrishnan contrasts Williams's notion of a "trans-contextual method" with a postcolonial "politics of location" based on the concept of "complex multiple rootedness." Pointing to the work of Lata Mani and Vivek Dhareshwar, among others, he concludes "that the travel thought up by these postcolonial intellectuals is less natural, more deliberate and self reflexive, and less self assured than the resources of hope that stem from a metropolitan assumption of universal experience."

The contributors to this final section of the book, "Culture's Others: Culture or Cultural Imperialism?" mainly direct our attention to the limitations of Raymond Williams's theoretical perspective and the shortcomings of the wider traditions to which he belongs. Yet no less than the contributors to the first two sections, these writers acknowledge the magnitude of his overall achievement. Their criticisms, like so many others in the book, reflect the belief that genuine appreciation entails rigorous scrutiny of the underpinnings of Williams's thought, that repaying our debt to him involves distinguishing between productive paths, dead ends, and routes never taken.

Part I

Culture Is Ordinary

1

Autobiography and the "Structure of Feeling" in *Border Country*

Laura Di Michele

Border Country (1960) is Williams's first autobiographical novel, which presents us his fictional self—Matthew Price—as a character moving between two very different worlds and pressed by the difficulty of that complicated situation to analyze the very significance of his own life.[1] It draws upon his boyhood and adolescence in Wales and upon his remembrances of the General Strike of 1926 as it is recalled time and again in the novel through the voices and recollections of his father, Harry Price, and his friend, Morgan Rosser.

The novel is deeply imbued with the author's feelings of longing for the ideal Welsh community life of Glynmawr and with the protagonist's anger at having left it to go to study at Cambridge University. *Border Country* is an autobiographical novel for many reasons. It is inspired by Williams's life in the time of his childhood; and it is a kind of continuation of the writer's ideas on "culture and society" as they had already taken shape in his *Preface to Film* (1954)—where Williams uses the expression "structure of feeling" for the first time in the sense of a general or shared culture[2]—and in *Culture and Society* (1958), wherein Williams discovers, so to say, a "culture and society" tradition which is explored by him through a cultural analysis that attends "to the experience that is otherwise recorded: in institutions, manners, customs, family memories."[3] The novel can be also perceived as an anticipation and, in fact, an extended critical reflection, in narrative form, of what Williams was to theorize in his fascinating book on *The Long Revolution* (1961).

It is in this more general and complex sense that *Border Country* may be envisaged as a work which mirrors Williams's whole way of life, and, at the same time, comments upon it. From this point of view, *Border Country* is a novel of self-exploration; a representation of the working-class movement observed from a Marxist angle; a revaluation of the "organic" rural community in the tradition of Hardy and the Welsh novels; it is a form of communication which transgresses generic boundaries, containing within itself different ways of writing, autobiography, cultural analysis and theory, and political assessment. It reveals how a structure of feeling is construed in the interconnections between the characters and the various situations they are in; it also shows how the "structure of feeling" can be used by the narrator to explain a specific sensibility and mentality, to reconstruct the culture of a period.

We know that Raymond Williams wrote *Border Country* seven times[4] before he could find a satisfactory narrative form wherein the complex internal processes, divisions, and conflicts which articulate the events and characterize the people who inhabit the small Welsh community of Glynmawr could connect deeply with wider issues and social pressure originating well beyond the borders of that locality and regionality, and yet penetrating far inward into it.

Metaphorically and structurally, this idea of an intense, dynamic relationship is conveyed quite early in the novel, in that episode where Matthew Price—the main character, and surely an emanation of Williams—is described while looking intently at the rail-map on the wall of the compartment of the train that is taking him to Glynmawr from London, back into Wales; back into Wales, from England. Significantly, as the rhythm of the train rattle changes, so does the speed and rhythm of the sentences; and the flow of writing slows down coming nearly to a halt, as if to capture the reader's attention and fix it on that specific moment, which then opens up a very wide range of interpretations.

> Abruptly the rhythm changed, as the wheels crossed the bridge. Matthew got up, and took his case from the rack. As he steadied the case, he looked at the rail-map, with its familiar network of arteries, held in the shape of Wales, and to the east the lines running out and elongating into England.[5]

The railway lines on the map trace the course of different routes that from Wales penetrate into England, crossing the frontiers between the two countries and, in fact, symbolically erasing any kind of border. One consequence of this description is that the train and the railway operate to alert the reader's attention. The railway—with the little country station, and the signalmen and the stationmaster—already retains a highly significant function in this initial part of the narrative, and it displays a symbolic quality similar to that it will disclose later in the novel when we reach the General Strike section.[6] Now, at this early stage, and in spite of the fact that the station is located in the periphery of the town, near the asylum "on the outskirts, where the Victorians thought they belonged,"[7] it occupies a very central, crucial place: it is a kind of magical crucible, where Matthew regains a lost sense of his belonging there and understands the reason why he does not feel any longer a stranger in Glynmawr.

His coming back to Wales becomes much more than "a break from the contained indifference that was still his dominant feeling of London."[8] There, in London, "you don't speak to people," because "there is plenty of time for that sort of thing on the appointed occasions—in an office, in a seminar, at a party."[9] Here, in Glynmawr and Gwenton alike, you speak to everybody; you know everybody; as a matter of fact, the whole community is in direct relationship and in face-to-face contact with you.

Perhaps, the complex meaning of Matthew's meeting with Morgan Rosser at the country station of Gwenton resides in the fact that the situation is presented through the two contrasting characters of Matthew and Morgan: Matthew seems to stand for the impersonal city attitude to human relationships, while Morgan illustrates the rural community attitude to personal relations. The scene is beautifully described and succeeds completely in communicating the intense feeling of the skepticism and disbelief which inspire the look, the gestures and the whole behavior on Matthew's part; by contrast, we discover Morgan's confident approach and natural gestures, and his penetrating stare at Matthew in search of direct confrontation. Not recognizing him, Matthew answers Morgan's questions curtly and goes on walking head down in the rain. Morgan does not give in and follows him with his car, while Matthew is thoroughly absorbed in his own private thoughts:

> He was set, now, on the walk. He wanted to come back like this; slowly, with obvious difficulty, making up his own mind.
> "You'll get wet, you know, Will!" the voice said suddenly.
> Matthew stopped, and swung around, arrested by the name. Always, when he had lived here, he had been Will, though his

registered name was Matthew, and he had used this invariably since he had gone away.[10]

From that moment, Matthew begins his voyage back *home*; from that instant onward, gestures, voices, sounds, colors, movements, landscapes, and friends do cohere in helping Matthew/Will to find out his own way through the difficult journey into Wales. The dialogue between Matthew and Morgan is not easy at first and Matthew feels uncomfortable, while Morgan knowingly tries to help him, though he cannot resist the temptation of being ironically reproachful.

> "I'm sorry," Matthew said. "I should have recognized your voice. Only sometimes we only recognize when we're expecting it."
> "You thought we'd leave you to walk then?" Morgan said, looking across at him.
> "I expect to walk. Nobody knew the time of my train."
> "We got timetables. Get in, Will. Don't stand in the wet."[11]

Gently, but firmly, Matthew is reminded of where he is and that there exists a reality he had almost forgotten. After the first exchange of words, Morgan explains what happened soon after the news of Matthew's father being seriously ill spread among the neighbors:

> "Your mam rung me," he said, settling again in his seat. "She said Mrs. Hybart rung you a quarter past five, you said you'd get the first train."[12]

In speech, too, Morgan draws on the oral and local tradition of Glynmawr; effectively, he shows how the spontaneous chain of solidarity among the members of that community got started and how natural the reaction of the neighborhood to the serious illness of Harry Price is. Matthew still tries to react and defends himself: " 'Well, thank you, anyway. I didn't expect it.' ";[13] but he has to capitulate quite soon and remember that he is in Wales now.

> Morgan did not answer, but with a hard movement sent the car forward. Matthew jerked back, then steadied himself. It is like that, this country; it takes you over as soon as you set foot in it. Yet I was sent for to come at once.[14]

Matthew *recognizes*, so to say, Morgan Rosser and the values of friendship, neighborhood, and, ultimately, of Welshness he incarnates as against those traits of Englishness (indifference, impersonality, and alienation) Matthew noticed at the beginning of the novel.

The meeting at the railway station, then, may be seen as the starting-point of the process of the growth of Matthew's consciousness, very similar to the painful awakening of the working class's consciousness which was shaped during the General Strike of 1926. It is in that year—both in the novel and outside of it—that a wider process of the growth of the working-class consciousness of the rural community of Glyn-mawr and other communities all over Wales developed amid the many contradictory and complex events. On the occasion of the strike, the country station of Gwenton (like many other Welsh country stations) became the nerve-center of the then rising working-class movement and one of the most important ways of communication, together with the telephone, the telegraph, and the radio.[15]

Raymond Williams's reflections on the General Strike will better explain the main function of the railway station as far as the formation of the working-class consciousness is concerned. Williams's words refer to the situation of the General Strike as it occurred in the Welsh mining valleys and as he knew it from his father; but these words are also perfectly suitable to illustrate the situation in *Border Country*:

> Consider first that specific situation. These men at that country station were industrial workers, trade unionists, in a small group within a primarily rural and agricultural economy. All of them, like my father, still had close connections with that agricultural life. One of them ran a smallholding in addition to his job on the railway. Most of them had relatives in farm work. All of them had gardens and pigs or bees or ponies which were an important part of their work and income. At the same time, by the very fact of the railway, with the trains passing through, from the cities, from the factories, from the ports, from the collieries, and by the fact of the telephone and the telegraph, which was especially important for the signalmen, who through it had a community with other signalmen over a wide social network, talking beyond their work with men they might never actually meet but whom they knew very well through voice and opinion and story, they were part of a modern industrial working class.[16]

From this perspective, then, the railway station in *Border Country* plays a crucial role in highlighting the social significance of the General

Strike, both at a personal and local level and at a national level, and also in facing the complex problems of consciousness and solidarity arising and spreading among the men at the country station of Gwenton. Again, Williams's words will clarify the meanings of the close and difficult relationship between the railway station and the strike. They interlocked very tightly indeed: "There, in that country station, there were real connections—of neighbourhood, of kinship, of trade—with the mining valley."[17] Again, Williams is referring to the real situation, when his father, the other two signalmen, and the stationmaster working in the old Great Western Railway Box of Pandy in 1926 took a very active part in the strike. They—like the characters in *Border Country*—suffered from many disappointments and recovered from betrayals, learning with mixed feelings and great difficulty of the social solidarity of the working class. That solidarity seemed to clash with another, larger idea of solidarity: that of a national cohesion and loyalty to their "country" to which they had all been trained and which could, and in fact did, exercise a powerful influence in smoothing away conflicts and obstacles, thus defeating the working-class movement.[18]

This mixture of hope and despair, of illusion and defeat is what characterizes the description of the attitudes and feelings of the people who inhabit the rural community of Glynmawr in *Border Country* at the time of the General Strike; as a matter of fact, the novel centers around the General Strike and the difficult relation between the Welsh working classes and the Trade Union Congress (TUC) in London. The events of 1926 are represented through the recollections of Matthew's memory, and they are commented upon in the dialogues between Matthew and his father, between Matthew and Morgan Rosser.[19]

It is in the intensely "liminal conjuncture of social, cultural, ideological and generational conflicts"[20] that the protagonist of *Border Country* is put to a severe test and succeeds not only—as K. Ryan maintains—"at last emerging, charged with a deeper understanding of his whole personal and social situation and with the renewed political energy and committed will to transform it";[21] Matthew is also a figure whose ability, from both a narrative and ideological point of view, consist in coordinating—that is, in connecting and serving as a condensed expression for—the series of ideological and cultural issues that have been important in the cultural life of Glynmawr and in Britain since the late 1920s.

From this perspective, *Border Country* represents a special type of industrial novel which discusses the ways through which Matthew climbs over the fence which separates him from Will (the Welsh part of his identity). In the process, Matthew/Will painfully achieves the full consciousness of himself and his self-identity, of his efforts to conciliate his Welsh roots and his sense of guilt at having gone off to England, away from Wales and its moral values and ways of life.

It is this deep split in Matthew's character that the novel tries to explain and overcome through the minute exploration of Matthew's dissatisfaction with himself and his work as a university lecturer in London, and through the sustained analysis of the difficulties he has both with his father's moral integrity and with Morgan's equivocal compromises.[22] In Williams's mind, Matthew/Will [Williams] is a kind of guinea-pig which is being experimented with throughout the novel in the attempt to produce—with the help of a partially autobiographical recollection of the author and the complex construction of the structure of feeling of that specific period in history—a new way of seeing and, also, a new way of writing.

From many points of view, it appears that the story of Matthew Price *is* the story of Raymond Williams: both were railway signalmen's sons from a Welsh village; both were professors at the university; both were deeply bound to their country, Wales. Both of them never lose touch in fact with their roots, with their Welsh origin, while at the same time living in England, beyond the border.

In a way, in reading his fiction and his criticism, his interviews, one gets the impression that Williams did always live *on* the border, in a sort of metaphorical "border country" of his own which allowed him to look deep inside, with great advantage, both at England and at Wales. He could look, as it were, from *there* and from *here* simultaneously at his two worlds, which never appeared to him as mere landscapes or places; they were in fact landscapes "with figures," living worlds and authentic communities, where people were socially and culturally present with their various types of fulfillment and despair, with their crises and successes, with their myths and beliefs, with their "full rich life."[23] From that privileged "border country" experience, Williams (and Matthew similarly) could conceive the idea of a multifaceted world-view which let him discover significant relations between people, which are not naturally "given" but have to be consciously pursued and brought out on the surface by tenacious, even harmful search and effort. These relationships must be lived and felt, in the first place; they must be worked out by the impartial and neutral observer, in the second place.

Both when he was elaborating his approaches to culture and society, and when he was writing his first published novel (*Border Country*), Williams was consciously and openly renouncing the safe role of the observer who does not know the object of his analysis from the inside.

27

Autobiography and "Structure of Feeling"

This position is something Williams shares, though partially, with George Orwell: both writers revisit their own cultures after long and difficult journeys in other countries and cultures. Writing of the two essays Orwell wrote about England in 1940 ("The Lion and the Unicorn") and in 1944 ("The English People"), Williams says:

> The eyes of the observer, of the man coming back to England, are eyes full of this experience of imperialism. But he is not coming to England in the same way as, say, an Indian or an African student: to a foreign country about which he has only read. He has been educated here; his family lives here. He is aware of the internal structure of English society, but from a class position which he has only theoretically rejected.[24]

Of course, many are the differences; they may be better illustrated when we think of Matthew Price and his role as a "visitor" in Glynmawr after going to live in England; Matthew does not accept to be considered a "stranger," although he appears like one to his old friends. As a matter of fact, Matthew is, until the middle part of the novel, the sort of *exile* of whom Williams writes in his *Culture and Society* (1958) and who is not yet ready, so to speak, to come home.[25] At this stage of the novel, Matthew is fighting strongly against the pressure of feeling, against the "knowable" and known community of his adolescence and, in the end, against any available form of commitment to his Welsh roots. Perhaps Williams thought of him in terms very similar to those he used to discuss Lawrence's type of exile: it was a necessary exile to gain the necessary distance and consciousness of oneself and of the other members of that community, to acquire the necessary sensibility to *feel* and *understand* the close relationships which connect the people of an "organic" community together.[26]

Once he has reached the end of the process of the growth of his consciousness, Matthew will be able to comprehend the complex significance of that world from inside its structure of feeling. At that point, he will not feel a stranger and will be ready to take a clear position, that of a detached analyst.

Matthew plays this double role, then; and, this dual presence—of being *there* and *here* at the same time— invites the reader to a dual movement: it is the to-and-from movement of the mind from distant memories to present details, from past slices of national and local history of the working-class movement and real people to present personal uneasiness and sense of estrangement which enables the reader, perfectly attuned to the characters and the narrator, to become fully aware of the vast significance of *Border Country* in the process of understanding and experiencing it.

As we have suggested earlier, the figure of Matthew has been partly constructed in terms of the whole way of life of Raymond Williams; the relationship between the figure of Williams and that of Matthew/ Will seems to work in a direction which enables Williams's thick intellectual image to overlay and resonate with the character of Matthew: Matthew becomes a part of "Raymond Williams's" identity, while Williams becomes a fragment of the identity of the character portrayed at different moments in the novel.

Of course, there is something to be asked: Has this kind of double vision something to do with his being Welsh? Has it to do with Williams's Welshness, or with Williams's attitude toward Wales?[27] The answer is not easy, because—although Williams "has always been loyal to Wales"[28]—his Welshness has always been problematic and shifting over the years. It has partially to do with his being Welsh and having received an English education; at one time he was deeply repelled by what he saw "as the extreme narrowness of Welsh nonconformism"[29]—as he admits in the *New Left Review* interviews of 1979; he also felt he was totally unprepared for Cambridge and could not easily accept it. As is well known, it was only after his discovery of the Socialist Club that things began to change. As he himself recounts, "Meanwhile, of course, I had to dine in Hall and the class stamp of Trinity at that time was not difficult to spot. But it did not have to be negotiated as the only context at Cambridge. The Socialist Club was a home from home."[30]

When Matthew is back in Wales, in the novel, he understands that he is undergoing a deep change of attitude toward himself and the people of Glynmawr; he feels like one who has never left Wales, "not really. Not altogether."[31] He understands that he has to adjust himself, to negotiate with the different situations he may come across, even to look at England from Wales. This is how England appears to him, while he is waiting to be received by Eira; the passage is highly metaphoric, naturally, and it serves to let the reader follow what happens in Matthew's mind.

England seemed a great house with every room partitioned by lath and plaster. Behind every screen, in every cupboard, sat all the great men, everybody. If you wanted to see them, you could see them; that was what they were there for. But you must cool your own heels first; a necessary part of decorum. If you went out of your own cupboard, to see a man in another

cupboard, still you must wait for the cupboard door to be
opened, with proper ceremony, and by a proper attendant.[32]

It is also a question of relating oneself to the others:

> Only sometimes, if your approach was right, the cupboard
> door would be opened with a flourish. If your approach was
> wrong—it's something you just know about people—then you
> could wait for a while, looking up at the cupboard door, get-
> ting yourself—and why not?—into a proper state of mind.[33]

It is a question of growing up, of acquiring consciousness, of being
able to accept the difficult relation between continuity and change,
between past and present, and to rework and represent in a new
perspective images and myths belonging to a certain cultural formation
at a certain fixed time. This is something Williams himself does, when
he looks back at his Welshness, for instance, and explains the particular
significance it had for him and the people living "on the border."

> Of course on the border, it was more problematic than in
> North or West Wales, in the still Welsh-speaking communities.
> They are that much further away from England. There was a
> curious sense in which we could speak of both Welsh and En-
> glish as foreigners, as "not us." That may seem strange, but
> historically it reflects the fact that this was a frontier zone
> which had been the location of fighting for centuries.[34]

As we have already noticed, the frontier does not mean division only;
the border offers a privileged angle of observation, a place from where
one can relate Wales to England and Wales to its own history and
myth, to the various "imagined communities"[35] which constitute the
idea of "Wales" as the nation experienced by different people at different times. From this point of view, in Williams's fiction, too, "Wales"
becomes a useful metaphor to fight against the image of a timeless,
mythical Wales and—at the same time—to throw light on dark England.[36]

In a way, *Border Country* is a novel which helps to construct an
authentic image of Wales as it is experienced by Matthew/Will and
narrated by Williams, especially in Chapter Ten. Here, Will is sitting
above the Kestrel, looking down across the valley and *seeing* fields and
orchards, houses and "the occasional train, very small under its plume
of smoke":[37] what he can *see* in reality is more than this, because the

whole place shows signs of life, of human life and history. "The patch was not only a place, but people, yet from here it was as if no one lived there, no one had ever lived there, and yet, in its stillness, it was a memory of himself."[38] That is an authentic landscape, affectionately and knowingly observed and remembered. Land and people mean also work, connections, change: Matthew/Will knows all this and that from that distance everything may look different. He can follow every single detail of the land as far as his eye can reach: the narrower valley of Trawsfynydd with its ruined abbey, the fields of potatoes, a farmhouse and a cart moving on the high-banked road, and many other concrete elements giving life to that landscape. But that is not all that his country is. That country has also a history imprinted on its ground and its history is one of domination and possession.

> In its history the country took on a different shape. On the high ground to the east the Norman castles stood at intervals of a few miles, facing across the wide valley to the mountains. Glynmawr, below them, was the disputed land, held by neither side, raided by both. And there, to the south, was Gwenton Castle, completing the chain.[39]

The history of the Norman conquest is written down on the soil, and the alternate movements of the fights are recorded and mapped out on the sites still occupied by the castles and the roads.

> All that had been learned of the old fighting along this border stood out, suddenly, in the disposition of the castles and the roads. There on the upland had been the power of the Lords of the Marches, Fitz Osbern, Bernard of Newmarch, de Braose. Their towers now were decayed hollow teeth, facing the peaceful valleys into which their power had bitten. All that stayed of that world was the memory, the decayed shape of violence, confused in the legend with the rockfall of the Holy Mountain, where the devil's heel had slipped as he strode westward into our mountains.[40]

In this beautiful mixture of history and legend—an "archeological sense of place," as the historian R. Samuel calls it[41]—comes out, stemming from Matthew's trade as a university lecturer in history: Matthew's ability to decipher the signs/documents inscribed in the terrain and to interpret the meanings of past events is a distinctive feature of his intellectual activity and research in the field of economic history.

Yet, at the same time, it derives from Williams's methods and ways of analyzing cultural history, as one can clearly perceive from many pages of *Culture and Society*, from the chapters which form *The Long Revolution*, from his book on *Television* which "doubles back on itself to show the play of cause and effect in earlier forms of social drama, and positions the new medium in very long sequences of development,"[42] and from his cultural theory as a whole.

The historical past of his country in *Border Country* is also a past of industrial exploitation, of difficult relationships between the agrarian and industrial worlds; again, it is the fictional self of Williams, Matthew Price, who *sees* that complex situation:

> Or look out, not east, but south and west, and there, visibly, was another history and another border. There was the limestone scarp where the hills were quarried and burrowed. There along the outcrop stood a frontier invisible on the surface, between the rich and the barren rocks. On the near side the valleys were green and wooded, but beyond that line they had blackened with pits and slagheaps and mean grey terraces.[43]

After this unsentimental description, Matthew goes on commenting dryly:

> It seemed only an accident of the hidden rocks, but there, visibly, were two different worlds. There along the outcrop had stood the ironmasters, Guest, Crawshay, Bailey, Homfray, and this history had stayed.[44]

It is a past Matthew can now understand and explain to himself and to other people; but it is a past which deeply connects with his own present; nearly at the end of the novel, Matthew comes to know that he cannot stay in Glynmawr: he has to leave Wales for the second time in his life and has to go back down there where he lives, in London. After this long crisis is over, he feels he is ready to resume his research on the population movements in Wales during the Industrial Revolution. He can come down to earth, as it were; only, he takes with him what he has learnt and experienced from the past history of the Welsh villages and from his own past life there. Again, it is the complex interplay between memory and present reality[45] which helps in making up his own mind. He remembers his meeting with Blakeley:

On the way down the shapes faded and the ordinary identities returned. The voice in his mind faded, and the ordinary voice came back. Like old Blakeley asking, digging his stick in the turf. What will you be reading, Will? Books, sir? No, better not. History, sir. History from the Kestrel, where you sit and watch memory move, across the wide valley. That was the sense of it: to watch, to interpret, to try to get clear. Only the wind narrowing your eyes, and so much living in you, deciding what you will see and how you will see it. Never above, watching. You'll find what you're watching is yourself.[46]

This is how Matthew [Williams] relates to his Wales during this phase of his life, after leaving aside—at least partially—his role of stranger, but retaining his function of a "guest from a different generation."[47] The process Matthew goes through is the same type of process as Williams describes in the second chapter of *The Long Revolution*, when he writes of the difficulty of getting hold of "a sense of the ways in which the particular activities combined into a way of thinking and living."[48] His words are also an illustration and guide to the interpretation of Matthew's growth of consciousness; in a way, what Williams writes in his *Long Revolution* is already written in the pages which narrate of Matthew Price in *Border Country*. His ideas on the "structure of feeling" are already sketched out in his novel which, among other things, is also the story of a contrast between generations. On this aspect, Williams says:

We are usually most aware of this when we notice the contrasts between generations, who never talk quite "the same language," or when we read an account of our lives by someone from outside the community, or watch the small differences in style, of speech or behaviour, in someone who has learned our ways yet was not bred in them.[49]

Of course, the case of Matthew Price—the "scholarship" boy— is slightly different, because he was bred within the community of Glynmawr and educated at Cambridge; nevertheless, the section of the narrative where Will—after a long and much suffered argument with his father about leaving school and getting a job—refuses Morgan's offer to work at his factory is extremely telling. Will opposes his own views to his father's and to Morgan's, while Harry opposes his opinions to Will's and Morgan's trying to understand both and, at the end of an exhausting discussion, he sides with his son against Morgan.

Behind the gestures, the looks, the words, the confrontation one can imagine the novelist and cultural analyst Williams busy watching, recording, commenting, and interpreting. He gives the reader the idea of what is passing through Matthew's mind during that passionate confrontation with Harry and Morgan.

> Will could not say anything. It was as if he had no breath. He did not know why he should feel this extraordinary tension. It seemed that something was trying to get through to him, some strange pressure that was not even a voice yet that carried an unmistakable attention and warning. He saw Morgan and his father sitting side by side, looking across at him. How would it have been, he thought suddenly, if Morgan had been my father? He immediately looked away, as if the thought had been spoken.[50]

Will knows the answer to that; though he is unsure of his position between Harry and Morgan, he seems to know that—with all their divergencies—Harry understands him and encourages his expectations; in his turn, Will comprehends his father's ideas and beliefs. Of course, after the quarrel about his job, he feels that something has changed: "The real substance, and its roots, seemed to lie far back. This was a border defined, a border crossed."[51]

Obviously, differences and conflicts are very important in giving shape and meaning to the new experiences of the "learner" Will; from this point of view, his friendship with Morgan is highly significant and it becomes more so, first when his father falls ill and then after his death. Morgan helps him to clarify his sentiments toward Harry, "a man that is more of a man, more interesting as a man,"[52] and to himself. Will tries to explain his feelings, his fears, and his dissatisfaction with his life as a "worker" and as a "son":

> I don't know. We don't understand it. But a part of a whole generation has had this. A personal father, and that is one clear issue. But a father is more than a person, he's in fact a society, the thing you grow up into. For us, perhaps, that is the way to put it. We've been moved and grown into a different society. We keep the relationship, but we don't take over the work. We have, as you might say, a personal father but no social father. What they offer us, where we go, we reject.[53]

But Morgan corrects his way of seeing things, which is wrong according to him, and tries to explain the quality and the dimension of the exemplary figure of Harry Price by referring to what happened to them both after the General Strike. Morgan starts by recounting the events of those days:

> "We fought that strike hard. We were together then, young, in the box. And when we went down—down, mind, because our leaders got frightened, I insist on that—well, it was never the same for me, after that. I knew I wouldn't live to see any real change. Improvements, yes, but not a change where I could feel it."[54]

When Matthew says that he and other historians are still debating about what happened during the General Strike, Morgan gets terribly angry:

> "Never mind your side of it, Will. I'm telling you what it did to me. What it did, in fact, was to give me a different direction. I gave up the box, and started the business. I did well."[55]

It is Morgan's lived experience of the strike that helps to clear up what happened then, in what way the defeat of the working classes affected people's attitudes and ways of life, and how in the end it had a strong bearing on personal changes and reactions. It is Morgan, with his sensibility and consciousness of what that period in history signified to him and to the other men working at the railway station of Gwenton, who can make Matthew accept, or at least understand, his father's firm loyalty to his work and refusal of the change the offer of a job at Morgan's jam factory would have brought him. It is through Morgan's words that we learn of Harry's differences and ability to build directly from his own feelings:

> "That's what I say, what I always have said, and why Harry's different. He changes a thing because he wants the new thing, and he settles to it because he wants it right through, not because the rejection is driving him."[56]

In a way, and without knowing it consciously, Matthew *is* both looking at his father as a model figure and trying to be different from him. Again, significantly, it is Morgan who helps Matthew to work things out.

"Would you change places? With him now?"

"You're trying to, Will."

"Change places?" Matthew said, and then stopped. As he hesitated Morgan got up, buttoning his heavy coat.

"It's late. I'd better be going."

"With nothing finished?"

"We shan't finish this, Will. It's a lifetime."[57]

It is only after his father's funeral and after his arrival in London that Matthew realizes how wrong he was:

"It was as if I stared straight at the sun. A sun that was blinding me, as I was learning to see. I had stared as a child, almost destroying my sight. And I was staring again, at the same centre."[58]

These words signal the end of the journey from Glynmawr and the past to enter a new, consciously laid hold of, present and future. Something crucially important has happened within Matthew, who is no longer opposed to Will: he can look back at his own past and at his people's ways of life in Glynmawr grasping the whole meaning of that community experience and with more confidence in the future. He has reached a new form of maturity and consciousness, as he confesses to his wife:

"Only now it seems like the end of exile. Not going back, but the feeling of exile ending. For the distance is measured, and that is what matters. By measuring the distance, we come home."[59]

The frank recognition points also to another kind of ending: the self-exploration has come to its end, because Matthew has reached the innermost springs of his feelings and, having dominated his impulses, he is ready to watch, to understand, to interpret and elaborate, ultimately to communicate to others what can become not only reflection but action.

Williams's *Border Country*—which owes much to the many variegated narrative traditions of nineteenth-century working-class writing, to Lawrence's *Sons and Lovers*, and to the working-class life novels of twentieth-century Wales—is then something more complex than mere autobiographical fiction. The novel (and the other two narratives, *Second Generation* and *The Fight for Manod*, which complete the

"Welsh Trilogy") is an exploration in a new narrative and cultural form elaborating on Williams's concept of a "knowable community" and anticipating his idea of a "structure of feeling." Being in the position of "the visitor, the learner, the guest from a different generation," Matthew is in the privileged position of the listener who attends to the various narratives the members of that community offer him about their lives. Such a condition allows him to develop from there and to assume the role of the cultural analyst/historian/sociologist who acts as a catalyst for a whole process of structured remembrance. The plunging into the cultural life of Glynmawr—as it is reconstructed in the flashback chapters, dominated by memory and worked and reworked through the dialogues between Matthew and his father, between Matthew and his mother, between Matthew and Morgan, and by Matthew's own meditations—enables both Matthew and the reader to establish the connections with all those values and social practices which combine to make up the general organization of their lives: neighborhood, family, school, friendship, work, class relations, communication.

The almost documentary reconstruction may surprise us, and, in fact, suggests that what happened in Williams's life happens in Matthew's life too, with slight differences. In a way, we are in a better position to understand the author's life and thought, his criticism and methods of analyzing literary and cultural texts, and his fiction, which is at the same time a piece of cultural analysis. His Matthew Price is a perfect model of a character who represents beautifully the new generation; Williams's *Long Revolution* may serve as a useful comment to that:

> [. . .] the new generation responds in its own ways to the
> unique world it is inheriting, taking up many continuities, that
> can be traced, and reproducing many aspects of the organization, which can be separately described, yet feeling its whole
> life in certain ways differently, and shaping its creative response
> into a new structure of feeling.[60]

2

Cultural Studies and the Crisis in British Radical Thought

Dennis L. Dworkin

Raymond Williams has been influential on literary and political discussions in so many different ways, but perhaps none of them has been as important as his pivotal contributions to the creation of cultural studies. In *Culture and Society* (1958) and *The Long Revolution* (1960), Williams attempted to circumvent the blind alleys represented by the literary and social criticism of F. R. Leavis and the orthodox Marxist tradition. His close readings of cultural practices were reminiscent of Leavisite critics without succumbing to their reverence for the "Great Tradition." He extended Marxists' insistence on the class basis of society, while resisting their tendency to reduce cultural practices to reflections of the economic base. Williams's negotiation between Leavisite criticism and Marxism helped to create a new intellectual space, one in which culture was the essential link between social organization and experience. From this perspective, culture included "high" and "popular" expressions but was reducible to neither—culture as "the whole way of life."

Partially because of its interdisciplinary nature, cultural studies has been very difficult to define. Yet if its definition has been elusive, its political nature has been beyond dispute, as Raymond Williams himself has reminded us recently in his posthumously published address, "The Future of Cultural Studies."[1] But while Williams's contention itself might be uncontroversial, his view of what this "politics" has consisted of—its origins and development—is highly provocative.

Williams's argument might be regarded as a veiled attack on Stuart Hall's quasi-Althusserian interpretation of cultural studies, the generally accepted understanding of its development.[2] While Hall linked the evolution of cultural studies to radical politics, he mostly saw its development in terms of theoretical influences and paradigm shifts: the tension between the "culturalism" of the late fifties and sixties and the "structuralism" of the seventies. He marked its origins as a "problematic" by reference to a series of "classical" texts: Richard Hoggart's *The Uses of Literacy* (1957), E. P. Thompson's *The Making of the English Working Class* (1963), and Williams's *Culture and Society* and *The Long Revolution*. Williams, on the other hand, emphasized that cultural studies developed as a radical theoretical and political practice within an alternative educational setting. He was referring to the English adult education milieu of the late forties: part of a long-standing tradition of British worker's and adult education that provided a unique forum for intellectuals and working people to communicate. For Williams, the classic texts of cultural studies did not so much embody a theoretical paradigm shift as represent the most salient expression of a much wider practice, shaped by numerous men and women who never put their ideas in a written form. As a consequence, Williams had a very different view of cultural studies in the 1970s. Where Hall believed that cultural studies came into its own during this decade, Williams was troubled by the fact that theoretical sophistication had been purchased at the expense of incorporation into an inherently conservative university system.

While Williams sheds some much needed light on the history of cultural studies, his observations need to be placed in a broad political context. Undoubtedly, the move of cultural studies from the fringes to the center, or near center, of the academy was fraught with political danger, but Williams left unexamined the historical conditions in which this move took place. Universities in the seventies cannot be regarded in any simple way as reproducing the dominant ideology. As is well known, they were sites of turmoil, scenes of ideological and hegemonic struggle; and no simple incorporation of radical intellectual practices ever took place. Moreover, the working-class educational milieu, so important to the origins of cultural studies, had itself undergone fundamental change, in large part because working-class life was more heterogeneous and fragmented. What is missing, then, from Williams's account, and only alluded to in Hall's, is not the recognition of the political dimension of cultural studies but a full representation of its scope.

It is my contention that the trajectory of cultural studies must be situated within the whole culture of the British Left. I argue that cultural studies, and cultural Marxism more generally, must be viewed in terms of the crisis of the Left, a crisis virtually coterminous with the postwar era.[3] British cultural studies grew out of the effort to generate a socialist understanding of postwar Britain, to understand changes that undermined traditional Marxist assumptions about the working class and the traditional Left's exclusive reliance on political and economic categories. Cultural theorists attempted to identify the contours of this new terrain and, in doing so, to redefine social struggle. They were concerned, above all, with redefining the relationship between structure and agency, for the agency of traditional socialism, the industrial working class, no longer seemed to guarantee a socialist transformation. To illustrate this general point, I would like to look at two historical moments critical to the formation of cultural studies: the late fifties and the early sixties, when the classical texts were published, and the decade of the 1970s, when cultural studies became part of the intellectual map. In the process, I shall also be examining Williams's own relationship to cultural studies.

Who Never Had It So Good?

However important the adult education context might have been to the development of a cultural studies outlook, it was only fully articulated in conjunction with the New Left politics of the late 1950s. Briefly, the British New Left was a heterogeneous group of ex-communists, disaffected Labour supporters, and socialist students hopeful of renewing socialist theory and practice. They were brought together as a result of the Suez and Hungary crises in 1956, and were consolidated by a shared commitment to the nuclear disarmament movement of the late fifties and early sixties. New Left activists attempted to create a democratic socialist politics rooted in English traditions but not bogged down by the orthodoxies of the past. Eventually "New Left" came to define virtually any radical tendency that was not in the mainstream of leftist politics. But in late 1950s Britain, where the term first came into usage, it had a very specific meaning: neither communist nor social democratic.

The major question faced by the New Left, like the Left more generally, was that socialists, despite having created the mixed economy and the welfare state, appeared doomed to endless electoral defeats. While the electorate might have relied on Labour to mold the postwar framework, Harold MacMillan's Tories repeatedly convinced voters that they were better equipped to administer the new "affluent society." The root of the problem was the reshaping of working-class consciousness and culture, a consequence of full employment, steadily growing income, the beginning of class mobility, and spreading mass culture. While the working class certainly did not become middle class in the way that many imagined that it would, transformations were undeniable. Most importantly, these beginnings of Britain's "Americanization" called into question one of the principal tenets of the socialist project: the belief that the working-class movement would inevitably bring about a socialist transformation.

Throughout the fifties, Labour struggled to find a way of appealing to an acquisitive and mobile working class living in a mass society. Its most original response was the "revisionism" associated with Anthony Crosland, John Strachey, and the party leader Hugh Gaitskell. For a thinker like Crosland, the 1945 Labour government had created the foundation for a postcapitalist society which rendered obsolete the traditional socialist emphasis on class struggle and ownership of the means of production. He argued that if Labour refused to formally endorse American-style liberalism, it would become a permanent and dwindling opposition.

While the New Left certainly objected to the portrayal of Britain as "postcapitalist," and strenuously disagreed that the conditions for class struggle were coming to an end, it recognized the sweeping and wide ranging transformations in postwar English society. New Left activists rejected the politics of revisionism, but believed that its analysis of the changing society could not be overlooked. Socialists, they argued, must acknowledge the profound impact of the new consumer society and welfare state, and create a socialist politics founded on everyday life and experience, not outworn myths and slogans. They advocated a totalizing conception of radical politics or "socialism at full stretch," one in which the cultural dimension was considered as important as the explicitly political. But if the New Left represented a distinct place on the political map, it was nonetheless the site of intense political and ideological conflict between ex-communist Marxists, who feared that the new politics threatened to displace the centrality of the working class, and the younger generation of intellectual radicals, who were eager to distance themselves from the politics of the past.

The New Left response to labor revisionism and the crisis in socialism was shaped by, and reflected in, the founding texts of cultural studies. *The Uses of Literacy* and *Culture and Society* were written just prior to the founding of the New Left, and played a central role in articulating the New Left agenda, while later works like *The Long Revolution* and *The Making of the English Working Class* were in turn influenced by the New Left experience. These works (as we shall see) may be regarded as being in friendly debate with each other, but they shared in various ways a rejection of the terms of the argument about working-class affluence. They argued that there was no simple or necessary correlation between a standard of living and a political response: working class affluence did not necessarily produce "embourgeoisement" and the end of socialist aspiration. This attitude about the working class is best summarized by Williams in *Culture and Society*:

> We all like to think of ourselves as a standard, and I can see that it is genuinely difficult for the English middle-class to suppose that the working class is not desperately anxious to become like itself. I am afraid this must be unlearned. The great majority of English working people want only the middle-class material standard and for the rest want to go on being themselves. . . . The working people, who have felt themselves long deprived in any adequacy, intend to get them and to keep them if they can. It would need more evidence than this to show that they are becoming vulgar materialists, or that they are becoming "bourgeois."[4]

For Williams, as for Hoggart and Thompson, it was not poverty that produced socialism but the collective aspirations inherent in working-class life. The emphasis was on "community."

If the founders of the nascent cultural studies outlook believed in the durability of working-class values, they were still clearly anxious about contemporary social trends. This is most clearly expressed as a pervasive anxiety about the corrosive effects of mass culture on the working-class way of life. Such an attitude is perhaps most closely associated with Hoggart's conclusion to *The Uses of Literacy*, which raised serious doubts about the ability of working-class people to resist the temptations of a vacuous commercial culture. But it was also true, if not as obvious, of Williams, who once described mass culture as "a synthetic culture, or anti-culture, which is alien to almost everybody"; and thus, not surprisingly, he was befuddled as to why working people were enthusiastic about it.[5] What Williams said about working-class attitudes toward newspapers and magazines could have been extended to their relationship to the whole of mass culture: "But there is still one surprising fact: that people whose quality of personal living is so high are apparently satisfied by a low quality of printed feeling and opinion."[6]

Underlying Hoggart and Williams's condemnation and anxiety about mass culture was the fear that Britain was going the American route. In part, such feelings were connected to British intellectuals' well-known contempt for American vulgarity, but they were also perhaps related to the pervasiveness of the myth of classlessness in American political discourse. Though Williams acknowledged that American culture was not uniformly inferior in quality, he was clearly dismayed that in certain respects Britain had become "culturally an American colony" and seemed to be heartened by the fact that the worst mass cultural products consumed by British audiences were American in origin.[7] E. P. Thompson manifested similar attitudes toward the growing influence of American culture on the English way of life. As a member of the Communist Party, Thompson actively participated in anti-American campaigns, including a conference on "The American Threat to British Culture" held in 1951. In his address to the conference—"William Morris and the Moral Issues of the Day"—he vividly captured the most worrisome aspect of American cultural imperialism.

> In place of the great proletarian values revealed in class-solidarity and militancy, we now have, even among sections of our own working class movement, the values of private living growing up—the private fears and neuroses, the self-interests and timid individualism fostered by pulp magazines and Hollywood films.[8]

Though Hoggart, Thompson, and Williams shared a common understanding of postwar changes, their differences were of equal significance. In many respects, Thompson's and Williams's conflicts were emblematic of the divisions in the New Left generally. Where Williams had left the Communist Party immediately following the War, and was skeptical of the continued relevance of Marxist politics and theory, Thompson was a loyal party member during the worst days of the Cold War, and conceived of himself as one of the few voices in the early New Left to speak for the Marxist tradition. For Williams, the New Left journal, *The New Reasoner*, edited by ex-communists Thompson and John Saville, was "still too involved in arid fights with the Party Marxists," and gave the impression that nothing had changed at all after 1956.[9] In Thompson's terms, Williams had admirably avoided theoretical sectarianism during the Cold War, but in the process had appropriated some of the assumptions and perspectives of his opponents. The result was that in *Culture and Society* he had adopted a reverential tone toward a tradition of mostly reactionary thinkers.

Thompson's and Williams's differences were most visibly spelled out in their conceptions of revolution. Williams conceived of revolution in epochal terms. He coined the term "long revolution" to describe the industrial, democratic, and cultural transformation of the last two hundred years. It was an oxymoron simultaneously conveying the radically innovative and protracted nature of the process. "It is a genuine revolution," he wrote:

> . . . transforming men [sic] and institutions; continually extended and deepened by the actions of millions, continually and variously opposed by explicit reaction and by the pressure of habitual forms and ideas. Yet it is a difficult revolution to define, and its uneven action is taking place over so long a period that it is almost impossible not to get lost in its exceptionally complicated process.[10]

Williams's faith in the "long revolution" was implicitly founded on the optimistic belief that the welfare state represented one more stage in the long march of the working class whose institutions would gradually become the institutions of society as a whole.

Thompson agreed that the creation of the welfare state unleashed possibilities for socialist transformation that were scarcely imaginable in the earlier part of the century. But like Terry Eagleton nearly twenty years later, he objected to Williams's gradualist assumptions.[11] Thompson was not attempting to create a rigid dichotomy between "gradualism" and "revolution," but he believed that Williams's position ignored class struggle. While finding the wish for a common culture admirable, he argued that cultural expansion in a capitalist society inevitably produced an intensification of class conflict as the real divisions of interest and power became more visible. Even in a long revolution, Thompson suggested, those social forces working toward common ownership, a common culture, and an organic community, must eventually confront the realities of class power. "My own view of revolution (I am often assured)," he wrote, "is too 'apocalyptic': but Mr. Williams is perhaps too bland."[12] Without some theory of revolutionary transformation—a conspicuous silence in *The Long Revolution*—the socialist project would be ultimately frustrated.

Since Hoggart's and Williams's most influential works were published virtually at the same time, it was often assumed that they developed their ideas in tandem. Williams himself once observed that their names were so frequently linked that it sounded as if it were a joint firm.[13] But despite the obvious similarities between them, there were also decisive differences. Indeed, the conclusion to *Culture and Society* may be read in part as a refutation of Hoggart's pessimistic prognosis of the working class's future, one in which Williams romanticized working-class values. Williams argued that the reason working-class culture remained an alternative to bourgeois society was not because of its everyday practices, which had never remained static, but because of its political culture—the collective and democratic institutions of the labor movement. He acknowledged that numerous working-class people felt pressured to take advantage of the "opportunity state" and that individual members had climbed the ladder offered them. Yet he was convinced that the collective democratic idea, the foundation of working-class experience, remained unimpaired. While liberal reform was ultimately based on the maintenance of inequality and exploitation, the extension of working-class values would lead to genuine democracy.

Thompson's writings in the late fifties and early sixties, including *The Making of the English Working Class*, were written not only as a critique of Williams's "culturalism" but also as a response to Hoggart's more sociological approach. For Thompson, the pessimistic analysis of the contemporary working class contained in the writings of Hoggart and his followers (including a young Stuart Hall) lacked historical perspective. Thompson pointed out that working people had been lured by social climbing and status since the middle of the nineteenth century, that they were the original consumers during the Industrial Revolution, and that church and state agencies had fought to control the people's minds as persistently as the purveyors of mass culture.[14] Throughout its history, the working-class movement, especially the militant activists of the trade union and labor movement, resisted forms of manipulation and control, and struggled in turn for democratic and social reforms. Yet if Thompson correctly criticized Hoggart and his followers for being ahistorical, and injected a much needed dose of historical perspective into New Left debates, his own position had problems as well. In stressing the continuity of working-class history, and suggesting that the working-class situation was neither unique nor radically different than during previous periods, Thompson avoided considering the unprecedented changes after 1945. Yet such changes would not go away.

Cultural Studies and Crisis in Radical Thought

Between Structuralism and Humanism

If cultural studies was produced by the climate surrounding Suez and Hungary, it was transformed by the countercultural politics of 1968. Not only were many of the leading theorists and writers who expanded the field affected by, and participants in, these events, but their experience of them influenced the way that they conceived of culture and ideology, and presented them with both objects to investigate and theoretical problems to solve. They attempted to understand both the emergence of countercultural and radical practices and the means by which the dominant ideological structures defined and defused them. This included the means by which an independent media helped to secure the hegemony of the ruling class and the State. But it was not only an intellectual shift. In a sense, cultural studies came to resemble a counterculture itself. Like the sixties subcultures, cultural theorists participated in a semi-autonomous intellectual culture founded in opposition to bourgeois norms. They escaped (what they saw as) the stifling effects of English bourgeois culture by bringing a new vocabulary into English radical discussions—French structuralism and semiology and Western Marxist thought, especially that of the philosopher Louis Althusser. The result was a radical intellectual culture larger than anything that existed before, but whose audience was considerably narrower, for it systematically excluded those not versed in its intricate, and sometimes difficult, philosophical discourse.

These changes dramatically affected the political debates surrounding cultural studies. While the cultural theorists of the 1970s were no less haunted by the crisis in radicalism, they were less confident than their predecessors. Taken together, the political counterculture's inability to challenge British institutions; the growth of political movements like feminism, ecology, gay rights, and antiracism; the apparently growing fragmentation and assimilation of the working class; the indisputable evidence for British economic decline; and the growing feeling that Labour's defense of capitalism was barely distinguishable from the Tories' further called into question the inevitable triumph of socialism and the "long revolution." Indeed, one of the principal characteristics of cultural studies during this time was a preoccupation with discovering social subjects that were an alternative to the traditional working class.

These shifts in the cultural studies outlook can best be seen in the Birmingham Centre for Contemporary Cultural Studies, whose work in the 1970s was as critical for the growth of the field as Hoggart's, Thompson's, and Williams's had been in the previous decade. The

Centre was founded in 1964 under the directorship of Richard Hoggart, and was originally part of the School of English at the University of Birmingham. Its original purpose, following Hoggart and Williams, was to use the literary critical approach to illuminate contemporary culture. Yet by the late 1960s, cultural researchers and theorists at the Centre had grown dissatisfied with the theoretical foundations of their project. They recognized that their method of close readings must be anchored in a wider understanding of society, an understanding that could only come from social theory. Moreover, their involvement in the Birmingham University protest of 1969 brought home the potential and limits of human agency, the specificity of ideological struggle, and the power of the media to shape events. After an initial attraction to modes of thought like Weberian sociology and phenomenological sociology, the Centre turned to Marxism and structuralism.

There are several possible ways to conceive of the Centre's multifaceted theoretical and empirical work at this time, but I will be discussing it primarily in two ways. First, I will be considering it as a political project, as an attempt to overcome the crisis in radicalism. From this point of view, the Centre's work may be regarded as an attempt to discover alternative agents to the traditional working class. Second, I will be looking at its project in relationship to that of the founders, especially Williams. In this context, Centre theorists in the 1970s may be thought of as trying to critically fuse two intellectual traditions often starkly counterposed: the socialist humanist impulse of writers such as Hoggart, Thompson, and Williams, and the structuralist perspectives of Althusser and Barthes. This balancing act, which was articulated in the second half of the decade, was achieved through the critical adoption of the thought of Antonio Gramsci.

This theoretical project of negotiation between "structuralism" and "humanism" was largely developed by Stuart Hall, and can be found in the Centre's best known work, its numerous contributions to subcultural studies. These studies were grounded in the socialist humanism, culturalism, and cultural Marxism of the pioneers of cultural studies. In the tradition of Williams, Thompson, and Hoggart, cultural researchers "listened" to and recreated the lived experience of cultural consumers and producers, especially that of oppressed groups. The Centre's recovery of the experience of youth subcultures showed as much respect for its subjects as any work within the tradition of *The Making of the English Working Class* and incorporated the method of close reading associated with *The Uses of Literacy*. Yet the Centre's approach was irrevocably altered by the Althusserianism challenge to the humanist tradition's impulse to conceptualize culture in terms of experience. They saw Althusser's theory as a way of grounding ideology in material conditions yet treating it as a discrete process. It allowed them to see cultural practices as not merely the expression of lived experience, but as a "field of signification" which was both determined by, and determinate of, consciousness and subjectivity. Centre theorists thus rejected both Thompson's counterposing of experience to ideology in *The Making of the English Working Class* and Williams's contention in *The Long Revolution* that a particular culture could only be truly known by those who lived in it. They saw culture as being pulled by both experience and ideology, a relationship that could only be negotiated theoretically.

In this context, Paul Willis's *Learning to Labour* exemplifies the position that the Centre eventually developed. The book was an ethnographic study of a group of white, teenage, working-class boys from the industrial heartland—"the lads"—living through the crucial transition from school to waged work. It told the story of how, in the act of opposing the dominant ideology of capitalist society, the lads eventually accepted a role which guaranteed their oppression. While Willis's study of working-class youth was situated within a debate on education, its perspective reflected the Centre's unique theoretical stance in contemporary debates on Marxism.[15] Willis steered a middle course between the extremes of structuralism and humanism. On the one hand, his recovery and celebration of contemporary working-class culture—his insistence that working people shaped their lives in the process of struggle—recalled the spirit of Thompson's *The Making of the English Working Class*. However, Willis's celebration of human agency (unlike Thompson's) was founded on a theory of reproduction. Indeed, his acceptance of the close relationship between the educational sphere and the ideological reproduction of the social formation was, in effect, an endorsement of the Althusserian concept of ideological state apparatuses. Yet it was not a wholesale endorsement. Willis echoed the socialist humanist critique of structuralist theory, attacking its functionalism and impoverished conception of human agency. For Willis, social agents were not merely bearers of structural forces; their experience of the social world was not reducible to external determinations; and the outcome of collective projects was not a foregone conclusion. Structuralist interpretations needed to be supplemented by a conception of the "cultural," the semi-autonomous domain through which social agents lived the meaning of structure, understood and represented it, resisted and transformed it, and frequently reproduced it.

Underpinning Willis's attempt to grasp the relationship between structure and agency was his preoccupation with the crisis in radicalism. Like other Centre researchers, Willis veered between celebrating the rebellious spirit of subcultures, whose practices at times (it seemed to him) presaged an alternative society, and making it clear that their opposition to bourgeois ideology was ultimately absorbed. Following the sociologist Phil Cohen (and his theoretical mentor Althusser), he saw subcultural response as ideological and "imaginary," unable to penetrate the real class contradictions which it resolved at another level.[16] Yet he held out the hope that working-class youth would eventually understand and act upon their situation.

This is apparent, for example, in Willis's first book, *Profane Culture*, an ethnographic study of two socially unrelated youth subcultures—working-class motorbike boys and hippies. Willis regarded these two groups as challenging in different ways the everyday values of the dominant order and, in the case of the hippies, the cultural politics of the organized Left. Though the groups lacked either the means or desire to topple the system, they provided "profoundly premature, post-revolutionary cultural responses to pre-revolutionary social, political and organizational problems." Willis's utopianism was mitigated by an awareness that the countercultures of the late sixties never really mounted a political challenge to the dominant order, that their radicalism had been defused and appropriated. Yet in defeat they provide a valuable political lesson. "A genuine politics must come from the people, from cultural politics, as well as down from theory, or the political party."[17]

What has been said about Willis is also true of Angela McRobbie, though she was an important critic of the dominant masculinist tendencies of Birmingham subcultural studies, including Willis.[18] McRobbie argued that male subcultural experience was poisoned by sexism, and male cultural researchers, in so far as they celebrated it, were implicitly endorsing it. Women, owing to their structural position in the sexual division of labor, could not share the same space as the men. But they could create their own distinctive subcultural practices derived from their own experience—what McRobbie and other feminists described as "feminine cultures of romance and domesticity." Yet if McRobbie had a different vision of subcultures than her male counterparts, she had the same identification with them. "As a pre-figurative form and set of social relations," she wrote, "I can't help but think it could have a positive meaning for girls who are pushed from early adolescence into achieving their feminine status through acquiring a 'steady.'"[19] Feminist cultural theorists, then, no less than their male counterparts, were haunted by the crisis in radicalism—the struggle to overcome the contradictions between structure and agency. They resorted to the same utopian solution of overcoming it.

While the Centre's work in the 1970s represented a critique of its own theoretical foundations, it is important to remember that the founders of cultural studies themselves did not stand still. Raymond Williams reformulated his cultural theory in the 1970s in response to the social upheavals of the late sixties and in recognition of a kind of Marxism unknown in Britain during the Cold War years. Williams was originally critical of Marxist cultural theory, but his later position, which he described as "cultural materialism," was conceived as a "theory of the specificities of material and literary production within historical materialism."[20] It contained a greater stress on both cultural and political struggle (a tacit response to Thompson's original critique) and on the "ideological" or, what was a preferable term to his mind, the "hegemonic." Williams, in effect, expanded his idea of culture by critically adapting Gramsci's concept of hegemony:

> a whole body of practices and expectations, over the whole of living: our sense and assignments of energy, our shaping perceptions of ourselves and our world. It is a lived system of meanings and values—constitutive and constituting—which as they are experienced as practices appear as reciprocally conforming.[21]

Hegemony was a process of cultural domination never static or total, but continually defended, challenged, reformulated, and reproduced.[22] It was in continuous conflict with oppositional forces: "emergent" and "residual" cultural forms which posed a threat to the dominant order, even if confined and marginalized by hegemonic constraints.

While Centre researchers acknowledged Williams's continuing contribution to the field of cultural studies, especially his attention to cultural contestation, they regarded his later work as a modification, rather than a transformation, of his original project.[23] By the end of the 1970s, they openly rejected Williams's conception of the social totality. For it was based on the idea that society was an indissoluble whole, founded on a single contradiction, capital and waged labor, linked to the various cultural and political practices by a series of "correspondences" or "homologies." Under the influence of Althusser, Hall emphasized the "specificity" and "autonomy" of practices in a social formation, their unity based on "difference" rather than "correspondence," linked together through "articulations." He argued that this conception of the social formation as a "structured totality" made it possible to understand "how social practices (articulated around contradictions which do not arise in the same way, at the same point, in the same moment) can nevertheless be brought *together*."[24]

Dick Hebdige's *Subculture* exemplifies the differences between the Centre and Williams's approach in the late 1970s. In *Subculture*, Hebdige doubted that there was a necessary correspondence between the constituent parts of the social formation. He implied that each level was structured by a unique set of determinants and linked to each other and the whole through "articulations." Social practices were not "determined" in the classical Marxist sense but "overdetermined." In Althusserian terms, Hebdige saw the social formation as being a "structured" rather than an "expressive" totality, meaning that its unity was constituted, not by the homologous relationship between practices, but by their differences.

Hebdige's view was sustained by his reading of Punks. While Punks were a product of working-class culture, they dislodged themselves from their own experiential location, relating to it as if from the outside. "In this way, although the punks referred continually to the realities of school, work, family and class, these references only made sense at one remove: they were passed through the fractured circuitry of punk style and re-presented as 'noise', disturbance, entropy."[25] Punk had a unity, but it was ruptural, dislocated, ironic, self-conscious. Hebdige was not suggesting that all subcultures could be explained in these terms, but he concluded that Punk culture demonstrated that the relationship between experience, expression, and signification was not necessarily homologous. His view of cultural practices was clearly at odds with Williams's contention that culture was the embodiment of experience.

Raymond Williams and Cultural Studies Today

In his recent book, Patrick Brantlinger has argued that cultural studies in the 1980s returned to its sources, that "the recent turn in cultural studies away from an emphasis on determining 'structures' to indeterminate 'practices' is also a return to the emphasis on lived experience in Hoggart, Thompson, and Williams. . . ."[26] It is difficult to see what Brantlinger has in mind. Cultural studies, as developed by the Centre, never ceased to be interested in "lived experience"; its work attempted to come to terms with both "structures" and indeterminate "practices"; and insofar as there has been a renewed interest in "experience" the greatly expanded and diverse cultural studies field in the 1980s has by no means entailed a return to the ideas of an earlier generation. If anything, it has relied on a combination of poststructuralist and feminist points of view.

This continued direction of cultural studies away from the founders includes a movement away from the thought of Raymond Williams. For although in such ideas as the "structure of feeling," Williams recognized that invoking the concept of ideology was too rationalistic to capture the forms of everyday consciousness, his own understanding of them has not been very useful for the most recent direction in cultural studies. There are undoubtedly many reasons for this. But the most important is that though a generous supporter of the women's movement, Williams never came to terms with the great diversity of feminist work on the construction of subjectivity and consciousness. Nor did his work easily lend itself to a critical modification from a feminist perspective. As Jenny Bourne Taylor has recently observed: "While the means to analyze the historical and cultural construction of gender identity seem to be there, where one tries to pin them down, they slip away."[27] It is not that Williams failed to recognize the interdependence of "structure" and "consciousness" but that partially because he was hostile to the individualistic biases of psychoanalysis, he never explored what they were. As Bourne Taylor points out, the result is that he has left out

> those difficult areas within the self or family simply in shadow, so that in an odd kind of way he ends up implicitly doing the same kind of thing that he accuses psychoanalysis of—by not subjecting those forms of subjectivity to "social" analysis he perpetuates the split between the public and the private, the personal and the political that in other areas he so thoroughly takes to pieces.[28]

But if cultural studies seems to have moved away from one of its most influential founders, like so much of its history, this shift must be understood in political terms. Williams's historical approach to understanding the politics of signification will undoubtedly continue to inspire students of culture. This has been recently underscored in the posthumously published 1986 dialogue with Edward Said, where Williams forcefully states the purpose of radical criticism:

> "If you analyze the representations with the history, if in the representations you trace their sources, you see what is absent

from them as well as what is present. And you then also see how the form of these images actually contributes to the way people perceive, and act within, those situations."[29]

Yet if Williams's understanding of the aim of criticism is still worthy of attention, his political ideas, rooted in the notion of a "knowable community," are a less reliable guide. In the end, they are founded on the same nostalgia for the organic community of the past as the Leavisites. This nostalgia can be found in his writings right up to his death, as in a 1987 talk when he argues that to overcome the ahistoricism of postmodernism it is essential to put forward an "alternative tradition taken from the neglected works left in the wide margins of the century, a tradition which may address itself . . . to a *modern* future in which community may be imagined again."[30] While Williams himself might have been open to a radical politics of diversity, his notion of community implies the homogeneous experience of a particular group bound to a particular place. As Dick Hebdige has written about the notion of community in general:

> The tendency to isolate, idealize and homogenize communities is matched by the assertion of the integrity and "purity" of cultural traditions. Cosmopolitanism—the register in which the "globalisation" of culture is today represented—is regarded as the inauthentic Other to all that is "local," "lived" hence "real."[31]

Such characteristics, of course, are present in the writings of Williams: the faith in the purity of working-class values, the dislike for mass culture, the suspicion of Americanization, and the stubborn insistence that authentic values will reassert themselves after the eventual dissipation of modernism.

When Williams first developed his ideas about the working-class community in the 1950s, the working class itself was already beginning to fragment. In retrospect, his solution to the crisis in radicalism was to insist on the myth of the working class, even when the evidence for the reality of such a myth was mounting. In contemporary Britain, as elsewhere in the advanced capitalist West, the crisis has accelerated at a frantic pace, and the myth of the working class can no longer be sustained. The politics of "difference," founded on the recognition of a necessary diversity of interests and grounded in the politics of race, ethnicity, gender, and class, has been a response to this crisis. The conception of such a politics has done much to contribute to the growth of radical thought. But it has so far produced no image of the future or strategy for getting there, in part because it has no unified concept of who precisely will transform society and for what reason. Moreover, while many socialists in the West have long distanced themselves from Leninist models of radical change, the clear failure of existing socialism in Eastern and Central Europe has been a severe blow to socialism as an economic system and as an alternative to capitalism. As we enter a world in which the traditional basis for radical transformation has been undermined, we might respect how much Raymond Williams has helped us to grapple with this new situation. But though he has only been dead for less than five years, he is already part of a different political age.

3

Placing the Occasion: Raymond Williams and Performing Culture

Loren Kruger

"Culture is ordinary." This idea unsettles a familiar, rather *literary,* notion of culture: culture as monument to special, usually artistic achievement of exemplary works, and the "arts and learning" necessary for their appreciation.[1] Instead of the "work of art" addressed to an enlightened minority, "culture is ordinary" offers us culture as common activity:

> It is not a question of relating art to the society, but of studying all the activities and their inter-relations, without any concession of priority to any of them we may choose to abstract.[2]

"Culture Is Ordinary" offers a radical departure from the minority culture known as the "great tradition." It challenges the mystique of the unique work of art by invoking the habitual aspect of activities common to all.

Conceiving of culture as popular "activity" does not simply expand the reach of culture beyond the specialized sense of the "great tradition." It questions the very notion of culture as precious *art objects* sheltered from the contingencies of social life. Moreover, the idea of art as an activity among others challenges the theoretical and evaluative priority of the tradition. In its place is the outline of culture as popular activities, as *signifying practices* in the life of society, alongside the *significant products* or works engendered by those practices that critically represent and act upon social life. This emphasis provides the impetus, in *Culture and Society* and *The Long Revolution,* for the study of the "ordinary processes of human societies" ("Culture Is Ordinary," 6) *as* signifying practices, so that the production and consumption of the electronic media and local subcultural group interaction may take their place as significant cultural products and pursuits.[3]

This dialectic between significant product and signifying practice emerges in Williams's early work on modern drama, in the relationships between the settled value of the work and the effect of its performance on the "structures of feeling" in society, to become a crucial problematic informing his perennial emphasis on culture as activity.[4] At stake in this project is Williams's conviction that people in society are their own cultural agents, transforming those situations by acting *on* and acting *in* them, in short, by performing them. Cultural practice is *symbolic action,* a sense of "strategies for encompassing social situations," to modify Kenneth Burke's formulation for making sense of social life through representing it.[5]

The invocation of performance is not a mere metaphor. The immediacy and the site-specificity of dramatic performance—staging an action for a particular audience in a particular time and place—enables a community to engage in what Williams calls *subjunctive action.* It provides the means, but also the *occasion* for marginalized community, affiliated, in his accounts, by class and region or, as I will later show, by race and gender, to *stage* their marginalization and to enact alternatives to the hegemonic center, which are meaningful and so common to that community. Culture is not universal or timeless, but multiple *strategies* that vary in response to the social, political, cultural affiliations of the people engaging with them. "Common culture" cannot mean that "all people possess an equal amount of so much cultural property,"[6] whose value is presumed universal, but rather that particular communities will choose, not merely consent to, those practices that make sense to them. The significance and even the audience's *perception* of cultural practice *as* culture arises out of the place and occasion, rather than the form, of its performance.

This emphasis on performance and participation in diverse cultural practices rather than "extension" of cultural property allows us to review drama as cultural practice. If certain forms, such as drama, appear to us to be *inherently* specialized artifacts of "high" culture, it is because the history of their *performance* and the conventions, including prevailing expectations governing their perception and reception, continue to secure their legitimacy. No small-scale form (such as drama) belongs inevitably to a dominant minority, anymore than mass-mediated culture is "popular" by virtue of large-scale consumption. By stressing the historical and social specificity not merely of cultural practice but also of its perceived value, it challenges the very commonplace that has excluded drama: the *essential* dichotomy between a "high" culture of special works and a "low" culture of leisure consumption. To a remarkable degree, this dichotomy still underpins canonical literary criticism and contemporary cultural studies, even though they may take opposite sides. Williams's reflections on place, occasion, and activity offer us a way beyond the opposition between the "selective tradition" and the "ordinary processes of human societies."

The Uncommon Pursuit: Exemplary Culture and the Legacy of Leavis

Yet, even as he prepares the way for a radical transformation of our study of culture, Williams hesitates at this critical border, at which culture is both "art" and "activity." Confronted with the radical leveling implied in the phrase "culture is ordinary," and concerned lest "culture is ordinary" (natural, common, popular) might produce only "ordinary (mundane, trivial, consumer) culture," Williams returns to the high ground of aesthetic *value* and the apparently inalienable concept of *art*. Although the works embodying this value may vary according to the final arbiter of experience, and the shape of the art may change according to the pressure of differing experience ("Culture Is Ordinary," 16), the categories "art" and "experience" themselves remain enduring touchstones of meaning.

This essentialism depends on an undifferentiated concept of "common culture" as *common sense*, which smooths over conflicts between antagonistic cultural practices. It does not, in other words, grapple directly with the fact that "culture involves power and helps to produce asymmetries in the abilities of social groups to define and realize their needs."[7] Before we can harness Williams's insights to a critical study of culture as performance in "community," we must investigate its association with an explicitly conservative "common pursuit."

The conception of art as the "special processes of discovery and creative effort" ("Culture Is Ordinary," 6), may seem to lead us to "ordinary processes of society," but the notion of the "finest individual meanings," accessible to those "members" who are "trained" to appreciate them, bears a startling resemblance to cultural critics known for their defense of elite culture. This sense of culture as *exemplary works,* somehow both universal and proper to "sensitive" minds, echoes Leavis' "sensitive . . . complete reader," Eliot's "critic [engaged] in the common pursuit of true judgment" and Arnold's "disinterested play of the mind."[8] This "common pursuit" pulls us away from the ordinary to the *exemplary* and the *exceptional,* and from there relentlessly to Eliot's and Leavis's "minority culture." Set against what these critics see as the tawdry materialism of the majority "mass culture," *common culture* takes on the image of its opposite: the patrimony of an embattled minority.

Williams clearly resists this minority's claim to represent common culture, but he shares their resistance to the common character of *mass* culture. His attachment to "art" as the "creativity in *all* our living" (*LR,* 37) is thus rooted in a desire to separate the "creativity in all our living" from what he sees as the *secondary* reaction of *leisure consumption* (*LR,* 38). In other words, he joins the conservative cultural critics in rejecting the idea that the leisure pursuits of ordinary people might amount to a "common pursuit" of culture. Even as he shares their indictment of the degrading aspects of mass culture, Williams refuses nonetheless to agree that the people themselves are merely a *mass* of passive consumers ("Culture Is Ordinary," 11). Instead, he maintains that ordinary people are as capable as elites of contributing to a common culture, once they are no longer excluded from it.

Having dismissed the claims of mass culture, Williams argues for greater access to "art" so that it may *become* common. He sees the relationship between culture and social organization as enabling rather than conflicting. Although he acknowledges the Marxist argument that prevailing economic and social discrimination continue to limit the impact of cultural democratization, he still asserts the desirability of that democratization and its potential impact on the whole society:

> To take our arts to new audiences is to be quite certain that in many respects these arts will be changed. . . . I would not expect the working people of England to support works, which, after proper and patient preparation, they could not accept. The real growth will be slow and uneven, but state provision . . . should be a growth in this direction and not a means of [preserving] a fixed and finished partial culture. . . . cultural growth . . . is a continual offering for common acceptance, . . . we should not therefore, try to determine in advance what should be offered, but clear the channels and let all the offerings be made ("Culture Is Ordinary," 16).

The argument for change seems remarkably accommodating. On the one hand, we have Williams's insistence that *we* (the educated Left) affirm the right of the "working people of England" to shape "our" arts; on the other, however, we cannot fail to notice that these working people (reified as *they*) are expected to "accept" "art" after patient preparation. Although the arts *"will be* changed," it is not clear that the "working people" are the agents of this change.

Even as he sets up this patrician dispensation, Williams claims that it is not patrician at all. He asserts that the "channels" are neutral and have only to be "opened" to let "growth" take place. Implicated in this benign view of neutral structures is not only a conviction that evolution and common "growth" will preempt the premature narrowing of offerings, but also that those with current access will be benevolent "persons of experience and goodwill"—as Britain's informal, but tightly knit, elite has historically called itself. This sanguine faith in government arts provision is at odds with the facts. In reality, the patrician practice of "maintaining standards" has regularly sacrificed extension and access (dubbed "dandelions for the many") to the promotion of "powerhouses of culture" serving the metropolitan elite ("roses for the few").[9]

In the light of this discrimination, the *conceptualization* of cultural democracy as "growth" obscures the actual barriers to democratization (in the restrictions on further education, for example) and the ways in which preserving "a fixed and finished partial culture" figures as the legitimate defense of *tradition*.[10] Moreover, the "selective tradition" is usually defended (whether directly by state support or informally by producers and audiences) *in the name* of common culture, which reinforces the self-evident character of that tradition and the hegemony of the minority group that claims possession of it.[11] It is precisely the *self-evidence* of this hegemony, its "common sense," that sustains dominance by consent of a particular social group or cultural formation, which defines both the terrain and the players in the contest for a *legitimate* "common culture."[12]

The cornerstone of "Culture Is Ordinary" is thus also its weak point. Williams would like to persuade us that his position is common sense, that culture *is* indeed ordinary and therefore not exclusive. Although he acknowledges that the actual restriction of cultural access means that "growth" will be "slow and uneven," he would like to claim that a truly common culture is the *natural* outcome of this inclusive and restorative growth, rather than the successive domination of different and exclusive notions of culture. The idea of a common culture is alluring but, in this accommodating form, it can only be insubstantial.

It offers little concrete engagement with the persistence of a culture held (and withheld) "in common" by a ruling group ("Common Culture," 35), or the violence this assertion of a hegemonic culture does to diverse "ways of life" of different communities. Nor does it address the possibility that people might experience both the consumption of mass culture and the participation in local activity as part of the "ordinary processes" of their lives.

From Common to Popular: Hegemony, Pleasure and Resistance

As we have seen, Williams's attempt to salvage the "art" in the "ordinary" reinforces this split. He calls art "ordinary" to redeem the "creativity in all our living" (*LR*, 37), in other words, to find "art" in everyday life. His attachment to "art" is thus rooted in a desire to separate this "creativity" from the habit of leisure consumption (*LR*, 38). His defense of the "special processses of discovery and creative effort" (*LR*, 6) as a standard that the majority's actual "common pursuit" of recreation cannot meet only leads him to *displace*, rather than heal, the breach between the creative and the mundane. He remains unwilling, at this point at least, to recognize not only that leisure consumption constitutes an integral part of daily life and hence of popular culture in contemporary society and so cannot be dismissed as degrading, but also—and crucially—that the production of and response to entertainment cannot be completely summed up by the "culture industry." The invocation of small-scale community participation in "Culture Is Ordinary" is powerful because it implies resistance to an oppressive central norm, but it cannot accommodate the view that contemporary leisure pursuits have in fact been shaped by centralized communications institutions. Nor is the notion of affirmative community ready to articulate a relation between the dominance of communication institutions (as opposed to a residual high cultural norm) and any emergent *critical* community.

Contemporary cultural studies, from cultural materialist work associated with the Birmingham school to the rather less critical "popular culture studies" in the U.S., address this issue by focusing primarily on contemporary leisure pursuits marginalized by Williams's paradigm on the grounds that these activities, not residual traces of traditions (whether "folk" or "high"), constitute "people's actual experience of contemporary culture."[13] Although this new emphasis on mass cultural consumption of, say, television and sport, or on subcultures of young men and women or racially subordinate groups, marks an explicit break with Williams's early emphasis on "art and learning," the Birmingham projects nonetheless take their cue from Williams's culture as a "whole way of life," as well as the "creation of conditions in which the people as a whole participate in the articulation of meanings and values" ("Common Culture," 36) and shares the concern of Williams's contemporary, Richard Hoggart (first head of the Birmingham Centre) with the recovery of *authentic* working class experience.[14]

Unlike Williams and Hoggart, Hall, Johnson, and their colleagues remain skeptical of any notion of an inclusive culture held in common by "all the people." Instead they argue that contemporary developed societies are marked by conflicting and overlapping cultural practices, competing for the legitimate designation of "common culture." The predominance of any one kind of culture does not make it common culture, but rather indicates its *hegemony*. Against this hegemony, contemporary cultural studies raises the standard of a *popular* culture whose critical force is grounded in its *difference* from common culture. This emphasis on difference is crucial because it reminds us that the legitimation of cultural practice is a result of struggle and not merely growth.

Valuable as it is, this critical definition of popular culture does not, however, overcome the opposition between the "creative" and the "mundane," between "art" and "leisure pursuits." It rather reverses it, attributing "creativity" to "leisure pursuits" rather than to "art," now reified as residual "high culture," by (unspoken) definition remote from the people. In the competing discourses within the field identified as "cultural studies," the precise *significance* of the "creative" aspect of popular culture is subject to debate. For Stuart Hall, popular culture "is the arena of consent and resistance," "one of the sites where the struggle for and against a culture of the powerful is engaged."[15] But there are those who stress consent rather than resistance:

> It seems quite difficult now to map the language of struggle on
> to a culture which is increasingly sophisticated and centralized
> in its production and dissemination, and which is increasingly
> experienced by the vast majority of its consumers as a comfort-
> able and largely enjoyable necessity.[16]

The "language of struggle" is insufficient, because it displaces enjoyment, to conjure up conscious resistance in the place where habitual recreation usually takes place, and because it proceeds too hastily from outrage at the historical exclusion of popular experience from legitimate culture to a speculation about the hidden power of that experience.[17] But do we therefore abandon resistance and critique at the threshold of the community of pleasure? Surely not, since that would land us in a hedonist fancy that pleasure is somehow prior to our experience as subjects of intersecting and interfering allegiances, and thus unconnected to question of power.

Instead we might argue that overemphasis of either resistance or pleasurable consent is problematic because it forgets the interpenetration of consent and resistance in the effects of hegemony. As Williams reminds us, hegemony—including the domination of mass-mediated culture—is lived as *consent*:

> [Hegemony's] forms of control are not those ordinarily seen as 'manipulation'. . . . It is the whole body of practices and expectations . . . a lived system of meanings and values—which, as they are experienced as practices, appear as reciprocally confirming. It thus constitutes a *sense of reality* for most people in a society.[18] (emphasis added)

Nonetheless, the "sense of reality" is not immutable. The concept of hegemony permits us to analyze the persistence of political authority and cultural legitimacy of a particular social group, but it also enables us to explore links between critical cultural practice and the emergence of a counter-hegemony.[19] It does not dictate *a priori* where we might find either dominant or emergent hegemonic projects.[20] While we can certainly track the evidence of hegemony in the historical exclusion of the majority from "high culture," we cannot assume that the association of certain forms with a privileged audience is categorically fixed, nor can we presume the shape of a "popular" alternative. In each case, we must investigate the historical emergence of particular forms, the occasion and place of their legitimate performance, and challenges to that legitimacy.[21]

Placing the Occasion: the Stage and the Public Sphere

The very opposition between "high" and "low" culture and the defense of autonomous art is a historically specific response to what cultural conservatives from Coleridge to Leavis dismiss as the cheapening of art in the interests of amusement.[22] For example, the burgeoning desire, over the course of the nineteenth century, to preserve the poet Shakespeare from the ravages of the stage, was not an overdue recognition of Shakespeare's literary genius after a century or more of neglect, but a historically specific response, by the so called "cultivated classes," to what they saw as the vulgarity of the stage and its motley audience.[23] Appeals to the poetry tend to be coupled with the assertion that it can *only* be compromised by the stage. Arguments over proper form are thus predicated on assumptions about the proper *occasion* and *place* for appreciating Shakespeare: contemplation in the study, rather than diversion in the theatre.

In practice, the popular response to Shakespeare was not that simple. Audiences combined a taste for spectacle and virtuoso solos on demand with an extensive knowledge of and pleasure in the language of Shakespeare and, in response, burlesques whose success depended on this knowledge proliferated.[24] The "cultivated classes'" aversion to the performances of Shakespeare in repertoire with burlesque and other variety shows was powerfully affected by their fear of the audiences that applauded them; this suggests that this disruption was interpreted as a social as well as cultural threat to minority domination. In this scenario of popular culture, pleasure and subversion are not at odds; in fact, they reinforce each other. The popular audience's *entertainment* encompasses their amusement but also their knowledge of mixed cultural forms, and their willingness to entertain subversion as well as sublimity.

While subversion of this sort may not add up to a systematic critique of hegemonic institutions, it certainly amounts to more than mere vulgarity on the one hand or elite exclusion on the other. In diverse performance contexts, the "object itself" is neither an immutable touchstone of universal value, nor a simple sign of class domination. In other words, its *critical* significance, its *identification* as "art" or "entertainment," changes with the occasion and the place and the *kind* of audience of its performance.

The performance and permutation of *Antigone* in contemporary South Africa is an interesting example. Performed by a number of theatre groups since the emergence of an alternative (urban, intellectual, mostly white) theatre in the late fifties, Euripides' play can be interpreted in canonical universalist terms as a courageous individual's resistance to unjust law in the name of justice. This interpretation is certainly apt, but it alone does not make the play accessible to a popular, *majority* audience, nor address the history of the troubled but productive symbiosis between "town theatre" and the majority.[25]

The first performance of *Antigone* by a black cast (the Serpent Players, 1965) represents an extension of access, rather than a *popular appropriation.*[26] The group had approached Athol Fugard, then South Africa's only "world-renowned" dramatist, for help and followed his advice in the production of primarily *literary* texts. Only once arrests and harassment made the use of published texts hazardous did they turn to improvised material drawn from the experience of group members. This experience included not only daily life under apartheid in the local township of New Brighton, but the experience of members imprisoned on Robben Island for political activity and their performance of *Antigone* for prisoners there. Drawing on this experience and its retelling, two other members, John Kani and Winston Ntshona, later devised and performed *The Island* (script and direction by Athol Fugard).[27] The piece shows a series of moments in the lives of two Island prisoners, from their absurd punishment routine to their preparation for a prison performance of *Antigone,* and concludes with Winston's rendering of Antigone's farewell speech directly at the audience.

Significantly, those metropolitan critics accustomed to praise Fugard for his "universality" (to wit, his place in the European tradition of Beckett and Camus) prefer to see a "change of heart" rather than a call for political transformation in the final stage image.[28] This reading privileges the isolated *character's* position as victim over the *actors'* collective defiance in performing "banned" information about the Island; it also erases the places and occasions of earlier performances invoked or reenacted in the text. The embedded performances in the first scene—from John's recollection of the very 1965 performance that planted the seed for *The Island* to his "call home" in which he names prisoners and their relatives—do not simply rehearse the climactic rendering of Antigone's "famous speech." The reenactment of "ordinary" acts are sharp reminders of what is not possible in South Africa. These moments, not the "universal [sic] implications for overseas audiences," concentrate the play's meaning. Judging by the Interior Ministry's attempt to ban the show (1973), this performance had the direct force of a political action, as well as the resonance of a creative act.

It is these *local* moments in *The Island* and in its companion piece, *Sizwe Banzi is Dead,* that make acting *in* the play an action *on* its audience. The *political* exigencies of "playmaking" (dispensing with a written script to avoid its likely confiscation) have *aesthetic* consequences: the spare quality of the action and in the performers' control and amendment of the performance in response to local stimulus. *Sizwe Banzi is Dead* begins and ends with the banter of photographer "Styles" around a client whose picture records his (temporary) victory over the vicious bureaucracy of South Africa's pass laws. A friend urges him to get rid of the "wrong" stamp by appropriating a dead man's passbook, name, and "proper" endorsement. Sizwe Banzi hesitates to give up his name ("the nation is strong") and is persuaded only when his friend acts out a series of skits to dramatize the urgency. If audiences in London were touched by the tragedy or bitter comedy of this predicament, those in New Brighton were moved to interrupt the debate and take sides. As Fugard notes:

> As I stood . . . listening to it all, I realized I was watching a
> very special example of one of theatre's major responsibilities
> in an oppressive society: to break . . . the conspiracy of silence.
> . . . The action of our play was being matched . . . by the ac-
> tion of the audience. . . . A performance on stage had provoked
> a political event in the auditorium.[29]

What is remarkable about this audience's participation in the remaking of *Sizwe Banzi is Dead* is not simply the urgent engagement with the subject matter; Fugard's stress on the "urgent and real" desire to "speak and be heard" oddly implies that this audience has never discussed the matter before. This intervention is powerful not because it "breaks the silence" or has immediately political effects, but because it acknowledges the symbolic character of the action, while using the fragile *public* occasion to enact alternatives. The audience's debate, like the show it interrupts, is a *performance*; its enactment here—in the border country between the familiar ground of the township and the occasional, unlikely character of the show—is significant precisely because it is impossible in the legitimate public sphere.[30] By intervening in the play, the members of the audience do not abandon the fiction, but *sustain* it. Their participation in a public *performance,* and not merely a public hearing, testifies to their ability to reenact the symbolic action and so entertain the hope of a culture in common.

Much as this account shows that the stuff of an apparently high art can be transformed into the symbolic action of a community in struggle, we might hear the retort that, while "poor theatre" functions as an intermediate technology of liberation in South Africa, it is high art in the metropolitan theatres of Europe and America and is therefore not likely to reach those whose leisure pursuits are heavily influenced by dominant mass-(produced) culture. With the development of an increasingly centralized capitalist culture and of global communication monopolies,[31] we can no longer talk about cultural activity *without* acknowledging (and not merely regretting) the large-scale capitalist penetration of leisure.[32] We should not stop there, however. We might remember that popular entertainments have emerged historically as complex, often ambiguous, amalgams of residual "folk" habits, dominant leisure *consumption* of commodities, and strategies for negotiating the border between.

Entertaining Alternatives: Strategies for Critical Community

At a time and place where centralized and rationalized power make large-scale appropriation of the media difficult, the intermediate technology of small-scale actions may provide an effective stage for alternative "strategies for encompassing social situations." But, to make the case for popular culture in local and decentralized practice, we need to scrutinize the opposing claim that, without appropriating the central institutions of communication or media, we can operate only marginally on the "unoccupied fringes of a culture."

In conversation with *New Left Review*, Williams defends this claim on two fronts. The first, in terms of political strategy, that "the left can never content itself with a cultural policy that does not attack quite centrally the dominant means of production,"[33] is grounded in a commitment to complete social(ist) transformation, which will inform if not guarantee cultural transformation. The second is more problematic, however: Williams claims that television offers greater social horizons to its viewers because of its greater *technical* capacity to represent social reality:

> The [movement of] the camera now allows television to do what theatre . . . could not. It permits the *resumption of public actions* in fully *realized* locations of history, moving drama out from the enclosed room . . . to workplaces, streets, and public forums. (*Politics and Letters*, 223–42, emphasis added).

He goes on to argue that the social distribution of television sets makes possible an unprecedented dissemination. This claim gives technical means a *moral and political* charge: the medium's capacity for reproducing scenes of social life is read as the *"resumption of public action."* This view obscures the formal intervention of editing and narrative, which make the reproduction seem like a resumption of action. Further, the *institutional* context where this "public action" is perceived remains the space of private habit; *watching* such reproductions, in a space quite different from their production, does not amount to critical participation merely because it is a "common" enough pursuit. It tends rather to replicate the illusion of immediacy on which the ideology of "live television" rests.[34] Although Williams gives greater weight than before to the technological media, his insistence that "communication" and thus transformation can be secured only at the center, by way of the appropriation of the dominant media and thus also of their large scale diffusion capacity belies the same problematic confidence as in his appeal for state "extension" of the arts: however powerful, the "channels" are themselves somehow neutral and so can be carried over in the institution of counter-hegemony.

As the *New Left Review* editors note, this view *defers* to the hegemonic use of the media, even as it infers that the only way forward is through them (*Politics and Letters*, 224, 226), and therefore neglects the role of small-scale local practices, like regional popular theatre, in performing alternatives to the status quo (*Politics and Letters*, 224–25). The NLR's example is John McGrath, whose theatre group, 7:84, has performed regional and popular material for audiences in pubs and dance halls. McGrath left a successful TV career (he wrote the popular series *Z-Cars*) to found a theatre for popular audiences on their own territory, in theme as well as venue. *The Cheviot, the Stag and the Black, Black Oil*, for example, enacts the links between capitalist exploitation of North Sea oil and England's historical expropriation of Scotland; it was well received by Highland audiences affected by this "development."[35] The success of 7:84 and other popular theatre groups who engage the interests of regional working-class communities stems from their recognition of their audience's competence—these people participate as audiences for a variety of shows, from television to panto—and of the value of making connections in performance between general subjects and local history informing the event.

Dismissing popular theatres on the grounds that they are inevitably marginal in a developed capitalist society ignores this potentially empowering relationship between place, community, and skepticism about the normative claims of the center. The argument that the margins are finally only "unoccupied fringes" and, therefore, that the center must be the site of common culture misses not only the possibility that commonality might emerge out of a concrete sense of place and of critical difference from the center, but also the value of the border as a site for *staging* alternative centers. Local popular theatres certainly don't reach millions in their homes simultaneously, but the directness of the enactment for a present audience, as well as the theatrical distance of the show, sets up better conditions for what Williams calls "subjunctive action" (*Politics and Letters*, 219, 224), than the habitual character of watching TV provides. Whereas the habit of watching blurs the difference between what is and what might be, and the construction of the narrative makes playing and replaying an action impossible, the occasion of performance creates a *liminoid* space in which alternative or *virtual* public spheres can be performed, tested, entertained.[36]

In his late essays on the politics of decentralized communities, Williams moves to recognize that subaltern groups not only can but must provide the political and cultural initiative when attempts to appropriate centralized power or cultural hegemony have failed.[37] At the same time, he acknowledges that people owe allegiance to diverse communities and thus that no single one can be uncritically affirmed. Although he does not explore in detail the cultural implications of these propositions, his remarks on decentralism, and the critical value of place, prepare the terrain for a critique of a "crucial form of imperialism"—at home:

> Right back in your own mind, and . . . inside the oppressed
> and deprived community, there are reproduced elements of the
> thinking and feeling of that dominating centre. . . . we [cannot]
> simply react by saying that the values of community . . . are su-
> perior to those values of the power centres.[38]

We have come a long way from the affirmation of "common meanings and directions" and "taking our arts to new audiences. . . ."

We have not, however, abandoned the impulse of "Culture Is Ordinary" to take as the material for culture the concerns of people's lives, nor have we forgotten cultural studies' skeptical response to affirmative community. Acknowledging as Williams does that the very term "community" is problematic precisely because it is so commonly used across the political spectrum ("Importance of Community," 112), we may still argue that the sense of place engendered by the performance of "subjunctive actions" retains, by virtue of its liminality, a certain critical distance from total identification, even as it rests on a sense of community. To sustain this critical identification with an occasion, a place, a cause, the best way of enacting common culture may not be the extension of "access," which continues, in Britain as in South Africa, to reinforce the legitimacy of metropolitan culture. The performance of *Sizwe Banzi is Dead* is important in that it shows that local popular performance can defy aesthetic as well as overtly political imperialism by declaring that daily life under apartheid is fit for performance. If "theatre [was] not part of the African vocabulary,"[39] but a colonial import, it has nonetheless been suited to its new situation. Similarly, theatre "imported" into places in Britain, where it does not "naturally" occur, can emerge as a means and occasion to entertain and represent an audience that may not see itself as such.

The Women's Theatre Group (WTG), a non-profit group of women performers, writers, and technicians based in London, seeks to address and represent an audience of working-class teenage girls in schools and youth clubs. The portrayal of the girls' daily concerns on familiar ground avoids glamorizing the event while maintaining its entertainment. *My Mother Says I Never Should* portrays the conflicting social pressures facing teenage girls who confront the double sexual standard, was performed for teenage audiences, their parents, and teachers.[40] Since their concern is to *represent* the audience members to themselves rather than to create a work of art, WTG made critical use of familiar forms—TV (sitcom and family drama) and panto (songs to traditional tunes and direct address):

> The way in which we wrote was affected both by the content
> of the play and the proposed audience; there was a wariness of
> experimental "art" theatre and stark agitprop forms, because
> we felt that the most effective way of making sense to an audi-
> ence whose principal theatrical experience had been mediated
> by television was to use a conventional TV style with a story
> and lots of laughs.[41]

WTG defends its decision on the grounds that *dramatizing* the contradictions and virtues in common attitudes to and of women is more effective than simply offering positive role models of feminist women, which would contradict this audience's experience. In other words, WTG recognizes the need to engage with the girls' intense, if ambivalent, participation in a "culture of femininity," if WTG is to engage them in a critical revision of that culture.[42]

My Mother Says shows teenage girls in a variety of social situations that make different demands on their allegiances. The action gives full play to the girls' involvement in a "culture of femininity," in particular their concern for their appearance and their interest in "boys," but it does not simply endorse these values. Aware that attitudes which are presented in order to be criticized can actually be reinforced, the performers also dramatize the disparity between the girls' domestic aspirations and their mothers' lives and to suggest differences among the girls as well. In addition to conflict over appropriate behavior for girls, the play shows us how this behavior is influenced by contradictory expectations at a school and the home, which tends to reinforce rather than challenge their entry into domesticity.

The feminism in the play lies not in any final or universal solution to the domestication of women, but in encouraging young women to "see themselves as agents capable of making choices about their lives." ("My Mother Says," 115) The ending, in particular, does not resolve divergent views on women's sexual and social roles, but rather juxtaposes the very different voices of several women in the play, including the doctor and teacher, as well as the teenagers and their mothers. The feminism in the *event* emerges not just in the play, but in the "ordinariness" of the performance. While the scenes themselves are performed naturalistically, the performers sit with the spectators when not on stage. The audience is encouraged to identify the dramatized action and the social situation, but not to succumb to an "imitation of life." The matter-of-fact, *disposable* (available as well as timely) text suits the occasion of the performance; it encourages the members of the teenage audience to recognize themselves in the action, while showing them how they might change it. The significance of the event depends on the audience acknowledging the story as its own *and* as the occasion for public representation. This articulation of local story and public sphere is both vital and contentious. We can see this in the enthusiastic support of the targeted audience—working-class girls, their parents, and teachers. At the same time, the ILEA Health Inspector's praise, "Excellent . . . I wonder if your next play could be about teeth," reinforces the performance's legitimate place in the public sphere, by hailing the *normality* of its subject, even as it provokes retaliation from those who dispute the subject's claim to public attention.[43]

The circumstances of this performance may well seem remote in Conservative Britain. In addition to narrowing the reach of Arts Council funding, the Conservatives' attacks on local government—from abolishing the Greater London Council to dissolving ILEA and other quasi-autonomous educational authorities—have limited the place and occasion for a counter public sphere. While official support for such alternative representation continues to dwindle, we should remember that *My Mother Says* was produced part-time by amateur and professional women and reached a substantial audience in schools and youth clubs before being endorsed and filmed by ILEA. This example of theatre in the community reminds us that work contesting the official line can operate without long-term subsidy, and suggests the critical potential of local initiative.

What brings these performances together is not that they enact the *same* popular culture or that they claim, explicitly or not, that popular culture always resists dominant metropolitan cultures. The meaning of popular culture lies in its *contradictory* but lively combination of traditions of high or folk art *and* the commodities of a variety of culture industries. The instances discussed here suggest the *necessary heterogeneity* of popular cultures, their origins in diverse and conflicting practices, and their potential to represent critical as well as affirmative community. At its most vital, popular culture *entertains* us: it diverts us from immediate daily tasks, not to distract us, but to grant us the space to entertain other ways of performing culture.

4

Realisms and Modernisms: Raymond Williams and Popular Fiction

Jon Thompson

> For tradition is in practice the most dominant expression of the
> dominant and hegemonic pressures and limits. It is always
> more than an inert historicized segment; indeed, it is the most
> powerful practical means of incorporation. What we have to
> see is not just "a tradition" but a *selective tradition*: an inten-
> tionally selective version of a shaping past and a pre-shaped
> present, which is then powerfully operative in the process of
> social and cultural definition and identification.
> —Raymond Williams, *Marxism and Literature*

Power of Tradition/Traditional Powers

With the notable exception of feminism, most schools of contemporary
literary theory have tended to accept established literary traditions
without challenging the values and ideologies that underpin and produce them. Indeed, in literary traditions influenced by hermeneutics,
phenomenology, semiotics, structuralism, and some forms of poststructuralism, canonical texts still hold sway. While the issue of canonicity has attracted more attention in recent years, many critics and
critical schools still habitually separate an autonomous "high" literary
culture from a popular or "low" culture, and on that basis either
implicitly accede to traditional literary traditions, or else explicitly
engage in the construction of ones which can then be valorized.

Raymond Williams and Popular Fiction

Much of Raymond Williams's own work constitutes a critique of these traditions and the systems of canonicity that underpin them. From the very beginning of his academic career, the work which was to culminate in *Culture and Society 1780–1950* (1958), Williams displayed an acute awareness of the ideological character of traditions, and literary traditions in particular. In *Culture and Society,* this is most evident in his critical dissection of romantic ideology in "The Romantic Artist," and it is this awareness of the selective nature of traditions that informs his plea for a common culture in the conclusion to that book.[1] Likewise, Williams's consideration of largely ignored country and working-class writers in *The Country and the City,* as well as marginalized authors and genres, attempts to problematize the "selective traditions" and canons that have become the recognizable borders of literary study.[2] In *Marxism and Literature,* that agenda becomes explicit and theoretical. Yet Williams's work is not irreproachable on this score: it is probably fair to say that it has been marked by a combination of blindness and insight. In contrast to his remarkable critical achievement, there are the almost infamous blindnesses: Williams's tendency to privilege British literature, his undervaluation of women's writing, and his propensity, as in *The English Novel from Dickens to Lawrence* (1971) to merely offer an alternate version of Leavis's Great Tradition.[3] Despite these, by the end of his career, as I shall argue, Williams developed a theoretical vocabulary capable of articulating some, if not all, of these cultural relations.

One area of cultural relations that always interested Williams was popular culture. Unlike many of his contemporaries, Williams did not dismiss popular culture as mere ephemera; indeed, *The Long Revolution, Communications,* his television reviews for *The Listener,* and his science fiction essays suggest something of the range and depth of this interest. Yet while Williams's work always emphasized the importance of human agency, sometimes to the extent that he undervalued what he later came to call hegemonic forces, he did not ultimately regard popular culture as the autonomous, untainted site of a people's self-making. Rather, he came to see it as the full range of commodified, technologically reproduced social, literary, and artistic practices and images that dominate society. These practices and images, he emphasized, exist in a conjunctural relation to hegemonic values, and even when largely incorporated, Williams steadfastly maintained that they engage certain real needs, desires, and longings.[4]

Raymond Williams's key term here, however, is not "mass culture" or "popular culture" but culture itself. As he argued in *Marxism and Literature,* culture is "a constitutive social process creating specific and different 'ways of life,'" which not only includes popular culture but also apprehends the role popular culture plays in the construction of culture generally.[5] For Williams culture performs this dialectical function inasmuch as it resists the critical tendency to fetishize popular culture by seeing it as a wholly autonomous sphere, detached from the equally autonomous but somehow superior sphere of high culture; significantly, this has been the approach taken by both critics on the Left and the Right, as the examples of F.R. Leavis and the Frankfurt School attest. Williams's approach, by contrast, effects a shift of attention away from the vexed question of literary *value* to an understanding of the full historical complexity and richness of literary *practices,* practices which are comprehensible only in terms of their relation to other literary, cultural, and social practices. I will return to this point shortly, but for the moment it is important to emphasize that for Williams, there is no actual division between high and low culture, only ways of seeing culture in this way.[6] For him, that is, popular culture and high culture are part of *one* cultural process and use similar techniques, forms, and ideologies.[7]

Thus, Williams's theory of culture not only situates high and low culture with one another, but it also dialectically relates the modes of representation and techniques traditionally associated with each. Because Williams's work accentuates the relationships *among* cultural practices, it is possible to use his theoretical insights in order to reconsider the relationship among realism, modernism, and popular culture.

Traditionally, these relationships have crystallized around three crucial assumptions: popular fiction (crime fiction, Westerns, romances, science fiction, etc.) is *genre* fiction, whereas modernist fiction is not; popular fiction is aesthetically inferior to canonical fiction; and lastly, modernism is a self-reflexive mode of representation, fundamentally different from realist modes of representation which were—and are— generally committed to engaging an external reality.

In his analysis of cultural formations in terms of "dominant, residual and emergent" forces, Williams offers a way of going beyond these paralyzing dichotomies and value judgments.[8] In allowing us to articulate the "residual" relations of realism to the institutionally "dominant" cultural field of modernism, his theory of culture and cultural formation enables us to theorize literary modernism as incorporating a much wider cultural space than avant-garde production. Williams's theory of cultural formations, in other words, allows us to see that different genres use the residual strategies of realism in conjunction with the institutionally dominant techniques and ideologies of modernism. In Williams's work, realism is theorized as residual in a very particular sense. It is residual in the sense that it is *ideologically* residual, minimized by ideologies of modernism that pronounce the aesthetic superiority of modernism and the aesthetic inferiority of realism. Of course, in film and television, indeed all the forms of fiction marketed and sold under the heading of "popular fiction," realism has for a long time been leading a healthy, subterranean existence. Yet the dominance of realism in the marketplace does not necessarily translate into *cultural* dominance. As Williams notes in "The Metropolis and the Emergence of Modernism," the dominance of modernism, and its aesthetic, intellectual, and psychological traits, is due to its "intellectual hegemony of the metropolis, in its command of the most serious publishing houses, newspapers and magazines, and intellectual institutions, formally and especially informal."[9] It is, in other words, domination of the *institutions* of art, and the cultural and educational apparatuses, and not sheer quantity which makes cultural domination and creates a dominant sensibility.

Williams's emphasis on the links between literary practices traditionally defined as high or low, as well as his acute sense of the select, ideological definition of modernism, can thus be appropriated to mount a revisionist rereading of literary modernism: whereas many theorists and critics tend to see the transition to modernism in terms of a rupture with the realist tradition of fiction, Williams's work on cultural formations and relations allows us to see the continuity of realist strategies *within* modernism. Modernist modes of representation did not abandon the realist tradition, as many modernist apologists suggest, but instead modernist novelists adapted and shaped realist strategies of representation for ends ideologically different from the conciliatory ends by and large promoted by the nineteenth-century realist novel. Modernism, then, can be seen as an *ideology* of literary production, often radically at odds with the doctrines espoused by its apologists and critics.

Realism or Realisms?

From his early empirically based notion that "Culture is ordinary" to his later theoretical refinement of that notion in Gramscian terms, Williams saw culture as a response to society, and criticized the attempts, whether made by John Stuart Mill or by modern-day television moguls, to make it either a consolation or an opium-like substitute for the injustices or disappointments of an inequitable, class-based society.

Raymond Williams and Popular Fiction

Underlying his life-long interest in film, television, drama, the novel, the media, and popular culture is the singular sense that all of these cultural forms *engage* reality. Implicit in much of his work, but never fully worked out, is a philosophy of realism—the notion that all cultural artifacts inevitably absorb and respond to conjunctural historical situations. Yet Williams rejected the dominant theories of realism. He rejected, for example, "reflectionist" realism, or direct representationalism, for not accounting for the mediating function of language. Nor did he entirely accept Lukácsian realism: although Williams's work on the novel has certain affinities with Lukácsian realism, his interest in what Lukács condemned as decadent post-realist forms—namely, naturalism and modernism—also suggests a certain distaste for the rigid categories of Lukácsian realism. At the same time, Williams was critical of the structuralist tendency to read language and literature as the passive product of a system, whether the system is one of language, culture, or politics.[10]

Williams's realism thus exists as an attempt to rescue realism from those who would valorize it at the expense of other modes of literary representation, as well as from those who would dismiss it as naive reflectionism: Williams maintained that realism *is* mediated by language and its own compositional processes and conventions, but that it nevertheless *engages* reality. Indeed for Williams, it is this realist basis to language and literature that produces a shared reality. Williams's realism is thus intimately tied to the idea of *community. The English Novel from Dickens to Lawrence,* for instance, is a study of realism in terms of what Williams calls a "knowable community." In it, Williams argues that the nineteenth-century classic realist novel is defined by its ability to articulate a full range of social and class relations. In interviews with the *New Left Review,* published under the title of *Politics and Letters,* Williams clarifies this position by suggesting that literary modernism articulates the breakdown of the privileged position of the nineteenth-century realist novelist to grasp society in its totality.[11] Modernism, for Williams, refers to a narrower, more restricted range of experience than that represented in the Victorian novel. Williams's situating of realism and modernism in terms of their social base, or the communities to which they relate, is elaborated in other essays in which he argues that the breakdown of the old realism arises out of the social, economic, and cultural dislocations—and their corresponding forms of alienation—that produced the twentieth-century metropolis.[12]

It would be wrong, however, to see Williams's work as exclusively valorizing the communities and social relations that produced nineteenth-century realism. Williams's work suggests that any attempt to build a new society will inevitably involve realist practices. Williams's approach to realism is not then a duplication of Lukács's fetishism of nineteenth-century realism, for Williams's sense of community and realism differ radically from Lukács. Williams's notion of community, significantly, develops *away* from an idealized, Golden Age organic society, toward a material conception of the relations and dislocations of late twentieth-century communities. Late in his career, Williams was developing a notion of communities not just as purely geographical entities, but as "communities of interest physically spread out from each other."[13] Williams's sense of the relations between realism and community, then, takes as its starting point the assumption that the kinds of communities that were typical in the nineteenth-century are no longer possible in the late twentieth century. This conjunctural sense of community suggests that contemporary economic transformations cut across old borders, old alliances; and that new alliances, relations, and communities are formed as much out of mutual interest as physical propinquity. Realism for Williams assumes a crucial role inasmuch as it engages and recognizes these new communities.

Yet it is important to emphasize that by "realism" Williams does not mean a mode of representation which pretends to merely reflect a pre-given reality "out there." Nor does he mean a single style. Instead he has in mind "a method or mode of social representation with many styles."[14] In "Realism and the Contemporary Novel" Williams begins to develop this theory of realism by arguing that the function of realism is in some sense to adequate reality, but not by mirroring it.[15] For Williams realism is a mode of registering experience which is fundamentally *evaluative*: "When I think of the realist tradition in literature, I think of the kind of novel which creates and judges the quality of a whole way of life in terms of the qualities of persons."[16] Thus Williams is a long way off from claiming that realism is a styleless transparent way of writing, the type of writing that Roland Barthes criticized in *Writing Degree Zero*.[17] Williams agrees in effect that realism is a form of *écriture,* a highly conventionalized way of writing that encodes certain ideological values. But he also differs from Barthes in that he maintains that art is not only perception but *communication*, and reality is not just the vision of the monad or individual:

But art is more than perception; it is a particular kind of active response, and a part of all human communication. Reality, in our terms, is that which human beings make common, by work or language. Thus, in the very acts of perception and communication, this practical interaction of what is personally seen, interpreted and organized and what can be socially recognized, known and formed is richly and subtly manifested.[18]

This theory of realism is anticipated and confirmed in the work of C.N. Volosinov and M.M. Bakhtin on language.[19] Like Williams's work, Volosinov's and Bakhtin's work acknowledges that language does not reflect reality in any direct way; rather, for them, language speaks about reality, engages in an evaluative discourse about it. Perhaps their most explicit statement on the subject is contained in an essay entitled "Discourse in Life and Discourse in Art":

> First of all, it is perfectly obvious that, in the given case, the discourse does not at all reflect the extraverbal situation in the way a mirror reflects an object. Rather the discourse here *resolves the situation,* bringing it to an *evaluative conclusion,* as it were. Far more often, behavioral utterances actively continue and develop a situation, adumbrate a plan for future action, and organize that action.[20]

The fundamental principle here, that the discourse of realism is not reflective but evaluative, seems to me to be extremely useful, inasmuch as it suggests the possibility of developing a new theory of realism, what might be called a theory of *evaluative realism.* First of all, the notion of realism as evaluative displaces the terms of the realism debate by shifting attention away from the vexed question of the veracity of realism to the social and moral *imperatives* registered in and through discourse. Second, the emphasis on the communicative function of realism, the fact that through the interchange of discourse reality is produced and made *socially recognizable,* means that realism need not be rejected as a naive medium, a pseudo-objective version of reality. Third, this formulation allows us to see that realism is *movable*—that realist strategies of representation can be combined with other modes of representation.

Using Williams's theory of cultural formation, it is now possible to read realism as a historically "residual" element within the institutionally "dominant" modernist mode of representation. Far from inventing itself anew, literary modernism took over, adapted, and problematized realist strategies of representation, all the while integrating them with modernist ideologies, forms, and techniques.

This notion of realism *in* modernism requires a rethinking of received notions of modernism, many of which, as I have argued, depend on the idea of a complete break with realism. The fiction of Joyce, Lawrence, Woolf, Faulkner, and other "high" modernists suggests that they were concerned with social existence and sought to evoke and evaluate it, albeit in forms and styles different from those deployed in the classic realist novel that Lukács fetishizes. Indeed, it is possible to argue that the realist strategies of representation *within* the dominant modes of modernism enable referentiality in the first place. If one of the primary features of these modernists is their tendency to embrace anti-Establishment values, it is possible to argue that this critical function becomes possible by drawing on the evaluative capacities of realism.

Modernism's Anxiety of Contamination

What, then, are the implications of reading modernism in terms of Williams's critique of traditions?

First of all, it is necessary to consider the *making* of the modernist tradition. Modern apologists, such as Edmund Wilson, tended to see literary modernism as antithetical to popular culture, particularly popular fiction. Indeed, the dense, complex, allusive, and self-referential style often associated with Kafka, Joyce, Lawrence, and Faulkner was widely seen in contrast to the more straightforward, less elliptical, realistic style of popular fiction. In the eyes of many critics, this "popular" style suffered in comparison not only because it lacked a dense verbal texture, but also because in its use in literary genres such as thrillers, science fiction, adventure, Westerns, and romance, it was used more in the service of describing outward events and action rather than in exploring the subtleties and nuances of "centers of consciousness." In this connection it is interesting to note that critics, not novelists, were harshest in their dismissal of popular fiction. Many "high" modernists were fascinated by popular fiction, and some, like Faulkner, wrote what many considered to be pulp fiction. It may be that many modernists sensed connections and similarities between the modernist project, which was officially recognized, and the work of popular writers, which generally was not. At any rate, modernism's relationship to mass culture was, and is, characterized by "an anxiety of contamination."[21] Modernism, that is, sought to define itself by what it was *not*. Accordingly, its apologists shaped a tradition (actually, *traditions*) by elevating certain literary and artistic qualities and by excluding and denigrating others. The question of the value of popular fiction, therefore, is not susceptible to resolution by adducing examples in which popular fiction can be shown to meet the standards set by modernist fiction—not merely because counterexamples can always be adduced, but more importantly, because this strategy leaves the premises of the modernist case unexamined. It is not, in other words, sufficient to say that popular fiction is as good as canonical fiction, because this leaves modernist aesthetic premises in the position of dictating what is and what is not good literature. This essentially defensive posture leaves modernist criteria firmly in place. Instead of displacing the modernist hierarchy, and the standardized modernist tradition handed down in schools and universities, this posture defers to it, and ultimately confirms it.

Another ramification of Williams's critique of traditions is that literary *value* ceases to be the dominant consideration. Literary traditions, as Williams reminds us, are constructed according to ideological principles, not according to universally accepted aesthetic ones. There is no universal, coherent set of criteria that will allow readers to make a distinction between popular and high fiction. There is no *ontological* basis for deciding what is literature and what is not; there are only *functional* reasons for doing so. A term like "literature" does not describe the "fixed being" of a complex range of writing practices so much as it signifies, in a casual and informal way, a kind of writing which someone values for one reason or another.[22] This is not a fancy way of saying that one man's meat is another man's poison: it is instead a recognition that literature, strictly speaking, is a relative term and that excluding other writing practices on this basis is a conventional or ideological operation.

Popular fiction has traditionally been excluded by critics and the academy from the canon of Literature by just these kinds of ideological operations. Yet this rejection is based on a fallacious view of literary value, namely that value inheres *in* the text, that it is an inalienable essence of the text. In actuality, literary value is largely a function of reading subjects who relate to texts in determinate ways. As Tony Bennett has put it: "Texts do not *have* value: they can only *be valued* by valuing subjects of particular types and for particular reasons, and these are entirely the product of critical discourses of valuation, varying from criticism to criticism."[23]

The question of the value of different writing practices, then, ultimately relates more to the *valuing reader*—and his or her interpellation by a given *tradition*—than the text in isolation; given this, the question of value ceases to be the paramount consideration in the analysis of writing. Looked at in this way, Literature, that body of writing which is canonized and otherwise institutionally affirmed, is no longer a uniquely privileged body of texts whose common factor resides in an undefinable difference from popular fiction, but instead signifies a wide range of writing practices differentiated by their strategic deployment of particular narrative strategies, modes of representation, registers of discourse, literary devices, conventions, forms, and so on. All writing practices avail of a common pool of literary and linguistic resources. Consequently, it becomes theoretically impossible to maintain a stable, objective distinction between genre and non-generic forms of writing, even though, of course, booksellers market and display their books according to these categories. In "Discourse in the Novel," Mikhail Bakhtin develops the notion of literature-as-genre by contending that all forms of writing are mutations of different genres—genres understood generally to mean "a horizon of expectations."[24] For him, every new form of writing is merely an extension of the possibilities of a known genre or a creative synthesis of two or more already existing genres. So, for example, *Madame Bovary,* that most modern of novels, often regarded as having no connection at all with genre fiction, may usefully be regarded as a particularly fine example of a genre which flourished in the nineteenth century, the novel of adultery.[25]

Despite the fact that there is no *essential* set of characteristics that we can point to in order to arrive at an objective description of Literature, the academy and the literary establishment in general continue to use and rely on, both explicitly and implicitly, many of the oppositions that I have been destabilizing—especially those of Literature/non-Literature, genre/non-generic forms of writing, "high"/"low" culture, "literary"/"non-literary" fiction. While these oppositions do not have any objective validity, it is necessary to acknowledge that they retain a *political* importance inasmuch as they designate the various ways in which existing literary institutions organize and value a multiplicity of writing practices into "selective traditions."

If it is true that many forms of modernism share this "anxiety of contamination" in regard to popular fiction, it is also true this anxiety has often manifested itself in the attempt to distance itself from the modes of representation taken to be typical of popular fiction. In practice, this has meant drawing a distinction between the "classic" realist tradition of fiction, which flourished in the nineteenth and early twentieth centuries (not to mention the unofficial tradition of realism in popular culture), and the radically different culture of modernism. Very often this has led to an accentuation of the differences between modernism and realism, to the extent that modernism has represented itself as coming into being by means of a rupture with realism. But more important than the destabilization of the opposition between realism and modernism is the recognition that just as there is not one realism, but a multiplicity of realisms, so too there is not a single, monolithic modernism, but multiple modernisms. The most significant implication of Williams's theory of tradition is that every literary tradition is more various and complex than the "selective" constructions put on it. And it is to one of these other modernisms, the popular American modernism of Dashiell Hammett, that I will now turn.

Popular Fiction: The Case for a Hard-boiled Modernism

Hammett's fiction embodies Williams's notion that "culture is ordinary." Indeed its ordinariness, its use of a form from "popular culture," has meant that it has always occupied an uncertain position within the literary canon. While his work has generally been relegated to a kind of second-tier status thought to be appropriate to "genre" fiction, because of its *stylistic* sophistication and existential atmosphere, it has attracted its share of literary admirers. And although Hammett's work predates that of Hemingway, critics often praise it for its stylistic similarity to Hemingway's minimalist fiction. Ultimately, however, it is misleading to read Hammett's fiction as a pale reflection of "high" modernism. Hammett's modernism, and the modernism of the hard-boiled school, is not based on a repudiation of mass culture, but on an embracing of its possibilities. The distinctiveness of Hammett's fiction consists of its recuperation of many dominant modernist themes and techniques in a realist form that was institutionally residual, but which Hammett made contemporary through his command of the American language. In the process, Hammett virtually produced the hard-boiled detective genre, a distinctly American genre. Hammett's modernism is thus different from the European modernism rooted in the avant-garde, but it is a modernism rooted in a deeply felt response to the modern urban American world of the 1920s and 1930s. Unlike the avant-garde in Europe, Hammett did not reject the artistic forms of the past; instead, he transformed a seemingly already exhausted form into a distinctively new genre, a genre with its own distinctive language and world-view. As Raymond Chandler testified in his essay "The Simple Art of Murder," "Hammett gave murder back to the kind of people that commit it for reasons, not just to provide a corpse; and with the means at hand, not with hand-wrought dueling pistols, curare, and tropical fish. He put these people down on paper as they are, and he made them talk and think in the language they customarily used for those purposes."[26] While Chandler downplays Hammett's stylization of ordinary language, his comments do suggest the transformations he made in the detective story genre. It is thus ironic that although Hammett's fiction was not regarded as serious in his own time, it succeeded in reaching the mass audience the European avant-garde coveted, but could never reach. Hammett was a modernist in his response to the post-World War I society he observed and criticized, and his work displays many similarities to that of other modernists, but he was, characteristically, a modernist on his own terms, an unorthodox modernist writing for pulp magazines, just as he was an unorthodox and independent-minded Marxist, democrat, and citizen.

If crime fiction exists as a response to the anxieties produced by a modern, industrialized, urban environment, it attempts to mediate that anxiety by producing reassuring versions of the relations between the individual and society. In the case of hard-boiled fiction this effort is at best only partly successful. Hammett's protagonists—the Continental Op, Sam Spade, Ned Beaumont *et al.*—generally exist on the margins of society, and while they are for the most part isolated and estranged from it, and its values and political systems, their interest as characters derives from their connection, antagonistic as it may be, with bourgeois society. Hammett's fiction thus is part of the tradition of crime fiction which grew out of and responded to the urban, industrial moment of modern history.[27] Like the most recognized representatives of "high" modernists, Hammett's detective fiction explores what it means to be "modern." Unlike many modernist writers, however, Hammett does not try to convey the meaning of this experience by accentuating subjective consciousness. Instead he evaluates the social and political forms modernity took in the early decades of the twentieth century. In *Red Harvest* he analyzes the gangland violence that consumes the industrial town of Personville, otherwise known as "Poisonville," a town which as its name suggests, is supposed to be representative of any middle-American town. In *The Maltese Falcon* the deceit and mistrust which erodes all social relations, even relatively nonpolitical ones like the one between Sam Spade and Brigid O'Shaugnessy, come under intense scrutiny; similarly, in *The Glass Key* official politics have become indistinguishable from the actions of gangsters: Senator Henry, it transpires, is responsible for the murder of his own son. Hammett's fiction calls into question some of the most fundamental distinctions by which bourgeois society operates. For Hammett, respectability—whether bourgeois or otherwise—is fabricated, is essentially *fictional*.[28]

Thus, while on one level Hammett's protagonists are as alienated from modern urban "civilization" as are D.H. Lawrence's, on another level they are deeply identified—and identify themselves—with it. It is almost impossible to imagine Sam Spade or the Continental Op working outside the city. For the Continental Op the city is the locus of corruption and vice, just as it is for Sam Spade and Ned Beaumont. And while all of these protagonists feel they have a duty to rectify these ills, all of them, to a man, feel the attraction of the criminal life, not merely because of the lifestyle that the dirty money supports, but because they have grasped that the facade of respectability that legitimate society puts up is also a fiction. This is why all of these detectives adhere so tightly to their own personal codes of behavior. In a world where order and integrity inevitably give way to disorder and corruption, it becomes all the more necessary to have a stable code by which the detective figure can operate in this morally equivocal environment. As the Continental Op confesses to Dinah Brand in *Red Harvest*:

> This damned burg is getting me. If I don't get away soon I'll be going blood simple like the natives. . . . I've arranged a killing or two in my time, when they were necessary. But this is the first time I've ever got the fever.[29]

For Hammett, the possibility of mastering the city by means of a superior intelligence, as was the case with Edgar Allen Poe's Dupin, no longer exists; the city has now become dominant, and threatens to crush the detective. The Continental Op, as much as Leopold Bloom, is adrift in the city, dominated by its rhythms, its pace, its mysteries, and as much as he professes to long for an escape from the city he is tied to it, is formed by it, and is endlessly fascinated by it.

The city is defined by what Steven Marcus calls "the ethical irrationality of existence, the ethical unintelligibility of the world."[30] It could be argued that Hammett made this modernist trait an intrinsic aspect of hard-boiled fiction in that he created a genre committed to the posing of questions. And if modernism as a literary formation can generally be characterized in terms of its obsession with questions (unlike, for example, the Victorians who focus much more on answers), Hammett's work can be said to be a part of this tradition. Like many high modernist heroes—and anti-heroes—Hammett's detective figures are obsessed with questions, questions that have more to do with the contradictions of existence in the modern world than with the purely local problems of who killed whom with what.

In *The Glass Key,* for instance, Hammett grapples with institutionalized corruption as a social and political force in American society during the Depression. Hammett's exploration of the role of the individual in this society is complicated by his choice of protagonist. Ned Beaumont is the lieutenant of the political boss, Paul Madvig. As such, he participates in the manipulation of big-city politics that the Continental Op attempts to end in *Red Harvest*. Beaumont is thus an unusual and complex protagonist—an amateur detective who sanctions political corruption at the same time that he uncovers more virulent forms of it than his own personal morality allows him to condone. In creating an obviously flawed detective in Beaumont, and in placing him in a situation that calls attention to a compromised social and political order, and the dilemma of the individual in that system, Hammett is able to question some of the most basic conceptions of morality at the same time that he destabilizes some of the most common assumptions about detective fiction. While Hammett's fiction does not offer any answers to the questions it raises, in one sense it does not matter because it suggests that the conventional imperatives of crime fiction—for example the "whodunit" convention—is less important than the questioning of all epistemological certainties.[31] It is partly this open-endedness to his fiction, this refusal to yield to pat answers and easy solutions, that marks his work's affiliation with the ideology of modernism most often associated with high modernists such as Joyce and Kafka. Hammett brought detective fiction into the modern world—not merely by seeming to be more realistic, as Chandler believed—but by introducing this modernist ideology into the genre.

In part, Hammett achieved this by undermining some of the oppositions typical of detective fiction. He not only brought detective fiction to a new level of technical and artistic achievement, but he also inaugurated the anti-detective novel: his fiction broke down the binary oppositions of detective/villain, good/evil, and order/disorder that characterized the rational moralism of the formal English novel of detection.[32] The dominant ideology of Hammett's fiction is thus relativistic; but it is not relativistic in regard to the social reality it evalutes. In this matter, hard-boiled fiction as a genre is critical of civilization, bourgeois law and property, and ultimately, the ideologies which assert that there is an absolute distinction between the criminal and the law-abiding citizen.

This is not meant to imply, however, that hard-boiled fiction is an *unmediated* representation of reality. Like any other fiction, it is a linguistic construct. Although it lays claim to being "realistic" (i.e. life like), it is no more so than the classic English novel of detection. Both are regulated by the demands of the genre, both are conventional (although they adhere to different conventions), both are stylized versions of ordinary speech. Hammett's fiction purports to use more ordinary English—and indeed one finds registers of English that one does not find, for example, in Agatha Christie's novels—but these registers have been reworked and tailored into a stylized version of lower-class speech. The tough guy speech in hard-boiled fiction, like the genteel diction of the classic English detective story, is a literary representation of types of ordinary discourse, but there is nothing natural about it. Take, for example, the famous first line of *Red Harvest*: "I first heard Personville called Poisonville by a red-haired mucker named Hickey Dewey in the Big Ship in Butte."[33] Few tough guys have the sense of pace, slang, alliteration, and syntactic control that Hammett demonstrates here. And while some critics argue that this sense of style gives his fiction the density and richness characteristic of modernism, a modernism which as Roland Barthes claimed in *S/Z* was distinctive in its being self-reflexive or "writerly" (*scriptible*),[34] Hammett's style also is oriented "outward," toward an assessment or evaluation of society.

Hammett's language is always used to suggest that everyone's point of view is *fictional,* or ideological. Hard-boiled fiction is thus particularly suspicious of bourgeois claims to represent a morally transparent order that the reader can take straight without having to read it as a fiction. This hermeneutic of suspicion in hard-boiled fiction assails a central tenet of institutionalized high modernism: that is, the modernist work's claim to be autonomous. Instead, hard-boiled fiction revels in its *negative* capacity, in its conventional tendency to evaluate the post–World War I urban American experience of modernity. While it does not have any pretense toward documentary truth, it is oriented toward an evaluation of this reality, and this suggests that Hammett's fiction does not see itself as a purely self-reflexive autonomous work of art, detached from the time and place of its production, but rather sees itself as engaged with contemporary society, as a part of it. The dialogic nature of Hammett's fiction thus goes against the grain of that brand of high modernist aesthetics which claims an *autonomous* status for genuine modern art. If the discourses in the texts that make up the official modernist canon are examined, for example, those in *Ulysses,* it is apparent that this claim of artistic autonomy is untenable. If anything, this is more true of Hammett. By incorporating slang, wisecracks, and more colloquial, vernacular registers of English, Hammett—like Joyce—not only enlarges the creative possibilities of fiction, but he also shows the possibilities for writing in a modernist mode using the language of the streets.[35] The language of Hammett's fiction asserts the dialogic nature of his fiction. Far from striving to appear to be independent of society, Hammett's hard-boiled fiction indicates the linguistic resources available in colloquial speech. Indeed, this connection with lower and working-class life, as well as with the criminal underworld, which is expressed in stylized versions of those discourses, is used to make a political point. Tough guy speech shows irreverence for authority at the same time that it establishes the hero's disdain for bourgeois norms. Hammett's use of language thus contains a class element which Hammett uses to criticize class society. While the hard-boiled world is made up of lower-class criminals and crooks, Hammett uses their language to impugn the pretensions of legitimacy, morality, and ethical behavior that characterize middle-class characters in his novels. Thus, the slang and colloquial language within Hammett's fiction exists as a marker between the "honest" (i.e. less hypocritical) crooks—the class defined as criminal by bourgeois law—and the "dishonest" crooks, which for Hammett includes virtually all of the middle classes.

Despite the acute sense of class consciousness that pervades his fiction, for Hammett there is no master epistemology which will allow his protagonists to solve the dilemmas with which they are presented, partly because the problems they engage are not limited to the solving of a "whodunit": a crime in hard-boiled fiction always signifies the presence of a wider, social or political malaise of which the corpse is merely the signifier. Ultimately, there can be no solution to a crime, because crime is not extrinsic to the system, but intrinsic, part of the system. Even if the detective discovers the identity of the murderer, the implications of the crime extend far beyond the matter of a mere corpse and are so endemic that they are, finally, intractable. If in the English formal novel of detection the resolution of the crime largely exonerates society, in hard-boiled fiction the ending almost invariably suggests the wholesale corruption of society. Individuals may be exempt, but the social order stands condemned. In most hard-boiled fiction, society itself is essentially unknowable. Instead of knowledge, the hard-boiled detective relies on gut instinct and his—or her—hunches. As Lukács has pointed out in *The Meaning of Contemporary Realism,* this state of unknowing is one of the cardinal traits of modernism. Kafka's fiction also sees the individual as dominated by contemporaneity, almost lost within it. It is this loss of perspective and knowledge, Lukács maintains, which leads to the *angst* of modernist protagonists and the alienation of modernist fiction. While more violent than most canonical modernist fiction, hard-boiled fiction shares this world view. What the hard-boiled detective learns is usually sufficient to solve the question of "whodunit"; but this knowledge never gives him a permanent grasp as to how society works. And this says as much about the heterogeneous body of writing practices we call "modernist" as it does about Kafka or Hammett.

Conclusion

It may seem paradoxical at best, and perverse at worst, to speak of Hammett in the same breath with Joyce or Kafka. Like most traditions, literary traditions have their borders, and their border guards, and attempts to redraw the boundaries, or eradicate them altogether, will inevitably seem to many to be the most self-aggrandizing kind of transgression—iconoclasm. And yet it seems to me that one of the central challenges of Williams's work is to rethink "selective traditions" of all kinds so as to come to an understanding of the social forces and hegemonic values that have created them, and then ultimately, reverse these institutionalized discriminations through genuine social transformation.

In terms of the cultural issues I have explored here, Williams's theoretical emphasis allows us to oppose those critics who have fetishized modernism as a largely avant-garde mode of literary production by seeing it instead as a broad, *intercultural* practice. To assert after Williams that "culture is ordinary," that Hammett's work is part of a culture of modernism, then, not only widens our sense of the possibilities and capacities of modernism, but it is also represents the beginning of a reassessment of modernism in terms of its previously undervalued connections to realism and popular culture. But perhaps most importantly, Hammett's fiction throws into relief the *conventional* character of high modernism and it suggests the possibilities for seeing, and resisting, the ways in which different traditions, whether literary or cultural, organize and interpellate texts—and subjects.

Part II

Education from Below?

5

Rebuilding Hegemony: Education, Equality, and the New Right

Michael W. Apple

Introduction

It is not possible to talk about the history of our growing understanding of the relationship between education and cultural and ideological struggles without giving Raymond Williams his due. No figure has been as powerful in setting the path that critical educational studies has taken over the past two decades. Given the overly psychologized discourse that has dominated education for so long, it is truly remarkable that concepts that Williams was so instrumental in developing, popularizing, and employing—concepts such as hegemony, selective tradition, effective dominant culture, residual and emergent culture, ideology, the long revolution, and so on—have now become cemented in the field.

Williams's influence on critical educational studies has not "only" been strongly felt in the growth of analyses employing this rich stock of concepts. By providing some of the most important foundational components that led to a strengthening of the broader cultural Marxist tradition, his work has had an impact in a more indirect way as well. Thus, knowingly or not, the development of educational scholarship that rests within this tradition owes a major debt to Williams.

Out of the vast array of questions he stimulated, I wish to focus on one area in this essay. In the context of major shifts in cultural authority and political alignments, how is an effective dominant culture maintained? How are hegemonic discourses and the social relations under-pinning them reconstructed during a time of political, economic, and ideological crisis in Western capitalist nations? I shall instantiate these questions in a study of the growing power of the Right in education and the wider social formation.

Focusing on rightist movements is not an oddity here. As early as the 1960s, within Williams's own writing there is an emergent analysis of the possibility that powerful rightist forces could alter the terrain on which ideological conflicts would take place.[1] I will examine the culture, language, and ideology—in many ways the "structure of feeling"—that the Right has struggled over. Following Williams's lead, rather than seeing such cultural forms and processes as epiphenomenal, as simply reflections of other more fundamental relations—as is the case in all too many discussions—I shall indicate how they provide very real sites of conflict that have material effects in education and elsewhere.[2] While my own discussion will extend beyond Williams to the larger cultural Marxist tradition, I am keenly aware that this analysis stands on his shoulders and could not have been accomplished without his pathbreaking work in this area.

The conventional Marxist approach to understanding how ideology operates assumes by and large that ideology is "inscribed in" people simply because they are in a particular class position. The power of dominant ideas is either a given in which dominance is guaranteed or in which the differences in "inscribed" class cultures and ideologies will generate significant class conflict. In either case, ideology is seen as something that somehow makes its effects felt on people in the economy, in politics, in culture and education, and in the home without too much effort. It is simply *there*. The common sense of people becomes common sense "naturally" as they go about their daily lives, lives that are prestructured by their class position. If you know someone's location in the class structure, you know their sets of political, economic, and cultural beliefs and you do not really have to inquire into *how* dominant beliefs actually do become dominant. It is usually not assumed that these ideas "should positively have to *win* ascendency (rather than being ascribed it) through a specific and contingent (in the sense of open-ended, not totally determined) process of ideological struggle."[3]

Yet the current political situation in many Western capitalist nations presents us with evidence that such a conventional story is wholly inadequate in its explanation of the shifts that are occurring in people's common sense. We are seeing a pattern of conflicts within dominant groups that has led to significant changes in their own positions and, even more important, we are witnessing how elements of ideologies of groups in dominance become truly *popular*. There is a rupture in the accepted beliefs of many segments of the public who have historically been less powerful,[4] a rupture that has been worked upon and expanded by economically and politically strong forces in the society. These ideological shifts in common sense are having a profound impact on how a large portion of the public thinks about the role of education in that society.

In this essay, I shall describe and analyze a number of these most important changes in popular conceptions. A particular concern will be how ideologies actually become a part of the popular consciousness of classes and class fractions who are not among the elite. In order to understand this, I shall employ theoretical work on the nature of how ideology functions that has developed over the past decade. I do not make such an argument because of some disembodied commitment to the importance of "grand theory." Indeed, as I have argued at greater length in *Teachers and Texts,* we have been much too abstract in our attempts to analyze the role of education in the maintenance and subversion of social and cultural power.[5] Rather, I intend to provide an instance in the use of theories to uncover the limits and possibilities of cultural and political action by actually applying them to a concrete situation that is of major importance today: the New Right's reconstruction of our ideas about equality.

Stuart Hall stresses exactly this point in his criticisms of the abstractness of much critical literature on culture and power in the last two decades. After a period of "intense theorization," a movement has grown that has criticized "the hyperabstraction and overtheoreticism that has characterized theoretical speculation, since . . . the early 1970s." As he puts it, in what seemed to be the pursuit of theory for its own sake, "we have abandoned the problems of concrete historical analysis."[6] How do we counteract this tendency? As Raymond Williams and those who have been influenced by him understood so well, theoretical analysis should be there to allow us to "grasp, understand, and explain—to produce a more adequate knowledge of—the historical world and its processes; and thereby to inform our practice so that we may transform it."[7] This is what I shall do here.

Reconstructing Education

We live in a period in which our educational system has been increasingly politicized. The curriculum and the values that underpin it, and that are included and excluded from it, are now being placed under intense ideological scrutiny. The Spencerian question, "What knowledge is of most worth?" has now been replaced with an even more pointed question, "*Whose* knowledge is of most worth?" That this latter question has become so powerful highlights the profoundly political nature of educational policy and practice. This is not simply an abstract issue. It is made strikingly clear in the fact that the curriculum of many school districts and universities throughout the country has been turned into what can best be described as a political football. Conservative groups in particular have attacked the school and, in the process, have had a major impact on educational debate not only in the United States but in other nations as well.

As is evident all around us, there has been a significant shift in public discourse around education. The rapid growth of evangelical schooling,[8] the court cases involving "secular humanist" tendencies in textbooks, the increasing attempts to "raise the standards" of teaching and teachers, and the calls in the literature to return to a core curriculum of a "common culture" all signify, among many social groups, a deep suspicion of what is going on in our classrooms.

Williams, too, was deeply concerned with a common culture. But to his mind the call to a "return" to a common culture in which all students are given the values of a specific group—usually the dominant group—was not a common culture at all. A common culture can never be the general extension to everyone of what a minority means or believes. Rather,

> the culture of a people can only be what its members are engaged in creating in the act of living . . . [It involves] the creation of a condition in which the people as a whole participate in the articulation of meanings and values, and in the consequent decisions between this meaning and that, this value and that.[9]

Thus, for Raymond Williams, a common culture is never finally realized; it is never complete. In speaking of a common culture, then, we should not be talking of something uniform, something all of us conform to. Instead, what we should be asking is "precisely for that free, contributive and common *process* of participation in the creation of meaning and values."[10]

This vision of a participatory process, and the project of equality that lies behind it, is decidedly not what is on the conservative agenda. There are very real fears—usually among right-wing groups, but also to be found in official statements coming out of the federal and state governments—that for the past decade things have gotten out of control. In this vision, we are losing control both of our children and of the pace of social and cultural change. We have gone too far in tilting our educational and social policies toward minority groups and women. This is not equality, but reverse discrimination. It goes beyond the bounds of what is acceptable. Not only is the search for a more egalitarian set of policies misplaced, but it fails the test of cost/benefit analysis. It is simply too expensive in practice to work and gives things to people that they have not really earned.

The position is especially evident in quotes from former Secretary of Education William Bennett. In his view, we are finally emerging out of a crisis in which "we neglected and denied much of the best in American Education. For a period, we simply stopped doing the right things [and] allowed an assault on intellectual and moral standards." This assault on the current state of education, which, as I noted above, the conservatives see as being connected with attacks on the family, traditional values, religiosity, patriotism, and our economic well-being, has led schools to fall away from "the principles of our tradition."[11]

Yet, for Bennett, "the people" have now risen up. "The 1980's gave birth to a grass roots movement for educational reform that has generated a renewed commitment to excellence, character, and fundamentals." Because of this, "we have reason for optimism." Why? Because "the national debate on education is now focused on truly important matters: mastering the basics . . . insisting on high standards and expectations; ensuring discipline in the classroom; conveying a grasp of our moral and political principles; and nurturing the character of our young."[12]

In essence, our educational system has become too committed to "equality." In the process, "our" standards, the cultural and intellectual values of the "Western tradition," our very greatness as a nation— and the "moral fiber" upon which it rests—are at risk. Just as much at risk is our economic stability and our ability to compete internationally in the global market.

All of these points are part of a contradictory bundle of assertions. Yet all are having real effects on education and on the language and conceptual apparatus we employ to think about its role in society.

Concepts do not remain still for very long. They have wings, so to speak, and can be induced to fly from place to place. Their context defines their meaning. As Wittgenstein so nicely reminded us, one should look for the meaning of language in its specific contextual use. This is especially important in understanding political and educational concepts, since they are part of a larger social context, a context that is constantly shifting and is subject to severe ideological conflicts. Education itself is an arena in which these ideological conflicts work themselves out. It is one of the major sites in which different groups with distinct political, economic, and cultural visions attempt to define what the socially legitimate means and ends of a society are to be.

To understand the concern with "equality" in education, it is necessary to see it as part of a larger conflict: to place its shifting meanings both within the breakdown of the largely liberal consensus that has guided much educational and social policy since World War II and within the growth of the New Right and conservative movements over the past two decades that have had a good deal of success in redefining what education is *for* and in shifting the ideological texture of the society profoundly to the right.[13] This entails seeing how new social movements gain the ability to redefine—often, though not always, in retrogressive ways—the terms of debate in education, social welfare, and other areas of the common good. At root, my claim will be that it is impossible to fully comprehend the value conflicts underlying so much of the debate in education and the shifting fortunes of the assemblage of concepts surrounding equality (equality of opportunity, equity, etc.) unless we have a much clearer picture of the society's already unequal cultural, economic, and political dynamics that produce the center of gravity around which education functions.

Between Property Rights and Person Rights

As I have argued at considerably greater length elsewhere, what we are witnessing today is nothing less than the recurrent conflict between *property rights* and *person rights* that has been a central tension in our economy.[14] Gintis defines the differences between property rights and person rights in the following way.

> A *property right* vests in individuals the power to enter into social relationships on the basis and extent of their property. This may include economic rights of unrestricted use, free contract, and voluntary exchange; political rights of participation and influence; and cultural rights of access to the social means for the transmission of knowledge and the reproduction and transformation of consciousness. A *person right* vests in individuals the power to enter into these social relationships on the

basis of simple membership in the social collectivity. Thus, person rights involve equal treatment of citizens, freedom of expression and movement, equal access to participation in decision-making in social institutions, and reciprocity in relations of power and authority.[15]

The attempts to enhance person rights partly rest on a notion of what is best thought of as positive liberty, "freedom to" as well as "freedom from." In industrial nations, this has grown stronger over the years as many previously disenfranchised groups of women and men demanded suffrage. The right to equal political participation would be based on being a person rather than on ownership of property (or later on being a white male). Further, person rights have been extended to include the right of paid workers to form unions, to organize a common front against their employers. At the same time, claims about the right to have a job with dignity and decent pay have been advanced. And, finally, there have been demands that economic transactions—from equal treatment of women and people of color in employment, pay, and benefits to health and safety for everyone—are to be governed by rules of due process and fairness, thereby restricting management powers of unrestricted use and "free contract."[16]

This last point is important since it documents a growing tendency to take ideas of civil equality and apply them to the economic sphere. Thus, "the right to equal treatment in economic relationships, which directly expresses the dominance of person over property rights, has been an explicit demand of women, racial minorities, immigrant workers, and others."[17] This, too, has been accompanied by further gains in which the positive rights of suffrage and association that have been won by women and by minority and working-class groups have been extended to include what has increasingly become seen as a set of minimum rights due any individual simply by the fact of citizenship. These include state-supported services in the areas of health, education, and social security, consumer protection laws, lifeline utility guarantees, and occupational safety and health regulations. In their most progressive moments, these tendencies lead to arguments for full-waged workplace democracy, democratic control over investment decisions, and the extension of the norms of reciprocity and mutual participation and control in most areas of social life from the paid workplace and the political life of local communities and schools to the home.[18] Taken together, these movements constitute at least a partial restructuring of the balance between person rights and property rights, one that would soon be challenged by powerful groups.

It is not surprising that in our society dominant groups "have fairly consistently defended the prerogatives of property," while subordinate groups on the whole have sought to advance "the prerogatives of persons."[19] In times of severe upheaval, these conflicts become even more intense and, given the current balance of power in society, advocates of property rights have once again been able to advance their claims for the restoration and expansion of their prerogatives not only in education but in all of our social institutions.

The United States economy is in the midst of one of the most powerful structural crises it has experienced since the Depression. In order to solve it on terms acceptable to dominant interests, as many aspects of the society as possible need to be pressured into conforming with the requirements of international competition, reindustrialization, and (in the words of the National Commission on Excellence in Education) "rearmament."[20] The gains made by women and men in employment, health and safety, welfare programs, affirmative action, legal rights, and education must be rescinded since "they are too expensive" both economically and ideologically.

Both of these latter words are important. Not only are fiscal resources scarce (in part because current policies transfer them to the military), but people must be convinced that their belief that person rights come first is simply wrong or outmoded given current "realities." Thus, intense pressure must be brought to bear through legislation, persuasion, administrative rules, and ideological maneuvering to create the conditions right-wing groups believe are necessary to meet these requirements.[21]

In the process, in the United States, as is the case in Britain and Australia, the emphasis of public policy has changed materially from issues of employing the state to overcome disadvantage. Equality, no matter how limited or broadly conceived, has become redefined. No longer is it seen as linked to past *group* oppression and disadvantagement. It is simply now a case of guaranteeing *individual choice* under the conditions of a "free market."[22] Thus, the current emphasis on "excellence" (a word with multiple meanings and social uses) is evidence of a shift in educational discourse in which underachievement is once again increasingly seen as largely the fault of the student. Student failure, which was at least partly interpreted as the fault of severely deficient educational policies and practices, is now being seen as the result of what might be called the biological and economic marketplace. This is evidenced in the growth of forms of Social Darwinist thinking in education and in public policy in general.[23] In a similar way, behind a good deal of the rhetorical artifice of concern about the achievement levels in, say, inner-city schools, notions of choice have begun to evolve in which deep-seated school problems will supposedly be solved by establishing free competition over students. These assume that by expanding the capitalist marketplace to schools, we will somehow compensate for the decades of economic and educational neglect experienced by the communities in which these schools are found.[24] Finally, there are concerted attacks on teachers and curricula based on a profound mistrust of their quality and commitments.

All of this has led to an array of educational conflicts that have been instrumental in shifting the debates over education profoundly to the right. The effects of this shift can be seen in a number of educational policies and proposals now gaining momentum throughout the country: (1) proposals for voucher plans and tax credits to make schools more like the idealized free-market economy; (2) the movement in state legislatures and state departments of education to "raise standards" and mandate both teacher and student "competencies" and basic curricular goals and knowledge, thereby centralizing even more at a state level the control of teaching and curricula; (3) the increasingly effective assaults on the school curriculum at all levels for its supposedly anti-family and anti-free enterprise bias, its "secular humanism," its lack of patriotism, and its neglect of the "Western tradition"; and (4) the growing pressure to make the needs of business and industry into the primary goals of the educational system.[25] These are major alterations, ones that have taken years to show their effects. I shall paint in rather broad strokes an outline of the social and ideological dynamics of how this has occurred.

The Restoration Politics of Authoritarian Populism

The first thing to ask about an ideology is not what is false about it, but what is true. What are its connections to lived experience? Ideologies, properly conceived, do not dupe people. To be effective they must connect to real problems, real experiences.[26] As I shall document, the movement away from social democratic principles and an acceptance of more right-wing positions in social and educational policy occur precisely because conservative groups have been able to work on popular sentiments, to reorganize people's genuine feelings, and, in the process, to win adherents.

Important ideological shifts take place not only by powerful groups "substituting one, whole, new conception of the world for another."

Often, these shifts occur through the presentation of novel combinations of old and new elements.[27] Let us take the positions of the Reagan administration, positions which by and large have provided the framework for the Bush administration's policies as well, as a case in point. For as Clark and Astuto have demonstrated in education and Piven and Cloward and Raskin have shown in the larger areas of social policy, significant and enduring alterations have occurred in the ways policies are carried out and in the content of those policies.[28]

The success of the policies of the Reagan administration, like that of Thatcher's and now Major's in Britain, should not simply be evaluated in electoral terms. They need to be judged also by their success in disorganizing progressive groups, in shifting the terms of political, economic, and cultural debate onto the terrain favored by capital and the Right.[29] In these terms, there can be no doubt that the current right-wing resurgence has accomplished no small amount in its attempt to construct the conditions that will put it in a hegemonic position.

The Right in the United States and Britain has thoroughly renovated and reformed itself. It has developed strategies based upon what might best be called an *authoritarian populism*.[30] As Hall has defined this, such a policy is based on an increasingly close relationship between government and the capitalist economy, a radical decline in the institutions and power of political democracy, and attempts at curtailing "liberties" that have been gained in the past. This is coupled with attempts to build a widespread consensus in support of these actions.[31] The New Right's "authoritarian populism"[32] has exceptionally long roots in the history of the United States. The political culture here has always been influenced by the values of the dissenting Protestantism of the seventeenth century. Such roots become even more evident in periods of intense social change and crisis.[33] As Burnham has put it:

> Whenever and wherever the pressures of "modernization"—secularity, urbanization, the growing importance of science—have become unusually intense, episodes of revivalism and culture-issue politics have swept over the social landscape. In all such cases since at least the end of the Civil War, such movements have been more or less explicitly reactionary, and have frequently been linked with other kinds of reaction in explicitly political ways.[34]

The New Right works on these roots in creative ways, modernizing them and creating a new synthesis of their varied elements by linking them to current fears. In so doing, the Right has been able to rearticulate

100

traditional political and cultural themes and has effectively mobilized a large amount of mass support.

As I noted, part of the Right's strategy has been to attempt to dismantle the welfare state and to roll back benefits that working people, people of color, and women (these categories are obviously not mutually exclusive) have won over decades of hard work and struggle. This has been done under the guise of anti-statism, of keeping government "off the backs of the people," and of "free enterprise." Yet, at the same time, in many valuative, political, and economic areas the current government is extremely state-centrist both in its outlook and, significantly, in its day-to-day operations.[35]

One of the major aims of a rightist restoration politics is to struggle in not one but many different arenas at the same time, not only in the economic sphere but in education and elsewhere as well. This aim is grounded in the realization that economic dominance must be coupled to "political, moral, and intellectual leadership" if a group is to be truly dominant and if it wants to genuinely restructure a social formation. Thus, as both Reaganism and Thatcherism recognized so clearly, to win in the state you must also win in civil society.[36] As Antonio Gramsci would have put it, what we are seeing is a war of position. "It takes place where the whole relation of the state to civil society, to 'the people' and to popular struggles, to the individual and to the economic life of society has been thoroughly reorganized, where 'all the elements change.'"[37]

In this restructuring, Reaganism and Thatcherism did not create some sort of false consciousness, creating ways of seeing that had little connection with reality. Rather, they "operated directly on the real and manifestly contradictory experiences" of a large portion of the population. They connected with the perceived needs, fears, and hopes of groups of people who felt threatened by the range of problems associated with the crises in authority relations, in the economy, and in politics.[38]

What has been accomplished has been a successful translation of an economic doctrine into the language of experience, moral imperative, and common sense. The free-market ethic has been combined with a populist politics. This has meant the blending together of a "rich mix" of themes that have had a long history—nation, family, duty, authority, standards, and traditionalism—with other thematic elements that have also struck a resonant chord during a time of crisis. Such themes include self-interest, competitive individualism (what I have elsewhere called the possessive individual),[39] and anti-statism. In this way, a reactionary common sense is partly created.[40]

Education, Equality, and the New Right

The sphere of education has been one of the most successful areas in which the Right has been ascendant. The social democratic goal of expanding equality of opportunity (itself a rather limited reform) has lost much of its political potency and its ability to mobilize people. The "panic" over falling standards and illiteracy, the fears of violence in schools, the concern with the destruction of family values and religiosity—all have had an effect. These fears are exacerbated, and used, by dominant groups within politics and the economy who have been able to move the debate on education (and all things social) onto their own terrain, the terrain of traditionalism, standardization, productivity, and industrial needs.[41] Since so many parents *are* justifiably concerned about the economic futures of their children—in an economy that is increasingly conditioned by lowered wages, unemployment, capital flight, and insecurity[42]—rightist discourse connects with the experiences of many working-class and lower middle-class people.

However, while this conservative conceptual and ideological apparatus does appear to be rapidly gaining ground, one of the most critical issues remains to be answered. How *is* such an ideological vision legitimated and accepted? How was this done?[43]

Understanding the Crisis

The right-wing resurgence is not simply a reflection of the current crisis. Rather, it is itself a response to that crisis.[44] Beginning in the immediate post-World War II years, the political culture of the United States was increasingly characterized by American imperial might, economic affluence, and cultural optimism. This period lasted for more than two decades. Socially and politically, it was a time of what has been called the *social democratic accord,* in which government increasingly became an arena for a focus on the conditions required for equality of opportunity. Commodity-driven prosperity, the extension of rights and liberties to new groups, and the expansion of welfare provisions provided the conditions for this compromise both between capital and labor and with historically more dispossessed groups such as blacks and women. This accord has become mired in crisis since the late 1960s and early 1970s.[45]

Allen Hunter vividly describes this accord.

From the end of World War II until the early 1970s world capitalism experienced the longest period of sustained economic

growth in its history. In the United States a new "social structure of accumulation"—"the specific institutional environment
within which the capitalist accumulation process is organized"—was articulated around several prominent features: the
broadly shared goal of sustained economic growth, Keynesian-
ism, elite pluralist democracy, an imperial America prosecuting
a cold war, anti-communism at home and abroad, stability or
incremental change in race relations and a stable home life in a
buoyant, commodity-driven consumer culture. Together these
crystallized a basic consensus and a set of social and political
institutions which was hegemonic for two decades.[46]

At the very center of this hegemonic accord was a compromise
reached between capital and labor in which labor accepted what might
be called "the logic of profitability and markets as the guiding principles
of resource allocation." In return they received "an assurance that
minimal living standards, trade union rights and liberal democratic
rights would be protected."[47] These democratic rights were further
extended to the poor, women, and people of color as these groups
expanded their own struggles to overcome racially and sexually dis-
criminatory practices.[48] Yet this extension of (limited) rights could not
last, given the economic and ideological crises that soon beset American
society, a set of crises that challenged the very core of the social
democratic accord.

The dislocations of the 1960s and 1970s—the struggle for racial and
sexual equality, military adventures such as Vietnam, Watergate, the
resilience of the economic crisis—produced both shock and fear.
"Mainstream culture" was shaken to its very roots in many ways.
Widely shared notions of family, community, and nation were dramatically altered. Just as important, no new principle of cohesion emerged
that was sufficiently compelling to recreate a cultural center. As economic, political, and valuative stability (and military supremacy)
seemed to disappear, the polity was itself "balkanized." Social movements based on difference—regional, racial, sexual, religious—became
more visible.[49] The sense of what Marcus Raskin has called "the common good" was fractured.[50]

Traditional social democratic "statist" solutions, which in education, welfare, health, and other similar areas took the form of large-
scale federal attempts to increase opportunities or to provide a minimal
level of support, were seen as being part of the problem not as part
of the solution. Traditional conservative positions were more easily
dismissed as well. After all, the society on which they were based was

clearly being altered. The cultural center could be *built* (and it had to be built by well-funded and well-organized political and cultural action) around the principles of the New Right. The New Right confronts the "moral, existential, [and economic] chaos of the preceding decades" with a network of exceedingly well-organized and financially secure organizations incorporating "an aggressive political style, an outspoken religious and cultural traditionalism and a clear populist commitment."[51]

In different words, the project was aimed at constructing a "new majority" that would "dismantel the welfare state, legislate a return to traditional morality, and stem the tide of political and cultural dislocation which the 1960's and 1970's represented."[52] Using a populist political strategy (now in combination with an aggressive executive branch of the government), it marshalled an assault on "liberalism and secular humanism" and linked that assault to what some observers have argued was "an obsession with individual guilt and responsibility where social questions are concerned (crime, sex, education, poverty)" with strong beliefs against government intervention.[53]

The class, racial, and gender specificities here are significant. The movement to create a conservative cultural consensus in part builds on the hostilities of the working and lower middle classes toward those above and below them and is fueled as well by a very real sense of antagonism against the new middle class. State bureaucrats and administrators, educators, journalists, planners, and so on all share part of the blame for the social dislocations these groups have experienced.[54] Race, gender, and class themes abound in other ways here, a point to which I shall return in the next section of my analysis.

This movement is of course enhanced within academic and government circles by a group of policy-oriented neoconservatives who have become the "organic intellectuals" for much of the rightist resurgence. Theirs is a society based on individualism, market-based opportunities, and the drastic reduction of both state intervention and state support; these currents run deep in their work.[55] They provide a counterpart to the New Right and are themselves part of the inherently unstable alliance that has been formed.

Building the New Accord

Almost all of the reform-minded social movements—including the feminist, gay and lesbian, student, and other movements of the 1960s and 1970s—drew upon the struggle of blacks "as a central organizational fact or as a defining political metaphor and inspiration."[56] These social movements infused new social meanings into politics, economics, and culture. These are not separate spheres of practice and action. All three of these levels exist simultaneously. New social meanings about the importance of person rights infused individual identity, family, and community, and infiltrated state institutions and market relationships. These emerging social movements expanded the "political" so as to include all aspects of the "terrain of everyday life." Person rights took on ever more importance in nearly all of our institutions, as evidenced in aggressive affirmative action programs, widespread welfare and educational activist programs, and so on.[57] In education this was very clear in the growth of bilingual programs and in the development of women's, black, Hispanic, and Native American studies in high schools and colleges.

There are a number of reasons why earlier social movements for gaining person rights viewed the state as their chief target. First, the state was the "factor of cohesion in society" and had historically maintained and organized practices and policies that embodied the tension between property rights and person rights.[58] As such a factor of cohesion, it was natural to focus on it. Second, "the state was traversed by the same antagonisms which penetrated the larger society, antagonisms that were themselves the results of past cycles of [social] struggle."[59] Openings in the state could be gained because of this. Footholds in state institutions dealing with education and social services could be deepened.

Yet even with these gains, the earlier coalitions began to disintegrate. In the minority communities, class polarization deepened. The majority of barrio and ghetto residents "remained locked in poverty," while a relatively small portion of the black and brown population were able to take advantage of educational opportunities and new jobs (the latter being largely within the state itself).[60] With the emerging crisis in the economy, something of a zero-sum game developed in which progressive social movements had to fight over a limited share of resources and power. Antagonistic rather than complementary relationships developed among groups. Minority groups, for example, and the largely white and middle-class women's movement had difficulty coming to an agreement over programs, goals, and strategies.

This antagonism was exacerbated by the fact that, unfortunately, given the construction of a zero-sum game by dominant groups, the gains made by women sometimes came at the expense of people of color. Furthermore, leaders of many of these movements had been absorbed into state-sponsored programs which—while the adoption of such programs *was* in part a victory—had the latent effect of cutting off leaders from their grass-roots constituency and lessened the militancy at this level. This often resulted in what has been called the "ghettoization" of movements within state institutions, as movement demands were partly adopted in their most moderate forms into programs sponsored by the state. Militancy was transformed into constituency.[61]

The splits in these movements occurred as well because of strategic divisions, divisions that were paradoxically the results of the movements' own successes. Thus, for example, those women who aimed their work within existing political/economic channels *could* point to gains in employment within the state and in the economic sphere. Other, more radical members saw such "progress" as "too little, too late."[62]

Nowhere is this more apparent than in the African-American movement in the United States. It is worth quoting one of the best analyses of the history of these divisions at length.

> The movement's limits also arose from the strategic divisions that befell it as a result of its own successes. Here the black movement's fate is illustrative. Only in the South, while fighting against a backward political structure and overt cultural oppression, had the black movement been able to maintain a *de-*centered unity, even when internal debates were fierce. Once it moved north, the black movement began to split, because competing political projects, linked to different segments of the community, sought either integration in the (reformed) mainstream, or more radical transformation of the dominant racial order.
>
> After initial victories against segregation were won, one sector of the movement was thus reconstituted as an interest-group, seeking an end to racism understood as discrimination and prejudice, and turning its back on the oppositional "politics of identity." Once the organized black movement became a mere constituency, though, it found itself locked in a bear hug with the state institutions whose programs it had itself demanded, while simultaneously isolated from the core institutions of the modern state.[63]

In the process, those sectors of the movement that were the most radical were marginalized or, and this must not be forgotten, were simply repressed by the state.[64]

106

Even though there were major gains, the movement's integration into the state latently created conditions that were disastrous in the fight for equality. A mass-based militant grass-roots movement was defused into a constituency, dependent on the state itself. *And very important, when the neoconservative and right-wing movements evolved with their decidedly anti-statist themes, the gains that were made in the state came increasingly under attack, and the ability to recreate a large scale grass-roots movement to defend these gains was weakened considerably.*[65] Thus, when there are right-wing attacks on the more progressive national and local educational policies and practices that have benefited people of color, it becomes increasingly difficult to develop broad-based coalitions to counter these offensives.

In their failure to consolidate a new "radical" democratic politics, one with majoritarian aspirations, the new social movements of the 1960s and 1970s "provided the political space in which right wing reaction could incubate and develop its political agenda."[66] Thus, state reforms won by, say, minority movements in the 1960s in the United States, and the new definitions of person rights embodied in these reforms, "provided a formidable range of targets for the 'counter-reformers' of the 1970s."[67] Neoconservatives and the New Right carried on their own political "project." They were able to rearticulate particular ideological themes and to restructure them around a political movement once again. And these themes *were* linked to the dreams, hopes, and fears of many individuals.

Let us examine this in more detail. Behind the conservative restoration is a clear sense of loss: of control, of economic and personal security, of the knowledge and values that should be passed on to children, of visions of what counts as sacred texts and authority. The binary opposition of we/they becomes very important here. "We" are law-abiding, "hard working, decent, virtuous, and homogeneous." The "theys" are very different. They are "lazy, immoral, permissive, heterogeneous."[68] These binary oppositions distance most people of color, women, gays, and others from the community of worthy individuals. The subjects of discrimination are now no longer those groups who have been historically oppressed but are instead the "real Americans" who embody the idealized virtues of a romanticized past. The "theys" are underserving. They are getting something for nothing. Policies supporting them are "sapping our way of life," most of our economic resources, and creating government control of our lives.[69]

These processes of ideological distancing make it possible for anti-black and anti-feminist sentiments to seem no longer racist and sexist because they link so closely with other issues. Once again, Allen Hunter is helpful.

> Racial rhetoric links with anti-welfare state sentiments, fits with the push for economic individualism; thus many voters who say they are not prejudiced (and may not be by some accounts) oppose welfare spending as unjust. Anti-feminist rhetoric . . . is articulated around defense of the family, traditional morality, and religious fundamentalism.[70]

All of these elements can be integrated through the formation of ideological coalitions that enable many Americans who themselves feel under threat to turn against groups of people who are even less powerful than themselves. At the same time, it enables them to "attack domination by liberal, statist elites."[71]

This ability to identify a range of "others" as enemies, as the source of the problems, is very significant. One of the major elements in this ideological formation has indeed been a belief that liberal elites within the state "were intruding themselves into home life, trying to impose their values."[72] This was having serious negative effects on moral values and on traditional families. Much of the conservative criticism of textbooks and curricula rests on these feelings, for example. While this position certainly exaggerated the impact of the "liberal elite," and while it certainly misrecognized the power of capital and of other dominant classes, there was enough of an element of truth in it for the Right to use it in its attempts to dismantle the previous accord and build its own.

A new hegemonic accord is reached, then. It combines dominant economic and political elites intent on "modernizing" the economy, white working-class and middle-class groups concerned with security, the family, and traditional knowledge and values, some of what Williams called the old humanists who want to return to or defend the "humanistic" corpus of knowledge, and economic conservatives.[73] It also includes a fraction of the new middle class whose own advancement depends on the expanded use of accountability, efficiency, and management procedures which are their own cultural capital.[74] This coalition has succeeded partially in altering the very meaning of what it means to have a social goal of equality. The citizen as "free" consumer has replaced the previously emerging citizen as situated in structurally generated relations of domination. Thus, the common good is now to be regulated exclusively by the laws of the market, free competition, private ownership, and profitability. In essence, the definitions of freedom and equality are no longer democratic but *commercial.*[75] This is particularly evident in the proposals for voucher plans as "solutions" to massive and historically rooted relations of economic and cultural inequality.

Will the Right Succeed?

So far I have broadly outlined many of the political, economic, and ideological reasons for the slow disintegration of the social democratic consensus that led to the limited extension of person rights in education, politics, and the economy. At the same time, I have documented how a new "hegemonic bloc" is being formed, coalescing around New Right tactics and principles. The question remains: Will this accord be long-lasting? Will it be able to inscribe its principles into the very heart of the American polity?

There are very real obstacles to the total consolidation within the state of the New Right political agenda. First, there has been something of a "great transformation" in, say, racial identities. Omi and Winant describe it thus:

> The forging of new collective racial identities during the 1950s and 1960s has been the enduring legacy of the racial minority movements. Today, as gains won in the past are rolled back and most organizations prove unable to rally a mass constituency in racial minority communities, the persistence of the new racial identities developed during this period stands out as the single truly formidable obstacle to the consolidation of a newly repressive racial order.[76]

Thus, even when social movements and political coalitions are fractured, when their leaders are coopted, repressed, and sometimes killed, the racial subjectivity and self-awareness that were developed by these movements has taken permanent hold. "No amount of repression or cooptation [can] change that." In Omi and Winant's words, the genie is out of the bottle.[77] This is the case because, in essence, a new kind of person has been created within minority communities.[78] A new, and much more self-conscious, *collective* identity has been forged. Thus, for instance, in the struggles over the past three decades by people of color to have more control of education and to have it respond more directly to their own culture and collective histories, these people themselves were transformed in major ways[79]:

> Social movements create collective identity by offering their adherents a different view of themselves and their world; different, that is, from the world view and self-concepts offered by the established social order. They do this by the process of *rearticulation,* which produces new subjectivity by making use of information and knowledge already present in the subject's mind. They take elements and themes of her/his culture and traditions and infuse them with new meaning.[80]

These meanings will make it exceedingly difficult for the Right to incorporate the perspectives of people of color under its ideological umbrella and will continually create oppositional tendencies within and across the black and brown communities. The slow, but steady, growth in the power of people of color at a local level in these communities will serve as a countervailing force to the solidification of the new conservative accord.

Added to this is the fact that even within the new hegemonic bloc, even within the conservative restoration coalition, there are ideological strains that may have serious repercussions on its ability to be dominant for an extended period. These tensions are partly generated because of the class dynamics within the coalition. Fragile compromises may come apart because of the sometimes directly contradictory beliefs held by many of the partners in the new accord.

This can be seen in the example of two of the groups now involved in supporting the accord. Following Williams's work on the politics of cultural history, we can see that there are both what can be called "residual" and "emergent" ideological systems or codes at work here.[81] The residual culture and ideologies of the old middle class and of an upwardly mobile portion of the working class and lower middle class—stressing control, individual achievement, "morality," etc.—has been merged with the emergent code of a portion of the new middle class—getting ahead, technique, efficiency, bureaucratic advancement, and so on.[82]

These codes are in an inherently unstable relationship. The stress on New Right morality does not necessarily sit well with an amoral emphasis on careerism and economic norms. The merging of these codes can only last as long as paths to mobility are not blocked. The economy must pay off in jobs and mobility for the new middle class or the coalition is threatened. There is no guarantee, given the unstable nature of the economy and the kinds of jobs being created, that this pay-off will occur.[83]

This tension can be seen in another way which shows again that, in the long run, the prospects for such a lasting ideological coalition are not necessarily good. Under the new, more conservative accord, the conditions for capital accumulation and profit must be enhanced by state activity as much as possible. Thus, the "free market" must be set loose. As many areas of public and private life as possible need to be brought into line with such privatized market principles, including schools, health care, welfare, housing, and so on. Yet, in order to create profit, capitalism by and large also requires that traditional values be subverted. Commodity purchasing and market relations become the norm and older values of community, "sacred knowledge," and morality need to be cast aside. This dynamic sets in motion the seeds of possible conflicts between the economic modernizers and the New Right cultural traditionalists who make up a significant part of the coalition that has been built.[84] Furthermore, the competitive individualism now being so heavily promoted in educational reform movements in the United States may not respond well to traditional working-class and poor groups' somewhat more collective senses.

Finally, there are counter-hegemonic movements now being built within education itself. The older social democratic accord included many educators, union leaders, minority group members, and others. There are signs that the fracturing of this coalition may only be temporary. Take teachers, for instance. Even though salaries have been on the rise throughout the country, this has been countered by a rapid increase in the external control of teachers' work, the rationalization and deskilling of their jobs, and the growing tendency to blame teachers and education in general for most of the major social ills that beset the economy.[85] Many teachers have organized around these issues, in a manner reminiscent of the earlier work of the Boston Women's Teachers' Group, a group of politically active teachers who fought against budget cuts, retrogressive educational policies, and the denial of teacher rights in the 1970s and 1980s.[86] Furthermore, there are signs throughout the country of multiracial coalitions being built among elementary and secondary school teachers, university-based educators, and community members to act collectively on the conditions under which teachers work and to support the democratization of curriculum and teaching and a rededication to the equalization of access and outcomes in schooling. The Southern Coalition for Educational Equity and the Rethinking Schools group based in Milwaukee provide but a few of these examples.[87]

Education, Equality, and the New Right

Even given these emerging tensions within the conservative restoration, and the increase once again in alliances to counter its attempted reconstruction of the politics and ethics of the common good, this does not mean we should be at all sanguine. It is possible that, because of these tensions and counter-movements, the Right's economic program will fail. Yet its ultimate success may be in shifting the balance of class forces considerably to the right and in changing the very ways we consider the common good.[88] Privatization, profit, and greed may still substitute for any serious collective commitment.

We are, in fact, in danger both of forgetting the decades of hard work it took to put even a limited vision of equality on the social and educational agenda and the reality of the oppressive conditions that exist for so many of our fellow Americans. The task of keeping alive in the minds of the people the collective memory of the struggle for equality, for person rights in *all* of the institutions of our society, is one of the most significant tasks educators can perform.

Of course, history is not simply *there,* available for all to see. Rather, it is constructed. What counts as an important past, indeed a past which is constructed and preserved, is never the result of a neutral process. As Williams so clearly reminded us, it is the result of a *selective tradition,* one that makes it so very difficult for people to find their place in that vast river of democratic struggle that Williams recognized as "the long revolution."[89] Constructing and reconstructing the collective memory of these struggles and connecting them again to the daily lives of people is essential. In a time of conservative restoration, we cannot afford to ignore this task.

This requires renewed attention to important curricula questions. Whose knowledge is taught? Why is it taught in this particular way to this particular group? How do we enable the histories and cultures of the majority of working people, of women, of people of color (these groups again are obviously not mutually exclusive) to be taught in responsible and responsive ways in schools? Given the fact that the collective memory that *now* is preserved in our educational institutions is more heavily influenced by dominant groups in society,[90] the continuing efforts to promote more democratic curricula and teaching are more important now than ever. This needs to be done in concert with other political movements that wish to extend the substance of democracy in all of our institutions. Action in education is made that much more powerful, and more likely to succeed, if it is organically connected to democratic social movements in the larger society.[91]

Yet, while action on the curricula and teaching that dominate our schools may not be sufficient, it is clearly necessary. For it should be clear that the movement toward an authoritarian populism will become even more legitimate if only the values embodied in the conservative restoration are made available in our public institutions. The widespread recognition that there were, are, and can be more equal modes of economic, political, and cultural life can only be accomplished by organized efforts to teach and expand this sense of difference. Clearly, there is educational work to be done.

This means, of course, that only communicating these perspectives with (notice I said with, *not* to) other educators is not enough. If we are to overcome apathy and cynicism, the effectiveness of the conservative restoration in transforming our discourse, and the rightist agenda in education and elsewhere, many more people must be involved in articulating and criticizing alternatives. The impressive socialist feminist arguments about how one should organize and engage in counter-hegemonic activity can teach us all a good deal here.[92] Most important, we must keep our feet on the ground, so to speak.

Successful ways of countering the rightist reconstruction cannot be fully articulated at the theoretical level. They begin and end in many ways at the level of educational practice. For these reasons, I do not want to end this essay with a set of abstract principles for educational strategies to stem the tide of the Right. As I noted, there *are* "models" of critical and emancipatory education being built currently in a number of places. And these are occurring in schools and universities, in community development, in many literacy programs, and elsewhere.[93] While these are in no way about to radically and immediately shift an entire country's consciousness to the left, I for one am certain that they provide ample amounts of insight into what is necessary and possible now. I am just as certain, however, that these principles and practices are not generated or learned from afar. They are learned by engaging in the thoughtful and committed daily activity of struggle for a more just set of economic, political, and cultural relations, something Raymond Williams knew not only intellectually but with his whole heart and soul.

There *is* educational work to be done and, perhaps, by joining in these ongoing struggles for democracy in schools and universities, in local communities, in paid and unpaid work, in the race, gender, and class relations in the multitude of institutions in which we now go about our daily lives, not only can we teach but we can be taught as well. The Right has succeeded in part by listening to and, of course, manipulating genuine feelings and, in the process, has demonstrated the power of the ideological. Here, too, we have much to learn. For only by engaging in the time-consuming, difficult, and draining—yet ultimately immensely satisfying—work of building communities based on varied but shared sentiments, and on programs that promise to take honestly the problems people face in their daily lives, can we start again on the path that Raymond Williams has so eloquently called "the journey of hope" toward the long revolution.[94] One of the places that journey of hope continues is in the real lives and experiences of those politically active teachers, parents, and students who are now struggling in such uncertain conditions to construct an education worthy of its name. We can join them, assist them, and be helped by them. In the process, the "we" can become larger, more inclusive, more democratic, a more decentered unity, thereby countering the Right. Too much is at stake if we do not.

6

Raymond Williams, Affective Ideology, and Counter-Hegemonic Practices

Wendy Kohli

Overview

It seems fitting for me to declare my working-class roots at the start of an essay on Raymond Williams. His work has touched me at a profoundly personal level. I find much to identify with in him—a man from the margins, from the "border country," who grounded his analysis of culture, class consciousness, and social identity formation in his own experience as the son of Welsh working people. The where and when of my life experiences (in)form who I am, how I think and see the world. Williams grasped the specificity of person and place in his novels, attending to the daily life of working-class people, to particular and multiple forms of consciousness among them, and to the generational shifts from parents to children.[1] At the same time, he theorized and *generalized* from his rich historical studies to develop analyses of culture, democracy, education, and communication that have laid the ground for much of the contemporary "cutting-edge" theoretical and empirical work being done in cultural studies in the U.S. and England.

In this essay, I draw on Williams's fiction as well as his cultural analysis and social theory to convey the power of educational institutions and practices in the process of class identity formation and the concomitant process of internalized oppression. I offer a critique of the rationalistic notion of ideology in most Marxist thought; one which assumes that social subjects create culture and consciousness in a

115

straightforward, rational, linear way proceeding to revolutionary action. To accomplish this critique, I will draw upon Williams's novels, *Border Country* and *Second Generation,* in which he explores in some depth the emotional ambivalences accompanying the contradictory material realities of working-class people moving on trajectories from working-class to middle-class interests. Williams opened the theoretical space for me to consider the contradictions of my own working-class experience and to conceptualize the relationship of affective ideology and contradictory consciousness to specific working-class histories.

Ironically, the open spaces for such a critique of Marxism that Williams provides in the novels are the very ones he closes or neglects, for the most part, in his cultural and social theory when he turns his attention to women's subordination and gender issues. Therefore, I will break from his gender-blind assumptions and draw on the work of feminists, particularly feminist educators, and show how a rationalistic model of consciousness inadequately conceives of the ways people make sense of their contradictory interests and cannot adequately account for the affective internalization of one's own subordination.

In moving beyond the limits of his thinking, I offer a transformative practice—a "practice of subjectivity"[2]—that can interrupt the internalization or "incorporation" process, the process that subverts one's ability to resist the dominating tendencies of capitalism.[3] Without interrupting and transforming this process, oppressed groups collude in their own oppression and in the oppression of others. Consequently, it continues to be increasingly difficult to create a new socialist politics; a politics that is just, democratic, and inclusive—that recognizes differences—as it promotes a "new form of the general interest."[4]

Remembering Ahead: Rereading "Toward 2000" in the 1990s

In the USA of 1990, Williams can be a source of hope for the future. In the last decade of this millennium—ten years before we reach that "fascinating round number" of the year 2000[5] that Williams used as a milestone for thinking about the future—I look to his vision of democratic socialism for inspiration.[6] I watch in despair as the "actual existing socialisms"[7] that Williams critiqued as "unilinear and singular"[8] turn to market economies for their resurrection in reaction to the Stalinized regimes of the past forty years. And I fight against hopelessness as I witness the increasing incidents of racist and sexist attacks and the "rolling back" of the hard-fought progressive gains of the late sixties in this country.

The dominant media has declared socialism dead. Williams would not be surprised at this "crisis of socialism." Neither, however, would he be thwarted in his defense of the possibility and necessity for "many democratic socialisms."[9] In the later years of his life, especially, Williams had a vision of a new politics—a new kind of socialism—that included a non-reductionist, non-essentialist understanding of class identity.[10] Drawing on the ambiguity and contradictions of his Welsh experience, he no longer accepted "those simple, confident, unitary identities which really belong to an earlier historical period."[11] Like many of his generation of "New Left" intellectuals who were beginning to grasp the implications of feminism and other liberation movements, he knew that the politics of the "Old" *and* the "New" Left no longer provided the analysis and action necessary to counteract the appeal of the Right or to deal with the increasing racism, sexism, and ecological destruction around the globe. It was time for the creation of a different politics; a politics that took the best of "the necessary economic struggle of the working class,"[12] yet moved beyond it to include other social formations in the struggle. Williams saw the possibilities for building alliances within and between the labor, peace, national liberation, feminist, and ecological movements.

Williams's work is an antidote to another "crisis" as well: what I see as an intellectual, moral, and political paralysis among the Left in the current climate of postmodern theorizing (and theoreticism). The debates between and among poststructuralists, Marxists, critical theorists, and feminists, and various combinations thereof, pose important challenges to our received political and cultural assumptions. These challenges raise the ethnocentrism, androcentrism, and Eurocentrism of the taken-for-granted positions of many Western, white (particularly male) academics. Yet, at the same time, the rush to embrace discourse theory and to move to a "post-Marxist discourse" threatens to depoliticize theory and subvert the possibility for political action.[13] I am convinced my working-class background prevents me from fully embracing the nihilist and relativist tendencies of the postmodern project. It has left an indelible mark on how I understand politics, education, and social change. And although my entry into the "professional academic" class distances me from my roots, I return frequently to the lessons of my childhood, to the concrete reality of the "haves and have-nots." Moving in and out of my different "spheres of struggle,"[14] I feel compelled to make sense of any liberatory theory in relation to my formative experiences and their material context.

Raymond and Me

I include an autobiographical passage as a "way in" to writing about the relationship between class identity and education because, as Williams's own work showed, class must be understood both as a theoretical construct and at the level of lived experience. One's biography influences how one comes to know the meaning of class. I read Williams from a particular standpoint, with a particular configuration of interests constructed through experiences growing up as a young white woman in a working-class family living in a small town in rural New York State during the "golden years of Rockefeller." I'm first-generation college-educated and the only one in my extended family to earn a Ph.D. Education was my "way out" of the working class.[15] I vividly remember deciding in second grade that I did not want the life of my father and mother—nor of any of my older siblings or cousins. And by "life" I did not mean simply economic position but a whole way of life defined by different social and cultural forms.

I was particularly resistant to getting married and letting a brood of children and a husband define my identity. At a young age, because of the material conditions of my existence, I was already on my way to developing a political awareness around gender and class. My father held many different jobs throughout his long life, including factory worker, greenskeeper, milkman, construction worker, and delivery man. He was anti-union, anti-communist, and anti-Rockefeller. With the gut instincts and raw energy of a revolutionary, he was just one more working person untouched by leftist politics. A "rugged individualist," he espoused populist slogans and praise for "the little guy" while condemning "the rich": a prime candidate for Reaganism and Thatcherism. My mother, with no affinity for politics, worked in the home until I, the youngest of her four children, went off to public school. Then she went to work as a cleaning woman in a county hospital, only later to "move up" to nurse's aide and then practical nurse. Hers became the "stable" income—government worker—while dad was at the mercy of a recessionary industrial economy. Lay-offs and unemployment "insurance" were a fact of life for the Kohli family, as we transferred our disappointments and fears to the new television in the center of the living room. No "Cleaver family" were we.

As a good student in the "high track" of our nearby city school, there was no doubt in my mind that I would go to college. My parents, however, declared early on that further education was out of the question. Money *cum* sexism[16] was their explicitly articulated reason, but I learned later that their resistance was also grounded deeply in an implicit, unstated fear: fear that I would change and leave them, breaking from all that counted as "our kind of people." Their fear was justified, though I resented it at the time. I *did* want to leave them—and much of what counted as their (my) way of life. I wanted distance between them and me. I wanted the "mobility" education was supposed to provide and the material life I thought a college degree could buy.[17] Ironically, I used the ideology of "rugged individualism" in order to pursue bravely a humble post-secondary education. Of course, classism played a determining role in my choice of colleges. Although in the "scholarship track" at a good academic high school, because of my family background I did not get the same college "advising" as did my upper-class classmates. And I did not have assertive parents to fight for me. Consequently, the only viable options open to me were several "teacher" colleges within the state university system. But history was on my side. What could have been a less than intellectually stimulating college experience at a regional campus was disrupted and transformed by the politics of the late sixties. Political activism became a significant part of my education—and my identity. Once again I was in oppositional relation to my family. I marched against the Vietnam War as my brother fought in it, and feelings of betrayal stewed beneath the family table.

Now a university professor, in my present material location I'm no longer part of the "working class," but my prior cultural understandings as a working-class person still inform my practical political connections to my work, including my reading of Williams. I live a "middle-class" lifestyle and, although I have moved "up" and "out," I still carry within me historical traces of my early life. These traces come in the form of emotional scars that hold me back as well as cultural resources that serve me well. I find myself returning to the images and experiences of my history, reaching down into that fertile ground to reclaim aspects of myself I had long ago buried. My career as well as my political and intellectual commitments reflect this history, albeit at times in contradictory, if not convoluted, ways. As a former classroom teacher and present teacher educator, I witness regularly the subtle and not-so-subtle ways schools reinforce and reproduce classist attitudes and practices. Teachers, as agents of cultural and ideological reproduction in schools, are expected to teach a "selective" curriculum that validates only certain knowledge and history, a distorted history that obscures and devalues the contributions of ordinary people, "my people."[18]

It has become increasingly important for me to understand, both intellectually and emotionally, the multiple layers of my desire to distance myself from my class background, while analyzing how my desire is created and reinforced in educational institutions. Yet, the more immersed I become in the alien world of middle-class academic culture, the more I find myself confronted by the pain and loss resulting from my move to the "middle class." While this move has brought material and cultural advantages, it has estranged me from many important aspects of my working-class community and family, including the traditional value placed on connectedness and loyalty. Like others who have had such a "border-crossing" experience, I was not prepared for the agonizing conflicts and ambivalent emotions that result from the mixed locations within my own class trajectory. Nor was I prepared for the confusing issues around "belonging" and "distancing"[19] that surface as I live out my life, a life so different from that of my family's. Most of the time, I feel "neither here nor there." I do not want to (and cannot) "go home again."[20] Nor do I want to fall prey to nostalgia as I address these feelings. To romanticize the "working classes" as if we are some undifferentiated heroic entity, neither desiring nor succumbing to middle-class material and cultural aspirations, is patronizing and distorts our conflictual histories of class experience. What I do want is to explore the cultural and structural processes that have shaped my class identity, to confront the deep ambivalence and shame associated with it, to validate the strengths and insights I have gained from it, and to engage in a process of transformation that will undermine the power of class oppression in all its forms.

This essay is not simply a personal journey into my psyche. The formation of class identity and the internalized class oppression many people carry around have political, social, and educational implications.[21] As someone committed to critical pedagogy, to the development of critical consciousness in students and teachers, I am eager to address the particular role education plays in the reproduction of classism and to offer a liberatory practice that can counteract the damaging individual and social effects of its internalized forms.[22] It is self-evident that classism, along with sexism and racism, serves to keep the unequal capitalist system in place. The more these forms of oppression are internalized by individuals, the more the "system" is aided in its efforts to maintain the status quo, thereby serving particular, dominant interests at the expense of all others. Raymond Williams's fiction and nonfiction provide a theoretical opening for me to further my work on classism and education.

The Influence of Williams

Williams's work serves as an important part of a foundation from which much of my thinking about class identity, democratic socialism, and the possibilities for social transformation has developed. Introduced to his work nearly twenty years ago, I continue to value the flexible, nonmechanistic, critical Marxism that informs his cultural materialism. Moving between his fiction and nonfiction, I have gained insight into the complexities of class-based societies and the contradictory moments in the "subjective" process of identity formation.[23] Raymond Williams understood the pain and possibilities that come with "crossing the border." He grasped, through his analytic and literary work, the subtlety and depth of class oppression, particularly as it was reinforced in and through the educational system. Drawing on the theoretical work of Antonio Gramsci, Williams provided an account of hegemony and cultural "incorporation" that laid the ground for much of the current critical work being done in educational studies in the United States and Britain.[24] Introducing this analysis of the hegemonic process into educational theory moved the radical critique of education away from a "mechanistic" Marxist interpretation of cultural and economic reproduction, an interpretation that could not account adequately for oppositional possibilities or for the "subjective" experience—the "lived reality" of people in all its complexity.

Through his novels, Williams conveyed this "lived reality" not only of working people but also of those like Matthew Price in *Border Country* and Peter Owen in *Second Generation*, who, through "higher" education, moved away from the physical work of their families to the intellectual work of the university. By engaging with real relationships and feelings, as experienced by actual people, Williams gave meaning to his abstract critique of capitalism and the structures of domination he analyzed.

Fact and Fiction

Williams's novels provide entrée to his own experiences and to how he understood class identity and class oppression. They also give me the theoretical space to consider my own contradictions of working-class experience and to conceptualize the affective dimensions of ideology. According to Williams, "a lived hegemony is always a process . . .

a realized complex of experiences, relationships, and activities . . . that has to be continually renewed, defended and modified . . . [and] continually resisted, limited, altered. . . ."[25] Through his fiction, Williams was able to convey this living process. His characters represented cross-generational instantiations of surrender *and* resistance to the prevailing systems of domination.

Encountering these characters, I saw moments of my own life, of my own subjectivity, particularly when working-class characters left home to go to university. I identified with a range of reactions: doubt, fear, betrayal, fraud, defiance, rage, isolation, detachment. His novels portray, in vivid detail, the lived experience of internalized class oppression. For example, in *Border Country* and *Second Generation,* the main characters grapple with the contradictions of university culture and the painful transitions they experience moving back and forth between "two worlds."[26]

In *Border Country,* Matthew Price returns to his hometown in Wales to visit his ill father, an active unionist. During these visits, he is forced to confront his choice to leave home and all the changes that come with that choice. Even his name, his literal identity, is different. While growing up, he was known as "Will" but took on "Matthew"—his actual birth name—when he arrived at university. Back home he is alternately alienated from both identities.

> "I've been away too long . . . I've forgotten it all, and I can't bring myself back." . . . As he looked away he heard the separate language in his mind, the words of his ordinary thinking. He was trained to detachment: the language itself, consistently abstracting and generalizing, supported him in this. And the detachment was real in another way. He felt in this house, both a child and a stranger.[27]

And he is reminded directly of his changes by an old love, Eira:

> "What's happened to you Will? . . . What's happened to make you like this?"
>
> [Will replies] "The usual things. I'm not quite so naive as I was."
>
> [Eira retorts] "You're not quite so human either. You seem to have forgotten every ordinary feeling. . . . You went away from us, you had to. And we accepted that, though in fact it meant losing you. It's just that it hurts now, when you come back as a stranger." (*BC*, 273–74)

And an old family friend follows this with a searing criticism, hitting directly one of Matthew's secret fears. The scene goes as follows:

> "I don't like what you're asked to grow up into, what you say you reject. . . . Your senior colleagues and masters: Just that lot Will. We still think of them as 'that lot.' "
>
> [Matthew/Will counters] "They're not bad. It's just they're like foreigners, when you come where it matters."
>
> [Morgan, the friend persists] "They're exactly like you, and that's the fact, Will. It's you think you're different, but you're getting more like them. With an occasional kick, you know. A rude noise round the corner when you're sure that they're looking. 'And please it wasn't me, sir, it was my background.' "
> (*BC*, 282)

The fear that he is turning into "one of them" grips Matthew as he struggles to carve out a line of research that will keep him tied to his working-class roots and to the political commitments of his family.

Similarly, in *Second Generation,* we find Peter Owen tormented by his own internal conflicts, which pit the traditional values of connectedness and solidarity with his people against the pull toward individual freedom, mobility, and "bourgeois" academic life. University education reinforces the latter, yet leaves him confused, impotent, and compromised. He rages at his mentor, also a "first-generation" university person.

> "Look Robert, what I'm asking from you I can't get from anyone. I'm asking for the connection, between work and living. I'm asking you to live in my work, and of course you can't. You have to detach yourself, or we'd overwhelm you."[28]
>
> [And the scene continues:]
>
> "You're scared Robert. You're scared of really meeting anyone. You're scared really, of being anyone. It might not fit the institution. . . ."
>
> "And you?" Robert asked, more sharply.
>
> "Yes, of course," Peter replies.
>
> "Then at least you can respect the difficulty, Peter."
>
> "Of course I respect it. I could even respect defeat. What I can't respect is surrender. Yet in a way it's nobody's fault. You were the first generation. And we can respect your work, your patience, your strength even. *But did you have to become like*

> them? Did you have to change your whole voice, your whole
> body, every bit of yourself?" (*SG*, 252; emphasis mine)

Williams, expressing his own biographical ambivalence toward university and middle- and owning-class cultures, was able to portray the pain of "selling out" to "them." Both Matthew Price and Peter Owen expressed their anguish at leaving behind the values of and connections to "their people." We see Peter Owen, for example, sitting with the manuscript of his thesis:

> . . . every page he touched seemed to suddenly, to belong in a
> quite different life. He could hardly recognize his own words
> . . . for his own voice, his own words, were not in this work at
> all. These were simply the words that he had learned to re-
> arrange and manipulate, that he had been paid for manipulat-
> ing. (*SG*, 136)

He had "surrendered"—to the values and attitudes of this new world—and it gnawed at him. Part of the work that he felt he had to do was to reclaim his own voice and reject the polite voice of the university. In a tirade directed at an academic who had an affair with Peter's mother, Peter revealed the depth of his anger and disgust toward this particular man and the world he represented:

> "You have this manner that's the ultimate weapon, that makes
> the rest of us feel so wrong and ridiculous we simply throw our
> own strengths away. We give up our causes and our voices to
> become like you, and then you congratulate us, and what
> sounds like England tells us we're right. I tell you the opposite.
> I tell you you're wrong. I tell you England must be won back
> from you, urgently and completely, or we shall all die." (*SG*,
> 318)

Throughout both texts, the tensions between and among different class identities surface regularly. Both families give their blessings to university education. Yet in both cases, they feel continuing ambivalence about the quality of the changes, of the meanings and values both sons learned in their "higher education." The "university lot" with whom their sons work are viewed, suspiciously, as corrupt and arrogant. Yet, at the same time, both families express feelings of inadequacy and inferiority in relation to them.

This sense of inferiority that many working people feel about themselves is reinforced systematically in our society—through formal institutions like the media and schools, as well as informally through the lived reality of daily life in communities. Classist practices encourage emulation of owning class habits and values, which in turn feed a consumer society and reinforce a sense of powerlessness and dependence. When educated to identify owning-class interests as their own, to become "like them," and to believe that mobility is not a myth, working people remain in competition with each other, ready to step on and over their brothers and sisters if it means "making it." This process is complicated by racism and sexism, which exacerbate the effects of classism. Not only are working people kept apart because of economic condition, they are further separated as a result of sexist and racist beliefs and practices. Williams's novels give us insight into the very powerful, personal process of incorporation, showing how educational institutions play a strong role in "implanting a deep assent to capitalism"[29] by, in the case of working people, undermining their value and mystifying owning-class interests as the interests of *everyone*.

Hegemony, Education, and Class Oppression

"Implanting a deep assent to capitalism": How and why is it that so many people assent to the fundamental inequities and oppressions dealt by capitalism? To begin to answer this theoretically, Williams drew on Gramsci's concept of hegemony to understand the ways the dominant classes maintained control of society, control that transcended power and property. He knew, as did Gramsci, that this dominance relied on the

> saturation of the whole process of living—not only of political
> and economic activity, nor only of manifest social activity, but
> of the whole substance of lived identities and relationships, to
> such a depth that the pressures and limits of what can ulti-
> mately be seen as a specific economic, political, and cultural
> system seem to most of us as the pressures and limits of a sim-
> ple experience and common sense.[30]

The concept of hegemony provided a sophisticated account of the process of domination, moving beyond "trivializing explanations of simple 'manipulation,' 'corruption,' and 'betrayal.' " This conceptual development helped clarify the process of *internalization*—how "relations of domination and subordination [take the form of] practical consciousness." And by understanding the extent to which given forms of domination are "experienced and *in practice internalized* . . . the whole question of class rule, and of opposition to it, is transformed."[31] What emerges are possibilities for many new forms of political struggle—for a "more active sense of revolutionary activity."[32]

Williams broke new theoretical ground in connecting education to hegemony.[33] He understood the power of "selective traditions,"[34] selections governed "by many kinds of special interest, including class interests."[35] His work in this area contributed greatly to a critique of the educational system, with its processes of sorting and grading, and to a radical analysis of the relationship between curriculum and economic formations.[36] With this critique came a better grasp of the way class identity and deep "structures of feeling" were lived—were experienced—particularly within and through educational institutions.[37] He maintained that the educational system, along with other social forces, "is involved in a continual making and remaking of an effective dominant culture."[38]

Williams analyzed schooling as a contradictory process, one inculcating people with dominant values and beliefs *as well as* providing openings for counter-hegemonic, liberatory action. However, he knew that "saturating" our consciousness—the process of hegemony—was much more complex than "merely impos[ing] ideology," so consequently it was that much more difficult to undo.[39] It required "the most sustained kinds of intellectual and educational work—a cultural process—'the long revolution.' "[40]

When Williams called for this "long revolution" in 1961, he argued for a "process of change [that affected] . . . our whole way of life . . . [including] deep social and personal changes.[41] At that time, he placed much faith in the role of the working class as a primary agent of historical change. By 1975, he no longer could rely on his fixed conceptions of class or traditional trade union practices. Other social formations had to be taken into account. And furthermore, he argued that any contemporary struggle had to be built on "feeling and imagination . . . as much as fact and organization" because "anything as deep as a dominant structure of feeling is only changed by active new experiences."[42]

Affective Ideology and Counter-Hegemonic, Feminist Practice

Contemporary work in critical educational studies, particularly ethnographic work documenting the contradictory role of schooling and critical pedagogy, offering theories to transform classrooms into counter-hegemonic spaces, has substantially advanced our understanding of the hegemonic process. In this essay, I want to push this critical work one step further to deal with the psychological and emotional levels of internalized oppression while taking into account the material conditions in which people consent to their subordination. I believe that when individuals and groups *internalize* the "meanings and values" of the dominant culture as their own and *believe* the cultural misinformation about themselves, they become accomplices in their own domination.[43]

As a counter to this internalization process, I believe such liberatory practices as the one Erica Sherover-Marcuse develops can extend Williams's work on hegemony, and that of the generation of critical educators who draw on it, in order to disrupt the patterns of powerlessness and mystification that serve the status quo. For too long, those of us engaged in Left criticism, critical teaching, and political organizing have come up against barriers—resistances to social change—and not just ones external to us. Many are located *within* ourselves.[44] We need to problematize our liberatory efforts and not assume that emancipation will automatically and necessarily follow from rational critique. If we are committed to transforming the dominating systems and cultures in which we live, we need to add to those rational forms of criticism to which many of us are so well-schooled. What is required is a process integrating the rational *with* the emotional, a process that is "a deliberate and systematic attempt . . . to *unlearn* the habits of thought and action that are the consequence of domination."[45] Through this "unlearning," and through an examination of the structural preconditions that accompany such unlearning, those of us committed to social transformation may be better equipped to create a new politics, a politics of "difference" that acknowledges multiple forms of political agency.

The challenge is to create the educational experiences and structures that can effectively work against the processes of cultural hegemony. Formal educational institutions must increasingly become sites of contestation and opposition.[46] And they must also support alliance-building among groups who are in subordinate relation to the dominant culture. But this is no small task. There are deep divisions among and between subordinate groups. Creating counter-hegemonic spaces requires a multiplicity of experiences: experiences that shift attitudes, beliefs, and emotions as much as cognitive understanding, critique, and analysis. Eradicating classism, sexism, heterosexism, and racism—all forms of oppression that exacerbate our differences and keep us separate—requires critical analysis, political organizing and struggle, *and* work on internalized, affective forms of oppression.

The Left, particularly the white male "Left" in the United States (including those engaged in theorizing critical pedagogy) has failed to grasp the importance of the affective dimensions of ideology in building a mass movement for social change. Understanding "the formations of feeling and relationship which are our immediate resources in any struggle"[47] will require new practices and commitments, practices that focus on subjective experience and that complement theoretical critique and political action.[48] The saturation of our everyday life, of our whole way of living—including our emotions and personal relationships— must undergo self-examination and transformation in order to create alternative practical possibilities. As Williams, in a self-reflective moment, put it:

> I learned the experience of incorporation, I learned the reality
> of hegemony, I learned the saturating power of the structures
> of feeling of a given society, *as much from my own mind and
> my own experience* as from observing the lives of others.[49]

Williams believed that it was possible to "defeat" the "experience of incorporation," but it required that "we make the effort, [that] we uncover layers of this kind of alien formation in ourselves, and deep in ourselves."[50] He was not alone in understanding the complexity of domination or in analyzing the importance of the psychological in creating revolutionary and oppositional movements. Wilhelm Reich, through his early work with psychoanalysis and politics, warned Marxists "that the ruling class disseminates and defends its ideology; the problem is why the masses accept it."[51] Critical theorists of the Frankfurt School were also clear that Marxism was "inadequate in comprehending the subjective dimension of social life" and turned to "Freudian categories to illuminate the dialectic of domination characteristic of modern capitalism."[52] But the richest source for addressing the "subjective" dimension of ideology and the contradictory moments in consciousness is feminist theory and practice, for it is feminism, particularly feminist materialism, that has moved the critique of Marxism beyond the abstract, universalizing account of hu(man) experience that subsumes all difference. Feminist politics, grounded in specific historical conditions, also legitimates the notion that the "personal is political" and provides the theoretical framework for naming and explaining women's experience (and, by extension, other oppressed groups' experience).[53] Williams, as sympathetic as he was to the affective side of ideology and to the complexity of subjective identity formation, "privatized" this sympathy by developing it only in his novels. His more "public" work, his theoretical work, did not incorporate the insights of his fiction.[54] I turn to feminist practices that are better positioned to grasp the integration of the affective and the rational in the formation of consciousness and in the transformation to a more liberated society.

The Practice of Subjectivity

I think it important to understand what experiences "taught" me to be embarrassed by and ashamed of my family: my father, a laborer, who came to the table in his tee shirt and my mother who worked outside the home, scrubbing other people's floors. How did I "know" so early in my life that it would pay to take on the habits and speech patterns of those with higher social and economic status than my own? What reinforcement did I get in school for these changes? What traditions and practices reinforce the reactionary stance of much of the white working class, particularly in the United States, so that they (we) actually become "engaged in preserving and reconstituting forms of domination"?[55] How is it possible that academics from the working classes spend lifetimes overcoming feelings of intellectual and social inadequacy, regardless of the "objective" evidence of their professional productivity? What price do we pay for relinquishing our voices and taking on "theirs"? What price do oppressed groups pay for "trying to pass"?

I believe these questions have political and personal import, and that all of us engaged in the struggle for progressive political alternatives must provide the theoretical and practical guidance to attack the devastating power of internalized oppression as we work to transform fundamental structural inequalities.

Williams concurred and recognized that these alien structures of feeling must be defeated, but, he argues, "to defeat something like that in yourself, in your families, in your neighbors, in your friends, to defeat it involves something very different . . . from most traditional political strategies."[56] Williams did not provide us with any practical direction in this area. His critique remained abstract and theoretical.

I look to Sherover-Marcuse's practice of subjectivity as one direction to take in our move away from "traditional political strategies." This practice, whose aim is "to *begin* the healing of wounds sustained in an oppressive society," focuses on the affective moments in ideology and hegemony but always within the context of specific historical, structural realities. The practice is designed to illuminate the tragic consequences of institutional inequalities on individuals and targeted groups and to analyze the differential effects of these structural inequalities. As people articulate the oppressive conditions under which they live(d), including how that oppression has been internalized, they express multiple levels of emotion—including rage, sadness, pride, happiness, and grief. By expressing the pain attached to their own oppressive situations and the multiple ways they are oppressed, and by *reclaiming* the pride and benefits of their specific cultural and material histories, they are then better able to *analyze* their conditions and to work to change them. The practice is an *empowering process.* Like individual psychotherapy, this practice works in a dialectical manner to uncover, express, and overcome the emotional pain resulting from particular oppressive conditions. *But unlike psychotherapy,* this practice embraces *social as well as individual interests*—"a commitment to human liberation"—that involves people from all walks of life, across all identities.[57]

Focusing on the release of deep emotional pain is not generally welcomed in most political or intellectual circles.[58] However, more and more people, taking the lead from various feminist practices, are becoming convinced that the repression of emotions is counterproductive to progressive social change.[59] These theorists maintain that safe spaces and structured processes are needed to encourage emotional release as a complement of any process of social transformation. Williams, more so than many Left male intellectuals, recognized the importance of feelings and relationships. What he did not grasp was the political importance of the *expression* of these feelings and the potential for rational, liberatory change that can result from this emotional process.

There are many ways to go about this practice. One place to start is to "speak my truth" to attentive people about my experience; to tell my story. Being listened to sincerely can provide a safe enough space for deep and old emotions to come out and for me to regain perspective on my true power and agency. A further process would be to join together with others from the working class to share our histories, to support each other in our development—individually and collectively—and to see how classism cuts differently across gender, race, and ethnicity. A third possibility is for several people, from different oppressed groups, to tell their stories—in a "speak out" format—to an attentive audience. In the telling, both the unique and the common

130

aspects of the various forms of internalized oppression are revealed. Consequently, bonds can be built across differences as individuals see that there are similar roots of oppression. A fourth option is for individuals from particular oppressed groups to boast about "our people" and validate the qualities we are proud of having gained through our particular experiences.

These and other practices would encourage the *affective unlearning* of the habits of oppression.[60] They would begin to subvert the tendency of oppressed peoples to defer to the beliefs and values of the dominant culture and to end the invalidation of their own talents and capacities. In other words, these practices could be counter-hegemonic, creating the necessary (but certainly not sufficient) preconditions for revolutionary action. These practices are fundamentally political in that they connect the socio-psychological processes of identity formation to specific historical, material conditions with the primary purpose of changing those conditions.

In order for this subjective praxis to retain its emancipatory force, it must continue "in the context of a developing solidarity." It is this context of solidarity that differentiates this practice from other psychological therapies which seek "happiness or self-realization *within* the established system."[61] The process, within a context of solidarity, works toward universal and particular emancipation as it acknowledges the real divisions that separate people, avoiding a "false humanism" in the process.[62] It is this "false humanism" that Williams struggled mightily to overcome in his unrelenting commitment to "a general interest." And he knew that this commitment to a "we" had to come through a socialist movement that respected and included differences. But his analysis did not take him to the point of creating a means to *work through and with* these differences. The practice offered here does provide a means to work through/with our differences, by getting at the embedded feelings that result from oppressive material conditions and providing a mechanism by which these feelings can be released.

Epilogue

Throughout his lifetime, Williams retained his respect for traditional labor politics, even as he recognized its failures, because he felt that at its core was the direction of the future:

The unique and extraordinary character of working class self-organization has been that it has tried to connect particular struggles to a general struggle in a quite special way. It has set out, as a movement, to make real what is at first sight the extraordinary claim that the defense and advancement of certain particular interests, properly brought together, are in fact in the general interest. That after all, is the moment of transition to an idea of socialism. And this moment comes not once and for all but many times; is lost and is found again; has to be affirmed and developed, continually, if it is to stay real.[63]

It is time once again to "affirm" this "moment of transition," making it "real" for *all* oppressed groups. This requires that we make sure that the specific and multiple forms of oppression we each suffer are not rendered invisible and subsumed by some abstract concept of general or common interests. A new politics must attend seriously and specifically to the grievances of each group as it provides theoretical and practical guidance for common social transformation. Williams was committed to keeping politics "real," to making sure that one's "lived reality" was taken into account in any analysis or prescription for change. By engaging in subjective practices to reveal the affective dimensions of the hegemonic process, people committed to social transformation for the next century may be on the way to "keeping politics real." I believe, as does Sherover-Marcuse, that these practices are "one essential component of an[y] emancipatory social movement."[64]

7

Williams on Democracy and the Governance of Education

Fazal Rizvi

Democratization of social relations is a consistent theme in most, if not all, of Raymond Williams's writings. Throughout his intellectual journey, from the late 1940s when he helped establish the journal *Politics and Letters* to the time of his death in early 1988 when Thatcherite cynicism seemed well entrenched on the British landscape, Williams was interested in examining the emerging forms of British politics in order to identify the conditions necessary for bringing about an achievable socialist democracy. For Williams, even a fully representative parliament was not a sufficient condition of a socialist democracy which must ultimately involve, he insisted, the direct exercise of popular power. Highly distrustful of bureaucratic and authoritarian solutions to social problems, he insisted that people ought to be given the power and resources to manage their own affairs. Williams's theory of democracy thus stressed the importance of "the distinctive principle of maximum self-management."[1]

Stated in this generalized manner, the similarities between these ideas and the language of recent initiatives taken by a British conservative government to reform educational governance are indeed striking. Indeed, in Britain, the introduction of the Educational Reform Act (ERA) in 1988 was supported by a rhetoric that utilized many of the concepts that would have once been assumed to have defined a socialist agenda. For notions such as devolution, self-governance, parent and community participation, and school-based decision making were all used by Williams to stress the need to overturn long-entrenched centralist decision-making structures, giving local schools and communities greater power to manage their own affairs. In this essay, I will discuss some of the ways in which the Right's understanding of the idea of self-management differs from the socialist agenda that formed the basis of Williams's political writings. I will argue that while the Right may use many of the terms which are integral to Williams's theory of democracy, it has succeeded in fundamentally rearticulating their meaning and significance.

Indeed, the current rhetoric concerning devolution and self-managing schools in Britain is illustrative of the extent to which a government of the Right has captured the popular vocabulary of the Left to serve a set of contradictory purposes. So while Williams proposed "self-management" as a central mechanism for releasing "a tremendous reservoir of social energy, now locked in resentment of bureaucratic and hierarchical organizations"[2] and for creating caring participative communities, in the hands of Thatcherism it has played a very different role in the organization of politics. While both the proposals that Williams put forward for a "decentralized socialism" and Thatcher's vision of a "popular capitalism" rest on a diagnosis of our social problems which suggests that they are rooted in the excesses of the modern paternalistic and highly bureaucratized state, what marks the current successes of the Right has been its capacity to translate these sentiments into a political rhetoric about "the rights of the individual" that masks many of the deep-rooted problems confronting Britain, most notably the vast social inequalities that are an inevitable consequence of a corporate capitalist economy. The Right's use of the notion of self-management stresses the capacity of individuals to manage their own affairs in an unconstrained market; in contrast, Williams's writings place a greater emphasis upon the distinctive socialist value of sharing within a framework that rejects the basic assumption of capitalism. For the Right, the notion of choice implies the autonomous preferences of individuals, viewed as Cartesian social subjects, who act in their own self-interest. For Williams, on the other hand, choice is something that is socially and historically formed; it is something that is exercised collectively, in communities that manage themselves in a climate of caring and sharing.

In Thatcher's Britain, this rearticulation[3] of socialist language has occurred against the background of an emerging realization that British capitalism faces a number of deep-rooted crises, and that the inherent contradictions upon which it is based require some form of resolution. Instead of attending to these contradictions, as Williams did, the social analysis upon which Thatcherism is based views the problems facing British capitalism in terms of the excesses of the welfare state that has been developed steadily since World War II. Thatcher's solution has been to "roll back the state"; and to do so by stressing the virtues of the "free market" and its capacity not only to generate greater national wealth but also to provide a more appropriate moral response to the social problems confronting communities. In this way, the Thatcher government has fed on the discontent, anger, and fears of people to suggest that a capitalism stripped of its expensive welfare commitments has a greater capacity to help actualize the values of "caring and sharing" than those ineffective proposals that the Left has so far put forward. Encouraging the belief that the state can never be in a position to support the initiatives and the creativity of individuals, Thatcherism has sought to give people a sense of control over their lives. But in doing this, it has stressed many of the virtues which Williams also celebrates—self-reliance, self-management, decentralization, and democratic control. What I want to suggest in this essay, however, is that Thatcherism's articulation of these values, as exemplified in the case of the Educational Reform Act, rests upon assumptions about the nature of human beings, social relations, and political organization which are diametrically opposed to those which Williams espouses. I want to argue that far from giving communities any real control over educational decision making, ERA represents an extension of the state's ideological powers of surveillance, and its participatory rhetoric masks an authoritarianism against which Williams's political program is squarely directed.

Central to Williams's theory of democracy is the distinction between "representation" and "popular power." In the socialist tradition, Williams argues, "democracy meant popular power, a state in which the interests of the majority of people were paramount and in which these interests were practically exercised and controlled by the majority."[4] But, suggests Williams, it has been the liberal tradition of representative democracy that has dominated thinking in Britain, informing popular conceptions about the form and extent of democratic possibilities. Most people in Britain now think of democracy as no more than a parliamentary approach to government with their democratic engagements restricted to casting a vote once every few years.

Williams defines a parliamentary democracy as "a system in which the whole government of society is determined by a representative assembly, elected in secret ballot by all adult members of the society, at stated and regular intervals, for which any adult member of the society may be an open and equal candidate."[5] For Williams, this definition represents a very weak form of democracy, though he hastens to point out that even if its narrowly defined formal conditions are accepted, Britain could not be classed as a genuine parliamentary democracy. For in Britain, legal sovereignty continues to reside with the monarchy, not with the people or their elected parliament; its second chamber, the House of Lords, is an unelected body, based on heredity and patronage; and it has an electoral system which produces a parliament that does not accurately reflect the actual distribution of popular votes. Of course, it could be acknowledged, as many political analysts now do, that the British parliamentary system needs reforming, and that it should look to adopting models from more modern systems, such as the United States.[6] But, to Williams, such proposals for reform are not sufficient, for he maintains that all representative systems are democratic only in a very limited sense.

Williams's survey of the problems of representative systems of government is both comprehensive and compelling. He argues that the idea of representation implies that in a society where it is not practically feasible for people to meet and make decisions themselves, representatives of various localities, opinions, or functional interests are appointed or elected to conduct the necessary negotiations to arrive at the best possible decision on their behalf. Thus a "legal representative" is one who acts on another's behalf. To an extent, this is what parliamentary representatives also do when they act for constituents in a range of dealings with governments and bureaucracies. Williams suggests, however, that this kind of parliamentary representation is mostly confined to local and personal problems. In major political arguments, in which matters of general community rather than individual interests are involved, it is the party "discipline" that becomes paramount. A "representative" is prevented from acting on behalf of views that are not in line with the dictates of the party hierarchy. Within the framework of all representative democracies, which are constructed around a tightly organized party system, diversity of opinion is discouraged; as is the free and unhindered dialogue between people and their representatives.

Williams argues that the current form and practices of "representation" conflate two distinct senses of the term: "making present" and "symbolization." The idea of "making present" entails the democratic principles of delegation, mandate, and revocability, while "symbolization" implies representation in a more abstract way. Symbolic representation involves acting on behalf of persons belonging to a generic category (such as the younger generation, the pensioners, the unionists, and the like). Thus a representative can claim to be acting on behalf of a group without any direct democratic mandate or accountability. Williams contends that increasingly it is the pre-democratic idea of symbolic representation that describes the current practices of parliamentary democracy in Britain. It is inherent in the rhetoric of "the national interest" to which "representatives" often appeal in contradicting the wishes of the people. Such rhetoric, of course, pre-empts all fundamental arguments about what the nation and its interests are and should be, as well as assuming a unity in those represented. Of course, such a unity seldom exists, but the system seems to perpetuate the present illusion of representation and consensus.

In a parliamentary democracy, representatives are elected on the basis of the aggregate of individual votes. Williams argues that since such a system "presumes the sovereign individual making his [sic] choice about the whole government of his [sic] country,"[7] it reduces the whole range of social relations to just two entities: the "individual" and the "nation." Other categories for organizing social relations, such as gender, race, and class, are thus assumed to be immaterial to the representatives who consider themselves to be working for either the individual or the nation. Once elected, moreover, most individuals have no further part to play in the decision-making processes of the government, even if circumstances change dramatically. The mandate which the government claims rests on a general package of issues that the representatives are expected to implement. But the packages themselves are extremely general and leave much room for later interpretation, diversity, and disagreement. To translate general sentiments into policies and programs, governments actively consult and negotiate with bodies outside the elected body of parliamentary representatives. Williams argues that this practice shows that the claim of representative theorists that parliaments "monopolize and exhaust the representative process" is, in actual conditions, manifestly false: that, in representative democracies, we are faced with "the practical co-existence of two different forms of represented interest."[8] One of these is the nominal and indirect interest of individuals who cast a vote at intervals of several years, the other is the powerful groups in the country who exert enormous influence over the day-to-day running of the government. Decisions are made by the cabinet, which, while it derives its authority from the representative process and in the end is answerable to the electoral process, is nevertheless autonomous between elections. The advice it receives, the groups it consults, and much of the information upon which it bases its decisions are seldom disclosed, either to the parliament or to the public. What transpires is a system in which, while the parliament retains some significance, it is the absolutism cabinet that is supreme; it is a system in which the "represented interest is effectively divided and distanced."[9]

Furthermore, the cabinet decisions themselves are taken in an environment dominated by the social power of capital. Behind the government's rhetoric of "consultation with those affected" lies a very different social process, which does not so much privilege the sovereign individual electors or their representatives as it does extra-parliamentary formations of political and economic power. Williams argues:

> Certain key political and economic decisions are of course made and contested through such (representative) systems, but always within the conditions in which control (and therefore decision-making) of major economic resources of the country remains firmly in "private" hands: in fact the hands of national and international capitalist corporations. The major decisions affecting the lives and livelihood of a majority of (individual citizens) are quite legally made beyond the reach of the system of political "representation."[10]

In the supposedly "neutral" consultations governments have with the public, it is the voices of financial institutions, corporations, and the press that are the loudest. They play key roles, both directly and indirectly, in the development and implementation of all major policies.

For Williams, then, these arguments serve to highlight the autocratic strains in the representative conception of democracy. They also demonstrate that even a fully representative parliament is not a sufficient condition of a self-determining democratic society. Insisting that cultural questions cannot be separated from political and economic questions, and that issues of cultural policy are issues about the conditions of social relations, Williams refers to existing representative political systems as bourgeois democracy because they allow the coexistence of political representation and participation with an economic system which admits no such rights, procedures, or claims. He argues that while it is important to acknowledge some of the historical achievements of bourgeois democracy—free speech, free assembly, and free elections—it is nevertheless necessary to point out that "the power of private (corporate) money can limit or at times overwhelm them."[11]

So what is the solution to the problems of representative democracy? For Williams, overthrow of representative systems is certainly not the solution. Indeed, he argues that we must mount "vigorous defences of parliamentary democracy against the strong current tendencies to bureaucratic and authoritarian solutions."[12] But at the same time he cautions us against the major deficiencies and evils of the present system, especially when it conspires with authoritarian forms, such as self-interested bureaucracies and the institutions of international capitalism, to further diminish democratic accountability. It should be stressed, however, that Williams is no less critical of those centralized states which practice "socialism" through an appeal to either efficient forms of expert administration or programs of "benevolent" authoritarianism. He is also critical of the Left in Britain, which he believes has repeatedly missed opportunities to develop enduring forms of democratic politics, assuming these to be somehow unrelated to the task of dismantling capitalism. It is this failure that has now allowed Thatcherism to assume a political space in which it has been able to rearticulate the language of socialism. The great challenge before us is "to show in very great detail why a socialist society would be more democratic, and this will involve being implacably clear about the failure of other kinds of democratic processes within socialist revolutions or labour movements." For Williams, then, the key to a socialist democracy must be "the direct exercise of popular power, rather than the internal management of a particular class-ruled state or those generalized means which are not democracy but simply its accompanying procedures."[13]

The central questions which concern Williams are how politics should be organized and how general interest should be served. In *The Long Revolution,* published in 1961, Williams argued that socialist politics should be organized around the pursuit of a "common culture" that had the capacity to unify the genuinely common experiences of people. In developing his idea of common experiences, he had turned to the traditions of English working-class culture, suggesting that it provided the resources for the transformation of British society. Rejecting the idea of individual advancement celebrated in bourgeois institutions, Williams had expressed a fundamental belief in collective and mutual development, and in the possibility of forming shared social identities and a sense of community for a future common culture. His view of democracy had called for a form of socialism in which the emphasis was on the need for the creation of an educated and participating citizenry. He justified this view both on the grounds of principle and efficiency—democracy was not only consistent with the highest moral principles of justice and equality but also provided a most efficient way of organizing social life.

In his later writings, in particular *Towards 2000*, Williams's commitment to a socialist democracy remains firm, but he now presents it with a greater sense of urgency. He argues that in a complex and interdependent society, general education, access to information, and positive and active involvement in decision making are absolutely necessary if we are to avoid the cultural, economic, and environmental crises that presently confront us. *Towards 2000* also presents the case for a socialist democracy with greater theoretical sophistication. Here he acknowledges some of the idealist and culturalist assumptions that characterized his earlier works. He concedes that his notion of "common culture" may contain a romanticized view of the English working class, and that a call for a class-based politics, divorced from other sites of political struggle, may rest on essentialist assumptions. Acknowledging these complex problems with his earlier work, later Williams explores the possibilities of resources for the "journey of hope" not only in traditions of the working class but also in the contemporary political and social movements, such as ecology, feminism, and peace. He recognizes the need to forge a new political project through the development of an effective hegemonic block. Williams leaves unexplored the issue of exactly how this is to be done, but it remains the greatest challenge that confronts socialism today.

In *Towards 2000,* Williams writes as a realist, concerned with identifying democracy's necessary and feasible forms. The central question he now asks is a pragmatic one. How should we sustain and extend existing forms of democracy? In pursuing this question, he is now prepared to explore conceptions of social relations other than those conceptualized around the language of class and class struggle. O'Connor has observed that "Williams's method assumes no fixed human nature, no simple nature of things, but a series of discourses through which we know each other and our world."[14] He engages with contemporary political conditions and is not reluctant to challenge the assumptions upon which his earlier analyses were based. This is hardly surprising, for, as Mulhern points out:

> Williams's work has always been distinctive for its tough-minded wariness in political response. He never accepted the analytic and the moral, the indicative and the optative, as truly sustainable alternatives. Williams's method of cultural analysis involves understanding the present and the future *historically.* His objective is to understand "the underlying problems, forces and ideas" of capitalism and its probable future and to indicate "some possible ways through them."[15]

So while in *Towards 2000* Williams reaffirms his contention that even a fully representative parliament is not a sufficient condition of a self-determining democratic society, he does not uncritically accept what have traditionally been purported to be the two defining principles of a socialist democracy. He argues that the familiar principles of a "Left government" and "self-management" are not self-evidently compatible. In defense of this contention, Williams takes up his long-standing argument with the British Labour movement, and particularly the Labour Left.

In post-World War II Britain, Williams believes, Labour governments had mostly squandered the opportunities to democratize institutions such as the local authorities, the housing estates, the nationalized industries, and the educational system. Instead of attempting to create a common and democratic culture, Labour had simply established mechanisms for the incorporation of the working class into the structure of the dominant culture. In this way, Labour's reformist program had rested on the assumptions of meritocracy, buttressed by a spurious concept of the nation. It had not challenged in any significant way the capitalist structure of British society: it had simply made the ladder of social mobility a little more accessible. The British Labour movement had moreover failed to create new democratic forums that might have provided people with greater opportunities to practice democracy. The failure to think creatively about the manner in which we might nourish and deepen democratic processes, Williams argues, had led inevitably to "a weakening of belief in the possibility of democracy."[16]

Williams maintains that, in effect, the Labour Party's proposals for the democratization of British cultural and political life have not progressed beyond the call for the abolition of the House of Lords. And he is particularly critical of those within the Left who seem perfectly content with the current undemocratic organizational structures of the Labour Party, which permit decisions to be made at the Party's conferences by the often nonaccountable votes of trade-union and constituency delegates. The Party, he contends, is run by an elite group of careerist politicians, more interested in preserving privileges than in seeking to involve the general polity in democratic processes. No party can claim to be democratic unless it offers more opportunities to open discussion and learning.

Labour's argument seems to be that once a "tight party government" has been elected, it will, using its command bureaucratic structure, be able to "deliver" self-management, popular democracy, community socialism, and worker control. Williams, on the other hand, believes that is muddled thinking. There is something odd, he says, about expecting a hierarchical bureaucratic apparatus to be able to implement radical democratic politics. It is to assume that bureaucracy is a neutral

141

phenomenon with no genuine interests of its own. Denying any clear distinction between politics and administration, Williams suggests that bureaucrats exercise a great deal of power in defining the goals of policies, determining priorities, mobilizing public support or opposition to particular policies, and evaluating the success or failure of programs. And their particular interests do not always coincide with the general interest. In view of the historical experience of Labour governments, which have repeatedly been captured by the dominant bureaucratic interests, Williams regards the belief that a tight Labour government will be able to deliver self-management "at best a pious hope, at worst a pathetic delusion."[17]

For Williams, self-management is not something that can be "delivered" by a government, a policy that can somehow be "implemented." Rather, it describes a social process that has to be fought for in every facet of social life. Self-management represents a conscious stage beyond representative democracy and involves the development of "new kinds of communal, cooperative and collective institutions."[18] Throughout his writings, Williams stresses the educative potential of direct democracy, which not only provides opportunities for people to participate in decision making but also enriches their cultural experiences through learning and sharing. Democracy is not simply a decision-making system; rather it is a moral principle for organizing social life, essential for securing human dignity and freedom. It is a way of defining social relationships. It affects everyday cultural life, and its popular form enables individuals to have a say in the way their lives are governed.

Williams recognizes, however, that in large complex societies not everyone can participate in decision making. He concedes that "certain industrial processes are necessarily complex, within both vertical and horizontal divisions of labour, and decision making in them cannot in all respects be assigned to elements of the enterprise."[19] Also, while some social policies have only local relevance, and should therefore be determined by everyone directly affected, others have much wider application. Williams suggests therefore that self-management "cannot be confined to isolatable enterprises and communities, for which some models exist, but must be taken as a principle, into what are necessarily more indirect, more extended and therefore more complex forms."[20]

According to Williams, then, in large complex societies, the distinctively socialist principle of maximum self-management can only be realized by the creation of many new kinds of "intermediate institutions" in which all necessary and extended relations are based on direct social relations, so that authentic power resides with the people "at the grass roots." Williams readily admits that "some considerations of economic viability and reasonable equity" would need to coexist with the principle of maximum self-management, but this, in his view, need not imply a commitment to the centralized state. Rejecting the often assumed imperatives of the capital or the centrally originated plan, Williams argues that it is perfectly feasible to imagine "new forms of self-management and of co-operative agreements between self-managed enterprises and communities." He insists that "we have to move beyond the *all purpose* political unit and the *all purpose* representative to a range of *specific and varying* political units and *specific and varying* representatives."[21]

The strongest single demand in Williams's theory of democracy is for self-management in our communities and workplaces. People, he argues, should have the power and the resources to manage their own affairs. Of course, it might be argued that this idea has already been incorporated into most contemporary theories of administration. The suggestions for wage-workplace and industrial democracy may be cited as illustrations of the moves toward direct democracy.[22] In the field of education, it might be said that recent attempts to devolve educational governance in Britain are borne precisely out of a desire to make schools "self-governing." Britain is not the only country where the ideas of self-governing schools, and the associated rhetoric of devolution, parent and community participation, and school-based decision making are strong. In the United States, Australia, and New Zealand, governments have legislated to overturn long-entrenched centralist decision-making structures, giving local schools new powers to organize their own affairs.[23] But are these developments consistent with Williams's theory of democracy?

In what follows, I want to show that, at least in Britain, the rhetoric of self-government sponsored by ERA is fundamentally incompatible with Williams's view of democracy. Indeed, a close examination of the Act, which came into force in Britain in the year of Williams's death, reveals the extent to which the Thatcher government has fed on the discontent, anger, and fear of the people. Its anti-bureaucratic, anti-hierarchical, and anti-authoritarian rhetoric has sought to give people a sense of control over their lives. Its rhetoric has stressed many of the virtues that Williams celebrates—self-reliance, self-management, decentralization, and democratic control. But ERA's *articulation* of these values has rested upon assumptions about the nature of human beings, social relations, and political organisation which are diametrically opposed to those which Williams espouses.

The central idea behind the changes in the governance of schools that ERA has unleashed is that of choice. This was most clearly stated by Kenneth Baker, the then Secretary of State for Education, in a speech he gave in the House of Commons on 1 December 1987. There he argued:

> If we are to implement the principle of the 1944 Act that children "should be educated in accordance with the wishes of their parents," we must give consumers of education a central part in decision making. That means freeing schools and colleges to deliver the standards that parents and employers want. It means encouraging the consumer to expect and demand that all educational bodies do the best job possible. In a word, it means choice.[24]

Baker went on to say that the main purpose of ERA was to give schools freedom to "make their own decisions" and to give "parents and governors a new opportunity, should they wish to take it, to run their schools themselves."[25]

Baker's theoretical justification of "choice" derives from his view of democracy. He subscribes to the classic liberal doctrine that collective social good can only be realized when opportunities exist for private individuals to pursue their aims in their own way with minimal state interference. Only the sovereign individual knows what is or is not in his or her best interest; neither the state nor the society is in a position to make judgments about individual aspirations or interests. Governments become coercive if they interfere with people's own capacity to determine their objectives. Their legitimate role is thus restricted to the enforcement of general rules which broadly protect the rights of individuals to exercise their freedom. In Baker's view, the notion of choice better embodies the principles of a liberal democracy than an arrangement which brings schools under direct state control. Choice will, Baker argues, produce what parents want and need for their children. It is therefore the consumers of education who make the ultimate judgments on schools. Within a free-market system, he suggests, there is not only greater choice and diversity in education, but there is also a mechanism of popular democratic accountability.

To translate these principles into practice, ERA has instituted a number of measures for unleashing a free-market approach to educational governance: among them, open enrollment, opting out of local authority control, and local financial management. The idea of open enrollment is a natural extension of the principle of parental choice. The Act states that no child should be refused admission to a school unless it is genuinely full. Schools can also apply to withdraw from the control of local education authorities and be maintained instead by direct government grants.[26] The initiative of "opting out" can be taken by representative school boards with the support of a majority of parents voting by secret postal votes. ERA has also devolved much of the financial management of schools to local governing bodies, who are now responsible for selecting principals and teachers, for promotions, and for allocating resources for services and maintenance.

The whole object of these "reforms" has been to change the system of educational governance from one where control is exercised by local education authorities to one where market forces reign supreme. But as many critics have pointed out, the changes envisaged will have disastrous social consequences.[27] Most significantly, the operation of market forces in education will inevitably mean the reproduction of social and economic inequalities. The idea of open enrollment will mean that well-off parents have access to all educational options, while others have no choice at all. There is, moreover, nothing in the Act that would prevent the creation of schools made up of homogeneous communities, serving narrowly defined cultural interests. The British Commission for Racial Equality has, for example, suggested it would be extremely damaging to good race relations if parental choice were based not on educational grounds but on some spurious racial considerations.[28] The possibility that the Act could result in a degree of de facto racial segregation in education has already emerged in Dewsbury, Yorkshire, where, under the auspices of the Act, a group of white parents sought to have their children removed from a school which had a student population of predominantly Asian background.[29]

But within its own terms, the Act contains numerous contradictions. It assumes, for example, that making parental choice paramount will in itself raise educational standards everywhere. But perhaps the most crucial contradiction inherent in ERA relates to its prescription of a national curriculum and standardized testing and assessment procedures, for the Act's central objective of creating something of a social market in education would seem to be an idea which is incompatible with a centrally dictated and managed curriculum. Here the Thatcher government's professed opposition to bureaucracy and authoritarianism would seem to be directly contradicted by the creation of an intrusive educational bureaucracy to sustain and defend the operations of the "free" market, with its radically uneven effects on the life chances of different social groups and classes. Thus, what ERA in fact implies is an alteration of the boundaries of the state—the "strong" center and greater political power going to the already privileged. What it "rolls back" are what Williams has called the "intermediate institutions," those localized structures of the state which had traditionally offered protection to the vulnerable. ERA does not so much represent a move toward the minimalist state as toward a more authoritarian state defined around a disingenuous rhetoric of devolution and self-management.

The concept of self-management which ERA assumes centers around the idea of the choice that individuals are supposed to be in a position to make in the social marketplace of education. Williams's writings imply an emphatic rejection of ERA's rearticulation of "self-management." His view of self-management would be linked to a different understanding of the nature of education and its relationship to cultural formation; of the notion of choice and the part it plays in decision making; and of the economic and social conditions which enable or prevent the exercise of choice. His principle of maximum self-management implies a different pattern of social relationships from that embodied in the ERA's notion of devolution, with its assumption of some authentic power located within a central bureaucracy that maintains effective control over communities.

For Williams, education is above all a cultural activity. In *The Long Revolution,* he argues that it is wholly misleading to speak of education as if it were "a fixed abstraction, a settled body of teaching and learning," to be distributed in institutions over periods.[30] Education, Williams stresses, is not a product but should be seen instead to express the wider organization of a culture; it is a process through which culture is expressed, struggled over democratically, and transformed. The content of education is a particular set of emphases and omissions which has an organic relationship to the social choices involved in its practical organization. Williams thus views education as a dynamic process which not only occurs in changing social conditions but is also a factor in contributing to social change; it has a transformative potential. Education has the capacity to enable more individuals and groups to be enfranchised and drawn into the full membership of society. For Williams, a socialist democracy both requires education and contributes to it. If a democracy is to be conceived as encompassing the broadest possible participation, then students need to learn the critical skills that will enable them to take control of their collective destinies. He argues that we cannot "call an educational system adequate if it leaves any large number of people at a level of general knowledge and culture below that required by a participating democracy and arts dependent on popular support."[31] But the relationship between education and democracy, Williams insists, is not an instrumental one: it is only when education itself is organized democratically, in ways that promote both learning and caring, that it can be said to have prepared children well for a life in a participatory democracy.

ERA, on the other hand, presupposes a very different notion of education, informed by the assumptions of instrumentalist consumerism. Education is seen as a means to an end, a service provided in response to the demands of the market. Tomlinson has shown how a market orientation to education requires it to be seen as a commodity, to be purchased and consumed.[32] ERA assumes a competitive relationship between schools to make the consumer's (the parent for the child) choice between a good school and a bad school apparent. The consumer is moreover assumed to require certain "objective" information in order to make informed choices, and hence there is thought to be a need for regular monitoring of school effectiveness and complaints procedures, should a school breach certain centrally dictated guidelines. The nature of the social relationship between parents and teachers is also revised, with teachers now responsible for "delivering" the educational goods. ERA does not thus view education as a cultural practice, but as part of a system of exchange in the marketplace, in which parents make the appropriate judgments on the quality of the services provided rather than negotiate with teachers and others about what is culturally significant.[33]

For Williams, all education expresses choice, a deliberate expression of values. The notion of "choice" thus plays an important part in his theory of democracy. But his notion of choice differs fundamentally from that which is embodied in ERA. The view of choice that Mr. Baker celebrates is derived from the notion of "preferences" in neoclassical economics and "interests" in modern liberal theories of democracy. Both these traditions assume that it is the sovereign individual who ultimately makes choices about which goals to pursue or which product to purchase. According to this view, democratic accountability can only be assessed against the expressed interests of individuals. To hold that institutions are democratic is to maintain that social choices are functions of choices which individuals make (counting each individual choice equally). Democracy is thus conceived within an essentially individualistic framework. The community is thus treated simply as a collection of individuals, not classes or groups of people of the same race or gender. Of course, it is recognized that this understanding of democracy conflicts with the plainly *social* character of political life. It is therefore conceded that social groups, constructed around such reference points as ethnicity, race, culture, religion, and gender, stand between the state and the individual. But the theory nevertheless maintains that such social divisions only matter if individuals are prepared to acknowledge them and choose to organize around them. In this way, individuals remain the ultimate unit of the political process. And if they have the freedom of political association, then the state can still be regarded as democratic, since the group choices are still a function of individuals' choices.

As I have already noted, Williams is highly critical of this view of democracy and of the notion of "choice" it embodies. To take the individuals' choices as given, he argues, is to obscure the fact that choices are culturally constructed, and that democratic institutions have a major role in fostering those capacities which enable people to choose intelligently and, thereby, secure some measure of control over their lives. Bowles and Gintis have developed this point further. They have argued that the liberal theory of democracy tells us that people make decisions, but it fails to acknowledge that decisions also make people. According to Bowles and Gintis, the liberal view presupposes a fundamental dichotomy between people as "choosers" on the one hand and "learners" on the other. How people learn to make choices is considered irrelevant to the liberal theory of democracy, as is the issue of how to distinguish a good choice from a bad one. In the aggregation of choices, all choices are counted equally. Thus, "choice is relegated to the arena of personal autonomy ostensibly devoid of developmental potential."[34]

In contrast, Williams's theory of democracy rests on an absolute rejection of the learning-choosing opposition. It stresses the formative power of action. In exercising choices, people do not simply express a preference, they *reason,* deliberate over possible courses of action, change their minds when better, more informed views are canvassed, argue against prevailing views, and so on. And through acting in the world in a variety of ways, they develop their personal powers. They become what they are in part through what they do. When individuals act at once as both choosers and learners, a different kind of social relationship prevails: not the one which normally exists between the producer and the consumer but one which highlights the reciprocal and communal character of social action. Decision making is no longer viewed as a privatized activity but one which affects, however indi-rectly, a whole range of other people.

That the notion of choice has a *relational* character is a persistent theme in Williams's writings. He argues not only that choices have a social character, but that people's capacity to make choices is affected by a range of political, material, and cultural conditions. ERA professes to give parents the right to choose the school to which they wish to send their children. But is this choice a real one? Do all parents have an equal capacity to exercise this choice? Clearly not: for the political settlement upon which the Act rests favors some and not others. The widespread inequalities which exist in Britain make it difficult, if not impossible, for some people to exercise the formal powers that the Act bestows on them. ERA is based on an assumption that there is no connection between the prevailing material conditions and the freedom to choose.

Various material conditions determine opportunities for choice and are, therefore, objective determinants of choice. Thus, as Williams has argued, while democracy is valued in most capitalist societies, it cannot be practiced in those societies in any more than the most minimal sense. Insofar as social inequalities are an inevitable outcome of capitalism, the well-off will always have the means of controlling the political process in a way the poor will not. In capitalist societies, the material conditions thus directly affect the options people have, as any Marxist realizes. But what is distinctive about Williams's analysis is his contention that issues about material conditions and processes cannot be separated from cultural considerations. Breaking radically from the traditional Marxist "base and superstructure" metaphor, which he judges to be excessively rigid and abstract, Williams counsels against the separation of the areas of thought and activity which the metaphor implies. He maintains that the economic or material relations in the processes of production should not be regarded in some way as the real or the primary condition of human social existence, the "base," to which cultural relations, the "superstructure," are ultimately reducible. Avoiding the dualism inherent in this formulation of Marxism, Williams suggests that social and material processes are inextricably related. Cultural questions are questions about the conditions of social relations—that is, questions of politics.

Johnson has pointed out that the key notion in Williams's cultural Marxism is that of "determination."[35] People's ideas, attitudes, beliefs, predispositions, and choices are culturally determined and cannot be understood as separate from the processes of material production. Williams explores his notion of determination through three sets of terms: hegemony; dominant, residual, and emergent cultures; and structures of feelings. The notion of hegemony, which Williams borrows from Gramsci, seeks to reveal the way consent to the ruling social order is secured through the construction of "common sense," and the way social processes are lived, rather than through an imposition of a particular set of beliefs on one class by another. Hegemony shapes our perceptions about ourselves and our world; it provides the framework within which we conceptualize, articulate, and explain our beliefs and act out and justify our values. But Williams insists that hegemony is not a passively existing form of dominance; it is a dynamic process, a lived system of meaning, which is continually "renewed, recreated, defended and modified."[36] Our choices are articulated through hegemony rather than totally constructed by it. There is thus always the possibility of resistance, challenge, and the emergence of counter-hegemony.

That hegemonic forms current in a society are constantly being recreated, challenged, and revised is an idea which underlines Williams's general contention that culture is always in a process of change. Stressing the notion that no dominant culture can ever include or exhaust all human practices, Williams suggests that there are always residual experiences, practices, meanings, and values which continue to survive in any community.[37] They often exist in a tension with the dominant culture, which in its emergent formations continually seeks to reinterpret their significance. Some elements of the residual culture are eventually rejected, sometimes through the creation of new hegemonic forces, while others are incorporated or modified into the dominant system of meaning. Through these processes, new features of the dominant culture emerge. But the processes of cultural change can also result in new practices, meanings, and forms of relationships that represent major alternatives or oppositions to the dominant culture.

Williams is thus highly critical of attempts to view culture as a fixed homogeneous entity, elements of which are somehow finished and closed. For him, the dynamics of cultural processes always contain consent and acceptance as well as conflict and struggle—conditions for both stability and change. The cultural relations of a society, Williams suggests, "will always tend to correspond to its contemporary system of interests and values, for it is not an absolute body of work but a continual selection and interpretation."[38] An understanding of culture hence requires attention not only to the specifiable political, social, and economic arrangements that are the outcome of selection and interpretation but also to those elements of culture that express its "distinct sense of a particular and native style."[39] Williams uses the term "structure of feeling" to describe "the most delicate and least tangible part of our activity." It is the structure of feeling that makes intimate communication between people in a community possible because it contains the taken-for-granted assumptions and the key ideas that give a community its qualitative coherence; it describes "a sense in which the particular activities combine into a way of thinking or living." In other places, Williams speaks of "practical consciousness" to describe peoples' sense of lived experience, within the structure of which cultures are constantly subject to qualitative change.[40]

What Williams's analysis of cultural formations reveals is that all exercises of choice are to a large extent "determined" by the public system of meanings and values within which we live. Furthermore, the character of choices is both social and material; choices involve both forming and formative processes. At an individual level, any exercise of choice depends on people's ability to envisage alternatives, formulate them clearly, and assess them rationally. This is an ability that human beings do not automatically have. Education, both formal and informal, has a vital role to play in helping people not only to acquire the relevant knowledge and experience necessary for decision making but also to develop faculties of imagination and the ability to predict the consequences of different courses of action and to compare them with one another. In these respects, the ability to make choices is extended or diminished by the education a person receives. The particular content of education reflects a certain structure of feeling and affects not only the ability of people to make decisions but also the kind of decisions they make. A narrowly focused education, as in the forms of religious indoctrination, political propaganda, and commercial advertising, can have the consequence of people uncritically accepting prevailing ways of looking at the world. On the other hand, a broad comprehensive education can help students acquire the knowledge, values, and skills necessary to make critical choices about the direction in which society is heading. Williams insists, however, that the processes through which these critical capacities are developed are inherently social.

Throughout his writings, Williams cautions us not to draw the fundamental theoretical division between the individual and the social, upon which the justification for capitalism rests. In *Marxism and Literature,* he demonstrates the extent to which it is the hegemonic pressures of capitalism that inform our practices and expectations,

> our senses and assignments of energy, our shaping perceptions
> of ourselves and our world. It is a lived system of meaning and
> values—constitutive and constituting—which as they are expe-
> rienced as practices appear as reciprocally conforming.[41]

It is the structure of feeling, engendered by capitalist hegemony, that molds and influences the ideas and expectations of ordinary people. Within a system of representative democracy, this has the effect of ensuring that items likely to threaten the interests of capitalism rarely appear on the political agenda. To a great extent, capitalist social relations account for the widespread political apathy and a lack of socially responsible participatory interest in the community. They encourage individuals to narrow the focus of their interest to the pursuit of private advantage. Under such conditions, people may even reject possibilities for collective action and often underestimate the significant influence of the wider social framework on their condition, choices, and opportunities for action. In turn, they may also conceive their relationship with other individuals and the world in purely instrumental terms.

Socialism, on the other hand, prescribes different human relationships. Williams argues that the

> first uses of *socialist,* as a way of thinking, were in deliberate contrast with the meanings of *individualist:* both as a challenge to that other way of thinking in which all human behaviour was reduced to matters of individual character and more sharply as a challenge to its version of human intentions.[42]

He rejects the view of life as "an arena in which individuals should strive to improve their own conditions," preferring to see it as "a network of human relationships in which people found everything of value in and through each other." The central socialist value, he argues, is an idea of *sharing:* it implies the well-being of a whole society and not simply of those isolated individuals or regions which prosper at the expense of others. But the notion of sharing can be understood in at least two ways. The capitalist understanding of "sharing" is based on the logic of consumption, in which processes of production are abstracted from other social relations. The distinctive socialist forms of the idea of sharing are, on the other hand, based not only on the idea of fairness in the distribution of what is produced but also in the specific ways in which "the work has been done, responsibility taken, care given. . . ."[43]

The principle of sharing thus refers to the entire spectrum of social activities in which human beings take part and through which they define themselves. For Williams, there are only two practical means of genuine social sharing—popular democracy and common ownership. Pointing, perhaps, to the experiments of the Eastern European countries, he argues that without popular democracy "the practice of socialism can degenerate to bureaucratic state forms or to the political and economic monopolies of command economies."[44] The older simplistic socialist formula which viewed planning as "rationality plus public interest" had, Williams suggests, led to "the arrogance of monopoly."[45] He is highly critical of those older socialists who assumed that there was a simple and abstract notion of "public interest" which could easily be translated into a system of rationality that stressed "centralized, expert, leadership plans and controls" for a diverse and changing society. Rationality, as we now know, is a much more complex idea, involving a variety of analyses and proposals and different mixes of priorities. Equally, "public interest is not singular but a complex and interactive network of *different* real interests." This recognition means that the principle of sharing, in its practical form, needs to rest upon an acknowledgment of diversity. Both the determination of rationality and public interest require "the true social processes of open discussion, negotiation and agreement." In a modern socialist democracy, all members of a society should therefore have "a practical share in the most fundamental organization of our common life. In practice, this sharing has to begin in the organization of our most basic forms—those of work and of community."[46] Williams insists that the power of private capital or the centralized bureaucratic state cannot be challenged without structures which facilitate active and local decision making. Exactly how we develop these structures remains our greatest challenge.

Williams remained optimistic throughout his life. In his earlier work, the resources of hope were to be found in the cultural traditions of the British working class. In *Culture and Society,* he argued for the pursuit of a common culture through which the general interest, as expressed in the common experiences of people, could be served.[47] In developing his idea of common experience he stressed the importance of the cultural forms associated with the working-class movement, including the trade unions and the central values of the community life in the small Welsh villages of Williams's childhood. These values—of reciprocity and equality and of collective and mutual development—were, Williams argued, being increasingly corrupted by a mass bourgeois society which rested on the assumptions of progress through individual advancement.

In his later work, Williams recognizes the limitations of this analysis. In particular, he accepts the criticism that the notion of common culture cannot have as its sole focus working-class culture; that class is only one of the facts that define social relations; and that, strategically, a vision of socialist politics should be more inclusive of other categories, such as gender and race. Also, against the assumptions of his earlier analyses, he maintains that all fruitful socialist thought and planning requires economic reason to be integrated at every level with ecological concerns. Socialist planning cannot be rational without an awareness of environmental issues. Toward the issues of peace, feminism, and alternative arts movements, too, socialism can no longer be ambivalent, because these issues pose a direct challenge to the traditional institutions of the labor movement and represent new conceptions of social relations.

Significantly for Williams, recent *social movements* have mostly emerged from outside organized class interests and institutions. But they represent a reality that has changed the nature of class politics because they are linked to the central systems of the industrial-capitalist mode of production in a radically different way. The new reality suggests that the socialist political struggle can no longer be confined to the overthrow of the capitalist forms of employment and wage labor. It also implies that socialist politics must now revolve around a "broader concept of human relationships with a physical world" than that defined by the notion of "society as production and reproduction." Such a concept should emphasize the interconnectedness of social processes, emerging social identities, and the lived experiences of people. Williams cautions us, however, not to look for a supra-logic to elucidate the nature of this interconnectedness. For the way in which various structures of feeling link up with each other remains an entirely contingent matter. Williams insists that any attempt to describe such a logic, of how effective communities are bonded together, in an a priori fashion would inevitably mean overlooking the complexities of social relations in contemporary daily life and politics.[48]

Abstract solutions to the problems of human relations, Williams suggests, have not served us well because they have failed to appreciate the fact that human allegiances are shaped by many different kinds of social bonds. Old socialism dictated a unilinear view of social relations, one that relied on abstract class determinations. Williams shows how that overconfident singular model has historically proved to be the root of so many of our contemporary problems. If socialism is to survive in some renewed form, then its practical politics must acknowledge diversity and become more exploratory; for too long it has been excessively Eurocentric and gender-blind. Williams thus insists that *"since there are many people and cultures, there must be many socialisms."*[49] Socialisms must emerge from the actual struggle for "full social identities" and "effective communities." Communities of many different kinds, which are interlinked around the socialist value of sharing, must be seen as a key resource for the future. For Williams, the idea of a community is related to "the principle of maximum self-management," with the view that decision-making powers should, as far as possible, reside amongst those most directly affected, in their work, localities, and other associations. Community is thus a normative notion, referring to social relationships of a certain type and quality, counterposed against the bureaucratic imperatives of both centralist communist regimes and international corporate capitalism.

Of course, Williams recognizes that the rhetoric of community is fraught with dangers. In *Keywords,*[50] he outlines the role it has played in conservative social thought. It has been used by conservative thinkers, such as Tonnies, to justify the preservation of class privilege and gross social inequalities.[51] And, as Mulhern has pointed out, the political polemics of community "can act very powerfully against the interest of workers—or women and oppressed minorities."[52] Also, the appeal to community can often become no more than an assertion of romantic localism. Indeed, Thatcher's Educational Reform Act also employs the rhetoric of community to justify its version of the self-managing school. The terms "decentralization," "devolution," and "local participation in educational decision making" feature prominently in the Act and suggest a commitment to the ideal of community.

But this rhetoric should not deceive anyone. While it shares with Williams a distaste for authoritarianism, bureaucratic intransigence, and the excesses of the centralist state, it rests upon views concerning social relations which differ markedly from Williams's socialist vision. As Hall has suggested, both social democracy and Thatcherism operate on a fundamental dichotomy between liberty and equality.[53] Thus, ERA privileges liberty over equality in such a way as to provide the wealthy with ample opportunities to participate in decision making, while giving the less well-off only an illusion of real popular power. The parental choice it offers is a choice only for those in a position to exercise that choice. Moreover, as I have already pointed out, the measure of choice (for some) and the opportunities to participate in decision making which ERA provides occur within the framework of a centrally prescribed set of rules—the non-negotiable national curriculum and a monitoring mechanism through regular and uniform state-wide testing as well as many other bureaucratic prescriptions to which all schools must conform. So, despite its antibureaucratic rhetoric, ERA places all kinds of restrictions upon the autonomy of schools and communities with respect to making their own decisions. In effect, then, it dictates cultural forms that may have little in common with the needs and aspirations of many communities. And the participation it does permit is mostly *managed* participation. As Hall argues, "participation without democracy, without democratic mobilization, is a fake solution. 'Decentralization' which creates no authentic, alternative sources of real power, which mobilizes no one, and which entails no breakup of the existing power centers and no real shift in the balance of power, is an illusion."[54]

In contrast to the ERA view, Williams maintains that genuine participation, and the realization of the ideal of a socialist democracy, is impossible without greater equality in the distribution of power amongst the older geographical communities and the communities now emerging as new social movements. Socialists, he argues, now need to realize that there can be no authentic center of power and that all reasonable planning has to be diverse, for the experiences of the socialist economies and the record of the capitalist corporations have clearly indicated that the assumptions of "an evident rationality of development and a self-evident general interest" are utterly unreasonable. This does not, of course, mean that there can be no policy coordination or that priorities cannot be determined. Williams's point is that we need to be more imaginative in creating new decision-making structures in which there is the widest possible participation in the institutions that direct society, and in which there is an overwhelming democratization of the complex machinery of the state. In his later writings, he envisages a "variable socialism" which is not only more local, enabling direct face-to-face deliberation of issues, but also interlinked with wider social movements and state institutions. Socialism, he argues, needs to stress not a uniform plan which responds to some presumed public interest but experiment instead with a variety of mechanisms of "complex participatory planning." We need to move, he says, "from the idea of socialism as a rationally simplified economy to the idea of a more complex political economy which can actually achieve rationality."[55]

What applies to the management of the economy is relevant also to educational planning. Education is a cultural activity, linked intrinsically to a whole range of issues concerned with social identities and relations. It occurs in communities which are everywhere, "not *places*, but *practices* of collective identification whose variable order largely define culture of any social formation."[56] Its planning therefore involves a complexity that the singular unilinear models, be they old socialist or of the kind that ERA represents, insufficiently recognize. In Williams's vision of a socialist democracy, educational planning would take place at a variety of levels, in forums which allow genuine debate based on public information and argument. Such information would not be so much an aid for individuals interested only in promoting their self-interest as a way of collectively determining the most general human and educational needs. This distinctively socialist form of planning would need to specify most general human needs in contemporary terms, with a recognition that different kinds of needs are themselves socially and materially constructed, and that responses to particular needs create new situations and relationships which require continuous observing and re-assessing. But most crucially in a socialist society the choices we make about education through such processes of reflection are a matter of collective social responsibility, premised upon the assumption of sharing and not based on a purported consumerist right bestowed upon parents in the marketplace of education.

8

"On the Ground" with Antiracist Pedagogy and Raymond Williams's Unfinished Project to Articulate a Socially Transformative Critical Realism

Leslie G. Roman

> [A] method of analysis on which you can base a method of teaching is put to the hardest test of practice . . . [when] you have to find it somewhere on the ground. . . . [A]ny analysis, however academic and theoretical, has to submit to that kind of test.[1]
>
> *Raymond Williams*

Radical intellectuals may read the closing words of Raymond Williams's essay, "A Defence of Realism," as prophetic when he says that "we live in a society which in a sense is rotten with criticism, in which the very frustrations of cultural production turn people from production to criticism. . . ."[2] Anchored in his deeper and more sustained body of work on cultural materialism, these words are part of Williams's larger provisional project to formulate a new socially critical and transformative practice of realism. In his elaboration of critical realism, Williams refuses to make a fetish of theory, refusing to privilege it over historically situated analyses of everyday life and practice.

Instead, following Brecht, he emphasizes the need for what he calls "the complex seeing of analysis"—a set of practices which alter people's consciousness of their own relationships to the material and ideological conditions that come to define their conjunctural realities ("DR," 239). "Active" cultural production rather than distanced "critical consumption" or grossly abstracted criticism are key terms in

Williams's own analyses of the contested cultural history of realist practices manifest in a variety of cultural and aesthetic forms, most notably American and European drama, cinema, television, the British novel, and contemporary cultural theory.[3]

This essay, written to the unfinished project of Williams's newly reconstituted realism, examines its efforts and promise to provide a framework within which a dialectic between critical theorizing and practice can be dramatized in our daily lives, as well as in the Brechtian sense, on the popular stage. I will engage in remembering Williams not by arguing that his vision of critically realist practices is free of the problems of masculinist treatments of gender, class essentialism, or Eurocentrism; for feminists and the others on the Left, the contradictions and failures of Williams's project are at once systematic limitations and pedagogical and theoretical resources that allow us to historicize the determinate conditions that produced them as symptomatic silences. In so doing, we may locate ourselves as interested subjects who have a stake not only in interpreting and re-presenting reality from our often conflicting standpoints but also in making emancipatory changes in what counts as *the real*.

My interest in Williams's defense of a new critical realism is not purely theoretical, although I certainly evaluate his work in light of my own prior feminist materialist theoretical and political assumptions.[4] My particular interest emerges from the relevance of Williams's ideas to concrete political and ethical problems that I have confronted while living and working amid the embattled reactionary politics of Louisiana. Like others who teach critical traditions or conduct qualitative research, I have the continuing opportunity to *test* and experience the moral and political consequences of certain theories in the context of their actual—and often asymmetrical—effects on differentially positioned groups.

First, I will consider the presuppositions of recent feminist debates influenced by postmodernism and variously referred to by terms such as *identity politics* (or the *politics of difference* and *voice*). I will foreshadow the kinds of stances they would authorize or delimit feminists from adopting in the struggle to advocate antiracist pedagogical positions in our teaching or research. I shall argue that one consequence of a feminism that would carry through in its practice postmodernism's a priori avowed relativism—often expressed as a rejection of all realist epistemologies—would be political paralysis. By the political paralysis, I mean the inability to make difficult critical choices that require taking what I shall later call *feminist materialist standpoint positions*.[5] When as feminists we adjudicate between, or find it necessary to distinguish between, the epistemic standpoints of fundamentally oppressed groups and of those in more privileged positions who claim to be oppressed, we are implicitly practicing a form of *critical realism* and hence demystifying both the pseudo-neutrality of objectivism and the reified celebrations of indeterminancy and relativism. By taking critical socially transformative stances, whether in our research or classroom pedagogy, we are ruling out the unacceptable knowledge claims of some to be included in one or more categories of fundamentally oppressed groups. In the current national reactionary backlash against the gains made by the civil rights and women's movements—one which is primarily characterized by members of more privileged groups erroneously claiming to be history's oppressed or disadvantaged victims by appropriating the rhetoric of the oppressed and discriminated against, I will argue that feminist practice increasingly requires us to evaluate these claims without lapsing into subjectivism or relativism. Instead, we must make such evaluative distinctions by weighing the person's or group's subjective claims against and in relation to adequate structural analyses of their objective social locations without also falling into objectivism or universalism. Put more sharply, even the practice of postmodernist feminists may not be as indifferent to *differences* or to different claims *to know* and *represent the real* as postmodernism's a priori theoretical commitment to relativism requires.[6]

In light of this, the second part of the essay will examine and critique Williams's reformulation of a critical socially transformative realism. I will show how Williams's ideas anticipate and contribute to the development of what feminist materialists such as Sandra Harding, Alison Jaggar, and others call *standpoint theory,* thus offering us a way out of the paralysis of postmodern relativism.[7] Here, I shall draw heavily—although not exclusively—upon his writing on critical realism in modern drama, particularly in the work of Brecht (because of its materialist standpoint critique as well as its relevance to pedagogical processes as performative communication).

Third, I also want to consider from a feminist materialist perspective how Williams's steadfast reliance upon a holistic understanding of culture as well as a "radically interactionist conception of totality" blocks the possibility to analyze the effects of asymmetrical power relations in people's concrete historical experiences.[8] I shall discuss whether this failure renders his emancipatory vision for critically realist practices obsolete. Lastly, in the final part of the essay, I extend and *test* the limits of Williams's explorations of Brechtian critical realism by drawing upon examples of my own attempts to formulate antiracist and feminist pedagogical stances in my teaching.

Antiracist Pedagogy and Williams's Unfinished Project

In the context of discussing *emergent* forms of *defensive racism* on the part of whites as they manifest themselves in the classroom, I will develop what I call a *critical socially contested realism* to discuss the ways in which individuals' and groups' phenomenological representations of reality are linked to their material interests in a struggle for hegemony. The extent to which those struggles become articulated with counter-hegemonic practices within larger emancipatory movements becomes a matter for critical pedagogy. In this way, I aim to provide a feminist materialist alternative that goes beyond some of the systematic limitations inscribed in Williams's own reformulation of a critical realism. Yet I aim to achieve the dialectic between critical theory and practice that Williams believed was necessary to effect a just society.

Postmodern Relativism: Whose Differences Speak For Whom?

Feminists, as well as others on the Left, face a material and self-definitional crisis that socialist feminist Jenny Bourne Taylor recognizes as being "at once theoretical and strategic."[9] Bourne Taylor characterizes the crisis confronting British feminism as "an impasse" that hinges most centrally and paradoxically on the insights produced by recent postmodernist debates over "identity and difference" ("GG," 298). She contends that having pluralized the category of gender by recognizing its intersections with the conflicting interests of "class, ethnicity, sexuality, region, age, and so on," it is no longer clear whether feminism as political practice and as a movement can transcend local contingent struggles and identities to propose radical social reform in a wider context ("GG," 299).[10] Thus, as she assesses the dominant view of the strategical consequences of postmodern theory, the impasse for feminism is that "it paradoxically undermines and is undermined by actual local contingent struggles for progressive change" ("GG," 299).

Only slightly less sanguine, poststructuralist feminist Linda Alcoff similarly argues against a ubiquitous "retreat response" among segments of Western Anglo-American academic and popular cultural feminism.[11] For Alcoff, this response involves the curious assertion that in all cases we can only speak for ourselves, thus articulating a pervasive skepticism about the possibility of ever adequately or justifiably taking advocacy positions. In her view the "retreat response" paradoxically arises out of the important recognition by feminists that the practice of privileged persons engaging in advocacy—or what she calls "the problem of speaking for" less privileged others—often further silences those whose voices it seeks to empower ("SFO," 1). Alcoff observes, however, that this important recognition has been taken to its paralyzing limits, denying feminists any epistemically salient conditions for advocacy as feminist practice. The inflections of postmodernism's assertion of a fragmented, individualistic, and particularistic self are clear in Alcoff's well-founded concern over the ascendance of the "retreat response."

While Alcoff locates the evidence of such a crisis in the debates concerning the "politics of voice"—or what she calls the problem of "speaking for" others, Bourne Taylor finds the crisis hinging on the terms of "identity and difference" ("GG," 298). One thing seems strikingly clear: their understandings of the symptoms and consequences of this crisis in varying degrees implicate the relativistic assumptions of variants of postmodernism in providing some of the conditions for widespread political and moral paralysis among feminists and others on the Left.

This pervasive skepticism and its attendant tendency to reduce complex political problems to aesthetic textual ones raises the question of whether or not postmodernism is compatible with feminism as a political movement and whether women's experiences of oppression are so divergent that no single feminist movement is possible.[12] Within feminist theorizing and the women's movement, many feminists have used postmodernism (at least as a *slogan system*) to show that it is no longer possible to accept in any a priori manner an essential or singularly interested category of *woman* or gender. Feminists have also employed the discourses of postmodernism to conceive of the social world and *reality* as plurally interested according to the determinants of race, not only to gender but also class, sexual orientation, and age. On this basis, the pluralism of postmodern feminism means to avoid resorting to modernism's alleged reduction of these interests to a coherent ensemble of social relations or what they see as the grand narrative of *social totality,* to which feminist discourses and politics have addressed themselves ("Difference," 41–42).

Instead, postmodern feminists have sought to pluralize the categories of difference and oppression while rejecting realist epistemologies and, indeed, suspending the need for (if not rejecting altogether) epistemology. Leading proponents of postmodern feminism tell us that, unlike modernism's discourses of Marxism and feminism, postmodern feminism avoids the master narratives of universality, totalism, and their dominating hierarchies of oppression.[13] By now, arguments attesting to the benefits of abandoning modernist projects of emancipation in favor of inflecting feminist discourses with those of postmodernism are well-rehearsed. Their typical formulations often entail the assertion that feminism and postmodernism can serve as important correctives to one another. For example, Nancy Fraser and Linda Nicholson emphasize the necessity for a critical encounter between feminism and postmodernism:

> Postmodernists offer sophisticated and persuasive criticisms of foundationalism and essentialism but their conceptions of social criticism tend to be anemic. Feminists offer robust conceptions of social criticism, but they tend, at times, to lapse into foundationalism and essentialism.[14]

Fraser and Nicholson's assertion implies that the "anemic" stances of postmodern discourses toward engaged social critique of prevailing theories and social structures are politically and ethically neutral. Thus they argue that postmodern discourses could be combined as unproblematically with feminism's commitment to social criticism and emancipation as with reactionary epistemologies and politics. While we might find it important to produce explanations that are the subjects neither of totalism nor of essentialism, to suggest that postmodernism's lack of robust social criticism is just as minor a deficiency as is feminism's essentialism is to treat all partialities as having relatively equal political consequences.[15]

Despite their conflicting epistemologies and conceptions of women's oppression, most traditions of feminism admirably recognize that all theories and epistemologies are *interested* and thus demand ongoing revaluations of the social world, including their own terms for representing feminism. I argue, along with Alison Jaggar and Sandra Harding, that with the exception of liberal feminism, which accepts liberalism's empiricist claims to value-neutrality, the major traditions of feminism (radical and materialist) offer us some moral, political, and epistemological principles to correct the terms of their essentialist tendencies as well as the gender, class, and racially specific blind spots of prevailing epistemologies. And they stand their different self-correcting grounds without recourse to the a priori relativism of a postmodernism that fails to locate its own perspective to celebrate indeterminacy of knowledge or reality claims in an interested *perspectival* way.

It is therefore difficult to fathom the ultimate value for feminist political practice of uniting feminism with a relativistic postmodernism. This becomes especially problematic when we consider the implications of relativism for the strategic decisions involved in building effective coalitions across diverse interests. Coalition building necessarily entails the ability of feminist activists to set priorities for interests that require immediate or long-term political attention—in short, to avoid treating all interests relativistically.[16] Nonetheless, the sloganeering around postmodernism as a complementary epistemology that ought to be married to feminism has reached a fevered pitch, extending into educational debates over what counts as critical and socially transformative pedagogy.

Education and the Conundrum of Postmodernism

Within education, Carol Nicholson takes the call for unification between the feminist and postmodernist discourses one step further than do Nancy Fraser and Linda Nicholson. After recognizing that the variants of postmodernism à la Lyotard and Rorty are not only *not* neutral but rather reinforce certain reactionary tendencies, she alleges that their appropriation within feminism will form the "basis of a new radical pedagogy."[17] As she puts it,

> A postmodern feminism that is sensitive to differences can serve as an important corrective to postmodernism's tendencies toward nihilism on the one hand and apologies for the status quo on the other. ("PFE," 203)[18]

But can we afford to presume that the relativism of particular postmodernist discourses is intrinsically neutral and, thus, able to be appropriated as a matter of willful voluntarism to effect progressive rather than reactionary pedagogical consequences?[19] Is it sufficient, for example, to follow the recommendation of feminist postmodernist Patti Lather that as educators we should "[j]ust say no to nihilism," and thus we can rest assured that nihilistic or reactionary choices and appropriations will *not* follow or be effected?[20] Such a response seems particularly inadequate, "especially insofar as the emblematic principle of postmodernism as such may be the 'principle' of never saying 'no' to anything" ("PP," 77).

Lather responds to the critics of postmodernism's relativism by suggesting that the relativity of truth and reality claims are not problematic in and of themselves; rather they are only a problem for those who are possessed by a "Cartesian obsession" with foundationalist epistemologies, causing them to engage in a "search for a privileged standpoint as the guarantee of certainty" (*GS*, 115). As a feminist materialist, I share Lather's cogent critique of privileged or universalizing stand-points authorized by objectivist accounts. But her response to critics of postmodernist relativism does not address the more dangerous impli-cations of cultural and political contexts in which all *reality claims* are treated as representing equally valid accounts of the social world.

There are examples, however, that strike closer to the heart of educational practice in the classroom than any of our speculations derived from abstracted theory. I will later treat one that is derived from my own experience teaching a racially mixed group of students in a graduate seminar on "The Principles and Practices of Critical Ethnography" at Louisiana State University. I write of these issues with some sense of urgency to understand the consequences of adhering to relativism, having witnessed the reactions of my students enrolled in this class to the October 1990 statewide campaign and election results in Louisiana, where David Duke, former Klu Klux Klan Grand Dragon and Nazi Party member, led a nearly successful bid for U.S. Senator, appealing to the anxieties of racial displacement among whites from middle- as well as working-class backgrounds, and appropriating the language of racial oppression with the support of his organization, the "National Association for the Advancement of White People."[21] Duke's political legitimation in his more recent campaign for the state's gubernatorial office underscores the need for critical analyses of impli-cations of relativism in such an educational context. Clearly, Louisiana is one place in which the Right understands all too well how to rearticu-late into its own hegemonic order of white patriarchal supremacy an a priori and dangerously relativistic language of inclusion and plural-ism in defining who constitutes the oppressed.

The example I foreshadow becomes the subject of a deeper analysis in the last part of this essay. For now, it is sufficient to raise some of the questions with which I have been confronted while teaching and practicing critical ethnographic research. How is a white middle-class feminist teacher to evaluate the claim of a white middle-class student that she has been the subject of racial discrimination simply because she and the three other white women students are out-numbered by the five African-American women taking the course? On what basis can such a teacher challenge the idea that whites are in this delimited context "racial minorities" and, hence, free to appropriate this category of oppression so as to then speak for or in the place of the African-American students in the class? How broadly can the categories of difference and oppression be drawn? Who gets to draw them? How might we recover the critically evaluative and historicizing uses of realism to discover whose standpoints have epistemic salience on both objective and subjective grounds? Conversely, whose standpoints are more blinded by their own sexist, racist, and classist ideologies by virtue of their interests and privileged social locations? What are the moral and political consequences of a teacher who resorts to postmodern relativism in the classroom, for example, failing to challenge the epistemic standpoints of white students claiming to be oppressed on racial grounds? Can critically realist practices avoid the worst fears of postmodernists, that is, the Lukácian imposition of socialist realist strategies as master narratives of authority over what counts as *the real* in the service of radical social change?

The political problems of practicing pedagogy that is both feminist and antiracist in such a context are an important part of the impetus for my return to Williams's reformulation of a socially transformative critical realism. Although his ideas on the subject are still indicative of the tendencies of Eurocentrism, masculinist dichotomies between the so-called public and private spheres of daily life, and class essentialism, they nonetheless provide a rich set of theoretical and pedagogical resources that help clarify what is at stake in struggles over knowledge claims and representations of *the real*. It is to Williams's work on the socially transformative possibilities of critical realism, elaborated particularly in his analyses of Brecht's endeavors to constitute "the complex seeing of analysis" or critically realist practices within popular theatre, that I now turn.

Williams Reading Brecht: Theatre as Political Forum

Like his defense of a realist tradition in relation to the British novel, television, film, and, more generally, cultural analysis, Williams's strong attachments to notions of Brechtian critical realism are meant to historicize the conditions under which particular aesthetic forms and cultural practices are produced as norms and therefore present themselves for our political transformation of them. Williams's essay, "A Defence of Realism," is, in part, set against absolutist rejections of realism—the "worst excesses" of which, as Stuart Hall suggests, can be found in film theory ("Politics," 63). Such rejections have been premised erroneously on the grounds that realist forms and works are inevitably and inextricably tied to modernist aesthetics and techniques. Arguing in the absolutist terms characteristic of the early 1970s, film theorist Colin McCabe asserts that realism is an inherently bourgeois form which creates an essentially unifying ideology that can neither deal with fundamental social conflict nor account for its own material production.[22]

Williams rejects MacCabe's formalist definition of the "classic realist text," arguing instead for historically and socially based analyses of variations of methods and intentions within and across realist works. He gives numerous examples in which the purported properties of realism pre-exist or exist well beyond the onset of eighteenth-century bourgeois culture. Furthermore, he shows that realism cannot be reduced to a single method, since the plays said to fit such a definition are historically variable and often disputed within their own terms. For Williams, realism must be understood both in relation to other methods in a play and to the intentions of the specific work in question. Williams argues that significant realist works, like his own unfinished analyses of Brechtian critical realism, are by no means finished projects: they necessitate social and historical analyses of the "quite unresolved problems" they raise ("DR," 239).

Williams establishes carefully the relationality between particular cultural forms such as realism and the sociocultural and political conditions under which they develop, warning us in his essay "Theatre as Political Forum" that

> [t]o abstract the specific methods or the theoretical phases
> attached to them, as determining forms without reference to
> their very specific and limiting social situation, is to confirm the
> actual development of the avant-garde, culturally and politi-
> cally, towards a new aestheticism. (*PM*, 91)

Such a forewarning seems especially apropos in light of particular contemporary debates in aesthetics, anthropology, and literary theory that return us to depoliticized notions of textual politics.[23]

What resounds most clearly in Williams's abundant writing in defense of a Brechtian critical realism is his appreciation of Brecht's aspiration to develop—although, Williams admits, Brecht did not always succeed—a notion of collective intention that dramatizes a common condition among subordinate class groups. We will have the opportunity to return to the problematic assumptions of Williams's efforts to situate and develop more fully Brecht's historicism through his particular conceptions of a "common condition" and "experience" of subordination formed primarily out of a specific set of class, gender, racial, and national cultural interests. At this moment, however, I will emphasize that Williams's examination of Brecht's critical realism reveals it to be much more than a series of technical or aesthetic innovations of dramatic strategies and conventions. He contrasts Brecht's critical realism with the more static and representational theatrical form of nineteenth-century naturalism. For naturalism, he argues, the aim was retrospection, that is, showing what *reality* for the working classes was like by *recording with precise verisimilitude* the historical impulses of the day as they affected and determined the lives of isolated and suffering individuals.

In *Drama from Ibsen to Brecht,* Williams highlights four decisive moves in Brecht's dramatic innovations that distinguish his critical realism from the dominant European drama following Ibsen.[24] Whereas naturalism is amenable to both heroic individualistic solutions and the determinism of merely recording the "evolutionary inevitability" of oppressive conditions, Brechtian drama calls each scene into question "as a thing to be looked at," in which spectators confront dramatic representations of reality (*DIB,* 278). Whereas the drama Brecht opposes engrosses audiences in the stage action and therefore consumes their capacities to act, Williams notes that Brechtian drama awakens the audience's capacity to act (*DIB,* 278). Whereas naturalistic drama presents experience by drawing audiences into a subjectivist identification with the action of the characters, in Williams's view, Brechtian drama shows human beings producing themselves and their situations in the course of enacting and evaluating different alternatives and courses of action. Instead of employing subjectivist identification strategies which do not give spectators the emotional distance to evaluate the dramatic action and world-views presented in the plays, Brechtian drama employs methods of writing, producing, and acting that enact critical detachment by both actors and spectators (*DIB,* 279).

For Williams, Brecht's critical realism breaks with naturalist drama by historicizing and denaturalizing the conditions under which people collectively suffer different forms of oppression. As Williams astutely argues, the depth of Brecht's contribution lies in his representation of social and material conditions as subject to moral and political critique, critical evaluation, and social transformation, not only by the socially located characters in his plays, but also by the audiences they actively engage.[25] Williams contrasts the dialogical openness of Brecht's "mature plays" of the late 1930s such as *The Good Woman of Setzuan, Mother Courage and Her Children,* and *The Life of Galileo* with the "bare exposition of morality" in some of his earlier didactic plays. He argues that it is in these later plays that Brecht's notion of "complex seeing" comes to its fullest fruition. Williams describes at some length the contradictory consciousness of Shen Te, the prostitute in *The Good Woman of Setzuan,* whose goodness is victimized and "exploited by gods and men alike," and yet who transforms herself into a victimizer, her tough male cousin, Shui Ta, who first appears in disguise and then, in Williams's words, "takes on an independent existence" ("AB," 157). Each of these dimensions of contradictory subjectivity—which Williams interprets through the binary opposition of goodness and badness—are coexistent possibilities for consciousness. They bear witness to Williams's appreciation for a notion of contradictory consciousness that is subjugated and yet remains an active subject. They defy more fixed or abstract interpretations of morality and realism that Williams shows to be associated with both naturalist drama and with the impositional critical realism of Lukács.

In a similar vein, what Williams finds most salutory in Brecht is his recognition of the interconnections between contradictory individual consciousness and moral and political dilemmas that are beyond the reach of individual solution:

> Brecht is always impressive, in his mature plays, in the *discovery of ways of enacting genuine alternatives: not so much as in traditional drama, through the embodiment of alternatives in opposing characters, but by their embodiment in one person, who lives through this way and then that and invites us to draw our own conclusions.* This is "complex seeing" integrated in depth with the dramatic form, and carried right through in that there is no imposed resolution—the tension is there to the end, and we are invited to consider it. ("AB," 157, my emphasis)

Williams's appreciation of Brecht's critical realism acknowledges a plurality of points of view that resists the temptation to secure a single resolution to complex and contradictory social dilemmas as a way of enacting genuine alternatives to the status quo.

In this regard, Williams is in sympathetic accord with explicit aspirations of postmodernism and poststructuralism to address a contradictory and multiply interested subject. Of paramount importance, what he emphasizes repeatedly in this essay and elsewhere the fact that Brecht's foremost achievement entails the effort to present the "embodiment" of socially produced contradictions and moral and political dilemmas within the consciousness of a single character or person. As Williams points out, what makes this particular effort on Brecht's part a significant break from naturalism is that it no longer accepts the idea that socially produced contradictions can be represented through oppositions between stable unconflicted characters with opposing

169

views on moral and political dilemmas. Unlike the dominant forms of European naturalism, Brecht's critical realism presents social subjects whose conflicted interests and selves are dramatized in the objective actions and consequences of their choices.

Throughout his body of work on Brecht, Williams rejects the didacticism of his earlier plays in favor of the pedagogical value of his later "teaching plays," in which he moved toward the development of consciously participatory and critical audiences—what Williams calls "an actual potential comradely public" in an important posthumously published essay entitled "Theatre as Political Forum."[26] Indeed, Williams acknowledges that Brecht's move toward or away from such critical engagement of audiences must itself be historically situated in the political, ideological, and material conditions for theatrical production of the time. In keeping with such a premise, he observes that Brecht moved much closer to the goal of participatory theatre by and for a working-class audience in the play *The Measures Taken*, which was performed by the Workers' Choir in Berlin before a predominately working-class audience, and which, unlike other avant-garde performances at the time, interacted directly with a militant working-class movement (*PM*, 90). Williams contrasts this example with what he calls "dissident minority theatre," or avant-garde productions whose theatrical revolts left institutional social relations of the performance and consumption of theatre in an unaltered state. At the same time, however, he acknowledges that the politics that brought about the emergence of fascism for the most part deprived Brecht of both a comradely public and the ability to confront directly the movement's political consequences, causing him to move more deliberately away from participatory theatre at this time and toward a more distanced and formalistic mode of theatre, as evidenced in the play *The Caucasian Chalk Circle*.

Although Williams's reading of Brechtian theatre is neither naively utopian nor impatiently dismissive, in *Politics and Letters*, the *New Left Review* interviewers challenge his assessments of Brecht on several fronts.[27] They take him to task for failing to account for certain irreconcilable tendencies in Brecht's work, tendencies they believe prove that Brecht's realism maintains certain affinities with naturalism. They argue that Williams himself offers inconsistent assessments of the potential of Brecht's work to break distinctively from naturalism and live up to his commitment to revolutionary socialism.

In particular, they remind Williams of his own critiques in *Drama from Ibsen to Brecht* that Brecht's work lacks a dimension of social realism capable of going beyond criticism to offer examples of "positive social liberation" (*PL,* 214). They point out that Williams merely acknowledges rather than comes to terms with the glaring contradiction between Brecht's explicit rejection of both the myths of autonomous individualism and determinism, and their implicit reinscription in his later plays, *The Life of Galileo* and *Mother Courage and Her Children* (*DIB,* 289). In a passage quoted somewhat out of context, that is, one which recognizes only one side of Williams's conflicting assessments of the complexities of Brecht's critical realism (as it was tied only narrowly to expressionism—a point they neglect to mention), the interviewers cite Williams's own assertion—again in *Drama from Ibsen to Brecht*—that "[Brecht] is hardly interested at all in intermediate relationships, in that whole complex of experience, at once personal and social, between the poles of the separated individual and the totally realized society" (*PL,* 214). The *NLR* interviewers fail to note that in the passage immediately following the one they quote, Williams also characterizes Brecht's expressionism as unusually open,

> . . . a development of possibilities and even at times a transformation of effective conventions, because he took up the position of explaining rather than exposing: an overall critical-objective position, rather than the intensity of pleading on behalf of the isolated individual. (*DIB,* 289)

Even taken in the narrow context he intended, Williams appreciates the idea that Brecht's expressionism rejects a *sensorial and sensational* approach to the representation of individual experience, while it favors critical analysis—"an overall critical-objective position." At the same time, though, Williams recognizes the limitations of Brecht having reproduced the polarities between the individual and the society.

It comes as no surprise, then, that when the *NLR* interviewers persist in calling upon Williams to defend his vision of Brecht's critical realism in light of these perceived inconsistencies in Brecht's work as well as Williams's reading of it, Williams offers a gentle but lucid and convincing reproof. He observes that what distinguishes Brecht's innovative realism from other forms of realism is its "subjunctive" rather than "indicative" or merely naturalistically descriptive approach to dramatic representations of reality. The "subjunctive mode," according to Williams, does not present an easy fatalistic dramatic resolution to actions entailed in representing oppressive conditions.

Rather, Williams argues, in Brecht's subjunctive mode—one which Williams believes is evident in *Fears and Miseries of the Third Reich,* among other of Brecht's plays—scenes are replayed that present alternative outcomes to the fascism of the times. Spectators are presented with several alternatives based upon the new elements introduced into the different scenes, such as the course of their own actions and how they affect the outcome of reality. They are also invited to take collective responsibility for evaluating these alternatives.

Williams also answers the *NLR* interviewers' criticism that Brecht leaves no concrete examples of "positive social liberation" whereby others might extend and test his ideas concerning socially critical uses of realist theatre. He takes great pains to describe just how the Brechtian television play, *The Big Flame* by Garnett and Allen, stages the possible alternative outcomes for the Liverpool dockers' strike. As Williams relates:

> At a certain point, the strikers say: suppose we went one step further, suppose we occupy, suppose we assert our own control over the docks? The whole sequence which follows is really a subjunctive one. Its form is this: If we did this, what would happen next? The occupation occurs. In the event[,] the workers are defeated, as the army invades the yard. Nevertheless, what the play successfully presents is an experience which is not realist in the *indicative sense of recording contemporary reality, but in the subjunctive sense of supposing a possible sequence of actions beyond it.* (PL, 219, my emphasis)

What makes Brecht's realism critical, according to Williams, is its *enactment,* rather than its *suppression,* of the conflicts posed by the varying alternatives. Unlike a Stalinist definition of socialist realism (which would warrant being called a Lyotardian master narrative), this kind of critical realism allows space for some vision of how subordinate groups might get from one possible alternative in the present to a desired and desirable social future. It would be wrong, then, to conclude that Williams either approves of or accepts a naively reflectionist view of realism that valorizes naturalism or resurrects the impositional tendencies of Lukácian realism. Far from constructing an *explicitly* universal practice of critical realism, Williams insists on the idea of interested subordinate communities examining each instance of critical realism, evaluating its moral and political implications for emancipatory social transformation. Thus, as I shall show, within Williams's unfinished project exploring Brechtian critical realism are some important connections both to feminist materialism and the critical consciousness and pedagogical practice it aims to create.

Antiracist Pedagogy and Williams's Unfinished Project

The Critical Realism of Williams and Feminist Materialism

Williams's reading of Brechtian critical realism anticipates several of the epistemological developments within feminist materialism, particularly those which feminists would later articulate as the effort to establish a collective feminist standpoint or the "standpoint of women." As Jenny Bourne Taylor observes, there are many unacknowledged affinities between Williams's insistence on the primacy of ordinary culture and lived experience in the 1950s and the writings of feminists such as Sheila Rowbotham in the early 1970s on the texture and politics of family life and waged work ("GG," 300). Michelle Barrett, Elizabeth Fee, Jane Flax, Sandra Harding, Alison Jaggar, Dorothy Smith, and other feminist materialists in the late 1970s and early 1980s would implicitly come to share with Williams the idea that conflicting knowledge claims or claims to represent reality begin with thorough examinations of one's own formative experiences and interests by class, race, gender, and national culture.[28]

At the same time, however, as I and others have argued, while Williams calls upon radical intellectuals to locate themselves as interested autobiographical subjects in the project of cultural analysis, he steadfastly rejects conceptions of a "realist standpoint" that reduce it either to a single point of view or to a haphazard combination of different and yet allegedly equally valid individual representations of reality.[29] For Williams, the vigor of his defense of critical realism hinges on the idea that its practice demands our ongoing evaluations of the conflicting material interests underlying claims to know and represent reality. His understanding of critical realism thus shares with feminist materialism a rejection of relativism and subjectivism. As I have shown, Williams emphasizes the dynamically discursive and empowering function of critically realist practices—particularly the effort of subordinate groups to use popular theatre as a pedagogical medium for *staging* and *realizing* social alternatives to the status quo. Through this effort he acknowledges that critical realism is not a fixed or monolithic system of representation: rather, it is socially produced through language and, indeed, struggled over in the effort of subordinate groups to stage a dialogue about the differences and commonalities in their experiences of oppression.

Similarly, feminist materialists would argue that the act of feminist theorizing is not a remote or abstract project: rather, it entails women becoming conscious theory-makers, that is, critically aware subjects and objects of their own experiences of oppression. As Jaggar argues:

> [A] way must be found in which all groups of women can par-
> ticipate in building theory. Historically, working class women
> and women of color have been excluded from intellectual
> work. This exclusion must be challenged. Working class
> women, women of color, and other historically-silenced women
> must be enabled to participate as subjects as well as objects in
> feminist theorizing. (*FPHN*, 386)

Just as Williams believes in testing theories against their practical everyday political and moral consequences, for feminist materialists, one goal of the women's movement and a test of its success would be to enable women of different social classes and races to join in dialogue over the commonalities and differences in their experiences of oppression. Feminist materialists have been more explicit and committed than Williams in their efforts to elaborate how racial and class divisions present serious obstacles to different groups' engaging in collective dialogue and the production of a common feminist standpoint. As Maria Lugones writes, "We cannot talk to you in our language because you do not understand it. . . . The power of white/Anglo women vis-à-vis Hispanas and Black women is in inverse proportion to their working knowledge of each other."[30] As Jaggar emphasizes,

> within a class-divided and racist society, different groups of
> women inevitably have unequal opportunities to speak and be
> heard. For this reason, the goal that women should begin theo-
> rizing together is itself a political goal and to succeed in collec-
> tive theorizing would itself be a political achievement. Women
> who theorize together can work together politically; indeed in
> theorizing together they are already doing one kind of political
> work. . . . (*FPHN*, 386)

Like Williams, whose aim was to pluralize realist strategies of representation, feminist materialists, like Sandra Harding, argue that women's different interests according to class and race, for example, can be theoretical and political resources to formulate alternative representations of reality and need not function exclusively as sources of division.[31]

Feminist materialists also share with Williams the epistemological assumption that alternative representations of reality will become more adequate by "constantly testing" their "usefulness in helping women transform that reality" (*FPHN*, 387). Williams gives evidence of this affinity when he speaks of the epistemological requirements and claims to knowledge that he believes ought to be applied to cultural theory in general, of which his own defense of critical realism is but one modest part:

> [C]ultural theory is at its most significant when it is concerned precisely with the relations between the many and diverse human activities which have been historically and theoretically grouped in these ways, and especially when it explores these relations as at once dynamic and specific within *describably whole historical situations* which are also, as a practice, changing and, [sic] in the present changeable. *It is then in this emphasis on a theory of such specific and changing relationships that such cultural theory becomes appropriate and useful, as distinct from offering itself as a catch-all theory of very diverse artistic practices.* (PM, 164, my emphasis)

Though written some years later, efforts to conceptualize a feminist standpoint resonate in Williams's aspirations to hold together the two tension-producing aims of critical realism: first, to grasp and represent the commonalities of subordinate groups' experiences as historically changing and changeable; and second, to do so without reducing their differences to an essential or universal standpoint. Shortly, we shall question whether these two aims and the tension they entail are addressed sufficiently by Williams. It is important to note that, on the positive side, Williams's project, like feminist materialism, is *provisional* in character and, therefore, remains open to revision based on rigorous testing of its adequacy and usefulness in producing emancipatory social change.

Cultural Holism, Experience, and Difference: Telling the "Whole Truth" or Nothing Else?

The spirit of provisionalism in Williams's work entreats those of us who consider ourselves to be constituents of the Left and of feminism to critique certain problematic assumptions and systematic silences that are characteristic not only of his work but also of the tradition of cultural materialism he so pervasively influenced. While we may wish to join with Williams in a rejection of relativism and defense of the socially transformative uses of Brechtian critical realism, it is important to challenge the grounds on which he often predicates these two emphases, namely, prior assumptions of *cultural holism.* By cultural holism, I mean the persistent implicit and often explicit tendency in Williams to understand processes of cultural practice and structures of lived experience as "describably whole" or encompassed by a *unified experience of lived wholeness.* Cultural holism erroneously presumes that cultural practices, formations, and experiences are unmediated by very different and often asymmetrical structures and interests of determination. What I consider to be Williams's problematic assumption of cultural holism becomes, in Stuart Hall's critique, Williams's "radically interactionist conception of the social totality" ("Politics," 62). In both cases, what we are arguing against is Williams's analytic conflation of very different and often historically uneven processes of cultural formation and structural determination. This conflation results in Williams's insistence that very different structures and practices cannot be separated analytically in order to determine how at a given historical juncture one interest, such as gender or race, might have a greater structural weight or determinateness than others, such as class.

In *Politics and Letters,* the *NLR* interviewers press Williams to revise his conception of the social totality, culture, and experience with the intention of challenging two main emphases at work in *The Long Revolution.* First, without explicitly naming the problem as one of cultural holism, they challenge the ineffectual notion of "determinancy" underlying his conception of the social totality, which, they note, is premised upon Williams's claim that it is impossible to analytically separate out in cultural practice or lived experience different systems of oppression according to any one prior determinancy. Second, they challenge the presumption of evenness, or what I call *symmetry,* at work in Williams's notion of experience and his understanding of processes of determinancy—a presumption that does not permit the possibility that differently weighted structural determinants accord quite unequal material and cultural consequences for groups.

With respect to both challenges, Williams makes certain noteworthy concessions. Yet, with each concession he backslides curiously into his earlier problematic formulation of cultural holism. Describing his concessions merely as "qualifications" of his earlier "definitions" of the social totality, culture, and experience, he now more explicitly acknowledges "marked" disparities between different systems of a society that, in his view, "necessarily limit the idea of the parity of structures" (*PL*, 138). Here Williams concedes that his earlier presumption of symmetry, what he calls "parity," is actually inadequate to describe the unequal interests at work in processes of historical change, determinancy, and social formation. In contrast to his earlier formulations, he also acknowledges a greater temporal unevenness in processes of historical change and the social formation of different structures.

But Williams offers two defenses for the apparent discontinuities between his former and current positions. With the first, he acknowledges that his previous vocabulary limited his ability to "theoretically negotiate" alternative conceptions of the social totality, culture, and experience, even though, as he relates it, he was "aware" of the problems created by his earlier formulations (*PL,* 138). The second is more problematic. He goes on to argue that his "present vocabulary of dominant, residual, and emergent patterns within any given culture is intended to indicate precisely the phenomenon of historical discrepancy" (*PL,* 138). Furthermore, he argues that these important changes in his vocabulary represent "a decisive change" in his thinking (*PL,* 138). I do not dispute the radical implications of his new language to distinguish the uneven and different struggles for hegemony over cultural processes and social formations. There is, however, scant evidence to suggest that in his subsequent work Williams radically revises his conception of culture based on the implications of asymmetric and contradictory power relations engendered in this new vocabulary as a set of theoretical propositions. In fact, Williams himself suggests the contrary in comments made subsequent to the supposed "decisive change" in his thinking.

Instead, he continues to insist that it is wrong to analytically separate different systems of oppression and structures of determination. The strongest reassertion of cultural holism occurs when Williams affirms that the "way he would put it today" is that different structures and practices are "indissoluble elements of a continuous social-material process" (*PL,* 138). For Williams, the veracity of the "indissolubility" and "wholeness of culture"—what I critique as cultural holism—is confirmed daily through an individual's own experiences of the interconnections among different structures of determination and practices of domination. Williams quite baldly asserts this thesis as a self-evident and auto-verifiable prophecy: "[W]e know this to be true about our own lives—hence, we can take it as a theoretical assumption" (*PL,* 138). While Williams correctly recognizes the interconnections among systems of domination, he undercuts the possibility of deconstructing their asymmetries and unequal effects in any particular historical situation. Instead, in an effort to valorize unanalyzed personal lived experience as theoretical knowledge, and thereby to avoid a certain fetishization of theory, Williams employs what Stuart Hall identifies as an "empiricist notion of experience" ("Politics," 62). Williams's empiricism pre-empts the importance of analytic abstractions by showing how apparent wholeness and commonality in lived experience as well as in culture are often fractured by different and conflicting structural interests. As Hall warns,

> [S]o long as "experience" continues to play this all embracing role, there will be an inevitable theoretical pull towards reading all structures as if they expressively correlated with one another: simultaneous in effect and determinancy because they are simultaneous in our experience. ("Politics," 62)

Given that Williams himself comes to reject the idea of a parity or symmetry of interests, it behooves us to recognize the essential role analysis plays in the deconstruction of the determinate conditions of "lived wholeness."

Missed Opportunities: Autobiography and Theory

Ironically, assuming that analysis necessarily results in gross theoretical abstraction, or that it obscures the interconnections among systems of oppression, Williams contradicts crucial innovations in his own expansion of Brechtian critical realism. In particular, his defense of cultural holism undermines the idea that occasions for critical analysis in popular theatre are a potentially empowering means through which subordinate groups can evaluate their own claims to know reality in relation to those emanating from dominant groups. One source of empowerment, for example, might come from a group determining that at a given historical juncture, race or gender, rather than class, is the primary or dominant means of their oppression. Although his theory of critical realism explicitly rejects universalism based upon any one a priori interest, his acceptance of cultural holism implicitly underwrites it.

As Jenny Bourne Taylor observes, throughout his writings Williams takes as normative and generalizable his own formative experience as a Welsh working-class male. Although he never explicitly universalizes his experience as the single point of reference, she argues that

> it manifests itself in different ways—[and] suggests that his analysis smuggles in a set of uncontested assumptions, a set of unexplored power relationships, within the "indissoluble element of a single socio-material process" most crucially in the

ubiquitous yet strangely absent status that the family (the fundamental meeting point of gender and generation) holds in his work. ("GG," 300–301, my clarification)

In Bourne Taylor's view, Williams frequently "naturalizes" the structural interests of his own identity as a working-class Welsh male, repressing their *salient inability to be generalized and universalized* to others of his generation, namely the girls and women. Cultural holism thus makes it possible to equate gender, race, or national culture with the interests of class, even when class is not the primary or exclusive referent for, or determinant of, a group's lived cultural experience. Moreover, in such cases, Williams's cultural holism denies the very historical specificities and dynamism his critical realism seeks to uncover.

In a similar vein, although Williams's cultural materialism often includes keen observations of gender-specific experiences of men and women, these observations do not rise to the status given to such subjects when they are systematically explored or analyzed. The frustration of encountering Williams's work as a feminist materialist is twofold. First, while it shares epistemological affinities with feminist materialism, these affinities are rarely made explicit as a dialogue with feminist work or concerns. Second, because Williams often relegates his keen observations of gender specificities to the largely unexamined realm of description, we are left with the task of deciding whether or not his cultural materialism can be extended to feminist issues and strategies for social transformation.[32]

One noteworthy example of how Williams's work discontents feminists will suffice. Bourne Taylor asks us to consider the significance of Williams's recounting, in *Politics and Letters,* an experience he erroneously characterized as the prototypical "structure of feeling" for his own generation, the experience of the scholarship boy. Here, he nostalgically reconstructs a working-class childhood, not as the exception for working-class males of his generation, nor as a categorically unthinkable experience for his female peers, but rather as the norm. The narrative involves a theoretical slippage, in which Williams uses the class and gender contradictions of his autobiography to stand for a fictive universal experience of class dislocation and crisis in the reshaping of his educational trajectory. Williams describes his experience as the winner of one of only seven scholarships awarded to attend the County school in Abergavenny. During one telling moment, he unself-consciously enjoys nostalgia for a fictive working-class community, which he renders as universal as his own case is exceptional:

> It happened that the village had its golden year when I sat for the scholarship. . . . There was a group photograph taken because it was such an exceptional event: six girls and me. But the girls—several of them were farmers' daughters—would usually only go as far as the fifth form and then would leave. . . . (*PL,* 28–29)

Like so many other occasions for the intersection of autobiography and theory-making, Williams only hints at the implications of an unequal gender experience for the girls. Ultimately though, he skips over them, assuming that his own class and gender experiences are the primary referent for his working-class village.

We must also remember that the occasion for this nostalgic recollection was an interview with other well-known and highly-educated male members of the British Left.[33] This would appear to be a context particularly vested in reproducing the ideology of masculine working-class heroism and the Left intellectual retrospectively exploring his organic roots from the exceptional and contradictory location of his identity as a new middle-class socialist educated at Cambridge. Noting the occasion, it is less surprising that, later in the interview, when Williams defensively asserts his over-identification with an empiricist conception of experience, he relies upon a residual form of working-class anti-intellectualism: the refusal to analyze or theorize one's own experience in the face of its over-theorization and commodification.

What theoretical opportunities might Williams have seized had he lived up to the promise of a "decisive change" in his thinking on these issues? We might expect to have found in his subsequent work the kind of theorizing and analysis that emerges from simultaneously analyzing the tensions between conjunctural moments and structural patterns in history. For example, we might have seen him make more of rich and suggestive empirical analyses of the conjunctures in power relations which cannot be read as the products of either a "common culture" or a "whole way of life" because they are indicative of asymmetries and conflicts of power within particular interests, such as the ways in which gender, race, and national culture divide the working classes. We would have seen Williams give the quality of attention many feminists and postcolonial critics have paid to the struggles of unequally oppressed groups to articulate their potentially conflicting interests in relation to the dominant centers of institutional power. We would have seen Williams pose questions concerning how socialist politics would be transformed by the effort to take seriously the issues being raised by the new social movements of feminism, peace, ecology, antiracism, and anti-imperialism. In each of these cases, Williams misses the opportunity to re-evaluate his presumption of "a common culture" and "whole way of life"—what Julia Swindells and Lisa Jardine sarcastically term the "minefields" into which he steps—in light of the fact that neither social subjects nor social movements are unitary or static in their identification with particular interests.[34]

Williams thus fails to connect his work on the possibilities for socially transformative critical realism to the very asymmetries and alliances that constitute, divide, and reconstitute communities and social movements. We need not, however, follow him down the romanticized path of *cultural holism*. Instead, we may seize these missed opportunities as challenges to explore and theorize *other sides* of cultural formations and their power relations, by showing how contradictorily interested groups may use their different forms of marginality to enact alternative and counter-hegemonic representations of reality.

Other Sides of Culture: Exclusion, Exportation, and Imposition

In conversation with Raymond Williams and the interviewers for the appendix to *The Politics of Modernism*, Edward Said distills the main problem of Williams's conception of culture. He recalls a moment in the interview for *Politics and Letters* when the *NLR* interviewers hold Williams accountable for his failure to address, in *Culture and Society*, the relationship between issues of Empire and British imperialism and the formation of nineteenth-century British culture. Said argues that throughout this work Williams mistakenly presumes that culture has been used almost exclusively as a "cooperative and communal term" (*PM*, 194). According to Said, the obverse is just as real, depending on one's location: *culture is also a term of exclusion, exportation, and imposition*. When culture is seen as such, the issues that move from the margins to the center are those created by the conditions of the contradictory social relations of postcoloniality: they reveal culture to be defined by an awareness of living in a society and yet by virtue of one or more subordinate or subaltern interests not being part of it. Experiences of *exile, marginality,* and *difference* from the hegemonic center foreground the realities of social subjects whose identities are not "describably whole" or unified in the terms Williams proposes; rather, they are conflicted *palpably* by contradictory structural interests and heterogeneous affiliations. They draw our attention to the realities of people belonging simultaneously to conflicting communities of interest and allegiance, and immigrating, by virtue of their conflicting loyalties, across and within their borders. Such a conception of culture and of social subjectivity directs our attention to the need to study how the often conflicting interests of class, gender, race, and nation cohere in lived experiences through an ensemble of ideologies and cultural practices. This coherence permits people to make common sense of objectively divergent interests. Yet while such ideologies may cohere under certain conditions, they can be destabilized and transformed within the context of specific hegemonic and political struggles, thus altering the terms in which relations of oppression and privilege are defined as well as the boundaries between and among groups.[35]

Said's reproof of Williams is also apropos of the dominant strands of cultural studies, which share Williams's cultural holism.[36] In light of the implications of Said's argument, as well as the arguments of postcolonial and feminist critics, what do we make of the systematic limitations of Williams's cultural materialism and his work to develop Brechtian critical realism? Are the limitations of Williams's cultural materialism intractable because they reinscribe many of the dominant terms of culture he sought to alter? Do they render his elaboration of Brechtian critical realism obsolete? How might we locate the theoretical, political, and ultimately practical tools and resources from the failures and insights of Williams's cultural materialism and his unfinished project to articulate a socially transformative critical realism? Given Williams's own commitment to testing theories "on the ground" and in relationship to their implications for teaching, it seems appropriate to submit his theorizing to such a test in a particular educational setting.

Williams on the Ground: Pedagogy as Critical Realism

The Relativism of Advocating Nonadvocacy

One indication of the hegemonic success of the Right in the United States during the Reagan and Bush era has been its forceful and yet wrongful representation of its own moral agenda, policies, and visions of a just society as neutral and interest-free, in opposition to those of the liberal and radical Left, which it casts as disqualifiable on the grounds of their instantiation in "extremist" discourses of advocacy, bias, and ideology.[37] Of course, while advocating nonadvocacy may seem like an oxymoronic project, as educators we cannot afford to ignore the implications of its relativism. Its relativism attempts to deny our pedagogical responsibility to engage students in critical evaluation of their own and others' claims to *belonging* to particular oppressed or privileged groups and, therefore, *to knowing* and *representing* their realities. Because relativism erroneously treats all knowledge claims as equally reliable guides to describing and representing the social world, it denies the interestedness of knowledge and unequal effects of representations emerging from different epistemic standpoints. As I shall show, when relativistic claims are *asserted* or *protected* by educators in the classroom, what emerges is an implicit endorsement, if not advocacy, of the existing social inequalities or, worse yet, of emergent practices that appropriate the experiences and discourses of the oppressed in order to deny their struggles for emancipation and equality.

To take Williams's theorizing about critical realism to "the ground" means examining specific national, regional, and local contexts in which struggles over whose knowledge counts as reality are manifest. In the context of discussing *emergent* forms of *defensive racism* in Louisiana, I intend to illustrate how and why a socially transformative critical realism is preferable, in its political, ethical, and educational consequences for the students and teachers, to the relativism of postmodernist discourses and to the allegedly antithetical reactionary discourses espousing nonadvocacy and neutrality. My argument shall suggest the potential and actual dangers of teachers either taking a priori relativisitic stances themselves or colluding with such stances—unwittingly or not—taken by students in the classroom. My argument shall also speak to the rewards for all concerned when teachers join with students to engage in the socially transformative practice of critical realism in order to evaluate in a *relational way* the objective and subjective bases for *conflicting claims* to *belong to, know, and represent the reality* of differentially oppressed and privileged groups. I shall offer a provisional feminist materialist alternative both to the impositional tendencies implicit in Williams's romanticized conception of culture as cultural holism and to the state of political and moral paralysis or collusion with the status quo that is authorized implicitly by postmodernism's a priori commitment to relativism.

Antiracist Pedagogy and Williams's Unfinished Project
Speaking With Rather Than For/Instead of Others

The provisional alternative I propose as a nontotalizing means to achieve a socially transformative practice of critical realism may be best expressed as *speaking with,* rather than *for,* the interests of oppressed groups who are engaged in critically evaluating and transforming existing social relations—whether or not members of such groups are physically present in the classroom. In contrast to the dominant meaning of *speaking for,* which implies that one group's voice can replace and stand for another's, I introduce the concept of *speaking with* to convey the possibility of tendential and shifting alliances between speakers from different unequally located groups. *Speaking with* refers to the contradictions of voices engaged in dialogue with one another, without suggesting that they are reducible to the same voice or epistemic standpoint. While the politics of *speaking with* cannot be defined in any a priori or absolutist way, we can specify the *relational politics of dialogue—or the lack thereof*—between unequally located groups. It also means that we can specify the conditions under which effective coalitions for social transformation may or may not be possible. To use the term relationally means avoiding the conclusion that we can only address each conjuncture of dialogue—or the lack thereof—between unequally located groups as dislocatable from a history of power relations in which they are embedded and thus necessarily subject to treatment only on a case-by-case basis. The concept of *speaking with* suggests that effective coalition politics relies upon groups rigorously evaluating the strategic value of their integrating with, or separating from, other groups in any decision to speak in behalf of the oppression of one's group or of others.

In the context of education, this alternative conceives of the aims of constructing, deconstructing, and transforming curriculum and pedagogy as dialogic in their form and democratically collective in their process—aims which do not result in teachers or students *imposing* their definitions of critical reality upon others in the classroom. As I argued at the outset, I use the notion of a *socially contested realism* to discuss the ways in which individuals' and groups' phenomenological representations of reality are linked to their material and ideological interests in a struggle for hegemony. Classrooms are one significant context in which struggles for hegemony amidst unequal power relations take place. By drawing upon feminist materialism and the work of Williams, I am arguing for an ontology of *socially contested realism,* one which aspires to democratize the production of theory in the classroom as pedagogy, research, and political process.[38] Such a process aims to treat as its legitimate texts for collective deconstruction all claims *to know* and *represent reality* made in the classroom, including those of the teacher, those manifest in the formal and hidden curriculum, and those implicit in classroom social relations.

I realize that my recourse to feminist materialism may produce multiple readings and misreadings, and that the standard complaint of postmodernist theorists to critiques of their work by critical theorists is that they have been misunderstood. But as critical theorist Thomas McCarthy says in defense of his recent critique of Derrida, I too cannot hope to avoid being misread.[39] If I must be misread, though, let it be in the direction of arguing against the imposition of any cultural analysis that does not acknowledge differences in the material stakes of all claims *to know* and *to represent reality* in the classroom—and *for* one that takes diverse material and ideological conditions seriously, both as the specificities of a given juncture and as practices locatable within a history of unequal power relations. Permit me to be misread as not advocating in the name of critical realism an authoritarian imposition of one group's ideological construction of democracy and a socially just society over others, but as refusing to accept the proposition that all claims *to know* and *to represent reality* have relatively equal consequences for the subjects of the claims.

As I will show, the politics of *speaking with* the interests of the oppressed confronts educators with the fact that social subjects occupy a range of contradictory and asymmetric interests that make it impossible to bracket or contain the pedagogical politics of *who* can speak for *whom* to an individualistic and essentialist conception. Such a conception assumes erroneously that "one can retreat into one's discrete location and make claims entirely and singularly based on that location that do not range over others" or do not have effects over those who are made or unmade the subjects of such speech ("SFO," 7). I must concur with Alcoff's argument that if such a definition governs the criteria under which people can engage in justifiable advocacy, then I should only speak for groups of which I am a member, or each of us should only speak for herself ("SFO," 7). Ironically, while this formulation sometimes stems from the desire to avoid committing "imperialist errors," it reinforces Western liberalism's erroneous presumption of the singularly interested autonomous self ("SFO," 5). But the retreat from advocacy begs many questions which arose in the context of my teaching in Louisiana, and which caused me to formally challenge its assumptions. For example, it does not tell us how groups themselves should be delimited or who gets to claim membership in them. How broadly or narrowly may the categories of oppression, difference, and privilege be drawn? Who gets to draw them? If educators accept the moral consequences of relativism, with its infinite capacity to treat all claims to be a member of an oppressed group as holding equal validity in explaining the social world, are we not then part of the problem of being in collusion with oppressive relations? How can we claim to teach critically when all bases for ruling out illegitimate claims to be oppressed have themselves been extinguished? How might we invoke the power of critical analysis and historicizing uses of realism to identify standpoints that have epistemic salience on both objective and subjective grounds?

The Dialectics of Prior Beliefs, Practice, and Theory

My rejection of the relativism of postmodernism is not premised upon a rigid or blind theoretical adherence to the critical realism of feminist materialism. Nor is it premised upon a naive first encounter with the practice of advocacy in an explicit, dialogic, and democratic manner within an educational context. As an ethnographer of young Punk women, I have confronted the impossibility and political untenability of adhering to certain stances of *neutrality* within naturalistic ethnography—which prescribe that ethnographers either conduct themselves as unobtrusive observers (*flies on the wall*) or as fully immersed (*gone native*) researchers.[40] I have shown how such stances reproduce the exploitation of research subjects through what I call *intellectual tourism* and *voyeurism* on the parts of ethnographers, the very practices of domination that feminist materialism strives to transform.[41]

Without the benefit of significant role models, I pursued what I now would call a *socially transformative praxis* of ethnography, similar to the general aspirations of *speaking with* that I shall describe shortly but specific to the relations that could develop between a middle-class white researcher and a predominantly white group of middle- and working-class young women. In this case, *speaking with* the young women necessitated my becoming increasingly forthright in disclosing to the Punks how my feminist materialism had come to shape my rationale for investigating them.[42] I came to call this process *double exposure* because it exposed my beliefs and structural interests in relation to those of the young women with whom I worked. As a consequence, they became something other than someone else's objects: they began to engage as active critical analysts of their own experiences of class and gender relations as well as of the descriptions, emergent hypotheses, and analyses I advanced about them. This profoundly affected my rethinking not only of methodologies for ethnographic research but also of the *critical* role of advocacy in all research and pedagogical acts.

I was, nevertheless, unprepared for many of the ethical and pedagogical dilemmas I would encounter as a consequence of teaching an explicitly antiracist and feminist course in a racially mixed classroom in a Southern university during this time of political retrenchment. As I shall show, had I adhered to relativism's implicit advocacy of the status quo in such a context, I would have entered into collusion with the production of *residual* as well as *emergent* forms of *defensive racism* that further silenced the racially oppressed African-American students in the class, while sanctioning and legitimating the appropriative speech of the white students.

Uncommon Biographies: Structural Institutional Racism and the Racially Divided Voices of the Women Students[43]

False Promises for Integration, Equality, and Dialogue

The social and political context for the two-semester graduate course I offered in the fall of 1989 and spring of 1990 entitled "Intensive Critical Ethnography" (EDCI-7811 & 7921) bears witness to this historical lesson of difference as a schism in the sisterhood, particularly across racial interests.[44] It underwrites the inseparable interrelation between racism and sexism, as bound in the biographies of the five African-American and four white women who enrolled in the course, and their unequal relationships to Louisiana's institutional biography of structural racism.[45] Teaching this particular course—a course designed to challenge students to develop alternatives to the conventions of naturalistic ethnography premised on colonialist, positivist, and masculinist notions of objectivism—in Louisiana's context of enduring and recently intensified racism, with a racially mixed group of female students, quickly disabused me of any lingering or occasional romantic presumptions of a shared history of educational experiences based upon a unified conception of the women's gender interests. It soon became painfully apparent to me that the five middle-aged African-American women who enrolled in the class were acutely aware of the university's history of structural racism. They told me their life histories against the backdrop of its recalcitrance, even in the years after the

Brown legal cases, to recruit African-Americans into its undergraduate and graduate programs.

For example, it is significant to note that four of these five women discussed with me being the official new recruits to an "outreach" and integration effort initiated only as recently as 1986. All four felt they bore this status as a burden as well as an opportunity. The effort, which previously had not been successfully undertaken, was designed to recruit African-Americans from private and public universities in New Orleans, whose populations are predominantly African-American, into the Department of Curriculum and Instruction. The five African-American students each commuted great distances on a weekly basis to attend class in Baton Rouge in order to pursue their doctoral work, in addition to meeting their full-time professional and familial responsibilities of child care and domestic labor.[46] I had learned, through conversations we had when they took previous classes with me in feminist theory and the sociology of youth subcultures, that the African-American women brought to the class their vivid memories of earlier unsuccessful attempts, by them or by their colleagues, to attend LSU in the early 1960s. They recounted that they or their colleagues had been harassed, scorned, or even shot at by white students.

In contrast to the African-American women, the four white women enrolled in the course had experienced neither the stigmatization of being the objects of special recruitment efforts nor the attendant fears and responsibilities of standing for the achievements of others of their group. All four were completing their doctoral requirements on a full-time basis without the demands of full-time employment or commuting to classes.[47] Instead, three of the four white women were middle-aged, long-term residents of Baton Rouge, who, through family members, maintained alumni associations with LSU. The fourth was a younger exchange student from Germany. Two of the middle-aged women had familial responsibilities of child care and domestic labor in addition to their coursework.

The Racially Privileged Naivete of My Teaching Voice

Although I was no stranger to the South's particular forms of regional racism, having grown up in Texas, and although I entered the classroom with the explicit aim of approaching pedagogy as an advocate of equality for different oppressed groups, I was unprepared for the specific manner in which already existing racial divisions would become manifest in the classroom dynamics, in relation both to the aims of the course and the pedagogical stances I would take as a consequence of these dynamics. Indeed, this *racially privileged naivete* on my part necessitated unanticipated revisions in my pedagogical stances as the first term of the course progressed. These were part of an effort (albeit not always successful) to maintain democratic conditions for dialogue between the white and African-American students. I came to realize, however, that conflicts between the African-American and white students over specific epistemic claims to know the realities of systematic racial oppression had not been resolved according to stated new awarenesses and understandings on the parts of the white students concerning the systematic bases of racism. Nor had the bases for trust and mutual disclosure of each group's different relationship to experiences of racial oppression and privilege been built in the context of the first semester. In retrospect, I can point to more evidence for unstated conflict between the two groups than I was able to recognize in the context of classroom social relations. As is often the case in Southern social relations, I found it difficult to pierce the *veneer of polite interchange and consensus* that appeared to characterize their interactions and my structuring of class discussions as well as other pedagogical choices with which I wrestled.

I first learned that the conditions for interracial dialogue in the classroom had ceased to exist after the first term ended. While at the outset and at the end of the first term white and African-American students alike had committed themselves to completing both semesters of the class, and all but one (African-American) student were eligible to receive credit for it in the second term, it was only these four African-American students who pursued the course in the second term.[48] Although none of the white students had completed all six credits of their methodology requirement, they withdrew after participation in the first term of the course.[49] Responding to my queries in the context of individual interviews, the white students politely offered various reasons for retracting their earlier commitment to continue in the course. Shortly, we shall have occasion to compare the reasons given by the two groups of students for their choices to continue or discontinue in the second semester of the course. Stark differences in the responses and relations to the course on the parts of white and African-American students led me to engage in a systematic analysis of the course's social relations and my pedagogical strategies, and, ultimately, to revise my thinking on what might constitute effective antiracist education in a racially mixed class of women in comparable political, cultural, and economic conditions.

Antiracist Pedagogy and Williams's Unfinished Project

Curriculum in Revision

Given the clear racially demarcated reactions to the course, I wished to understand my own location in relation to the processes of intensified and defensive racism. I asked myself questions I believed at the time to be "tough," regarding whether I had overcompensated out of racial guilt in my attempts to take antiracist stances in the classroom and, thus, unnecessarily alienated the white students.[50] I have struggled with my role as an educator, not wanting to dismiss these white students and yet wondering how I could have more successfully engaged them in reconsidering the bases of their (our) racial privilege without silencing or further marginalizing their African-American colleagues. My understanding of what had transpired was deepened by rereading the notes and observations I made as the class progressed and through a series of informal conversations during the first term, followed by more formal ethnographic interviews which I conducted with eight of the nine students[51] in the months following both terms of the course.[52]

I hoped to know retrospectively how they framed their perceptions of classroom interactions and their own positions as both students and subjects, according to interests of race, gender, and class, in the conduct of such interactions. Given some time to reflect on the stances they had taken in class, I wondered what they made of the conflicting epistemic claims made by white and African-American students to know the reality of systematic racial oppression. I asked whether they modified their stated positions and, if so, how, and to what effect. Equally, I was concerned to know the students' perceptions of *my* interests and pedagogical stances. How did they experience my authorial voice as both teacher and white middle-class feminist taking antiracist stances? How could I learn from the insights gained by the students into the contradictory nature of taking antiracist stances? How did these two groups of students perceive the aim and effects—both intentional and unintentional—of my pedagogical stances and choices? I hoped to discover how I might systematically revise and transform my approach to antiracist pedagogy in terms of building effective coalitions among groups interested in combatting both racism and sexism.

The Relation Between an Anti-Imperialist Critique of Ethnography and the Problem of White Jealousy and Displacement

When I examined my observations of the class along with the texts of the interviews, it became clear that my choice to focus the class readings and discussions, at least in part, on anti-imperialist critiques of ethnography, as well as my choice to take antiracist stances as a white woman professor, affected the kind of dialogue and rapport—or the lack thereof—I could establish with students of different racial backgrounds. As I discovered within a few short weeks after the first term commenced, the explicit aim of introducing the students to the postcolonial and feminist critiques of Western ethnographic narratives and practices produced racially differentiated, even polarized, responses from the students. These responses were often heavily veiled. For example, *emergent defensive racism* expressed by the white students often manifested itself in the form of jealousy over my tendency to legitimate the African-American students' epistemic claims to know what it means to be the subjects and objects of racial oppression. They correctly perceived that a curriculum focused by an anti-imperialist, feminist, and anti-positivist critique of ethnography presented the African-American students with the opportunity to become the central subjects who could legitimately identify with the colonial or racially subjugated subjects of texts such as Edward Said's *Orientalism,* among others.[53] As I learned from the interviews with the white women students, they viewed me in several ways. At times they saw me as someone whose antiracist stances derived from a "liberal desire" to engage in a special, if not charitable, form of communication with the African-American students. This was evidenced by Marsha's statement, "I thought when one of them [speaking of Coretta, an African-American student whose ideas and intellectual accomplishments I wished to give special mention in class] gave a paper at some conference thing, it was nice that you were trying to honor the achievements of the black girls, especially the stamina they had to commute from New Orleans" (Interview, Marsha, 10/14/90). At other times they saw me as a sympathetic audience for their own claims of being racially oppressed. When I was not sympathetic to such claims, I was viewed alternatively as someone whose antiracist stances threatened their sense of polite conversational decorum and classroom etiquette, a view best expressed by Dana when she said, "You kept focusing on all that race stuff, and it just gets in the way of people getting along" (Dana, 9/15/90), or, as someone to whom they felt prepared to lend their white racial support in the event that I would be falsely accused by the African-American students of racist treatment—an accusation which, I might add, *never* was made.

At first, the African-American students' claims took the form of strongly expressed identifications with colonial or racially subordinate research subjects, who, according to postcolonial and feminist critics, have been described and analyzed as *inferior others* or *exoticized projections* of the imaginations of Western anthropologists or sociologists.[54] Initially, and with good reason given the history of LSU, such claims by the African-American students were not expressed with the confidence that they would be taken seriously. Instead, they were issued tentatively, like trial balloons sent to test the receptivity of all the whites in the room to hearing them. I quickly came to realize, though, that the white students met such claims with a variety of responses that had the collective effect of redirecting the analytical energies of the class to themselves. Sometimes this redirection took the form of the discourse I now call *racially-privileged incredulity,* that is, time-consuming expressions of disbelief and horror that *other* whites had such racist attitudes or that racism still persists as a present-day phenomenon. In a noteworthy example, during the second week of class, Susan, a white woman, shifted attention away from Ceciley, an African-American, when Ceciley recalled an event from another class in which white students had called African-Americans "welfare leeches" and the white male teacher had taken the decision to "let it go." Susan prefaced her lengthy remarks, expressing horror by saying, "I just can't believe what I am hearing! I thought we had gotten beyond all that racial stuff when slavery was abolished" (Field notes, 9/89). A second more disturbing strategy of redirection, however, emerged in the third week of class. This involved whites appropriating the category of racial oppression by making similar claims to be victims of racial oppression or to be minorities. Such strategies appeared to coincide with my assignment to the class to read Edward Said's *Orientalism*. My aim was to engage the class in extending Said's analysis of the ideological functions of Western narratives to the implications for educational ethnography in the United States. I prefaced our discussion of the book with some introductory remarks concerning the undeniable role of the researcher's authorial voice and interests—interests that are written into ethnographic descriptions and analyses of the research subjects, but which rarely are acknowledged or challenged.

I asked the students to break into small groups to consider how educational ethnographies might perform the function of dehumanizing, essentializing, or "Orientalizing" particular groups in ways that paralleled Said's critique of Western anthropology and area studies programs. The students approached the task with eagerness, sliding chairs into circles and speaking excitedly about how they liked the book. I was struck by the fact that two groups formed: one, composed of white students; the other, initially formed by the African-American students and, after a moment's indecision, joined by Dana, a white, middle-class woman.

I requested that the groups take notes on their discussion so that they could bring their reflections back to the class as a whole. During the commotion of students breaking into groups, I overheard Dana exclaim, "Now, I get to be a minority!" She laughed anxiously, but no one else laughed with her. Though stunned at her attempt at appropriation, I was unprepared to interrupt the flow of the class at that time to draw attention to the relativizing implications of her claim. I spontaneously decided to postpone raising the issue of this problematic appropriation until I could formulate a way to do so without putting her or others on the defensive. While the students talked, I moved back and forth between the groups to answer questions and listen. I walked up to the group composed of African-American students and Dana. I overheard Alexa, one of the African-American women, drawing a connection between Said's analysis of "Orientalizing" practices and the ways "minority kids get labelled by ethnographers as 'underachievers,' " raising the question within the group as to which racial groups get described by whom in a pejorative manner (Field notes, 9/25/89). I noticed that Dana took an active role as officiator, transforming into her own words what she heard the African-American women saying, and persisting with the claim that she, too, was a minority in groups predominated by "black individuals." I was pleased to observe that the African-American women judiciously and diplomatically confronted what one of them later characterized as her "insults" (Interview with Faye, 10/13/90). I overheard the group composed of white women making similar claims concerning what it feels like to be a member of a racial minority. These claims suggested that in some way, as Marsha stated, "We all take our turns being discriminated against," or, as Susan added, "Yeah, like you can be discriminated against for wearing this or that weird clothing, or for just acting different in school. Lots of kids get treated that way, the nerds, the latchkey kids, and just about anyone who is different is a minority these days" (Field notes, 9/25/89).

The nature of the claims I heard the white students make, and the tones of voices in which they made them, seemed to minimize the difference between experiences of systematic racial oppression—with its dimensions of economic deprivation and involuntary cultural and political marginalization within society's power relations—and those experiences of what I would call *incidental stigmatization* of one individual under an isolated set of circumstances that may have involved some degree of choice to be different from others. I wondered whether such claims expressed the white students' sense of displacement and jealousy at being decentered subjects in a discourse challenging such issues as racism and imperialism. Was the appropriation of the category of racial oppression thus a strategy to regain control of the classroom discourse? Had the topic itself—a postcolonial criticism of Western imperialism in representations of non-Western groups by Western scholars—called into question their own location as white Western subjects? Did the white students feel defensive because I had recognized the legitimacy of the African-American women's claims to be subjects of racial oppression? I began to realize that if I failed to challenge the relativism of the claims made by white students, I would be in collusion with their deduction that to be a subject of racism was merely to volunteer for it, to simply choose to be a *consumer of difference,* rather than to know how systematic racial inequality positioned one outside the most basic of human rights for decent health care, housing, education, and employment.

As Raymond Williams's project to articulate a critical socially transformative realism distinguishes between relativistic claims and those that collectively express the interests of oppressed groups, I found myself standing on familiar ground, determined to open both sets of claims to dialogue, critical scrutiny, challenge, and, hopefully, transformation. In an effort to begin engaging the white students in a self-critical analysis of evaluating their claims, I asked the class to reverse their logic and consider the consequences of the assumption that all groups are *equally privileged.* Coretta, one of the African-American students, smiled with approval at my question. Immediately, one of the white middle-class women, Marsha, blurted out, "Well, we teachers know that isn't true because men in our schools who coach, teach social studies, and get principalships get paid more than us and get heard at the staff meetings!" (Field notes, 9/25/89). Building on her point, I asked the class to consider how they would feel if a man teaching social studies or acting as a principal spoke out at a staff meeting and complained that "with all this women's lib stuff, the real issues of sex discrimination against men were getting side-tracked." Marsha again chimed in that her husband said such things all the time and they "really pissed" her off because "he didn't come home after work all day, feed the kids, and get them off to bed." Karina, also white, mentioned that she was taking a women's studies course in sociology and had learned that many women were mostly making low wages because they were in secretarial and other service jobs (Field notes, 9/25/89). From these critical responses, I was able to outline for the class on the blackboard some of the structural elements of women's oppression: "double-work of wage work and family, low wages, dead-end and insecure service jobs." This provided the class with some basis upon which to evaluate the difference between the objective material conditions of their own experiences, or knowledge of gender oppression, versus the subjective and defensive claims of men in dissimilar positions, who did not *know* the reality of women's oppression.

Staging with my own students what I understand Williams to mean by staging the dialectic between their own critical theorizing and practice, I then asked the class to reconsider claims they had heard being made by themselves or others, during the course of their discussions, to be racially oppressed. I also posed the question of whether or not growing up as a slave, being forced to sit at the back of the bus, or going to inferior schools carried the same consequences as being left out of a social group because "people" thought one wore "weird" clothing. The white students' nonverbal expressions of downcast eyes and heads nodding "no" confirmed their recognition that the analogies being drawn were unfair and even wrong. Moreover, none expressed disagreement when Marsha said, "I guess that would be like saying you can't ever tell the difference between the pain of burning your finger on the stove and someone setting fire to your house." It was not the analogy I would have chosen, but it was evidence of new understanding among students in the class, particularly among the white students—one that acknowledged there were some fundamentally different consequences in the claims of whites and African-Americans to be victims of racial oppression. In the end, no one went away feeling as if the issues had been resolved adequately; on the contrary, our dialogue was merely opened, tested, and redefined.

Destabilizing Postmodernist Relativism: Not All Differences are Equal

After this meeting of the class, the African-American women students as a group collectively approached me with their analyses of what had transpired. They focused on the effects of being positioned in Dana's discourse as the subjects of white students' appropriations of the experience of racial oppression. Their words and insights clearly refused the relativizing treatment of this type of defensive racism, with its claim to "know" the reality of systematic racial oppression:

(Coretta): Dana positioned herself outside of us. We [referring to the African-American students] took it as a racial position, as a racial and cultural position. She was from the Northeast [and held] a superiority attitude towards minority groups and that was obvious to us. While I was trying to give my opinion in the group, she would interrupt a lot—try to put words in my mouth, such as, "What you meant to say was this." I think this may be a habit of hers. So, finally I just became annoyed and told her . . . [interrupting her own train of thought and trying to sound less assertive], I mean I asked her to be quiet. So it was that kind of intrusion, she was asserting herself based upon her own racial and cultural perspective. (Field notes, 9/ 25/89. Clarification mine, my emphasis)

Faye affirmed this observation:

In our small groups she [referring to Dana] had this need to talk *for* us. When she said, "Now I get to be a minority," it was a way of announcing her power to speak for us. It was clear that she was not in any way demonstrating or experiencing the characteristics of being a minority, of having no power. She transposed the air of superiority within her claim to be a minority.

In response to my query about how the students felt themselves to be positioned in relation to this, there were two responses:

(Faye): At that moment [laughing sarcastically] I was very annoyed with her, to be honest. I felt she used the ideas of the group to come off with this minority stuff, while taking this air of superiority—this air of "*I'm more important because I have all the right language as a white woman.*" (Field notes, 9/25/ 89, my emphasis)

(Ceciley): You could see, Dr. Roman, that we have a pretty interesting racial mixture in this class and that reading *Orientalism* was going to produce some pretty interesting groups for discussion. But when Dana gleefully made the remark that "for once, I get to be a minority," all she meant was she was outnumbered by blacks . . . she was the only white in the group. We all noticed that she joined our group. And when she made that remark, we all heard it—heard the racism. So, we kinda noticed that she wanted to control the group. (Field notes, 9/ 25/89)

This interaction fails to enact the doomsday scenario of some variants of postmodernist theory, which predict that, in the interest of taking antiracist stances in the classroom, I as a critical theorist would *inevitably* impose my own version of reality on the class; or, that as a white woman, I would easily or inescapably effect the rescription and ultimately disempowering effects of yet another master narrative of white supremacy.[55] While it is important to be wary of the potential for benevolent disempowering "regimes of truth" to emerge from the actions of purportedly liberatory pedagogy, it does not follow that repressive and silencing effects are inevitable outcomes of all forms of advocacy. Whatever insights I had about how racism works or whatever mistakes I made in taking antiracist stances, I clearly did *not* tell these African-American women anything about which they were not astute critics themselves. Nor did my antiracist stance diminish their epistemic claims in objective and subjective terms. But I was left to wonder whether and how such a conversation could be *enacted* in the classroom with other white students.

Racism in Resurgence

Southern Politeness: Interchange Without Dialogue

In the next months, the course focused on the assumptions and criticisms of feminist ethnographies, attempting to stage alternative courses of action for the practice of ethnography. Students were assigned research forays into groups they were interested in studying. We compared feminist critiques, such as those of Anne Oakely, Judith Stacey, and my own work against the assumptions of naturalistic ethnography, with its emphasis on the neutrality of the researcher, or what I earlier called *intellectual tourism* and *voyeurism*.[56] I asked the students to choose between embarking upon the conventions of naturalism and the dialogical participatory modes of research praxis, and to begin to explore the methodological and ethical stances that would follow from such a choice.[57]

My observation at this point was that in terms of the public interchanges between the African-American and white students, the class was well on the way to connecting the issues of democratic practice in research with those of respectful interchange between racial groups. Later, I would learn of other interchanges, and subtly nuanced communications, that occurred in the interstices of classroom social relations and that stirred discomfort and displeasure on the parts of each group at having to share the classroom speaking space with the other in the context of the white students' racial defensiveness. By the end of the term, however, the conflicts over who could claim legitimately to belong to a racially oppressed "minority" group resurfaced in the class. I discovered that *speaking with,* or aligning with the interests of the African-American women by challenging the *emergent racism* of the white students in the classroom, was not in and of itself a sufficient act or gesture. As a feminist materialist, I never thought the work of antisexism would be completed in one stance or a single coalition with other women. In this situation, though, my *racially privileged naivete* permitted me to underestimate how the recent resurgence of racism in Louisiana, and on the LSU campus in particular, could have eroded the ground on which the class would be able to stand, to reveal that ground as cloaked in the *veneer of Southern politeness:* interchange *without* candid dialogue, trust, or reciprocity.

The Problem of Ethnography as "Going Slumming"

During the months in which the class explored more dialogical modes of conducting ethnographic research, David Duke's political success as a viable candidate for senator legitimated a frightening rise in racist and sexist incidents as well as the appropriation by whites of the rhetoric of affirmative action to promote pro-racist and sexist groups and ideologies.[58] Thus, the recurrence of a white student appropriating the category of racial oppression would not have been out of context in this environment. Nonetheless, I was again to be surprised by its recurrence. On the last day of class, I had invited students to present their final projects after a potluck in the more informal atmosphere of my apartment. They were to present the short descriptions and analyses from their field forays of the groups they had selected to study. I explicitly asked students to note in their presentations the times when they felt particular conventions of ethnography drew them into the stances of *intellectual tourism* and *voyeurism*. The class agreed that oral presentations to the group would allow them to obtain feedback from the variety of perspectives represented by each of us as situated social subjects and analysts.

As the students began to arrive, the group of African-American students who commuted together from New Orleans reported to me that two white male college students, neighbors of mine, upon seeing them had called out racial slurs to them from their doorway and then slammed the door. Despite this incident, which was reported matter-of-factly, the atmosphere in the room was one of end-of-semester relief and friendly interchange. I saw no overt evidence of racial polarization. Before the student presentations began, the students exchanged stories about exams, the vacations they hoped to take, and how much they had looked forward to this opportunity to be together informally. Dana, who had earlier in the term said, "Now, I get to be a minority," announced excitedly that she was very proud of her ethnographic foray and eager to make the first presentation. The class agreed at once to accommodate her request. With enthusiasm in her voice, she began narrating her sojourn to a soup kitchen run by a parish in another inner-city neighborhood, where she solicited the permission of soup kitchen personnel to be one of the regular servers on the line. Representing herself as a *neutral observer* who blended in with the homeless people she researched, she described in detail how they dressed, moved through the line, spoke to each other, and ate. The pseudonyms she chose for the research subjects were stereotypical first names usually given by whites to African-Americans. Noticeably absent in her discourse was any analytic interest in, or mention of, the social backgrounds of the people she had observed. This fact did not go unnoticed by the African-American students or myself. Ceciley, one of the African-American students, interrupted her to ask, "What were the racial backgrounds of the people you studied?" Dana replied, somewhat chagrined at the question: "Black. Black, of course. Didn't you realize they were black?" Again, I was appalled at the explicit pride she took in this most graphic example of *intellectual tourism* and *voyeurism,* now recalled at the expense of all the African-American students who listened. Before I could gather myself for a critical response, she turned directly to me, saying,

> Dr. Roman, I really believe I understand what you mean by critical ethnography now because I went to this soup kitchen and I was amazed to see that these poor homeless people have a social order. I watched how they dressed, who got in line first, and who could give the signal for the meal to be eaten. I sort of have a feeling now about what it's like to be on the line, to be one of them. It was fascinating to see them make culture. I mean, *I really felt in touch with the real world just by going there.* I was surprised to see how complex just getting

food is at the soup kitchen, how it's a society all its own. (Field notes, 12/14/89, confirmed later in interview, 10/10/90, my emphasis)

I waited briefly to see whether any white students would challenge her *going slumming* approach or any of her other assumptions. None did so. Their reactions were an even greater source of interest to me when I observed that the white students were not making eye contact with Dana or with the other white students. They appeared to be uncomfortable. One of the white students maintained downcast eyes throughout Dana's presentation. The two other whites made fleeting eye contact with the African-American students, as if to check out their reactions. Failing to see any challenges to the racism of Dana's report, I felt I could not keep silent—even in the interest of avoiding speaking as the voice of teacherly authority. Judging from the stunned silence in the room, all seemed to have been powerfully affected by the account and summation of this foray. With much less detachment than the previous occasion had afforded me, I passionately countered her assumptions with a series of questions. I asked who benefitted from her foray, with the aim of challenging Dana's assumption that it was acceptable to peer into the lives of subordinate *others* and give nothing back that they define as useful knowledge or insight into the conditions oppressing them. I asked her to consider what kind of institutional structures make it possible for middle-class whites to be unaware of, or insulated from, dire poverty or to have so little contact with the world she described in her discourse as "so real," presumably in contrast to her own. Because my comments directly responded to her work, and I did not wish her to feel singled out, I specifically mentioned that she was not alone in making such assumptions. Structural inequalities of race, class, and gender relations, I argued, made possible the discourse of her ethnographic foray. Despite my interest in maintaining a non-threatening exchange, she reacted defensively, reiterating her earlier claim that her point of view was that of an "unbiased observer" and not as a white middle-class researcher. The other white students did not join Dana in publicly expressing similar experiences of having "gone slumming" in an African-American context. Nor did they verbally voice approval for the idea of conducting her foray and its presentation in this manner.

The reactions I heard from the African-American students immediately after the class and later in interviews concerned how they felt hearing her naturalizing the idea that it ought to be understood that "blacks, of course" were standing in soup kitchen lines, or that she, as a white, had the right to essentially "go slumming" in a soup kitchen. They frankly volunteered their readings of Dana's racial representations and the effects of my intervention on classroom dynamics. They focused in particular on what it felt like to identify with the racially stereotypical subjects of Dana's foray. They discussed the anger they felt when she presumed all those who frequented the soup kitchen to be naturally "black, of course." As Ceciley commented,

> What makes me annoyed and amazed is that Dana really thought she should be congratulated, patted on the head by you—by all of us—for having sacrificed this time and effort to go see those pitiful little black people at the soup kitchen. Had you [referring to me] not brought out the reality of how she appeared, then she would have misled herself and the other whites for life. And what's really amazing is that after invading these people's lives, she pretends to know them. You know, she does not know us. We . . . [referring to herself and Ruby, another African-American student in the class] conducted a little experiment recently to see if Dana would acknowledge our presence in another class we all take together on Fridays. She didn't even speak to us. We went into the restroom at break to freshen our faces after being on the road and she was there, and of course, made no effort to speak with us even though we have this class together. (Field notes, 12/14/89 and confirmed later in interview, 10/12/90)

Faye added to Ceciley's comments:

> I thought Dana assumed that it was natural for black people to be homeless. She kept telling the story—oral stories of each research subject as though they were characters in a play, like a folktale. And then she used only their first names. That's what gave me the feeling she thought all the homeless were black and at soup kitchens. And I thought it was strange how she presumed to be so comfortable with these people so soon after meeting them—so comfortable being an expert of their culture. You know what I mean? This was more exploitation than anything else. Here was an example of an ethnographer invading the privacy of black homeless people because they are not thought to have any privacy, being homeless. (Field notes, 12/14/89 and confirmed later in interview, 10/12/90)

And Coretta joined in:

> I just can't believe how angry and annoyed I feel to hear her
> once again position us [referring to the African-American
> women students] as subordinates. It was quite a surprise to
> hear her say that all the people she observed were "black, of
> course!" because, I thought, well, they could have been white! I
> mean I was visualizing white skid row bums in a downtown
> segment of the city where you often find soup kitchens catering
> to white skid row bums, winos, or whatever. But again, there
> we have it, a white is saying this false reality to us and we're
> supposed to sit there politely and listen. (Field notes, 12/14/89
> and later confirmed in interview, 10/11/90)

After they had expressed these feelings and insights, with which I
concurred, I asked the African-American women how they perceived
my intervention concerning Dana's discourse; whether it too constituted what Faye had just identified as a form of exploitative speaking
for others. They commented that Dana appeared to be in "a state of
disbelief" that her presentation was not going over positively because,
as Faye put it, Dana had expected to find common ground with me as
another white and was hurt and surprised that I had not aligned with
her.

There was a consensus among them that my intervention was a
necessary critique of Dana's racist assumptions. They welcomed the
advocacy of my antiracist stance, which prevented them from having
"to go out on the line with white liberals," as Coretta aptly stated. But
they also expressed discomfort at what they took to be an almost
unavoidable result of my confrontation of white students regarding
their racism in a mixed racial context. Although they mentioned that
the intervention was necessary to begin any genuine interracial dialogue
in the classroom, they believed it had the contradictory potential for
deepening racial tensions in an already polarized set of racial relations:

> I thought your intervention was a dose of reality. . . . I don't
> think she or many other whites here have ever been confronted
> with the consequences of what they're saying, especially in Da-
> na's case. I mean it's very different to get that feedback from a
> white, publicly, in front of us. I think considering the history of
> LSU, of the different races of people and their different histor-
> ies here, your intervention could have had polarizing effects for
> whites. And I don't know how you get out of that. Perhaps, if

Dana had been in a class only with other whites, maybe she would have felt more comfortable with the challenges to her racism. But rarely is there any confrontation of that sort made here in Louisiana, in the classroom, in education. Rarely is there a possibility to make dialogue possible. That's what I value from this class. (Field notes, Faye, 12/14/89 and later confirmed in interview, 10/12/90)

Ceciley stated:

You were speaking against racism, most definitely speaking for us in the sense of not tolerating racism, but your speaking was not a speaking that prevented us as African-American women from speaking for ourselves. The problem is whites don't want to hear that kind of speaking, especially when we're [African-Americans] in their presence. (Field notes, 12/14/89 and later confirmed in interview, 10/12/90, my clarification)

And Coretta spoke of my intervention as a necessary step to take for the benefit of whites, making sure I understood that my critique of Dana's practices was not news to the African-American women:

The thing that will really sticks with us is your intervention. We watched your body language and we could all tell you were becoming uncomfortable with her taking the voyeur position. Your intervention was an important one, a necessary step for you as a white to take with the white students. But we were reading her well already. So, we welcomed your critique of her practice and your solidarity with us, even if it made some of the white students a bit defensive. (Field notes, 12/14/89 and later confirmed in interview, 10/11/90)

The comments of Ceciley, Faye, and Coretta impressed upon me the implications of silence on the part of a white teacher in the perpetuation of racism. Yet they also reminded me to be mindful of not furthering the polarizations of existing racial divisions through my speaking out against racism. The insights of the African-American students suggested that it might be appropriate, on occasions when racist comments are made in the class, to create contexts for racially specific focus groups to analyze the personal and structural effects of racism. In other words, in order for dialogue to occur across very different racial histories, it might be necessary and advantageous for groups to have autonomous as well as integrated spaces within the class to consider the effects of particular classroom dynamics of racism.[59] Had I been aware of the need for such an approach and therefore in a position to practice it in the class, perhaps the white students would have been less inclined to withdraw before the second term.

Antiracist Pedagogy and the Problem of White Resistance to Racial Equality

In retrospect, it is not surprising that the white students did not continue the course. It is clear, from the polite conversational interracial rapport during the class and with me when I later interviewed the white students, that their resistance to reflexively challenging their own relation to a system of white domination was *tacit, persistent, and subject to little public discussion,* particularly in the presence of the African-American students. Well after the time when grades were posted or they need fear my reprisal, I asked each of them why they discontinued the course, how they perceived specific interventions and pedagogical choices I made with my antiracist stances, and how they felt and what they learned as a consequence. They politely and deferentially gave the following telling reasons for discontinuation:

> (Susan:) I just couldn't handle all that talk of the racial stuff and oppression. It's too depressing *they* [referring to the African-American women] *made me feel uncomfortable.* But it wasn't anything you did. Do they [referring to the African-American students] think you were being racist? Cuz, most of us [referring to the white students] thought you were very fair, always open to different interpretations?

> (LGR:) I am curious. How did the African-American women "make you feel uncomfortable"?

> (Susan:) *By just having to look at their faces when things got uncomfortable in class.* (Interview, 10/13/90, my emphasis)

* * *

> (Marsha:) My schedule got screwed up and I have to take statistics. I realize it would cut out *the commuters* [referring to the African-American women who were the only commuters], but is there any way you could offer the second semester course early in the day?

(LGR:) Why? Does your statistics class overlap with critical ethnography?

(Marsha:) [After an awkward pause.] No. I just don't want to get into the racial [issues] again. It's too real, too depressing, and what can I do about it anyway? (Interview, 10/11/90, clarification mine)

***

(Karina:) I'm trying to focus on feminist electives now before I have to go back to Germany. I want to take more Women's Studies courses that look at gender and not so much at race.

(LGR:) Do you think racial issues are not women's issues?

(Karina:) Well, not in the other Women's Studies courses I have taken. (Interview, 10/13/90)

***

(Dana:) I just couldn't take it anymore. *You were partial to the black girls from New Orleans. I can't remember their names,* but you were partial to them, which is unfair because everyone today is a minority in some way. Besides, my children need family around them and I decided to move back to the East for that reason. (Interview, 10/13/90, my emphasis)

Recurring themes structure the discourses of the white women as racially privileged subjects, such as a desire to avoid public confrontation or to rethink and challenge their own stances within such unequal power relations. Their reasons for retreat and withdrawal varied: from a sense of helplessness, to not seeing the relevance of racial issues within feminist gender concerns; from scheduling problems, to competing interests to which they gave higher priority. Most of these appeared to simply mask the underlying reasons for not returning to face other encounters with the African-American women, whose names some of them could not remember or perhaps never learned.

It is significant that within the discourse of white privilege my antiracist stances were not cited by the white women as attempts to confront racism or as alliances with the African-American women. Instead, they were framed in terms of how they affected my treatment of the white students. My having taken racism seriously was either seen as my ability to be "fair and open to different interpretations," despite an imagined accusation of racism by African-American students as the reason I would ask the question, or, conversely, as my being "partial to the black girls from New Orleans" and, thus, unfair to the white students. Private expressions of racism appeared to work effectively beneath the polite public reasons given for discontinuing in the class.[60]

In follow-up interviews with the white and African-American students, I pursued discovering whether or not an informal consensus had developed among the white women not to return, specifically because my challenge to Dana's soup kitchen foray broke the unspoken rule of not challenging racism directly, particularly in the presence of African-Americans. Although I was not able to confirm any informal discussions among the white women directed at deciding to discontinue, I learned of another compelling emotional dynamic underlying the white students' decisions not to take the class the second term. In a word, *shame* was the feeling three students expressed—a feeling they experienced when they heard Dana describe underclass African-Americans in racially pejorative terms. As Susan expressed it:

(LGR:) How did you view my intervention with Dana on the last day of the class?

(Susan:) It's like, when [pauses, takes a deep breath]—I remember that instance with Dana the last day of class very clearly. I remember thinking she's [speaking of Dana] really got an attitude of superiority, but that's not racism. I remember thinking that was typical of her. She was thinking of the racial aspect when she told us of her foray. At that moment I felt ashamed, ashamed to be white, ashamed to look at their black faces [referring the African-American students who were the receivers of Dana's narrative]. I didn't want to look at their black faces in the room.

(LGR:) You felt ashamed because you sympathized with the pain the African-American students may have felt while they listened?

(Susan): Yes. That's why I couldn't look at their faces or go on taking the class. I didn't know what to do. I felt helpless. (Interview, 10/13/90)

I found Williams's appreciation of Brecht's ideas about contradictory consciousness to go part of the way in explaining how the discourse of white racial privilege works. Williams recognized that there are interconnections between the contradictory individual consciousness of individuals and the moral and political dilemmas that are beyond individual reach. The white students simultaneously had material and ideological stakes in maintaining relations of racial oppression and in ashamedly witnessing its unjust consequences. Finally, when the self-exposure of witnessing Dana's narrative became intolerable, they withdrew. Contradictory subjectivity explains why and how the white women could not face further interaction with the African-American women after hearing their own implication in the racism of Dana's narration.

This, of course, raises the important question of what educators ought to do with that moment when white students recognize not only that racism exists at levels deeper than the expression of individual prejudices but also feel ashamed to be implicated in its structural practice—ashamed to face those who have suffered from racism. Williams realized that systemic problems such as racism were beyond individual solution, but he did not use this realization to argue for inaction, retreat, or shameful helplessness. Ashamed contradictory white subjects are not absolved of their responsibility to build effective social alternatives to structural racism. If white students are to become empowered critical analysts of their own claims to know the privileged world in which their racial interests function, it strikes me now that such privileges and the injustices they reap for others must become the *objects* of analyses of structural racism, to the effect that subjects move from paralyzing shame and guilt to stances in which we/they take effective responsibility and action for disinvesting in racial privilege.

Speaking With as the "Complex Seeing of Analysis"

Culture Talks Back: Re-Writing "Desire"

In contrast to the experience of white students discontinuing their participation, the African-American students firmly and vigorously pursued their research interests in the second term, developing a greater solidarity with one another and with me. This was evidenced by the fact that class differences among them were now open for discussion, differences which had to go unmentioned the previous term. Because the classroom was not consumed by having to deal with overt racism, theoretical and political differences among the African-American women could emerge as part of thoughtful classroom dialogue without provoking defensiveness. These differences proved to serve as resources in their critiques of each other's work.

Throughout the term, I was acutely aware of the arduous commute the students made to Baton Rouge. I offered, and they readily accepted, the idea of holding our last class in New Orleans, where four of the five lived and worked. The class was to be held at Southern University (SUNO), where Ceciley worked.[61] Although I was given excellent directions, I managed to take a wrong turn after exiting the freeway in my approach to the general area in New Orleans. I found myself suddenly an *accidental tourist* and *voyeur,* driving into the *Desire Housing Project.* I was uncomfortable seeing dilapidated wooden structures, railroad tracks, and a wire fence walled in and separating this neighborhood, peopled predominately by underclass African-Americans, from other, white neighborhoods. Many of the houses stood on stilts, whose function I could not fathom. I noted not only the lack of regular street signs at corners, but also the fact that the street names appeared on telephone pole-like posts, barely visible even in daylight. Certainly, I thought to myself, this was a neighborhood designed not for visitors but for people meant to be kept apart from their wealthier, more privileged others. What struck me most, after the appallingly depressed conditions, were the names of the streets themselves: *Pleasure, Humanity, Benefit, Desire,* and *Abundance.*[62] What an ironic set of metaphors for this occasion of my token attempt to hold the class outside the white-dominated context of LSU in Baton Rouge.

Upon finally reaching SUNO, Ceciley greeted me with a hug in the main administrative building. Again, I was struck by iconographic and symbolic reminders of place and my temporary re-[or dis-]location to an educational institution with a very different historical relationship to structural racism than that of LSU. I was not at LSU, where one of the two faculty dining halls was unapologetically named *The Plantation Room,* where the Anglo-American museum proudly announced its effort to preserve the "heritage" of particular white ethnic groups, and where only recently were half-day holidays legally permitted to honor Martin Luther King's contributions to the civil rights movement. As I stood facing a large painted collage-like mural depicting civil rights leaders from different eras, including Martin Luther King, I felt inspired by their community activism and struggles for racial equality. Yet I also felt appropriately haunted and discomforted by the living ghost of my racial privilege. I wondered to what extent any retelling of my drive through *Desire* could later satiate the pleasures and fascinations of white readers to consume representations of horrors we allegedly oppose.[63]

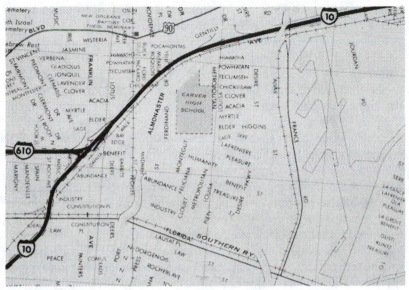

Figure 1 Desire Housing Project
From ©Rand McNally Map of New Orleans. (Photograph by Bill Wong.)

As we entered the room Ceciley selected for our class discussion, I mentioned to the class what must have seemed obvious: my feeling of being shaken by the drive through *Desire,* with its reminders of my privileged racial location. I apologized for my lateness, explaining to the class how I had gotten lost in *Desire.* Not the least surprised by my awkwardness, Ceciley responded knowingly, using a prophetic phrase, "It was meant to be that you got lost in *Desire.* That's where we take white middle-class parents when we want them to vote in favor of raising property taxes for the public schools" (Field notes, 5/3/90). I confessed that I felt like an *intellectual tourist* and *voyeur,* having been struck by the obvious contradiction of the street names to the very material conditions they stood against. Coretta immediately seized upon this, saying, "You know, I never really thought about this contradiction but it's true!" The class began an interesting semiotic analysis of the street names and their political history. Some, such as Ceciley, who were long-term residents of the city in various neighborhoods, commented that all of the streets were named by the white city council. They recalled the ways neighborhoods were bounded and demarcated in racial terms, separating who went to what schools, and how they knew as children that their schools were the ones without material resources, understaffed, and consequently thought of by most white and African-American teachers and parents as "inferior."

This discussion prompted Coretta, who was from a middle-class background and who was close friends with Faye, who was from a working-class background, to remember that Faye had grown up in the Ninth Ward near the *Desire Housing Project* and knew all too well the human costs of such material conditions. While Coretta told the story in Faye's absence, it was spoken with the utmost of respect for Faye's experience. Faye, some of us learned for the first time, lost her seventeen-year-old brother in the floods and tidal waves caused by the 1965 hurricane *Betsy,* when white property owners from a wealthy part of the city decided, rather than to suffer property damage from the flooding, to pressure city officials and the Army Corps of Engineers into diverting the overflowing waters of the Mississippi through the Industrial Canal and into Lake Pontchartrain, thus flooding the impoverished area surrounding the *Desire Housing Project.* As Coretta told us, and most of the African-American students similarly began to recall, the floods had been staggering. In Faye's neighborhood, they had reached beyond stilts designed to keep houses above water. Faye's brother, who was among the few residents who knew how to swim, nonetheless drowned, in the undercurrent while trying to get help for his family members, who were perched on the roof for safety.[64]

Coretta did not narrate this story in the sentimental or defeatist way that might characterize the recordings of a naturalistic ethnographer. Nor did she claim her own middle-class experiences of racial oppression were identical to Faye's. Yet in the animated discussion that followed, the African-American women all spoke of knowing in different ways what it meant to grow up in the segregated neighborhoods of New Orleans. A *regenerative collective engagement* became apparent to all of us in the context of this exchange, not because the "weness" constructed was one free of asymmetries of power and authority between and among us. Quite the contrary, the critical analysis of our different class and racial relations to a larger system of racial oppression began to transform the quality of our dialogue from one of conflict masked by false polite consensus into one that established more common ground for an open exchange of views, risk of conflict, and productive criticism.

Establishing Common Ground: Dialogue Through Conflict

One example of a persistent unstated conflict between us became more explicit on this occasion. In the context of daring to ask what it would mean to build a multiracial feminist coalition, Alexa reported why she felt wary of, and at times weary from, dialogue with well-intentioned whites, especially feminists. She began by complaining of exhaustion from having to live up to her family's expectation of her being the mythic "matriarchal figure" in the family.[65] She pondered why and how a mythology she believed originated in white authors' reports on "black welfare mothers" could now circulate so freely among her own family members as a stereotype she ought to fulfill. This generalized criticism of white authors' representations of African-American families then moved to the particulars of our classroom dynamics, to my attempts at taking antiracist stances, and my follow-up attempts to solicit students' feedback. She observed that after I had confronted Dana with the problem of narrating her soup kitchen foray as an *intellectual tourist* and *voyeur,* Dana "made the rounds," seeking emotional support from the African-American women in class, including herself. She asked to be reassured in *liberal terms* that she had not been racist in that moment—reassurance Alexa and the other African-American students felt was inappropriate and exhausting to give. Upon hearing this, I asked them whether my attempts to take antiracist stances were not also hopelessly reinscribed within the same dynamic of bearing well-meaning liberal intentions that come to no effect and, further, how I could know from them what constituted effective antiracist stances on my part unless I solicited their feedback in a dialogical way. Coretta quickly let me know that she appreciated the difference between my stances regarding institutional racism and the lack of them in Dana's presentation, which barely acknowledged racism on any level. But she also issued the important criticism that I expressed too much doubt about the effectivity of my stances, which was, after all, another way of paralyzing oneself with racial guilt—a guilt that easily translated into overly needy demands for their emotional support and validation:

> We realized you were alone up there in the class with all that white racism to deal with—that you had needed us too for emotional support. Every time I drive into the campus area, I think of that moss hanging on the big trees. I get this creepy feeling of history and I'm thankful that at the end of class I get to drive back to New Orleans. But I think of you having to work there. One thing you should know is that you shouldn't think that every time you ask me for feedback about whether your teaching went far enough in challenging racism . . . assuming that I won't be straight with you. Sometimes though, I

don't have the answer. But, it's exhausting to me if you can't trust what we've built. (Classroom conversation, 5/3/90)

Difficult as it was to hear, I learned from this criticism that the problem was *not* that I *had* solicited their feedback regarding the effectivity of particular stances I had taken; rather, it was the exhausting manner in which I sometimes practiced my dialogical research methods. Paradoxically, by confronting them with my suspicions at every turn that my actions were merely expressing the well-meaning intentions of the white enemy "other" instead of the directed and self-assured efforts of someone whom they recognized was self-consciously *doubly voiced* with the aim of working *against* her racial privilege, I wore them out. I was gently forewarned that if I did not avoid the excesses of racial guilt, I would gradually strain the trust and grounds for dialogue we had built.[66]

Despite the undeniable asymmetries that were and are between us, I would now argue that collective *speaking with* one another was possible because lived conditions of difference and cultural location were being acknowledged, honestly discussed, and then collectively theorized as the living social texts of the class. The narrative of Faye's brother's death emerged from self-censored and yet imposed silence, from *unspeakable so-called private pain,* to become *publically legitimate classroom knowledge.* This knowledge now informed a group effort to elicit evidence of the hidden structural barriers to understanding. The class's critique did not speak of the causes of Faye's brother's death as a tragedy resulting from a natural disaster of hurricane floods; rather, the event was renamed as a social and political injustice. It was spoken of as the consequence of inequalities that permitted one neighborhood to suffer loss of life and homes so that another could attempt to avoid property damage.

Unfinished Postscript: Cautionary Notes and *"Resources of Hope"*

Postmodernist relativism was not revisited by the students who took to task its standard for treating all claims to be racially oppressed as equally valid representations of *reality.* They reconsidered the racial oppression claims of white students from the previous semester and weighed them relationally against their own. Ceciley led the class in a discussion of Dana's earlier self-satisfied exclamation, "Now, I get to be a minority!" She expressed how she remembered it with new insight but also with renewed anger. Dana's misidentification of herself as a subject of racial oppression could no longer be seen as separable from the story told of Faye's loss. It was another symptom of the narrative of structural racism: like the misnaming of the streets of the *Desire Housing Project* by white city council members, it was a misnaming that unnamed those who lived with the actual condition of a racism rendered *unspeakable*.

Although I was implicated *in* the story Coretta told of Faye's loss, I was reminded by feminist literary critic Amy Gordon, who, following the significant insight of Toni Morrison, argues that this telling was not *for* me; rather, I was "invited to eavesdrop," to listen to a story told for and by the African-American women for their own purposes of *solidarity* (*GS*, 246). This "invitation" was at once a symbol of the unequal power relations and a gesture of emerging trust between us. And although they invited me to listen, my acceptance of the invitation committed me to struggle with the discomfort of hearing what they said and to confront the ethical and political dilemmas and responsibilities of "translating" adequately what I heard into revisions of my own pedagogical practice. Because it is not enough to listen privately or vicariously, to merely enjoy the special status of being the one white allowed to overhear, I am obliged to negotiate the important distinctions between a story of which I am a part and a story written for someone else (*GS*, 246).

Faye's story was not told for the racially privileged consumers who will read this essay, but nonetheless, as Gordon says, "the ghost-writer passed it on anyway and now it lingers. Uneasily between the story-teller and the one who is listening for the 'inner ear sound,' the story lingers somewhere [we] can barely reach" (*GS*, 246). I continue to be in the story to the extent that it is my responsibility to speak against *emergent* forms of *white defensiveness* and *appropriate speech*. To remain silent leaves African-American women, as Ceciley told me, "to mop up after white folks' racism" (Interview, 12/10/90). I am also in the story to the extent that I have much to learn about how to work with white students to transform their (our) desire to be included in the narrative of racial oppression as its disadvantaged victims into one that fully accounts for the daily ways we (whites) benefit from *conferred* racial privilege as well as from our complicity in the often invisible institutional and structural workings of racism. As a white teacher it remains my responsibility to work with racially privileged students (and educators) to foster an understanding that their (our) attempts to assume the positions of the racially oppressed are also the result of our contradictory desires to misrecognize and recognize the collective shame of *facing* those who have been *effaced* in the dominant texts of culture, history, and curricular knowledge. Such (mis)-representations, or the allowance for them to speak in the name of the *real,* are only successful if we as educators permit them to go unchallenged. Left unchallenged, they may silence, or, worse yet, eclipse any memory of the historical, economic, and cultural conditions under which they were produced. But my task as an educator is not to reproduce demogogic theories of exclusiveness, in which only African-American or other racially subordinate students can be allowed to comprehend the experiences of racism. As I learned, this only intensifies existing white defensiveness rather than promoting knowledge of one's role in the structural story of racism.

I am in this story, but only to the extent that I can begin to hear that neither myself nor the white students are its central subjects. The biographical narratives the African-American women dared to tell me were *not* the texts of *my redemption.* Yet "having surrendered to the story," I am, as Gordon says, "still recovering, having to acknowledge" that its authors and their texts raised questions for me that they "could not and should not have to answer for me" (*GS,* 246). I once again realize that working with others to produce possibilities for more socially just realities promises no narrative closure. Perhaps I have learned and listened well enough to know that all the work of *retelling* and *rewriting* culture has yet to be accomplished. And, if for some feminism is the happy "victim of the postmodern breakdown of authority," then "ironically it can benefit from the modernist virtue of risk-taking" in the act of deciding with whom we shall speak, how we shall listen, and what we shall now do.[67] On the occasion of *teaching with* this class, I was reminded in a most powerful way why Williams devoted so much of his life and work to taking the risks entailed by his unfinished project in the attempt to establish a practice of socially transformative critical realism.

Part III

Culture's Others: Culture or Cultural Imperialism?

9

Raymond Williams and British Colonialism: The Limits of Metropolitan Cultural Theory

Gauri Viswanathan

The failure of the British Left to conceptualize cultural practices in relation to imperialism is most pronounced in its unproblematic conflation of the terms "national" and "imperial." One would least expect to find this tendency in such works as Brian Doyle's *English and Englishness* (1989), Alan Sinfield's *Literature, Politics, and Culture in Postwar Britain* (1989), or Robert Colls and Philip Dodd's *Englishness* (1987), where the "naturalness" of English culture is rejected as a false premise obscuring a history of invented discourses and disciplines.[1] But the ways of reading the "invention" of national culture are as varied as the discourses themselves, and when read as ideologically motivated by social currents and institutional developments exclusively within England, as by these critics, English "national culture" acquires a narrow and limited definition whose generative events are safely circumscribed within local boundaries. This restriction thus makes it possible, for instance, for Brian Doyle to argue that English studies "embodied not only the high culture of 'polite society' but also the 'national character,' " to the point that the discipline of English came to be promoted as "uniquely suited to a mission of national cultivation"[2]; and for Sinfield to observe that the cultural monuments of England served as an instrument of "national domination" elsewhere.[3]

What makes imperial culture possible, both Doyle and Sinfield suggest, is an already existing national culture that is itself a product of mediation between local class tensions. For these critics, the success of

217

national culture abroad is attributable to a comparable negotiation of competing demands in a colonized population reorganized to correspond to English class structure. Here it can be seen that one of the unfortunate effects of conflating "national" and "imperial" is the elimination of important historical distinctions that would make a simple equation between class and racial ideologies more difficult, if not impossible. For instance, when the tensions between secular and religious tendencies in British culture are studied from outside the parameters of English society, it soon becomes apparent that British class conflicts are not fully explanatory of those tensions, and that they do not satisfactorily constitute the only, or primary, point of reference. The importance of the colonies for diffusing, maintaining, and redefining these conflicts makes it all the more urgent to consider English culture first and foremost in its imperial aspect and then to examine that aspect as itself constitutive of "national" culture. Such a project challenges the assumption that what makes an imperial culture possible is a fully formed national culture shaped by internal social developments; it also provokes one to search for ways to reinsert "imperial" into "national" without reducing the two terms to a single category.

The tendency to work with both "national" and "imperial" as interchangeable terms is noticeable in the work of Terry Eagleton, Chris Baldick, Brian Doyle, and Alan Sinfield, among others. But we would have to go back to Raymond Williams to trace the genealogy of a critical approach that consistently and exclusively studies the formation of metropolitan culture from within its own boundaries. Williams has written on Western culture with such brilliant insight and illumination that to cast aspersions on his work for its neglect of imperial influences might seem churlish at best. My intent in this essay is not to harangue Williams for his failure to account for imperialism's shaping hand in English culture—indeed, there is no novelty or originality in finding fault with Williams on this point—but to examine how and why Williams's analysis of sociocultural processes in nineteenth-century England, with its primary focus on English class formation, left a nebulous space that at one level seemed to allow for the potential broadening of that analysis to include colonizer-colonized relations but at another implicitly resisted such further refinements. My view is that Williams's "silence" about imperialism is less a theoretical oversight or blindness than an internal restraint that has complex methodological and historical origins. These require illumination and explication, since they are symptomatic of persistently obstinate problems in the serious study of imperialism and culture.

Questions are periodically raised about Williams's alleged ambiguity toward culture and imperialism, and they range from the genteel to the querulous: Does such ambiguity mean that his cultural theory is flawed to begin with? Are the intellectual paradigms for discussing imperialism simply unavailable to him? Can Williams offer an effective alternative to studying culture exclusive of imperial relations?[4] At first glance it would seem that these questions lose some of their contentiousness in the context of *The Country and the City*. This work stands out as the exemplary text linking English social formation with the economics of imperialism, and it does so through the characterization of the metropolis as the site of political and economic control. The connection between the two, however, is built on more than simply the power of analogy: if the city's relation to the country can be understood as replicated in the relation of the imperial metropolis to the subject colony, then the capitalist accumulation at the metropolitan center, "the extension to the whole world of that division of functions which in the nineteenth century was a division of functions within a single state," points in the direction of an appropriation of global economic power by one and the same class. As Williams asserts, "the model of the city and country, in economic and political relations, has gone beyond the boundaries of the nation-state. . . . What was happening in the 'city,' the 'metropolitan' economy, determined and was determined by what was made to happen in the 'country': first the local hinterland and then the vast regions beyond it, in other people's lands."[5]

And yet, as Williams is quick to point out, colonial territories do not function merely as an analogous term to "country." Williams takes great care to stress that the relation of the metropolis to the country on the one hand and to the colonies on the other cannot be understood as interchangeable; quite the contrary, he emphasizes that colonial developments had a more direct and immediate effect on the ascendancy of the metropolis, contributing in the long run to the eventual decline of England's rural base. The profits that successfully transformed Britain into an industrial and urban society were generated by the new rural economy of tropical plantations and the whole organized colonial system of which it was a part. Williams insists on the inseparability of the decline of England's rural areas from these developments in the colonies. That decline, he notes, was further hastened by newly created problems of poverty and overcrowded cities, in partial solution of which the colonies acquired new significance as places of emigration.

But this is as far as Williams's analysis goes, despite the theoretical status accorded the colonies as vital influences on British society. The relationality of British imperialism and culture is not further theorized;

wherever connections are suggested between the two, they tend to take the form of ironic observation, as, for instance, when Williams traces the way that the colonies came to be constructed in nineteenth-century literature as at once the source of the problem and the solution to it. A tone of understatement and paradox governs his description of British fiction (curiously left unnamed) in which emigration functions thematically as the point marking the novel's dissolution, by which is meant that characters whose lives were not compatible within the system were "put on the boat." Williams interprets this pattern as a simple strategy for resolving the conflict between personal ethic and social experience, while at the same time obviating any further questioning of either the ethic or the experience.[6] The effect of such an interpretation, however, is that colonial territories remain without material presence or substance. The colonies as an actual place impinging on the lives of these poor characters in powerfully direct, immediate ways cannot be accommodated to Williams's location of dramatic conflict in the self-delusions of characters; the colonies are turned into a vanishing point, the symbolic space for dissolving all problems that cannot be solved at home.

In describing imperialism as one of the "last models" of city and country, Williams obfuscates imperialism's relation to British economic production and, by extension, its cultural formations, by suggesting that British influence extended outward rather than that the periphery had a functional role in determining internal developments.[7] At some points, as, for instance, when he alludes to the country house system as built on the profits of European expansion in the sixteenth and seventeenth centuries, Williams acknowledges that British local developments were vitally affected and shaped by imperial activity. But by and large his understanding of imperial influence is limited to the *effects* of economic profits, and his commentary rarely goes beyond a description of British global involvement as an extension of socioeconomic developments that had already been set in motion within nineteenth-century England. This is all the more remarkable in light of the fact that he is aware that events in the peripheries reshaped and determined domestic relations, as when he writes in *The Country and the City* that "from at least mid-nineteenth century, there was this larger context (of colonial expansion) within which every idea and every image was consciously and unconsciously affected."[8]

Given this insight, why does Williams refrain from studying those ideas and images as factors shaping not just the economic organization of English society but, also, the particular forms in which metropolitan culture was expressed? If, as Williams himself points out,[9] the idealiza-

tion of empire following rural decline and urban concentration constitutes the structure of many industrial novels of the mid-nineteenth
century, why does his own discussion of these novels in *Culture and
Society* and elsewhere exclude empire? Is his reticence an expression
of self-imposed limits, a concession to the practical difficulties of or-
chestrating a sustained cross-referential analysis of English and imperial culture? Or is there some complex inhibition that restrains him
from speaking about English culture and the culture of its imperial
possessions simultaneously, as if speaking about them in the same
breath were tantamount to simplifying or, worse still, distorting their
relations? To put it another way, what is entailed in analyzing these
relations that will make that effort more than a juxtapositional exercise
and will produce not merely description but also explanation of the
particular forms in which English culture came to be expressed?

As these questions suggest, some of Williams's internal restraints are
related to problems of methodology. Edward Said has drawn attention
to Williams's methodological self-consciousness, citing the latter's
comments on Lucien Goldman as an instance of Williams's troubled
awareness that certain theoretical frameworks that had powerful local
appeal were too elusive to offer genuine insight into a global view of
cultural politics: "There was this obvious difficulty: that most of the
work we had to look at was the product of just this work of reified
consciousness, so that what looked like the methodological breakthrough might become, quite quickly, the methodological trap."[10]
What impresses Said most about this passage is that Williams, "as a
critic who has learned from someone else's theory . . . should be able
to see the theory's limitations, especially the fact that a breakthrough
can become a trap, if it is used uncritically, repetitively, limitlessly."[11]
Perhaps the thorniest problem for Williams was how to grapple with
those forms of analyses, both liberal and Marxist, that rely on cause-
effect models for explanations of cultural and social phenomena. Base
and superstructure, to take one example, are two terms that, for Williams, are heavily implicated in theories of causal relations, and he is
acutely aware of the difficulties of pursuing a project that seeks to
go beyond non-deterministic explanations of society, while himself
remaining bound by an obligation to retain some of the more useful
features of such Marxian categories. Williams's own particular contribution to cultural criticism is his construing of culture and society as
activity, through which he challenges the reading of base-superstruc-
tural relations as fixed abstractions. In insisting on a more fluid description of base, Williams set out to study culture and society as active
process, in the broad-based sense that superstructural institutions and

forms of consciousness can equally claim to influence the economic structure as the other way around. Ideally, his approach had the capacity to release critical theory from adherence to notions of predetermination and descriptions of culture and society exclusively from within the parameters of that same society. Indeed, Williams's criticism of Lukács in "Base and Superstructure in Marxist Cultural Theory" is aimed precisely at the latter's hermetic approach to social system. Williams makes it clear that he has no use for a static or highly determined, rule-governed model, in which the rules of society are highlighted to the exclusion of the processual and the historical.[12]

No doubt, the specific relevance of Williams for colonial discourse studies derives from his long-standing quarrel with Lukács and other materialist critics that led to his questioning of economic structures as the sole determining factor of culture and his favoring a model of contestation between dominant and subordinate classes in cultural formation. It will be recalled that Williams's project in *Keywords* was to increase our awareness of the hidden conflicts covered over by words like "democracy" or "culture." As he reminds us, "The book was organized around the new kinds of problems and questions which were articulated not only in the new sense of *culture* but in a whole group of closely associated words. Thus the very language of serious inquiry and argument was in part changed and changing, and my purpose then was to follow this change through in the writing of the very diverse men and women who had contributed to this newly central argument."[13] Contestation as Williams presents it is embedded in the very language of intentions. In "Base and Superstructure" Williams stresses that the specific organization and structure of society are directly related to certain social intentions, "intentions by which we define the society, intentions which have been the rule of a particular class."[14] But though intentionality, as Williams uses the word, may seem merely another term for determination, it would be a mistake to infer that by this he means prefiguration or control. Rather, he sees the determinative principle in intention as more closely allied with the notion of "setting of limits" and "exertion of pressure." By defining intention in these terms, Williams sought to get away from the crudely reductive idea that the direction a society takes is already prefigured and that it is merely following the course laid out for it at some prior, indeterminate, untraceable point. Also, his reading of intention as a "setting of limits" allows for the possibility of conflict, for the crucial nodes where constraints are placed are more readily identifiable as the places where resistance may occur against the gross "exertion of pressure." Indeed, Williams's main contribution is in offering a dynamic model that will permit one to study culture and society in terms of how social will or intention (the terms are interchangeable) is engaged in an unceasing activity of circumscribing human behavior, on the one hand, and diluting resistance to the authority that it represents, on the other. To know the "social intentions" by which a society is defined is thus to identify not only the potential places where the collective will seek to assert itself but also where it is most subject to the fracturing and dissipation caused by extreme pressure.

Williams's chief insights lie, I think, in pointing to the inherent instability of hegemony, particularly its vulnerability to external assaults and its defensive mechanisms of establishing authority. Hegemony, Williams reminds us, is never monolithic or uncontested. As he emphatically states, "it is misleading to reduce all political and cultural initiatives and contributions to the terms of the hegemony."[15] But in a seriously inhibiting way, Williams's model of contestation does not adequately incorporate the dynamics of his proposed cultural materialism, as is especially evident in his reluctance to extend his notion of contestation to transcultural or cross-referential solutions. While his theory of culture has the potential to produce a reading of England's colonial adventure, his cultural analysis is seriously inhibited by the framework of economic determinism within which that reading is produced. Suspending contestation altogether, Williams's scattered comments on empire in *The Long Revolution* and *Culture and Society* suggest that Britain had achieved dominance through the power of a fully formed cultural and institutional system whose values are simply transplanted onto the colonies. That system is subsequently identified as the "national" culture, but it partakes little of the contingencies of the colonial situation it confronts and remains hermetically sealed from the continually changing political imperatives of empire. What is quite striking is that Williams, while appearing eager to break away from the weaknesses of Marxian theory (and, indeed, he does come uncannily close to proposing a method of analysis of nineteenth-century culture that would have to incorporate empire to be complete), remains peculiarly reticent in pursuing imperialism as that single crucial factor which would invalidate totalizing descriptions of any kind and favor process over system—two critical objectives to which Williams has otherwise shown himself to be seriously committed.[16] Instead, what has the potential to be a liberating methodological insight, and a critical tool for resetting the boundaries of cultural study across societies, remains curiously undeveloped by Williams in his own critical practice.

The inefficacy of Williams's cultural materialism accounts for the shortcomings of a cultural theory that attempts to include imperialism

223

in its sphere of discourse but is inherently incapable of accounting for it as a function of metropolitan culture. Williams is pulled in two directions: on the one hand, he wishes to dispense with the rigidity and two-dimensional abstractness of certain Marxian analytic categories, such as base and superstructure, but at the same time he is interested in saving what he considers to be some of their more useful insights. Though he rejects the *language* of base-and-superstructure, he retains their interpretive value in yielding historical understanding. With regard to the practice of imperialism, the theoretical argument of base-and-superstructure proved invaluable. Consequently, Williams's reading of Britain in relation to global power suffers from the reintroduction of both the language and the concepts of economic and ideological determinism in the absence of a relational and conjectural analysis of imperialism. Despite Williams's life-long commitment to contesting purely abstract categories of analysis that draw on system rather than history, his critical practice paradoxically reproduces them in the context of imperialism.

In a sense, the contradictory impulses in Williams's work run parallel to what he perceived as the central contradiction of British Marxism, which he describes as an "historical interaction" between Romanticism and Marx whereby the value of culture is sought to be retained for its role in the "activation of energy" and the creation of individual consciousness, while remaining passively dependent on economic and social development.[17] Singling out Christopher Caudwell as the worst offender, Williams takes British Marxists to task for their unwitting defense of liberal-humanist ideas of cultural value in response to what came to be seen as Marx's diminution of the value of intellectual and creative activity. Linking Marxism as practiced in England with the Romantic tradition of the poet as creator of consciousness, Williams brilliantly reveals how British Marxism has always sought to give a high value to culture by adhering to a dynamic view of art as an active instrument for uncovering a suppressed history.[18] Williams considers it pertinent to interrogate English Marxists "who have interested themselves in the arts [as to] whether this is not Romanticism absorbing Marx, rather than Marx transforming Romanticism."[19]

But what Williams may not have realized is that his own work reflects aspects of the Romantic temperament, especially with regard to the reading of English culture as process; from the volatile, uncertain middle ground of history, art is conceptualized as both reflecting the economic structure and affecting attitudes toward reality "to help *or hinder* the constant business of changing it" (emphasis in the original).[20] In continuing to work with concepts such as "consciousness" and "agency" to describe the transformation of society and individual experience by nineteenth-century social forces, including those of industry and democracy, Williams reveals his interest in salvaging the more useful aspects of the Romantic idea of culture as a site of resistance, without having to subscribe to the Romantic belief in the power of art to change human beings and society as a whole. Because Williams sees art as occupying a middle ground, he is able to read in the industrial novels of Dickens, Kingsley, and George Eliot the possibilities for social action, not through legislation (which are bound to be doomed), but through what Williams calls "the instinctive, unintellectual, unorganized life" against which the hegemony of industrial life must contend.[21] At such points in *Culture and Society* Williams clearly oscillates between a view of culture as coeval with social process, always fluid and indeterminate in its meanings and definitions, and a more obdurate, anti-Romantic reading that gives more power to the forces of economic change.

Empire further dramatizes the tensions in Williams's cultural theory. In his analyses of British culture Williams radically questions that same analytical framework of economic determinism by which he simultaneously explains British imperialism. Time and again Williams undertook close readings of Marx and Engels to show how these two thinkers themselves resisted crude economic reductionism. In *Culture and Society* Williams quotes a significant passage from Engels to illustrate his point:

> According to the materialist conception of history, the determining element in history is *ultimately* the production and reproduction in real life. More than this neither Marx nor I have ever asserted. If therefore somebody twists this into the statement that the economic element is the *only* determining one, he transforms it into a meaningless, abstract and absurd phrase. . . . There is an interaction of all these elements [political, legal, and philosophical theories, religious ideas, etc.], in which, amid all the endless *host* of accidents (i.e. of things and events whose inner connection is so remote or so impossible to prove that we regard it as absent and can neglect it) the economic element finally asserts itself as necessary. Otherwise the application of the theory to any period of history one chose would be easier than the solution of a simple equation of the first degree.[22] (emphasis in the original)

As Williams understands this passage by Engels, the task for cultural criticism is to accept seriously the challenge of dealing with what is concretely manifest—the "way of life" as a whole—without isolating economic elements from the totality or interpreting economic change as occurring in neutral conditions. Williams claims that the "one vital lesson which the nineteenth century had to learn—and learn urgently because of the very magnitude of its changes—was that the basic economic organization could not be separated and excluded from its moral and intellectual concerns."[23] If Williams was openly hostile to the *Scrutiny* version of culture as the guarded possession of a minority isolated from the general society, he was equally critical of the totalizing tendencies of Marxian analysis (viz., his critique of Lukács). In work after work Williams repeatedly attacked static descriptions of culture as unilaterally determined by economic conditions and even went so far as to say that there can be no such thing as an *already existing culture* "because culture cannot be democratized without thereby being radically changed."[24] That is to say, the consciousness of a whole society is too diverse to be circumscribed by the self-definitions of the economically dominant class.[25] The "whole way of life" thus is both determined and determining, and it is to that, rather than to the economic system alone, that literature has to be related.

Yet there remains the peculiar paradox of Williams's critical position: at the very moment he sought to disengage culture from deterministic explanations, he was locked into a reading of imperialism as the end-point of European market forces. The element of creative tension present in his interpretation of English cultural formation is displaced by more deterministic modes of explanation in his discussion of empire. Is it any wonder, then, that, having defined culture and imperialism in noninteractive terms, and through mutually exclusive analytical categories, he should so detach one from the other? In wishing to suspend economic determinism in his analysis of English culture, while at the same time adopting its theoretical argument to account for Britain's imperialistic involvement, Williams is caught in a methodological trap of his own making from which there is no escape. The result is well known: the idea of culture as it is produced by imperialism receives little emphasis, and at best, only a tenuous, arbitrary relation is established between them.

Given the conflictual ways in which Williams's cultural materialism is worked out, it is not surprising that Williams has so little to say about British imperialism and its effects on English culture. To advance a different but related argument, his reticence in naming colonialism as a shaping factor in English cultural formation can be interpreted as a reluctance to consider the economics of imperialism as having a final determining power over culture. This is by no means to make apologies for Williams's omission of colonialism. Rather, it is to gesture toward the enormously complex situation Williams finds himself in as a result of a commitment to a revision of Marxian analytical categories that refuses to comply with notions of economic determination as fully explanatory of culture. Williams's uneasiness in working with exclusively economic categories causes him to give scant attention to the reciprocal and determinate relation between culture and imperialism, which he mistakenly reads as the end-point of established economic motives that get transplanted from Britain to its colonies rather than as a test site for a culture in formation. But that same uneasiness, we have to remind ourselves, is responsible for his studying English culture and society as historical process rather than the end result of fixed economic imperatives. We can only conclude that if Williams chooses to "ignore" imperialism, it is because the terms of his analysis preclude such analysis.

Williams's peculiar reticence in naming imperialism restricts him to a form of essentialism that robs his cultural model of much of its potency. At the most basic level, Williams's failure to incorporate the historical reality of empire into both his theoretical analyses and his readings of literary texts exposes a conception of society that is rendered in isomorphic terms, and cultural ideas appear as if produced *sui generis* rather than by external conditions. This is glaringly apparent in Williams's account of the origin of national culture and character, which he locates in the Germano-Coleridgean school.[26] Williams reads the distinctions made by Coleridge between culture and civilization as an attempt to interweave a philosophy of society with a philosophy of history and so to root human perfectibility in social conditions; but by introducing the notion of "cultivation" Coleridge, and Williams as well to some extent, reworks culture into a general condition or habit of mind. As a genealogy of culture, *Culture and Society* wavers unsteadily between the two critical positions with which Coleridge comes to be associated in Williams's reading: culture as process and history, subject to flux, discontinuities, modifications, which is set against culture as social value, expressed independently of radical change and historical disjunctions. Standards of perfection acquire two meanings: in the first instance, they are drawn from society and in turn influence it; but in the other, they are set apart to judge it. This movement of culture from social process to social arbiter, which Williams undertakes to chart as the history of English culture, limits him to a model of structural continuity for which he must take responsibility. Even though Williams militates against a model of continuous, organic history, that is precisely the kind of impression his work produces, for in tracing culture (prefigured as English) from its own conceptual base—as the pursuit of perfection—Williams's description precludes the possibility of foundations existing outside it. An historical practice such as imperialism can appear merely as a context for the promotion of culture, not as a condition for its generation nor as a determinant of its content and shape.

The trap closes in on Williams more definitively at this stage. Having chosen to conceive of art and social process as products of the same society, Williams frees himself from the obligation of tracing their development through contexts other than those in which (he presumes) they originated, contexts that must inevitably lead him (in the deepest historical sense) to imperial relations. To take a very simple example from educational history that Williams discusses in *The Long Revolution,* industrial schools were set up in the first quarter of the nineteenth century to provide manual training and elementary instruction in the Bible and other moral subjects. Williams reports on a revolution in teaching method that came to be known as the Lancaster and Bell monitorial system of instruction; this method consisted of the use of monitors and standard repetitive exercises, which allowed fewer numbers of teachers to teach greater numbers of pupils. Education in an era of mass democracy had found its first effective medium, observes Williams, documenting the growth in enrollments—and moral selves—that had been made possible by what many of us today might consider a fairly mundane innovation. The new pedagogy marked a significant moment in British social history, writes Williams, for "a national system of elementary schooling . . . had been set going."[27] The monitorial system, which rests on the concept of the few teaching the many, is a raw prototype for the more developed Arnoldian formulations of a hegemonic culture filtering downward through the agency of a carefully chosen elite.

What Williams fails to note is that the success of the Lancaster and Bell method in managing and controlling a mass population was partly assured in England because *it had been introduced and tested elsewhere.* The experiment began almost fortuitously in colonial India, where the problems of governing a large population were greatly exacerbated by limited English manpower available for the task. Dr. Andrew Bell, who had been an Anglican chaplain in the Indian Army, tried to cope with his many duties as superintendent of the orphan asylum at the Egmore Redoubt at Madras and as chaplain to five regiments. Frustrated by the meager resources available to him, he employed a better-than-average pupil to teach his fellow pupils to write and draw in the sand of the classroom floor. The boy proved as capable a teacher as he had been a pupil. Bell publicized this "discovery" in *An Experiment in Education*.[28] The Madras system was introduced into the Charity School of St. Botolph's, Aldgate, in 1798 and in the Kendal industrial schools the following year. But the system made little headway until Joseph Lancaster began in 1801 to use it in his one-room school in London, where he taught over a thousand children through a system of "drafts not classes" and published his results in *Improvements in Education as It Respects the Industrial Class of the Community* (1803).[29]

I do not mean to suggest, by citing this example, that for every social or cultural movement enacted in England there was a corresponding event that preceded it in the colonies. (It would be equally disastrous to infer, from these transfers of movements and ideas, that sustained analogies can be drawn between class relations and colonizer-colonized relations in the two societies.) Nor do I wish to imply that all errors of omission are ideologically motivated. But I do think that the fact of omission itself suggests a problematic relation between theory and history, or system and process, of which Williams could not have been ignorant. Earlier I suggested, taking my cue from Williams, that the contradictions in his position on imperialism can be read as internalizations of historical contradictions inherent in British Marxism, with its origins in the cross-fertilization of Marx and Romanticism wherein culture is understood as alternatively controlled by and independent of economic structures. This double focus on passive dependence and active contestation puts culture in the position of either affirming those structures or, in an enabling exercise of individual will, challenging them. The ambivalence of culture's trajectory is what Williams liked to think of as process or history, and his readings of English culture are informed by the dynamic interplay of event with social and economic reality.

But if the legacy of Romanticism left an uneasy mark on British Marxism, which responded by moving in the direction of theory and system-building to restore the primacy of economic determinism, the legacy of British Marxism thus construed left a similar mark on Williams, who, too, has shown a tendency to move toward system when unable to contend with the historical fluidity of economically engendered realities such as imperialism. Aware of the impossibility of accommodating system *and* process, Williams's answer is to address the reciprocal relationality of culture and imperialism in deliberately arbitrary and fragmented ways, producing in turn a systematic misrecognition of "Englishness" as an imperial construct.

As in the work of his successors, "national" culture takes the place of imperial formations, but it turns out to be a choice that creates new problems for cultural analysis, in that its fully constituted character obscures the heterogeneous fragments out of which it was constructed in the first place.[30] As Williams must have been aware, the greatest danger lies in the fact that cultural identity as a value takes precedence over the historical discontinuities and asymmetrical developments from which it emerged. In the end, what we are left with is a disturbing reminder that there is, after all, no view like the one from the other country.

10

Country and City in a Postcolonial Landscape: Double Discourse and the Geo-Politics of Truth in Latin America

Julie Skurski and Fernando Coronil

Raymond Williams's path-breaking work on the integration of materialist history and cultural analysis is nowhere more evident than in his discussion of class formation and literary production in *The Country and the City*. Building on this suggestive work, we discuss here the role of the "country and the city" model in the articulation of a nationalist project and in the constitution of political knowledge in Venezuela. We first analyze the novel *Doña Bárbara* (1929) as an allegory of national unity and as an intervention in the construction of populist discourse. Written by Rómulo Gallegos, acclaimed novelist and proponent of liberal democracy who was the nation's first freely elected president (1948), this national romance was widely read as an allegory of the attainment of progress through the civilizing union of the reformist, educated urban elite with the instinctual "pueblo" ("the people"). With the ascent of the nascent mass-based party system, the novel became canonized within dominant discourse as the legitimizing myth of the modernization project. We then examine the case of the Amparo massacre (October 1988), in which the ambiguous terms of the union between enlightened leader and backward pueblo, as imaged in *Doña Bárbara* and inscribed in dominant discourse, were polarized and re-combined. Official discourse presented the military attack on a group of fishermen on a river at the border with Colombia, resulting in the death of fourteen of the men, as an instance of the state's civilizing control of an unruly, subversive pueblo; opposition discourse interpreted the attack as an expression of state barbarity against the pueblo and, thus, against the nation's source of authenticity.[1]

In our discussion we seek to problematize the analytical opposition between internal and external factors that commonly informs discussions of the periphery by drawing attention to the mutual constitution and transformation of these factors on a postcolonial terrain and analyzing how, in a peripheral nation, the country and city model encodes relations of ambiguity as regards the bases of collective authority. The postcolonial city is defined domestically as a civilizing center in relation to the nation's primitive countryside. Yet since both country and city are located in the "country," or the global hinterland of the metropolitan centers, they are subsumed within an internationally inclusive category of backwardness and colored by the hostile meanings associated with the colonized.

How does this double articulation of city and country in the periphery affect the hierarchical relationship between them as sites of social power and sources of knowledge? On what basis can the dominant sectors claim to rule or represent authority if, as products of a peripheral society, they too are "backward"? DuBois and Fanon suggest that colonized subjects are formed through a "doubling" of consciousness, as they see themselves in fractured form through the eyes of the dominant. How is a dominated dominant class constituted at once as an agent and as a subject of this doubling?[2] We direct these questions to the history of a country once on the periphery of the Spanish empire, in which the identification that Spanish colonialism impressed upon its subjects between the city and civilization, the country and barbarism, has continued to inform the ruling elite's populist development project throughout much of this century.

Metropolitan Country and City

Country and city are at once interrelated forms of human settlement rooted in particular locations and times, and evocative images of social life that circulate beyond their source and inspire the social imagination in widely differing societies. As Raymond Williams shows in *The Country and The City,* these emblems of sociality have accumulated divergent meanings which cluster around familiar contrasts, suggesting that opposing qualities reside within them:

On the country has gathered the idea of a natural way of life: of peace, innocence and simple virtue. On the city has gathered the idea of an achieved centre: of learning, communication, light. Powerful hostile associations have also developed: on the city as a place of noise, worldliness and ambition; on the country as a place of backwardness, ignorance, limitation.[3]

Taking England as his focus and paradigm, Williams examines how representations of country and city as distinct ways of life are related to the transformation of rural and urban settlements under the impact of capitalism. By discussing literary conventions and their social roots, he problematizes familiar imagery associated with rural and urban domains, revealing the tendency of dominant representational forms to isolate and naturalize aspects of reality, obscuring the real movement of history and displacing responsibility from the agents of capitalism's expansion.[4] The construction of divisions between these domains, Williams argues, should be seen as the product of a unified process by which social practices and forms of consciousness are at once mutually constituted and become separated and opposed. Thought about these domains has tended to abstract their features and to give them a metaphysical status, presenting as natural and autonomous that which is social and interrelated. Williams suggests we examine the historical encodings of country and city so that we may trace the hidden connections that reside within these concepts.

These hidden connections weave together the ordering of the national and the international domains through colonial and imperial expansion; as Williams observes, "one of the last models of the 'city and the country' is the system we now know as imperialism."[5] At the global as well as the domestic level, one finds the tendency to obscure the mutually constitutive relationship between center (city) and periphery (country), and to represent them as separate entities whose characteristics appear as the consequence of intrinsic attributes. Accordingly, the division between metropolitan nations at the center and peripheral nations which are their "effective hinterland" has been made to seem the natural measure of a universal movement of each nation toward industrial development propelled by a worldwide rationalization of social life. The transformation of the national model of country and city into an international model has helped draw a map of the world from the perspective of the dominant centers. This model has operated as a central element in the triumphant ideology of modernity, replicating within nations oppositions between a dynamic center and a backward periphery, and establishing a ranking of nations along a hierarchical scale of seemingly intrinsic qualities.

Williams counters unilinear models by relating the center's progress to the periphery's backwardness. Furthermore, he indicates that the internalization of the country and city model involves its transformation along lines that polarize its multivocal meanings. The multiple associations attached to city and country as they developed within England become, at the international level, concentrated and fixed around two opposite poles: the city is unambiguously presented as the source of progress, and the country becomes a locus of backwardness, no longer made the object of idealization regarding past sources of order and community.[6]

Williams's understanding of capitalism, however, is rent by a tension between his conception of its universalizing form and of the specific forms it assumes in the context of imperialism. Consequently, he tends to reinstate a homogenizing centrist view, for he assumes that capitalism's disruption and reordering of rural society in widely differing nations creates "essentially similar" historical experiences within center and periphery.[7] The search for unity of process which motivates this assertion, and which fruitfully permits Williams to recognize similar experiences even when addressed in different idioms, may also obscure the distinct historical paths traversed by societies that occupy different positions in the international division of labor. Within this narrative of history, the metropolitan "country" and "city" appear as differentiated social landscapes which actively participate in struggles over competing visions of society. Nations on the periphery, in contrast, appear as an imperial hinterland whose mimetic development takes place in response to the demands of advanced capitalist powers. Their transformation, initiated by imperial dominance, follows "the lines of the alien development. An internal history of country and city occurs, often very dramatically, within the colonial and neo-colonial societies."[8] These statements suggest that processes induced by the demands of imperial powers and that reiterate their own history are repeated within the colonies. In this respect, the history of the periphery becomes derivative.

The model of country and city that Williams seeks to deconstruct and contextualize reflects the rise to dominance of the Enlightenment conception of history associated with the expansion of northern European societies, a concept that assumes reason triumphs over obscurantism as light over darkness, as mind over body, as interests over passions, as city over country. In contrast, colonial urban centers in Latin America were established as the product of an early experience of modern state-building that linked the spread of Catholicism to the consolidation of a transcontinental kingdom. These cities were civilizing outposts set in the vast territories of an empire for which the control of its subjects was a recurrent cultural and political problem. Enlightenment ideas in Spain and Latin America achieved a limited hold on historical terrains where neither trade, industry, science, nor religion could lend support to the promise of a luminous future cast in terms of the conceptual oppositions and rupture with the past that became imaginable in northern Europe. The domestic elites in Latin America, in their effort to attain national independence, defined Spain as an obstacle to progress, and yet they resisted the transformation of colonial economic and social relations called for by their turn toward northern Europe and the United States as models of rationalizing civilization. Thus an ambivalent relationship toward metropolitan centers as sites of civilizing order marked the foundation and consolidation of these nations.

The following discussion of the country and city model as an element in the construction of a populist discourse of national development in Venezuela suggests that categories arising in an imperial context are altered by their local appropriation and representation and by their projection in new form onto the domestic and international spheres. They are given historical content and relative political weight within societies having their own grid of associations with country and city divisions that may reflect a history of conquest and colonization, and for which the center and periphery classification is inextricably bound to hierarchical relations of control.

The Double Discourse of National Identity

The model of country and city in Venezuela expresses and reinforces what we call the double discourse of national identity, which at once assumes, conceals, and recreates the fractures of a colonial legacy. Built around principles of disjunction and ambiguity, double discourse negotiates the ambiguous and shifting meanings attached to center and periphery, and elite and pueblo, in terms of embedded notions of social, political, and cultural hierarchy. Informing official and quotidian practices, it encodes as natural a split between word and practice, the public and the private, statement and intent, and links claims to truth to the power to construct the appearance of knowledge.[9]

Populist nationalist discourse in contemporary Venezuela has sought to elaborate images of a tutelary relationship between the reformist educated elite and the backward pueblo on which to found its popular support. This has been particularly problematic given that the oligarchic nationalist ideology preceding it lacked images of social union from which notions of shared identity and a common past could be constructed. The liberal republican ideas advanced by Simón Bolívar and the Creole oligarchy in support of the Independence War (1811–21) rejected indigenous and Spanish concepts of community as elements on which to draw for the construction of a new national polity and defined the rural populace as a source of barbarous anarchy and despotism.[10] Narratives of the republic's origins constructed from the elite's perspective in the post-independence period presented the Creole independence leaders as the heroic agents of liberation, whose goals were frustrated by the pueblo's backwardness, and subsumed the divisive social struggle through which independence was achieved within an abstract account of the quest to create a new republic which owes nothing to its past. Thus they offered to the pueblo but a reflection of its marginality to the creation of an imagined national community.

The oligarchic elite's defense of its right to rule over the fractured society of the post-independence era merged the Enlightenment promise to bring progress to the backward population with the Spanish colonizing mission to achieve the triumph of civilization over barbarism. However, the stark decline of the countryside, the rise of rural rebellion, and the incapacity of export agriculture to bring material progress in the nineteenth century rendered the claimed link between urban life, civilization, and the right to rule highly problematic.[11] In response to these conditions, an anti-elite discourse exalted the land as the source of natural energy and located authentic national identity within the barbarous masses, providing caudillo strongmen with a language of popular revolt that mobilized support for their repeated assaults on power. The reproduction of the economic elite thus became dependent on its alliance with caudillos, regarded as "men of the people," who could command popular support and wield anti-elite discourse. With the establishment of the oil enclave in the 1920s and of mass-based parties in the 1940s, this language of conflict between the economic elite and the pueblo, in which the man of action was the mediator, was not erased but, rather, was incorporated into the politics of populist clientelism. At the same time, the land became an abstract figure for the nation, as the nation was urbanized and the national project valorized industrialization.

Doña Bárbara and the Amparo massacre were constructed as representations of the national community during two periods of major social transformation.[12] In the 1920s, at the time of the novel's publication, Venezuela's impoverished coffee and cacao export economy was changing rapidly. The establishment of a petroleum export industry by foreign capital provided the elite-controlled state, headed by a "caudillo" dictator, with a source of expanding and stable income, and channeled into the cities resources that stimulated the growth of the middle and working classes. With the expansion of the oil enclave and the consolidation of a centralizing rentier state, a competitive electoral democracy was established and has been sustained since 1958, and an expanding economy brought levels of urbanization and economic growth unprecedented for Latin America.[13] Nevertheless, income and social inequalities remained pronounced and the economy was highly subsidized and dependent. During the sudden financial abundance of the 1970s oil boom, the governing elite promised to vanquish backwardness through rapid heavy industrialization, but this illusory goal was quickly followed by a slide into debt crisis and political closure in the 1980s, at which time the Amparo massacre occurred.

During the period of transition to an oil-export economy, when *Doña Bárbara* was written, changing social and economic conditions began to undermine Juan Vicente Gómez's (1908–35) monopoly of political power. The book's rise as the national novel accompanied that of the leading mass-based party Acción Democrática (AD), of which its author was a leader. When AD occupied power from 1945–58, the project of promoting class unity, domestic capitalism, and universal education was regarded by its followers as mirroring the novel's vision; its civilized hero and his barbarous enemy became icons for the continuous struggle to contain savagery within the polity. The Amparo massacre, October 1988, occurred at a moment of crisis for this model. The state, under pressure from lending agencies and domestic capital to withdraw support from state protectionism, had intensified the economic exclusion of popular sectors and was about to initiate the elevation of market rationality to the center of its project. Spanning the sixty years between the initiation and the rupture of the tutelary populist project, *Doña Bárbara* and the Amparo massacre address the relationship between power and authority on a postcolonial terrain, making visible the space of ambiguity within which competing representations of national identity are constructed.

The Territoriality of History: The Llanos

The national territory acts in Venezuelan political discourse as a map of the nation's cultural landscape and as a stage for the dramatic enactment of its history. The Llanos (savannas, or plains, make up a large portion of the nation's territory) have occupied a privileged place in this territorialization of history. They have been enshrined within official and popular imagery as the emblem of the continuing struggle between barbarism and civilization, ignorance and knowledge, instinct and law. With the emptying and decline of the countryside under the impact of oil rents came the elevation of the Llanos as the source of the nation's heroic struggle for freedom. The improvisational and syncretic music and dance of this vast region are the emblems of national culture, while the figure of the independent and brave "llanero" (inhabitant of the plans) is the emblem of national political identity. In official rhetoric and ceremony, in presidential campaign, and in "folkloric" performances, the Llanos are identified with the nation's origins and authentic character. The leadership of Acción Democrática and of the military together claim this territory for the memorialization of the pueblo's already achieved liberation.

As William Roseberry argues in his analysis of the country's place in the Venezuelan national imagination, the notions of backwardness and development that orient the modernization project have centered on the petroleum industry, making of the agricultural past an historically empty and ambiguous zone and the countryside an area onto which notions of authenticity are projected. Yet this ambiguity configurates all the dimensions around which "national identity" is built, making of neither city nor country, petroleum nor agriculture, a certain source of order. "The image of the peasant and countryside emerging from the coffee economy is that of a disordered past, but the migrant moves from a disordered countryside to a disordered city. The city that presents itself as a symbol of modern Venezuela also creates its critical opposite: the pastoral countryside. . . . Petroleum and the city that is a product of the petroleum economy simultaneously symbolize backwardness and development. The countryside, purged of its own history, comes to represent the true Venezuela."[14]

Doña Bárbara and the tale of the Amparo massacre, both of which open with a canoe's passage up the Arauca River in the southwestern Llanos, are informed by the Llanos's sedimented associations with disorder and freedom, danger and vitality. But if the novel elaborates these associations into a tale of progress achieved through the romantic union of elite and pueblo, the official version of the Amparo tale assumes that progress requires the elite's control and containment of the pueblo. In the novel, the land renounces its wildness and willingly submits to domestication by a caring tutor. In the official version of the Amparo drama, the land spawns anarchy that only a forceful leader can control. However, if the novel seeks to contain through its authorial voice the tensions within the tutorial relationship between leader and pueblo, the emergence of a nonofficial version of the Amparo tale indicates that the transformation of this bond implies a questioning of elite authority.

Doña Bárbara: The Geography of Backwardness and Redemption

> If we wish to synthesize schematically the characteristic differ-
> ence between these two symptoms of social illness, while refer-
> ring to their origins, we could express it with these two anti-
> thetical terms: the city and the bush, thus indicating not only
> the places where they usually occur, but also their very nature,
> the circumstances which produce them, the spirit and tenden-
> cies that move them, which is the same as saying: civilization
> and barbarism.[15]
>
> Rómulo Gallegos

Doña Bárbara examines the bases of despotism in Venezuela by constructing the lawless cattle plains frontier as a metaphor for the nation
under autocratic rule. Seen in terms of the starkly simplified social
relations of the Llanos, Venezuelan society appears as an unformed
hybrid descended from the conquest, product of the disorderly union
between a backward Indian population and brutal Spanish adventur-
ers. The origins of this society have been lost to history, but the memory
of conquest is carried as a psychic wound that draws people to
violence and stunts their moral and political development. The
novel's social landscape resembles that painted by the positivist
social theorists and historians of the period, who drew on European
evolutionary theories to argue the necessity of despotism in Venezuela. Ideologues of Juan Vicente Gómez's regime, they maintained
that Venezuelan society, formed through the hybridization of three
unruly races, required a rural autocrat, a "necessary gendarme," to
control the anarchic impulses of its "semi-barbarous" population and
to achieve modern statehood.[16]

In dialogue with oligarchic official discourse, Gallegos sought to
reconfigure the relationship between leader and pueblo in a "semi-
barbarous" society by linking the taming of barbarism to the leadership
of reformist intellectuals and to the establishment of civil authority.
Bringing to bear ideas current in Europe concerning the vitality of the

primitive, he depicted barbarism as an undifferentiated natural force that could be directed toward positive ends. By granting creative potential to undomesticated physical and human nature, Gallegos recast the project of social evolution as the transformation of peoples' souls through the process of "education" or the formation of individuated subjectivities ruled by higher reason. It was the task of enlightened leaders to achieve through the "hegemony of culture" the "containment of barbarism," whose "dark instinctual tendencies" are energy which "rushes like a river overflowing its bed."[17]

When Gallegos wrote *Doña Bárbara,* Gómez had ruled for twenty years, monopolizing land, manipulating rural symbols of power, and demanding the allegiance of the educated urban elite. The novel's hopeful depiction of national transformation became possible at this time, with the oil industry's expansion and the creation of new prospects of ascent for the emergent middle class. An immediate critical success, both official and opposition intellectuals sought to claim it as an expression of their civilizing vision. With Gallegos's voluntary exile to Spain and his support for centrist anti-Gomez forces led by his former students, *Doña Bárbara* became a template for action for reformist leaders and was appropriated by the emergent populist discourse as a charter for a democratizing project based on clientelistic political incorporation rather than on caudillo-led coup or socialist revolution. Canonized after a time as a foundational nationalist myth, it has long been evoked in official and popular discourse as an image of the ever-present battle against backwardness.[18] Yet this charter, building as it does on conflicting historical memories, has been interpreted from differing class perspectives: conservative discourse constructs it as a ratification of the dangers of unruly populism, while in popular language it images not only the menace of backwardness but the pueblo's own vitality and strength. Through the double discourse of national identity the political leadership has attempted to construct itself as the mediator of the triadic set of relations contained within this representation of benevolent rule.

The Rivers of Barbarism

The past offers no image of unity, no source for the construction of an authentic "mestizo" (mixed race) identity in the novel's landscape. Yet the lack of an ordering past makes possible the existence of the feature most typical of the indomitable llanero: the assertion of individual will, bound neither by conscience nor by responsibility. For barbarous life on the Llanos is sustained by the absence of stable boundaries and institutionalized rules, by the freedom for instinct to direct individual action without obstruction, constrained only by those individuals who can assert their will through the use of force. Like the limitless plains uninterrupted by natural barrier or man-made boundary, individual consciousness is undivided by the moral categories and self-reflective activities that organize the civilized psyche into a complex unity distinct from its surroundings. Thus it cannot know the past or construct a future; it is caught in the cyclical present ordered by the pendular fluctuations of time on the Llanos, summer drought and winter floods, that alternately disperse and bring together cattle herds and men.

The novel argues that the capacity to sustain divisions between domains of life and of consciousness and, thus, to achieve a synthesis between the extremes of sentiment and individual interest in the service of collective order cannot develop in this domain. This is the barbarism of a truncated rather than a primitive society, one that defeats the advance of civilization by manipulating and emptying of content the rules that civilization constructs. Nevertheless, the shallow and morally unformed mestizo llaneros, unlike the Indians who fatalistically submit to nature's domination, have the impulse to attain an elementary freedom. But they are caught in the logic of rivalries between contending personalistic leaders, "caciques," a logic that demands violent retribution, for it does not recognize the law as a social mediator.

The novel's opening line, "A canoe goes up the Arauca River," locates the reader on a journey backward in time and at the social edges of the nation in the sparsely populated state of Apure, once inhabited by cattle hunters and caudillos who were the troops for the Independence War and the rebellions of the nineteenth century. The river represents in this tale the ever renewed source of barbarism. The hero, Santos Luzardo,[19] is a lawyer from the capital who returns to the land of his origins to regain control of his family hacienda from the predatory maneuvers of Doña Bárbara. She is a cacique who has monopolized land and corrupted authority, using Indian sorcery, legal manipulation, and force to expand her power and create belief in her invincibility.[20]

The journey from the capital to the hinterland awakens in Luzardo the resolve to defeat Doña Bárbara and to replace the "rule of force" by the "rule of law." He seeks to civilize the Llanos by establishing state authority and modern production, a project that entails the division of domains in all spheres of life. In this undifferentiated society, cattle and horses run wild, money is hoarded rather than invested, law is a tool of the powerful, and sexual union and reproduction occur in the absence of a domestic realm. Marisela, the illegitimate, untutored daughter of Doña Bárbara, personifies such wildness, for she has the beauty of the innocent but lacks civilized speech and consciousness as a result of social dissolution. Abandoned by her mother and neglected by her alcoholic father, who is Luzardo's cousin, Marisela grew up on the margins of this peripheral society, next to a swamp that embodies the principle of dissolution.

In the mutual transformation of the mythic trio comprised by Luzardo, Doña Bárbara, and Marisela, the women represent the two dimensions of barbarism. As the civilizing agent, Luzardo must at once prove himself to be strong in a realm ruled by violence, and he must exert the force of reason over that violence. This civilizing virility requires him to defeat Doña Bárbara by establishing respect for the law without succumbing to the use of force and to domesticate Marisela by instructing her in polite speech and feminine behavior without yielding to simple physical attraction. His task is to create differentiation within people and society so as to achieve a synthesis between the forces that constitute them.

Luzardo's relationship with Marisela is the template for his civilizing mission. Through his care she progresses from a new awareness of her backwardness, to the refinement of her speech and manners, the creation of an ordered domestic life, and the capacity for altruistic sentiment.[21] As an image of the potential for good that resides within the pueblo, Marisela brings to Luzardo an appreciation for a people he once disdained. Their announced marriage at the novel's end, together with Doña Bárbara's retreat as a result of the transformation she undergoes through her encounter with him, signals the beginning of a new economic and social order shaped by reproduction within marriage and production within capitalist relations.

Ambiguity: An Alternative Reading

Doña Bárbara has conventionally been presented as a straightforward narrative in which archetypical characters, placed in a realistic historical setting, portray the triumph of lawful rule over violence, urban progress over rural backwardness, and love over instinct. Doris Sommer's innovative analysis of national romances in Latin America brings out the underlying allegorical level of the narrative through which new forms of national identity and political organization are made to seem desirable.[22] Ignored by standard interpretations and denied by most postmodern readings, this level expresses an idiom shared by a wide range of post-independence novels, one which joins history and sentiment to explore different solutions to the problem of national integration.[23] These "foundational fictions" legitimate the "nation-family" through a rhetoric of desire that intertwines the fate of a couple, whose members come from divergent social sectors, with the destiny of a fractured polity. A populist version of this national romance model, Sommer argues, *Doña Bárbara* presents the legitimate marital union as a signal that productive sexual and economic relations have become socially possible, and it imposes unambiguous polar divisions between the categories of civilization and barbarism, order and disorder, male and female.

Certain deconstructionist readings attempt as well to right reductionist interpretations and to recognize the allegorical construction of *Doña Bárbara*. However, they read it as an allegory of the writing of texts and, thus, divorce its imaginary representation and reordering of the social world from the social conditions within which the novel's literary conventions were employed and have been reinterpreted over time— what Williams calls "the means of the production and the conditions of the means of production"[24] of the novel. González Echevarría, a leading proponent of this approach, captures the dilemmas posed in *Doña Bárbara* by the ambiguous bases of social authority; but he dismisses the novel's apparent "social concern" as but a nod to the "superficial dialogue of the moment" that conceals its true "critical substratum," i.e., the deconstruction of language and signification.[25]

As our discussion shows, *Doña Bárbara* was written and has been historically received as an intervention in the construction and reproduction of a populist political project.[26] In our view, the novel speaks in the idiom of a project which constructs the appearance of clearly demarcated categories through the continuing negotiation of ambiguity. The novel nervously broaches issues of moral uncertainty, attraction and repulsion, and cooptation and repression while seeking to sustain principles of authority within an unstable hierarchical framework. Thus the solution it offers can be neither singular nor unambiguous; it presents both marriage based on romantic love and the defeat of a feared and desired enemy as being necessary for the creation of a civilized order. The defensive stance of the populist project, which seeks to unite the nation in the face of threats, is imaged in the triangular relationship between the inwardly divided civilizing leader and the polarized embodiments of the pueblo. Bonds of harmony and of hostility, represented by the union of the tutelary leader and the pliant pueblo, and the antagonistic tie between the disciplinary leader and the savage pueblo, justify and cement each other.

The narrative's subtext can be seen as modeling the transactions between the populist leader and the pueblo that are necessary in order for bonds of loyalty and obedience to be achieved. This concealed tale has passed without significant critical comment, as the novel's narrative voice seeks at each instance to re-establish clarity and closure, to assert the normative principles that act through these highly schematic characters. Yet it is precisely this tension, and the glimpse it provides into the attractions and the demands of barbarism, that has made the novel an allegory for the construction of national identity as a continuing project.[27]

The omniscient narrator guides the reader to identify Santos Luzardo with an unambiguous conception of reason and progress, and to view Doña Bárbara as a figure of instinctual impulses and elemental anarchy. Given their identification with opposing forces, the tale of their combat appears to recount the urban elite's struggle to defeat the nation's backwardness. But there develops at the margins of this abstract tale a more complex version of the struggle, one which suggests that these two figures are historically interrelated and necessarily bound to each other. For Luzardo's claim to represent reason, or "the law," is itself arbitrary, since he is the product of an artificial center—the city as it exists in the hinterland. And Doña Bárbara's seemingly monstrous hunger for power is revealed to have derived from her history of violation rather than from her essence as the primitive.

Thus, Luzardo, as a member of the mimetic elite, is ambiguously positioned as a token both of metropolitan civilization and of its simulacrum. This tension propels the story of his quest for identity. The novel's commentary equates Luzardo with the defense of reason against the forces of anarchy and reiteratively interprets social and natural events in terms of the conflict between order and disorder. This seeming attempt to impose a single unambiguous reading of the text can also be seen as an examination of the question that motivates the narrative: from whence is to come civilizing authority in a society founded on violence and marked by the disjunction between law and justice, power and morality? The divided levels of the allegory suggest that while the civilizing elite must transact with and be energized by the pueblo it seeks to change, this dangerous process must be contained by the assertion of superior knowledge from a position of power.

The narrative commentary demonstrates that the control of the interpretation of events based on the elite's claim to represent civilization is both arbitrary and justified in a backward society. It illustrates through its redundancy and artificiality that the silencing of alternative voices through the learned discourse of the state is effected through the violence of representation. Rather than either imposing a single political meaning or deconstructing signification itself, *Doña Bárbara* seeks to demonstrate that populist double discourse, through which the national project incorporates and hierarchically controls popular knowledge, is a social necessity. The official voice of the narrative's commentary replicates the official imposition of meaning in the name of a higher reason. Its use of redundance and its suppression of alternative meanings that are present in the text, rather than undermining its authority, call attention to its ability to establish truth from a position of power.

Ambiguous Identities

There are signs that the qualities the narrator attributes to the principal characters are ambiguous and socially constructed. Luzardo's original intent in reclaiming his ranch was not to redeem the Llanos but to sever himself from his origins. After his mother took him from the Llanos to Caracas as a youth in flight from a murderous family feud, he lost his "regional sentiments" as well as "any feeling for his fatherland." The city "erased from his spirit his attraction toward the free, barbarous life of the ranch; but at the same time it had created a desire that this city could not fully satisfy. Caracas was but a big town . . . with a thousand spiritual doors open to assault by men of prey, something still very far from being the ideal city, complicated and perfect like a brain" (509). He resolved to emigrate to "civilized Europe," where the city seemed to fulfill this ideal.

Luzardo's return to the Llanos causes him to re-evaluate this goal. But his decision to rescue the Llanos from barbarism confronts him with unexpected demands to transform himself as well, as the contingencies of rural life undermine his certainties concerning standards of truth and justice. This allegory of civilization's triumph over barbarism thus appears at the same time as an allegory of their union. His cousin, Lorenzo Barquero, is presented as mirror of what Luzardo might become, for he is the product of a city built upon artifice, a secret servant of barbarism. Barquero was once a brilliant law student in Caracas, yet he left his promising career and succumbed to the seductive powers of Doña Bárbara, with whom he fathered Marisela. He exists in an alcoholic delirium next to a devouring swamp on disputed land, a location which symbolizes the retrogressive and nonreproductive condition of his class. Briefly aroused to lucidity through his interactions with Luzardo, Barquero reveals that his own demise began in the city. He had once earned high marks on his university oral exams, while being ignorant of the material, solely because he could speak articulately and create the appearance of knowledge. At that moment he realized that his intelligence was but a "mirage of the tropics" (578). Consumed by self-loathing, he left the university and became prey for the "insatiable" Doña Bárbara, who used Indian aphrodisiacs to leave him "an organism devoured by the basest vices, a destroyed will, a spirit in bestial regression" (519). Like Cardenio in *Don Quijote,* he became a Wild Man, a civilized person whose descent to madness outside society mirrors to the civilized the savage impulses residing within him.[28]

Barquero reflects the schism within his class, which had adopted the external signs of civilization while ceding power to despotism. Swinging between lucid skepticism and delirious paranoia, he encapsulates the link within the elite between paralyzing self-awareness and hallucinatory belief. Having perceived the fictive character of learned discourse, he derides the claim that learning and truth are related, and delivers himself to the horror of a "prediscursive" swamp which devours animals and men. González Echevarría reads Barquero's critique of learning as an "insight into the nature of language," which deconstructs signification.[29] In our view, Barquero reflects Gallegos's critical view of the metropolitan-oriented elite that refuses to construct meaning amidst ambiguity and delivers itself to political impotence as a class, a position which Luzardo demonstrates can be changed through the combination of authority with principle.[30] The narrative argues for the union of tutelary leader and malleable pueblo as the means to shape meaning out of local materials. It does not deconstruct "writing" but elite writing—which essentializes truth and evil in a land created by conquest.

Like the cursed swamp where Luzardo's grandfather had long before destroyed an indigenous village and taken its land, Doña Bárbara's origins reveal that in the Americas it is impossible to divorce good from evil, truth from illusion, the civilized from the barbarous.[31] Doña Bárbara is both seductive and "monstrous," a "repulsive" mixing of gender attributes, passions, and forms of knowledge—"witchcraft and religious beliefs, spells and prayers, were all mixed and confused in a single mass of superstitions."[32] The "daughter of the rivers," she is the creation of a double rape: that of her Indian mother by a Spanish river pirate and her own rape as an adolescent by the crew of his river boat. These men also killed her bestial father and the young man she loved, who had instructed her to read. After the destruction of hope ("education" and "love"), she obtains Indian magical knowledge so that she may pursue her revenge upon men. Although Doña Bárbara is presented as savage, her soul is shown to be a historical creation; while she cannot be redeemed, she can be contained. In a series of transformative episodes, Luzardo challenges her control of the Llanos through virile demonstrations of civilizing action which awaken her desire and tame her spirit. At the conclusion, she recognizes in the union of Luzardo and Marisela her own lost potential for love (i.e., civilization), and she relinquishes her power, disappearing downriver from whence she came.

Marriage: Power and Knowledge

Santos Luzardo's struggle culminates with two episodes in which his abstract relationship to the principle of order is ruptured, and he is obliged to negotiate partial and shifting truths constructed through local relations of power and forms of knowledge. These episodes demonstrate that Luzardo cannot solely represent civilization, for in this half-formed collectivity civilization and barbarism are fluid principles that demand synthesis rather than divorce. Seen in this light, Luzardo represents civilization as it exists in a backward nation, a noble impulse that runs aground on its own abstraction, plagued by society's endemic disjunction between thought and action, authority and will. The promise of the New World is that, through the synthesis of this impulse with primitive energy, an original form of civilization can be achieved.

The narrative's development places Luzardo in an unviable situation: he awakens within others the desire to reform, but they bring to life within him the desire for barbarism. He succumbs to this desire after his enemies murder his peon and his attempt to fence the plains is sabotaged. Luzardo demands that the district chief treat the death of his peon as a crime to be investigated, as required by law, rather than ruling that he had died of natural causes, as the official wishes. The official, like Gómez, manipulates the law in accord with his own standard of justice, as an adjunct of local power relations and a product of the knowledge he acquires "in the street" rather than in the court. He teaches Luzardo about this kind of justice with a story. "There once was one of those men who are called stupid; but who was far from a fool." He didn't know how to spell, and he pronounced words beginning with a J as if they began with an H. When his secretary wrote his words with the spelling that fit proper pronunciation, he ordered the secretary to "put a dot over that H for me!" (731). As a result, street knowledge is written into the book and the "stupid" man prevails over the educated one. Luzardo concludes from this story that he must act outside the state, since it is institutionally corrupt, and decides to combat barbarism using its own violent methods. Given the logic of the Llanos, violence inevitably escalates as a consequence of his violent acts. In an armed encounter with Doña Bárbara's evil henchman, the "Brujeador" (the Sorcerer), he shoots and apparently kills him. Although he drew in self-defense, he realizes with horror that he is now controlled by barbarism's limitless desires.

In parallel episodes, Luzardo is saved from moral decline by a synthesis of civilization and barbarism that grows out of his interaction with the pueblo. In the first, this synthesis is imaged in the private realm, through the attainment of romantic love between Luzardo and Marisela. Luzardo recounts in despair to Marisela how he had murdered the Brujeador. However she argues that, given the angle of the bullet, the fatal shot must have been fired by Luzardo's loyal peon Pajarote. Because Marisela has faith in Luzardo, which is the product of his "refinement" of her spirit, she intuits the correct explanation; her gesture returns to him his self-respect, and he responds with his love. The truth she gives him saves the Llanos from continuing barbarism, for he renews his faith in civilized behavior and recommences his unfinished mission: "to discover . . . the hidden sources of goodness of his land and of his people" (781).

The second episode, which takes the reader from the zone of sentiment into the peon's social world, unites Luzardo with his peon Pajarote. Pajarote relies on his practical knowledge of Llano life to evaluate the meaning of his loyalty to his patron. Thus he had told no one, despite Luzardo's anguish, that it was he who fired the fatal shot, for he knew that "when it was time to establish responsibility before the law, it would be easier for Luzardo to get off free" (784). Although he had risked his life for Luzardo, he was not foolish enough to incriminate himself and be jailed. But now Pajarote learns that the judge has ruled that Doña Bárbara's foreman, who is dead at her orders, was the murderer of the Brujeador and that the case is closed. Once out of danger, Pajarote pragmatically admits the truth to Luzardo concerning his role in the shooting. Taken aback, Luzardo insists they admit their own guilt to the judge so as to remove from the written record a murder accusation against an innocent man. Pajarote impatiently replies that the judge has no interest in changing the record and argues that this verdict is actually a just one because it is God's means of settling accounts for the foreman's previous murders. In case Luzardo still plans to turn them in, Pajarote comments with apparent innocence that perhaps Luzardo had actually shot the Brujeador after all. Luzardo recognizes that Pajarote's God, like the district chief, alters rules to fit his interests, and that as a patron he must make concessions to his subordinate; bemused, he consents to accept the collective fiction. The official history will have dots placed above the H's.

The episode with Pajarote is a climactic but overlooked moment in the many-layered story. The civilizing project is presented as a process of transaction and negotiation, in which elite principles are constrained by popular practice, and elite leadership is strengthened through the appropriation of popular knowledge. Luzardo is wed to a double image of the pueblo: as the ideal object of his civilizing action, it is a humanizing source of sentiment; and as the foundation of his reform project, it is an ambiguous source of unwritten knowledge and primitive energy. In both episodes Luzardo becomes more clearly defined as a class subject through interaction with a subordinate figure from the pueblo. Yet the episodes differ as far as the relationship they depict between the educated elite and the pueblo. When seen as "love," the relationship is imaged as a harmonious romantic union based on the natural bonds of affection between man and woman. Seen as loyalty, it is presented as mutual respect based on the necessary interdependence that leader and subordinate recognize as binding them. The development of these two images of a tutelary bond, and their intersection at the moment of Luzardo's redemption as an agent of social transformation, set out a two-level allegorical model for the populist project of nationalist reform.

Doña Bárbara's return to her river origins marks the subsiding of the barbarous currents with Luzardo and Marisela, but it indicates as well that she remains a submerged presence. The pull that Doña Bárbara exerts as a repressed force demands that containment be continually practiced, for as the narrator observes, she has a seductive mythic attraction for the popular imagination. Through the oft-told tales of her "loves and her crimes, many of them solely the invention of popular fantasy," she has become a "somber but at once fascinating heroine, . . . she was almost a legendary figure who excited the imagination of the city" (787). As a story of transformation, *Doña Bárbara* configures the populist project of reform as the idealization and domestication of the popular by the educated leader. The attainment of civilization in America requires him to marry principle with instinct, so that the pueblo may be domesticated and confined, and the river of barbarous energy may return to its bed. This linear tale of progress that maps straight fences upon the hallucinatory circularity of the Llanos is at the

249

same time a tale of the river that always lies at the border, exerting its attraction, rising to dissolve boundaries if not carefully contained.

The Amparo Massacre

The town of Amparo lies on the Arauca River, on the southwestern edge of the Llanos. The river legally divides Venezuela from Colombia but, in practice, provides a fluid path that connects the two border zones, linking families and economies through trade in cattle, fish, and consumer goods which travel in different directions in accord with changes in the economies. Whether in the form of individual purchase or wholesale smuggling, much of this trade is regarded officially as contraband. Drugs joined the flow of goods across the river, en route to northern continents, when the Colombian drug cartels came under pressure. The river has been crossed as well by members of Colombia's guerrilla organization, the ELN (Ejercito de Liberacion Nacional), to kidnap Venezuelan landowners for ransom.[33]

Following what the government claimed were the kidnappings of several ranchers, President Lusinchi created a counterinsurgency brigade, the CEJAP,[34] in October 1987. While the CEJAP was under the command of Army General Humberto Camejo Arias, it was headed by a DISIP intelligence agent notorious for his direction of paramilitary operations.[35] During 1988 the CEJAP claimed on several occasions to have encountered and killed Colombian guerrillas and to have prevented further kidnappings. Its first year coincided with increasing political unrest; protests against rising prices, police repression, and abuses by authorities spread across the country. Arrests and government harassment of critics rose, as did the use of the military against demonstrators. President Lusinchi explained the use of force as a response to the attempts by subversive groups to destabilize democracy.[36]

As this was a year of intense campaigning for the December 1988 presidential election, Lusinchi's actions were largely directed toward preserving his positive image as president in the face of declining economic conditions and of a challenge to his faction's control of Acción Democrática's leadership. AD's presidential candidate, and the predicted victor of the election, was the charismatic former president Carlos Andrés Pérez, Lusinchi's arch rival.[37] Lusinchi's response to rising criticism and unrest was widely interpreted as being mediated by his determination to defend his image and that of his close aide and spokesperson, his mistress Blanca Ibáñez. Withstanding scandal for several years, they had controlled the means to win public support and quel criticism.[38] The DISIP was one of those means.

The Official Story: A Military Confrontation

On October 29, 1988, General Camejo Arias informed reporters attending an army seminar near the Andean border that a clash with Colombian guerrillas had just occurred. Reporters were flown to the scene on a remote branch of the Arauca River outside of Amparo, where they were shown the bullet-ridden bodies of men wearing uniforms and insignia from the Colombian guerrilla army ELN and lying next to guns near a canoe. The general announced that according to intelligence reports, the guerrillas were headed to sabotage Venezuelan oil pipes and to kidnap ranchers. The CEJAP had intercepted fifty heavily armed insurgents in their boats and had defeated them in a military confrontation. Sixteen guerrillas were killed; the CEJAP suffered no casualties.

This sensational news was reported throughout the country, and President Lusinchi, who presented himself as defender of the pueblo, congratulated the general for protecting democracy from subversion and the nation from the violation of its borders. The event seemed to vindicate Lusinchi's hard line against subversives and against threats to the integrity of Venezuela's territory. His approach contrasted with his rival Carlos Andrés Pérez's policy of incorporating leftist leaders into his political camp and negotiating with Colombia concerning a border dispute.[39]

The People's Story: A Massacre

A series of factors converged to create around this event an alternative narrative—known as "the people's story"—which redefined the "confrontation" as a "massacre." This story was constructed through dramatic display and action, and the acceptance of its credibility was inseparable from the conditions of its production. Townspeople from Amparo asserted that sixteen men from their town (only one of them a Colombian citizen) had set out by boat on a Saturday morning to spend the day fishing and to share "sanchocho" (peasant soup) and rum by the banks of the river. Hours later the boat owner's wife, who resided near the tangled "Colorado" (Red) branch of the Arauca river, heard heavy gunfire and saw military helicopters overhead as she prepared the soup for the group's arrival. Nobody returned from the outing. The next day the press and television announced a government victory outside Amparo against foreign guerrilla forces, leaving sixteen dead. The military knew there were only fourteen casualties but assumed that reality would soon match the official facts.[40]

However, the police chief of Amparo unexpectedly escorted back to town, at their request, two members of the outing who had survived the attack by swimming through the swampy stream and hiding overnight at a nearby ranch. Wollmer Pinilla and José Augusto Arias[41] told of the fishing group's ambush by a heavily armed military unit, of troops shooting their unarmed companions point-blank, and of their flight while pursued by helicopters. Certain they were in danger, they remained in the police station for protection. Local residents, confronted both with their loss and with the denial of its reality through media reports that transformed the dead men's identity, sought to save the victims from being written into history as subversives. Members of the DISIP and the National Guard repeatedly attempted to remove the survivors from the jail "for questioning," but the police chief refused at gunpoint to release the two men, and a large group of townspeople surrounded the police station, singing the national anthem and waving the flag, in order to obstruct the efforts of the security officers. To avert civil unrest, authorities called Congressman Wálter Márquez, known in the border area as a defender of agricultural workers, to mediate.[42] Relying on his parliamentary immunity, he took the survivors in custody and initiated their defense. The bodies of the dead men had already been buried by the military in a collective grave without autopsies having been performed as required by law. The survivors, everyone knew, were essential for the rewriting of the story. The townspeople's collective defense of the survivors, and the two men's decision to speak out rather than hide, were central to the conditions of production by which the tale of the military confrontation became the Amparo massacre.

Contending Explanations

Both official and opposition discourse interpreted these conflicting stories in terms of the dominant paradigm of state-mediated national unity, but they built upon opposing strands of meaning that are present within the foundational allegory of civilization and barbarism. Official discourse depicted the Amparo confrontation as a call for the civilizing state to defend the nation against threats to order. Opposition discourse presented the Amparo massacre as a sign of barbarism's emergence within the governing elite and as a call to restore, through civilizing intervention, the tutelary bond between leader and pueblo. In asserting popular innocence, opposition discourse evoked historic associations between the country and authenticity that are inscribed within populist discourse. The official effort to cast the pueblo unambiguously as a threat was caught on the other term of the polarity it had long attempted to contain.

In the contest between official and opposition explanations, contrasting images of the political landscape were projected onto partial information, as the ensuing investigation was blanketed in secrecy by a military court and government silence. But the evidence of a massacre and an attempted cover-up sufficed for the opposition argument to be taken as valid, for the public did not expect that its claims to truth be backed by complete knowledge. Within a political landscape in which truth appears irremediably contingent, actors recognize the unavoidable incompleteness of their knowledge. Accustomed to murky political waters, they swim in them with ease.

Contention over the events rested heavily on the credibility of those who spoke about them. Officials invoked their status and access to restricted knowledge to claim the truth of their account. President Lusinchi and General Camejo Arias made ceremonious televised speeches a week after the attack, in which they supported the official story with their word as respected leaders. While Lusinchi acknowledged the dead men were Venezuelans, he cited secret intelligence reports in support of his claim that they were a threat to the polity. The sight of the grieving, impoverished relatives of the dead men—largely women and children—had created a public impact, as had the personal plea for justice a group of them made to Lusinchi on behalf of men who they asserted were innocent rural workers. Photographed with his arm around the shoulder of an aged mother, the president assured them the law would be fairly applied. But on television he dismissed their word and, presenting himself as more knowledgeable in issues of politics, asserted that the men were in fact allies of Colombia's ELN, engaged in a mission kept secret from their families.[43] "A golden rule of the clandestine struggle is that you cannot tell even those most closely related to you what you are doing." Further, he presented them as men with ample criminal records—for guerrilla activity is often recorded as crime—and linked the security threat in the border areas to threats to democracy in the domestic arena.[44] Lusinchi's denial signaled that the townspeople's version of reality would be discredited, a tactic which rested on notions of backwardness and disorder attached to the hinterland.

The executive and the military throughout the following months attempted to keep information confidential and to discount as invalid evidence offered by other sources.[45] They questioned the credibility of the victims and their relatives, seeking to create a belief in the victims' guilt through dramatic actions that treated them as criminals. The bodies of the dead were denied a family burial, and only after a month's delay were they allowed an autopsy at the Congressional Commission's insistence. The director of the Judicial Police announced that the victims had extensive criminal records (a charge which was shown to be false), and Camejo Arias stated that "everyone living in Amparo is in some way a criminal."[46] Above all, the two survivors were treated as subversives.[47] Despite mounting evidence and nationwide protests, the military judge charged the survivors with military rebellion and ordered them jailed.[48]

Political leaders opposed to the president criticized the official story but within set limits. Most defined the massacre as an abuse of power and presented themselves as concerned protectors of the pueblo. Carlos Andrés Pérez signaled this stance within days of the attack; he called it an "unjustifiable event" which was mishandled by the DISIP and offered as evidence the fact that several of the dead men were AD members "involved in my electoral campaign."[49] A multi-party Congressional Commission (which was headed by a Pérez supporter and included Wálter Márquez) organized an investigation.[50] Several newspapers, primarily those which had conflicts with Lusinchi, sponsored investigative reports of the case.[51]

As information about the attack and its planners emerged, there arose a consensus—outside conservative circles—that the CEJAP had massacred unarmed townspeople and had presented the assault as an encounter with guerrillas.[52] The evidence was not hard to find. There had been, in fact, a notable lack of effort to construct a plausible armed encounter and to dissimulate the massacre. Aside from the fact that the victims were Venezuelans whose relatives could claim their identity, there were many signs indicating the nature of the attack. As journalists and congressmen saw at the site and at the autopsy, the dead men's guerrilla uniforms had no bullet holes; there was evidence of torture; they had been shot at close range in the head and back and defaced with acid to make them unrecognizable; few weapons were found with them; and the scene was strewn only with casings from arms used by the DISIP.[53]

The explanations accounting for the attack, though limited by political convention and by fear of retaliation, converged with stories of political repression occurring during the administration of the apparently affable Lusinchi, with quotidian experiences of manipulation, and with newly exposed corruption scandals implicating both Lusinchi and Blanca Ibáñez. For many, the Amparo massacre confirmed what they implicitly knew. The opposition argued that the DISIP had planned the attack in an effort to expand its power and autonomy in the border region. Márquez asserted that the Amparo massacre, timed to coincide with the election, was the climax in a series of massacres on the border in which agricultural workers, primarily undocumented Colombians, had been presented as guerrillas.[54] He claimed that the DISIP and landowners, many of whom were retired military officers, were allied in this effort. The DISIP backed the ranchers in their takeover of peasant lands, and it charged them for the protection services it offered against kidnapping by guerrillas. In some cases, widely publicized kidnappings had been staged, for proof of a guerrilla threat bolstered the DISIP's claim to be a necessary presence in the region and won it freedom to act unchecked. An unspoken suggestion was that the DISIP and its superiors were involved in the drug trade and related illicit activities.[55]

These and other questions, however, were not pursued. The issues of why this form of terror was being practiced, or of how a counterinsurgency brigade with historic ties to international intelligence agencies and close to the presidency could have such "autonomy," were not raised, and the reputation of the military was carefully protected. The possibility of uncovering the truth was treated as the achievement of necessarily partial and partisan approximations to a concealed reality. The opposition explanation of the Amparo massacre was collectively constructed from fragmentary information and from the ceaseless gossip that is vital in a system of restricted and personally controlled knowledge. It was plausible to the public, for it rested on principles of political plotting and the construction of appearances which recurrently pattern political life. Those closer to power knew of links to an intricate network of powerful interests that made the establishment of the truth quite unlikely. But the premise that knowledge was obtainable only through the partialized views of those linked to power, and that it was always incomplete, did not lessen the story's power.

Country and City in Postcolonial Landscape

An Allegory of Rupture

The Amparo massacre had its greatest impact as an allegory of the pueblo's marginalization. While this allegory was developed in dialogue with the opposition account, it countered the terms of the dominant allegory of the tutelary union that the opposition account accepted. Instead, it represented the relationship between the pueblo and the elite as having been fractured by the disjunction between political power and truth. Rural and lower-class people became emblems of the truth that the powerful attempt to erase; in an inversion of the terms of the country and city model, the source of truth and moral order was located within the pueblo. This critique presented the people from Amparo (which means "protection") as being "desamparados" (abandoned), like the pueblo. Contesting the official attempt to construct the appearance of a popular threat, public protests redefined the Amparo men as victims rather than subversives and reconfigured the pueblo as vocal rather than passive. The people could speak truths which were independent of the center's knowledge. "I felt as if a block of ice was stuck in my heart when I heard the President call our sons guerrillas during our visit to the Presidential Palace," said Elda Mosqueda. "I interrupted him, 'I might be illiterate, but I knew my son very well, and he was not a guerrilla.' "[56]

Before the election, student-led demonstrations swept through cities, and in a large "March for Life" in the capital, the Amparo fishermen were depicted as symbols of a martyred pueblo, pawns in a system of inverted values. The survivors and the relatives of the dead men, with the aid of activist clergy, visited churches and Christian base groups in the working class "barrio" sectors of the city, where videos recounting the massacre circulated as well. The massacre prompted the establishment of new human rights groups, which for the first time addressed larger issues of political rights.[57] The survivors' odyssey transformed the Amparo massacre into an open-ended story of innocence abused by power. When Arias and Pinilla were ordered detained on charges of subversion, in fear for their lives they sought political asylum from Mexico.[58] They returned to Venezuela in January 1989, after President-elect Pérez promised they would be safe and the law would be fairly applied, but they found themselves again trapped by legal maneuvers, as a new accommodation was sought between the Lusinchi and Pérez political factions and military and intelligence agencies.[59]

Through these actions and statements, the Amparo case was made a symbol of the hidden quotidian experience of powerlessness at the hands of authorities, a form through which to recognize unacknowledged relations of power. Thus configured, it created an image of the pueblo united horizontally across rural and urban divisions rather than an image of the pueblo's union with a benevolent elite which mediates its common ties.

As an allegorical tale, the Amparo massacre was widely seen as resonating with the foundational tale of civilization and barbarism on the Llanos. People were quick to relate the events to Gallegos's novel and to note the inversion of the geography of truth. For the canoe which went up the Arauca River carried "people of the pueblo" ("gente del pueblo") in the image of Marisela, and their assailants resembled Doña Bárbara's henchmen rather than agents of a civilizing state. If, in dominant ideology, the union between elite and pueblo was based on the elite's provision of protection and tutelage, then the persecution and abandonment of people who embodied the national icon of the pueblo—humble villagers from the Llanos—were taken to signal the rupture of that union.[60]

The Geo-Politics of Truth and Double Discourse

In Latin America, a colonial legacy of political instability and deep social inequalities has forged modes of representing knowledge adapted to shifting political arrangements and fluctuating standards. On the public stage of politics, truth claims seldom achieve the appearance of independent natural facts but are colored by their social markings. The social space of Latin American nations is what de Certeau calls a "piling of heterogenous places" that are not homogenized, even on the surface, by modern forms.[61] In this multilayered space, a "forest of narrativities" is created not only by a multiplicity of media stories but by multiple modalities of narration, all creating a dense and often impenetrable sense of the real. The mode of "information"[62] disseminated by the media, which seeks to fabricate "realities out of appearances," competes with modalities of communication premised on a recognition of "the great silence of things" and dependent upon the value of experience and the force of beliefs formed in variously organized spaces of face-to-face social interaction.[63] The media itself, molded by the place in which it operates, does not just impose a modern mode of impersonal or objective communication; it does not necessarily appear as an anonymous code but as a magnified extension of voices that come from other social places, etching with visible threads the recognizable faces of power. In societies fractured by colonialism, a double discourse serves to mediate among these heterogeneous social places and modalities of narration, fixing unstable meanings through the deployment of power.

Our analysis of *Doña Bárbara* and the Amparo massacre suggests that the construction of a populist project in Venezuela has been premised on the implicit recognition of the fundamental instability of local sources of authority. In the absence of stable standards, truth claims are constructed on the basis of situational and contingent considerations, which are nevertheless presented as fixed and absolute. In some respects, the duality of double discourse is similar to the play of simulation and concealment characteristic of most political life, particularly when relations of domination and subordination are involved. Moureau argues that dominated groups, as they identify with and dissociate themselves from dominant groups, develop a "split subjectivity."[64] Their discourse, which is permeated by and yet distinct from dominant discourse, partakes of this division. Yet the distinguishing feature of colonial double discourse is the pervasive and perverse inscription of this duality within a colonial logic that deauthorizes the collective foundations of local knowledge. There is an unresolved tension between the requirement that states represent themselves as sovereign political units and the tenuous basis of their authority within neocolonial contexts.

In terms of Williams's model, it is as if both country and city remain trapped in an unstable colonial landscape which continually undermines national sources of identity and knowledge, particularly as local forms are defensively projected as authentic against a coveted metropolitan culture. Thus double discourse expresses and organizes the split between the appearance of national sovereignty and the continuing hold of international subordination, a split inscribed in the truncated character of domestic productive relations as well as in the mimetic form of consumption values, in the production of political knowledge as well as in the formation of collective identities.

Double discourse mediates oppositions that constitute dominant representations of national identity. Acting as a code of identity formation, its primary focus concerns the effort of the dominant class to negotiate the tensions produced by the dual sources of its identity as the leader of the populist development project. This class claims to govern both from the *city,* as the representative of metropolitan progress which derives from the center, and from the *country,* as the representative of "the people" on the basis of an anti-centrist nationalist ideology. These conflicting claims, and their inbuilt ambiguity, establish the basis for the deauthorization of the dominant alliance as a source of knowledge, undermining the authority of its actions and accounts. Its promise to bring modern progress fuels the notion that it is but an imitative importer of knowledge from the center, a backward pretender to the status of civilizing agent. And its promise to redress the domination of the periphery by the center strengthens anti-elite discourse and, with it, the notion that the dominant alliance is an anti-national and anti-popular agent of the center.

If it is difficult to found authority and identity on a stable social grounding, such as class or religion, then the principle of mediation itself, of holding together the disparate and contradictory while partaking of them, becomes impressed with positive images.[65] That this mediation is one of containment rather than of integration is part of what these images attempt to conceal. Power is made to reside within the mediator, within those who look in both directions—inward and outward, toward the future and the past, speaking the languages of the elite and the pueblo, of modernity and tradition. This Janus-faced character, Tom Nairn asserts, is constitutive of peripheral nationalism, marking its attempt to appropriate and to reject progress in the face of industrialization's overwhelming disruptions, and sealing it with a deep ambivalence.[66] Within Venezuela, Janus-faced populist nationalism, which speaks the Enlightenment language of universal progress and national harmony while asserting colonizing practices of control and marginalization, has historically implied the public construction of appearances linked to the concealment of relations of power. The Amparo massacre marks this project's growing inability to preserve the appearance of national unity in a world increasingly fractured by the movements of international capital.

11

Raymond Williams and the Inhuman Limits of Culture

Forest Pyle

> No idealistic but only a materialistic deliverance from myth.
> —Walter Benjamin, "Karl Krauss"[1]

To Walter Benjamin, Karl Krauss is the "messenger" depicted in the "old engravings" who "rushes toward us crying aloud," much like the "angel of history" engraved in the ninth of Benjamin's "Theses on the Philosophy of History." Surveying the wreckage of history accumulated before him, the messenger Krauss cries out for "public judgments."[2] Something of this messenger is inscribed in what Raymond Williams "came to say." For Williams, as for Benjamin, the messages that we must learn to hear are written in tenses of the future and the past: only the committed historical reading of all forms of "writing in society" can hope to salvage what Benjamin calls a "materialistic deliverance from myth."

This essay, written to the memory of Raymond Williams, addresses his efforts to achieve a "materialistic" deliverance of culture. Not that we will remember Williams by the achievement of that redemption: at once inevitable and compelling, the failures of that project are failures which disclose in turn the very limits—linguistic, political, colonial—of "culture" itself. My interest here is not to offer a comprehensive account of the concept of culture, or even to make a thorough inventory of Williams's own accounts of the concept. I am concerned instead with the nature of Williams's investments in and commitments to this term: I am interested in the kinds of critical analysis made possible by "culture," and in the critical intertwining in Williams's work between "culture" and "community." I want to consider how Williams's reliance on the pervasive and elusive concept of culture produces some unavowed but unavoidable confrontations with what I will somewhat elliptically at this point call the "inhuman." These theoretical confrontations open, moreover, a critical reading of the situation of empire and colonialism within Williams's map of culture. The incompatibility between "language" and "culture"—to give this confrontation a shorthand definition—discloses the nature of the symptomatic absence of empire in the work of Raymond Williams, and thus implicates in its entirety the fate of his cultural analysis.

Articulations of Culture

It has become customary to pay tribute to the remarkable reach of Williams's work; the impressive body of his critical writings extends from the British novel to the British labor movement, from modern European drama to theories of nationalism, from television to Marvell. But to any reader of Raymond Williams, what soon becomes as striking as this range of interests is the sustained coherence of its critical vision. We are bound to applaud such a compound of rigorous consistency and extensive intellectual "worldliness," situated as we are in this period of well-documented and widely deplored academic specialization. The singular combination of critical range and coherence that characterizes the writings of Raymond Williams is made possible by the consistent work of the concept of culture. The word and the concept "culture" assume a significance in Williams which is considerably more than thematic: "culture" often appears to be as much the author as it does the object of Williams's research. To write of Raymond Williams is thus to write in more or less explicit terms of what Walter Benjamin would call the "constellations" of culture.

To note but one critical tradition for which the work of this Welsh critic has made a difference, Raymond Williams's treatments of the concept of culture have contributed considerably to the debates within Western Marxism over the theoretical and political validity of the spatial metaphor of base and superstructure.[3] Williams is by no means the first "within" Marxism to stress the mutual reciprocities of base and superstructure: he is always quick to remind us that the distinction of that discovery rests with Marx himself.[4] But the decisive and recurring element of Williams's initially implicit and later overt engagements with the texts of Marx and the discourse of Western Marxism can be traced to the singular significance Williams assigns to the concept of culture. Any genuine materialism must, according to Williams, learn to engage and to theorize the formative processes of culture. The success or failure of Williams's materialism rests with the proposition that culture is not a stable domain or sphere but a fundamental human activity. This repositioning of "culture" from a domain or sphere into a human activity or process is a consistent feature of Williams's work, and is informed by the rigorous historical and etymological research that culminates with his volume of *Keywords*. The cultural analysis that characterizes *Culture and Society* (1958) as well as *Writing in Society* (1981) is formed by a persistent historical grappling with the concept of culture. Indeed, Williams will go so far as to assert in the opening pages of *Marxism and Literature* that "it is . . . impossible to carry through any serious cultural analysis without reaching towards a consciousness of the concept itself: a consciousness that must be . . . historical" (*ML*, 11). The conception of culture which sustains cultural analysis is itself thus sustained by the commitment to a historical consciousness which Williams never abandons. Such a historicism is organized on the premise, as Williams declares in 1977, that one can "understand the term [culture] itself" through "a return to the modulations of the term through history."[5] By virtue of this historicist "return," argues Williams, culture can be understood and, by this understanding, redeemed. We will have occasion to return to the premises and promises of this historicism, but it can be stressed at this point that Williams's genealogical labors reveal "culture" to be significantly more than a principal "idea" of nineteenth- and twentieth-century intellectual history. Culture is for Williams a term which no "history of ideas" can accommodate, because "culture" names the very process by and through which history, including the history of ideas, is made. At the same time, however, the viability of this notion of culture is predicated on the assumption that history is not forever lost to the past, and that it may be recovered by the present.[6]

If the word "culture" names for Williams the material processes of history, this necessitates an historical analysis which must recover the various social, economic, and political investments made in culture's name. "The development of the word *culture*," writes Williams in the 1958 introduction to *Culture and Society*, "is a record of a number of important and continuing reactions to these changes in our social, economic and political life, and may be seen, in itself, as a special kind of map by which the nature of the changes can be explored."[7] Culture is conceived as a form of "mapping" of the particular historical configurations of "social, economic and political life." Culture thus becomes for Williams the critical and historical template through which genuine interpretation of a specific work or an extensive practice is made possible. We cannot, in other words, understand the development of Victorian narrativity, the ascent of modernism, or the advent of television without the cartography of culture, for only the concept of culture can make readable the connections between artistic form and social relations. What first appears to be philological research turns out to be the elaboration of a fully social hermeneutic.

But to describe Williams's recurrent interest in culture according to this hermeneutical model fails to do justice to his decisive "interventions," as they have come to be called, in the historically and politically charged debates regarding the meaning and function of culture. Throughout his writings, Williams is consistent in his desire to wrest "culture" from its installation in a conservative tradition, and to restore to the notion of culture its critical capacity. But to "refunction" culture demands the most careful understanding of its various historical functions. This explains in part Williams's oddly sympathetic assessment of Matthew Arnold, a critic whose hostility to political activism is embedded in the title of his most influential work. But for Williams, if Arnold is read against the grain of his more mandarin pronouncements, the critical *activity* of culture can be restored even to such a work as *Culture and Anarchy*.[8] Divested of its aestheticism, a critical character of culture is, according to Williams, implicit in Arnold's work and present in various forms throughout the "culture and society" tradition. This reworking of culture culminates in Williams's 1982 proposal for a "sociology of culture." In Williams's eyes, such a proposal demands that culture be approached from the outset as a formative aspect of that which we call the "social." Culture must, writes Williams, emphasize "a whole social order"; it cannot be conceived as "simply derived from an otherwise constituted social order."[9] Culture is proposed here as nothing less than "constitutive": it is "the *signifying system* through which necessarily . . . a social order is communicated, reproduced, experienced and explored." (*SC*, 13). Culture becomes, in other words, constitutive of our social being; and any social hermeneutic must ultimately rely upon the "signifying system," the language of culture.[10] The "experience" and "communication" of the social order is made possible or, in other terms, *articulated* by culture. While "articulation" does not belong to Williams's vocabulary of social and cultural analysis, it is perhaps the most adequate term to describe his sense of the work and activity of culture. This notion of articulation relies on both senses of the word: the "linking" of the individual with society and the language "articulated" by this linkage. By this "articulation" of culture, the social is "reproduced"; and by learning to read the articulations of culture, the social may be *critically* "explored."

Such a critical explanation of culture can be understood to be at the heart of the recent emergence of "Cultural Studies" in North American universities. This incarnation of cultural studies has a deeply variegated and international genealogy, owing more perhaps to certain Continental names than it does to the postwar British tradition of Williams, Hoggart, Thompson, and Hall. But however one reckons the theoretical debts of cultural studies, the work of Raymond Williams remains both formative for it as an institutional project and symptomatic of its limits. The initial enthusiasm which greeted "Cultural Studies" has been tempered considerably by the (perhaps inevitable) circumscriptions of its more radical political promises. Though the enthusiasm may not have been altogether warranted in the first place, cultural studies and its methodological correlate, "cultural materialism," continue to pose a significant challenge to the more conservative models of teaching and scholarship by contesting persistent formalist models of exegesis and evaluation. From the perspective of literary studies, the turn to the "cultural" proposes a displacement of the "literary" as the term which orients the practices of reading and interpretation. Within the horizons of contemporary critical discussion, "culture" has come to designate a more extensive ensemble of texts and institutions through which a society is, to return to Williams's formulation "communicated, reproduced, experienced, explored"—and perhaps even remade into something resembling "community." The project of "cultural studies" thus promises more than a hermeneutics of culture: by positing culture as an agent of both social knowledge and social change, it harbors the ambitious, if implicit, promise of transforming both the subjects and objects of reading. What remains to be determined, however, is whether or not such a social and political promise can ever be fulfilled in the name of "culture."

Community: Culture's Narrative

The function of culture in Williams is invariably linked to the possibility of "community," to the prospect that a common existence—a shared subject position "we"—can be formed or recovered from the reified social relations of the present; that "culture" can, in other words, make the "communal" body of a people. Hence Williams's sympathy for Victorian fiction: from the Brontës through "Dickens to Lawrence," the British novel exhibits a consistent concern, both formal and thematic, for the problems and projects of community. It is no coincidence that when Williams asserts that "most novels are in some sense knowable communities," he makes this quietly polemical assertion regarding the ontological status of the novel in the opening sentence of his treatment of George Eliot.[11] Such a description makes the claim that the novel is inherently epistemological and social, and that these epistemological and social aspects of narrative are themselves intertwined. George Eliot would no doubt recognize and even espouse such an account of the novel. The project of a "knowable community" is a matter of real formal and thematic urgency for Eliot: her novels repeatedly register the crisis of a narrative "community" poised perpetually on the brink of a dislocation of such severity that it would disrupt our ability to "know" it. Responding to this condition, Williams demonstrates that the notion of the "knowable community" exists in George Eliot primarily as a *desire*, one which often takes the form of nostalgia. Thus, "knowability" is a formal narrative *project* and not a given condition; it is a task which the novel must undertake but which it by no means necessarily fulfills. What makes George Eliot so decisive for Williams's understanding of Victorian fiction is her recognition of the strained, tenuous link between available narrative modes of "knowing" and the community to be "known." Describing the failure of Eliot's attempts to represent an assortment of subaltern characters, Williams points to the "very recognition [in Eliot] of conflict, of the existence of classes, of divisions and contrasts of feeling and speaking" (*CC*, 169). Such recognition is, Williams argues, produced at the expense of any "unity of idiom" in the novel. It turns out that the linkage in Eliot between "knowledge" and "community" depends upon a narrative idiom which, internally divided, proves incapable of sustaining either "knowledge" or "community."[12] The fragility of "knowledge" and "community" explored by Eliot's novels is thus a fragility of language itself: "The problem of the knowable community is then, in a new way, a problem of language" (*CC*, 171).

The disunity of idiom, this "problem of language" encountered time and again in George Eliot, leads Williams to posit the distinction between the "knowable" and the "known" community:

> The knowable community is this common life which she is glad
> to record with a necessary emphasis; but the known commu-

nity is something else again—an uneasy contract, in language,
with another interest and another sensibility. (CC, 172–73)

The distinction between "knowable community" (the shared horizons
of a "common life," the idea of a common culture) and "known
community" (the deeply reified social relations) is inscribed in and by
language: the linguistic markings of these "uneasy contracts." Williams
recognizes that the passage from the "known community" to the
"knowable community"—the passage projected by "most novels"—
can be achieved only by way of this "uneasy contract" in language.
But the prospects of this passage are made more "uneasy" by the fact
that this "contract" must be negotiated through a language which
appears at times intractable, a language which always harbors other
"interests" and "sensibilities." Williams understands these latter as
properly *class* "interests" and "sensibilities" which register their social
contradictions and divisions in language; but this particular condition
demonstrates the perhaps inevitable difficulty of making an always
interest-laden language the reliable voice or medium of a "knowable
community." Though Williams never abandons that project, never
relinquishes the hope that a "knowable community" can find its appropriate narrative idiom, his essays on the Victorian novel continue to
record the forms of its failures. These are registered as formal as well
as thematic divisions; they are "the source," writes Williams, "of the
disturbance, the unease, the divided construction of the later George
Eliot novels" (CC, 174).

We can read this recognition of divisions and disturbances as the
sign of a recognition that "community" is not there to be "known";
what Williams calls the "knowable community" is that which must be
produced by cultural narratives such as the Victorian novel. This is
certainly a conception of the social work of the novel shared by George
Eliot, who considers the novel to be a form of "aesthetic teaching."
These divisions are not the inventions of George Eliot; they are the
problems embedded, as Williams demonstrates, in the narrative form
Eliot inherits, problems which she must confront "in almost every
sentence she writes" (CC, 169). In spite of what Williams regards as
this genuine and almost painful engagement with the problems of
narrating a community, and in spite of his evident dispositions for the
narrative mode of realism, Williams's concluding judgments of George
Eliot stress the politically conservative aspects of her novel-making.
According to Williams, Eliot's project—to remake through the materials of narrative itself the community that appears to have vanished—
remains designed to keep a genuine community "ideally in the past"

(*CC*, 180). If community exists in George Eliot as a figure of nostalgia, the wistful effect of a narrated past, in Williams's judgment these novels become the ideological correlate and support of a social order predicated on the withdrawal and abolition of an "authentic" community. The tone of disappointment registered in Williams's final pages on George Eliot is unmistakable: the disillusionment he exhibits toward the later novels derives from the belief that community itself has been betrayed by Eliot's resignation to insurmountable division.

Williams's interpretations of George Eliot deliver him (and those of us who follow his movements) to the verge of a disturbing recognition which he cannot acknowledge. Betrayed by the tone of Williams's disillusionment with the late and divided novels of George Eliot is the deeper recognition that the notion of community is irreducibly beset with divisions which are simultaneously linguistic and social. Through a confrontation which never quite takes place, we begin to recognize that "community" is constituted as the effect of what Williams calls "the paradox of language" in the novel. Raymond Williams must, in other words, refuse the recognition made possible by his own interpretation: he refused to acknowledge that the social and linguistic divisions in which "community" is entangled are not the temporary conditions of a narrative mode in crisis or transition, but the inextricable elements of community's appearance. Such a disavowal does not on the face of it seem necessary; for Williams's critical and historical project should accommodate the disclosure that the real social and ideological effects of "community" are produced by the narratives that sanction or even construct the community they ostensibly represent. A "cultural materialism," in other words, might be expected to pursue an analysis of the *constitutive, material* capacity of narrative. But for Williams, theoretical positions are always achieved through careful practices of reading British novelists such as Eliot, and are thus inseparable from the particularities of the interpretation. In this case we are delivered by Williams's analysis to the discovery that narrative language, beset by division, cannot be made into the reliable voice or medium of a "knowable community," that community is a story written in divisive idioms which cannot sustain it. For as sensitive a reader as Williams to acknowledge the narrativity of community would result in the acknowledgment that, strictly speaking, community is impossible.

"The Inhuman Rewriting of the Past"

The thematic of community makes it possible for Williams to narrate the complicated historical passage from a "realist" to a "modernist" paradigm. By this light, modernism gets written as the collapse or, more precisely, as the renunciation, both formal and thematic, of the Victorian project of community. Though Williams is more often associated with the interpretations of the nineteenth-century novel than with the analysis of modernism, significant critical reflections on the ascent of modernism are present throughout his work, from *Culture and Society* to his last writings. For instance, the very title of Williams's book on the English novel "from Dickens to Lawrence" proposes a trajectory from realism to modernism; and *The Country and the City* draws to its conclusions with an unanticipated leap from English realism to contemporary post-colonial fiction, the novels of "the new metropolis." But Williams returns most systematically to the questions of modernism and its aftermath in the significant late essays published posthumously under the title *The Politics of Modernism*.[13]

While the essays collected in that volume are not necessarily consistent in their assessments or interpretations or, for that matter, definitions of modernism, they return insistently to the distinctions of modernism and modernity. Adhering to a conventional model of cultural history, Williams characterizes modernism as a cultural movement associated with the practices and pronouncements of the European avant-garde. At these moments, Williams's most pressing concern is to discern and distinguish the politics of modernism, and his conclusions are not surprising: "The politics of modernism can go either way." These political judgments result in a predictable mapping of modernism as "progressive" (Brecht, Picasso, Mayakovsky) and "reactionary" (Eliot, Pound, Lewis). More important, however, are the speculations, anticipated by *The Country and the City*, on the definition of the "modern" and its historical relationship to the metropolis. "The emergence of modernism," asserts Williams, is inextricable from "metropolitan perceptions": "We can see how certain themes in art and thought [those that later become identified as "modernist"] developed as specific responses to the new and expanding kinds of the nineteenth-century city" (*PM*, 39). But the formative "character of the metropolis," "the key cultural actor of the modernist shift," is more than thematic:

> [T]he decisive aesthetic effect is at a deeper level. Liberated or breaking from their national or provincial cultures, placed in quite new relations to those other native visual traditions, encountering meanwhile a novel and dynamic common environment from which many of the older forms were obviously distant, the artists and writers and thinkers of this phase found

the only community available to them: a community of the medium; of their own practices. (*PM*, 45)

The historical conditions for the emergence of a modernist aesthetic are presented as the break-up of traditional or inherited communities by the profoundly disorienting and disruptive encounter with the city. Modernism takes shape in the desire to recover "the only community available to them: a community of the medium." Community is thus not abolished but displaced; and modernism is the name of the attempt to reclaim on the aesthetic level that which is denied socially and politically. However displaced, the *desire* for community remains, a desire which is for Williams inseparable from the activity of culture itself.

Williams historicizes the modernist encounter with a material opacity of language as the consequence of immigrations: for immigrant writers and intellectuals, "language was more evident as a medium" (*PM*, 46), a medium which promises the recuperation of community. What remains unexplored, however, is the possibility that these eruptions of the material sign that characterize the modernist text are not attributable solely to the social fact of immigration. Williams's historicism does not permit him to entertain the possibility that this historical condition of modernism, the engagement with a language which is not one's own, is less an exception than an inevitable feature of our insertion into language. Perhaps, in other words, modernism represents a particular *thematization* of inherent properties of language. To conceive of language as irreducibly opaque and alien would, of course, render it unstable and unsuitable for culture and the workings of a community. Williams's conceptions of culture and community demand that one understand language as a human instrument. Unless the modernist confrontation with a noninstrumental capacity of language can be ascribed to a specific historical phenomenon, and thereby contained, the project of culture is made highly suspect. The prospect that certain aspects of language cannot be reduced to language's communicative functions, that there may be a nonphenomenal, nonhistorical materiality of the linguistic sign, or that there exists a rhetorical element of language always to exceed its role as "medium" between human subjects—linguistic elements that cannot be redeemed in the name of culture—will strike Williams as "inhuman."

The piece which opens *The Politics of Modernism* is the historical reconstruction by students of a lecture Williams delivered at the University of Bristol in March 1987. This lecture, titled "When Was Modernism?," is primarily a historical assessment and critique of the modernist movement; but it concludes with an extraordinary and polemical paragraph which presents Williams's understanding of the relationship between modernism and postmodernism, and gives voice to the threat posed by the latter to the prospects of culture and community.

> [T]he innovations of what is called Modernism have become
> the new but fixed forms of our present moment. If we are to
> break out of the non-historical fixity of *post*-modernism, then
> we must search out and counterpose an alternative tradition
> taken from the neglected works left in the wide margin of the
> century, a tradition which may address itself not to this by now
> exploitable because quite inhuman rewriting of the past but,
> for all our sakes, to a modern *future* in which community may
> be imagined again. (*PM*, 35)

Whatever their state of reconstruction, these highly compressed sentences are indispensable for a critical reading of Williams and of the legacy of cultural materialism. Such a reading could begin by recording the predetermined but lucid hope voiced here for a meaningful negotiation between self and world; the passage resonates with the altogether human desire for a human "community." The desire for community is thus presented as the desire to free human subjectivity from the "inhuman rewriting of the past" that Williams identifies with the "non-historical fixity" of "post-modernism." The imagination of human community can be restored, Williams urges, only if this "inhuman rewriting" is effaced by the recovery of an "alternative tradition" of culture. But we might read this urgency as a sign that Williams is facing the same "paradox" of language and community which he had revealed to be at the heart of George Eliot's novels. It may be the case, in other words, that what Williams identifies as a "post-modern" disposition— the "inhuman rewriting of the past"—is not a critical disposition of hegemonic temperament which can be corrected or resolved by the project of historical reclamation; instead, this "inhuman rewriting" may well be what Paul de Man in his reading of Walter Benjamin discloses to be an inherent feature of language itself, a "nonhuman aspect of language." As de Man characterizes it in an exchange with the literary critic M. H. Abrams, "language does things which are so radically out of our control that they cannot be assimilated to the human at all, against which one fights constantly."[14] The material properties and rhetorical activities of the sign exceed the capacity of the subject to master them; there is an irreducible aspect of language which resists accommodation with the concept of the "human." What we call the "inhuman," continues de Man, is "linguistic structures, the play of linguistic tensions, linguistic events that occur, possibilities which are inherent in language—independently of any intent or any wish or any desire we might have" (*RT*, 96). These claims for the radical alterity, brute contingency, and compulsive force of language run counter to an Enlightenment and "humanist" tradition which posits language as a human property. Abrams's response to de Man in this exchange is exemplary of this humanist position: "Entirely the product of human beings," Abrams replies, "language is the most human of all the things we find in the world" (*RT*, 98). But de Man's disclosures suggest that such invocations of the "human" represent the ultimately idealist attempt to recuperate—to "humanize"—this "prosaic materiality of the letter" as phenomenal or instrumental or historical.[15]

Though Williams would by no means accept de Man's insistence on this "inhuman" linguistic dimension, his historical account of modernism and its aftermath delivers him to a confrontation with this "inhuman rewriting." Williams's invocation and denunciation of postmodernism thus refers less to any cultural or theoretical movement than it does to a crisis in the methodological assumptions of his own cultural materialism. By the name "postmodernism," Williams reveals, if only to disavow, an unredeemable materiality of language, the "inhuman rewriting" that from the perspective of Williams's resolutely redemptive historicism can only appear as "non-historical fixity." Williams's polemical encounter with postmodernism possesses far-reaching implications, since it turns out that in the elaboration of an ostensibly cultural materialism, culture and the longing for community are in fact predicated on the very denial of materiality.

The Empires of Culture

If this inherently anthropological concept of culture cannot account for the nonhuman forces of language, it may well be the case that Williams's concept of culture, like the concept of community with which it is so closely linked, is the name of an impossibility. The conceptual limits, the theoretical incapacities of culture—disclosed and disavowed by Williams himself—do not, of course, prevent rich and compelling work from being carried out in its name, notably by a critic such as Raymond Williams. The recognition and disavowal of these conceptual limits in the closing paragraph of a reconstructed lecture may, given the breadth and "worldliness" of Williams's concerns, appear as a trivial, almost theological dispute. But these theoretical difficulties involve genuinely significant and acute *political* consequences, particularly when the "idea of a common culture" must confront the history of colonialism and its aftermath. To put it as a matter of incapacity, "culture" cannot read the question of empire.

Edward Said has written recently on this absence in Williams's work of a sense of the broad and structural impact of empire. In "Jane Austen and Empire," Said argues persuasively that "something like an imperial map of the world in English literature" is ideologically pervasive, "turn[ing] up with amazing centrality and frequency well before" the period designated as "the great age of empire."[16] Said proceeds to develop an interpretation of Austen's *Mansfield Park* which stresses the constitutive thematic signs of an ideology of empire, a consideration missing in Williams's own treatment of Austen in *The Country and the City*. Said's interpretation of Austen is presented primarily as an extension and correction of Williams's approach: "I should like to be understood as providing greater explicitness and width to Williams's fundamentally correct survey" ("JAE," 153–54). I should like, by contrast, to argue that it cannot be restricted to a matter of "correction": Williams's sense of culture, posited always as the means to establish community, cannot account for the historical and structural forms of colonialism and its aftermath. This should be construed not as a personal but as a structural limitation; no apologist for empire, Williams would write trenchant passages about the shameful politics of colonialism and neo-colonialism.[17] But such discussions cannot in Williams's work proceed under the conceptual auspices of "culture."

To approach the relationship between culture and colonialism in Raymond Williams, we might return once again to an unlikely source, to the critical morphology of Paul de Man's *Blindness and Insight*.[18] The critical insights produced by way of the concept of culture are inextricable in Williams from culture's blindness regarding colonial (and linguistic) matters: to paraphrase de Man, the blindness of Williams's notion of culture to colonialism is not a mere oversight, but is constitutive of the considerable critical insights Williams will achieve in the name of culture. Contrary to Said's assertion, the absence of a treatment of empire in Williams's writings on culture cannot be reduced to an oversight which might be "corrected." It is, rather, the very rigor exhibited by Williams that presses the thinking and writing of culture to this simultaneously internal and historical limit: Raymond Williams opens a reading of those limits within which his work, and our own, remain inscribed.

Raymond Williams and the Inhuman Limits of Culture

When the Cuban poet and literary critic Roberto Fernandez Retamar subtitles his moving essay on the legacy of Shakespeare's "Caliban" as "Notes Toward a Discussion of Culture in our America," he points to the colonial and neo-colonial history that is internally inscribed in the elaboration of any Latin American culture.[19] Fernandez Retamar's critical writings, of which "Caliban" is the most celebrated, demonstrate that for those nation-states or "peoples" or "communities" emerging from and constituted by their relation to colonialism, culture can never be approached as something given, even in the form of a process or activity which must be reclaimed; culture will always be posed in the colonial situation as a question of an antagonistic difference. To frame a discussion of culture in Latin America with the figure of Shakespeare's "monstrous" Caliban, this "thing of darkness," is to cast doubt on the status of culture as a sign of unity or coherence. To ask the question of a Latin American culture in the Cuban context—singular convergence of "first," "second," and "third" worlds—is from the outset to ask a geopolitical and historical question. Fernandez Retamar responds to the question posed by a European journalist—"Does a Latin American culture exist?"—with considerable urgency: "To question our culture is to question our very existence, our human reality itself, and thus to be willing to take a stand in favor of our irremediable colonial condition, since it suggests that we would be but a distorted echo of what occurs elsewhere" (C, 3). Fernandez Retamar's response begins by equating culture and humanity—to question one's culture is to question one's existence—but proceeds beyond that equation to question the presumption of a cultural coherence which inheres in the West. It turns out that the colonial and neo-colonial theatres disclose the inscriptions of an otherness harbored within Western culture, an otherness in which Fernandez Retamar reads his own history. "What is our history, what is our culture," concludes Fernandez Retamar, "if not the history and culture of Caliban?" (C, 14). But how are we to understand this "culture of Caliban"?

The Tempest, it will be recalled, is staged on what is immediately recognizable as the "Mediterranean" displacement of a "Caribbean" island. Shakespeare's final play concerns the legitimacy of power and revolves around the deposed Prospero's efforts to regain—and eventually to extend—his sovereignty. Prospero establishes control of the island of his exile through the "magic" of his books; this control includes the enslavement of the island's inhabitants, Ariel and Caliban. The play devotes considerable attention to the "civilizing" force of culture and language: but to the "deformed" and "monstrous" Caliban, the cultural forms of the West have brought only enslavement. In the celebrated lines of a defiant Caliban: "You taught me language, and my profit on't/ Is, I know how to curse. The red plague rid you/ For learning me your language."[20]

Fernandez Retamar records the long history of critical interest in this figure of rebellion, by turns eloquent and brutish. "Our symbol then is not Ariel," asserts Fernandez Retamar, "but rather Caliban"— this resistant, nonhuman figure inscribed in a great monument of European culture. The most adequate term for this "culture" to be reclaimed through a reading of Caliban is thus precisely what Williams had called the "inhuman rewriting of the past," not the "idea of a common culture" but what Fernandez Retamar, following Jose Marti, calls "mestizaje" or "intermingling." This is not the place to pursue an analysis of Fernandez Retamar's term, though it should be noted that even this emphasis on an "originary" mixing does not result in the conclusive displacement of the concept of culture. It must suffice to say that Fernandez Retamar's "notes toward a definition of culture" refuse the nostalgia—even in its critical forms—of Williams's invocations of a shared culture or "knowable" community, and thereby discover instead the insistently "mulattoed" or "hybrid" nature of any Latin American "culture."[21]

If we find ourselves by this unexpected trajectory—from Paul de Man to Roberto Fernandez Retamar—at a considerable remove from the author of *Culture and Society*, it is nonetheless by way of Williams's rigorous and unyielding explorations of the term that we can continue to confront the internal limits of culture, even if this means that we will arrive at positions that Williams would only regard as "inhuman." What remains unimaginable in the present conjecture is a materialist concept or metaphor that might—to return to the passage from Walter Benjamin with which we began—help deliver us from the idealist myth of culture. But we will have to look elsewhere than the work of Raymond Williams to meet the truly formidable demands of that compelling task.

12

Cultural Theory and the Politics of Location

R. Radhakrishnan

It is unfortunate that we will not have the advantage of Raymond Williams's insights into the changing nature of the Left in the Eastern bloc countries. It would seem that the optimism and the sense of agency that Williams strove to keep alive during difficult and daunting times, with the poverty of ideology, on the one hand, and the sense of determinism produced by technology, on the other, have in a sense found concrete historical shape in the emancipatory subaltern movements throughout eastern Europe. Of course, there is both a relationship of affinity and asymmetry between Williams's projects of hope and those emerging from the erstwhile U.S.S.R. (CIS), Czechoslovakia, Poland, and Hungary. Whereas Williams's oppositional courses of action are in search of a viable Left politics in the context of Thatcherite Britain, the people's movements in eastern Europe find themselves deconstructing a repressive and dictatorial official Left politics: an originally emancipatory politics betrayed by the authority of the State, the Party, and their bureaucratic apparatus. But, despite the locational dissimilarity, there are a number of themes, issues, and anxieties that are common to both situations. My purpose here is to evaluate the "resources of hope" that Williams cherished and nurtured throughout his long and distinguished career as a committed public intellectual, and provide an appreciative critique of Williams from a point of view that is simultaneously postcolonial and poststructuralist. I will begin then with a selective analysis of the situation in eastern Europe by way of framing my discussion of Williams.

The ongoing "tectonic" changes in Eastern Europe and the erstwhile/ CIS U.S.S.R. would seem to demonstrate (1) that a politics of change is possible and (2) that subaltern movements can succeed in toppling "dominant forms without hegemony"[1] and initiate their own histories in opposition to all forms of top-down historiography. Clearly, these events have a global significance. The erstwhile/CIS U.S.S.R. is renegotiating its identity in response to long suppressed ethnic and nationalist claims. Europe too is in the process of reconceptualizing its geopolitical identity both along national and pannational lines. Even the U.S.A., whose custom it has been to remain ideologically insensitive to anything but its own interests, has been forced to open its eyes and restructure its foreign policy that has long been entrenched in the Us-Them logic of the Cold War.[2] Developing nations in the so-called Third World are watching these happenings with great interest, wondering how best to contextualize the lessons learned from these transformations.

And yet, it is not quite clear what the lessons to be learnt are. Ideologues of capitalism and free enterprise rejoice in the demise of Marxism and socialism. Defenders of individual rights are eager to announce the death of all forms of collective political endeavor and organization: we are now supposed to have discovered the only authentic bottom line—individual growth, desire, and profitability. Jeffersonian critics of "government" are busy glorifying governments that govern least. Poststructuralist theorists are only too happy to point out that all their critiques of "identity" and "totality" and their passionate advocacy of "difference" and "heterogeneity" have been right on all along; for, haven't they, ever since May 1968, been arguing against a monolithic and monothetic Marxism? On the other hand, Marxist theorists who wish to remain Marxists, but with a difference, offer the interpretation that these huge changes are to be read as autocritical moments within the history of Marxism and not as total leaps out of the Marxist horizon into a nonideological human history.[3] Postcolonial readings in general would tend to notice with approval the subaltern nature of these changes: a characteristic that is so relevant in the context of postcolonial interrogations of elitist nationalisms.[4] At the same time, the postcolonial perspective would be wary of the Eurocentric character of these revolutions.[5] To put it briefly, these events do have undeniable potential for global meaning, but this meaning itself is by no means univocal. In fact, there are multiple contradictory and contested meanings that depend upon the regional or positional reception and interpretation of these processes or change. It is of the utmost importance that a theoretical understanding of these historic changes not simplify the many tensions, disjunctures, and asymmetries that underlie these vast structural realignments. On the one hand, there is the dire need to retrieve and salvage possibilities for global meaning; on the other, there is an equally urgent need to protect the differential play of regional and subject-positional politics from the dominance of a false globality or totality. And of course, we cannot afford to be insensitive to the irony inherent in this entire scenario, i.e., the fact that these emancipatory subaltern movements are pitted against an ideology (Marxism) whose intentions have always been to bring together and synchronize the regional and the global through a series of carefully coordinated revolutions.

There are many points of convergence between contemporary Eastern European politics and the agential and transformative cultural practices that Raymond Williams theorized and practiced throughout his long and brilliant career. I would now like to identify a few of these themes before I go on to a fuller analysis of Williams's contributions to the politics of cultural theory and cultural studies. First, there is the question of Raymond Williams's subject position and the politics that are available to such a position. Here is Williams operating as a revolutionary cultural critic, but from a position well within the international metropolitan axis. He speaks from within the English tradition even as he questions and problematizes it from his borderline position as a Welshman and a socialist activist. Such a position raises the same kind of issues that I have raised in the context of Eastern Europe. Williams's work also speaks with many voices and valences, and, furthermore, its significance is vulnerable to a range of regional and subject-positional receptions and appropriations. And yet, the singular appeal of Williams's theory is that it does push forward notions of a common humanity and visions of general solidarity that seek a way out of the impasse of local islands of resistance and political change. Attractive and welcome as these visions may be, they raise a few questions. For example, what are the limits of Williams's theory, and how and under what conditions can his theory be made to travel from the center to the periphery, from the First World to the far-removed postcolonial situations? Would the postcolonial situation be in any way enabled by Williams's analysis, and if not, what happens to his idea of solidarity and complimentarity across national and other barriers? How self-reflexive is Williams about his own theories, and, is his mode of self-reflexivity sufficient to prevent his well-meaning intervention from degenerating into yet another act of colonial violence from the center?

Secondly, what promise do Williams's projects hold out for the Left, now that the Left seems to have been thoroughly deglobalized? Deprived of the guarantee of a global Left, how are different pockets of Left politics to communicate with one another? How should the politics of any one location be articulated with that of another in a situation of "unsutured global reality"?[6] What is the nature of "location": is it autochthonous or moveable? The logic of location is informed by a rich and contradictory logic. On the one hand, it represents a poststructuralist demystification of a total politics of global coordination as well as a politics based on essentialism. By this logic, meanings and political possibilities are assumed as a mode of subjection to a particular location, and, as such, they are strongly determined. By definition, locations are perspectival and not global, limited and not infinite, produced and not free or natural.[7] On the other hand, by virtue of being positional and not intrinsic, identitarian or essentialist, such a politics is nothing if not moveable; its very meaning is the function of its travel and mobility.[8] To put it in Bakhtinian terms, locations are characterized by an internal "exotopy," as such the logic of displacement becomes a corollary to the logic of position. Also, by virtue of its itinerant nature, any position is liable to take on charges that are simultaneous and contradictory. For example, deconstructive theories may be considered transgressive and radical within the European context, but these very theories, caught up within the ideology of Eurocentrism, cannot claim any radicality when placed, say, in an ethnic, feminist, or postcolonial context. The controversy over Salman Rushdie's *Satanic Verses* and the debate in France over the right of Muslim women to wear the veil thematize fully the difficulties of assuming a homogeneous norm in adjudicating claims that are contradictory and multidirectional. These issues also demonstrate the inability of any one macropolitical ethos such as nationalism, feminism, or Marxism to contain or represent one another: no single horizon is capable of subsuming or speaking for the other, nor do the different politics of ethnicity, sexuality, class, gender, and nationality add up into one unifiable political horizon. The problem then is: how should theory help in translations among and across different and uneven political terrains?

Thirdly, and this is as much a political issue as it is epistemological, in the wake of poststructuralism and the Eastern European movements, what meaning can we give to the term "representation"? The ability of the people's movements not just to be adversarial, but hegemonic in their own interests, the emergence of artists, intellectuals, writers, and "non-political" leaders such as Vaclav Havel, the fundamental distrust of official rubrics and systemic mediations such as the "party": do these trends announce, in the manner of Foucault and Deleuze, the end of representation?[9] Are we witnessing a post-representational politics here? Are these intellectuals of the "organic" Gramscian variety, or has the people's movement succeeded in superannuating the very category of the "intellectual," for now, theory has become praxis in action? Fourth, how will the nascent subaltern subject find unimpeded access to its own agency, and, how and in what manner is this issue to be mediated?[10] What will be the ideological nature of these mediations, and, what sort of institutional forms and structures are to bear the burden of this newly historicized agency? Has the purity of the people's movements entirely transcended the problem of institutional and other secondary structures, or is the problem, in the words of the subaltern historian and theorist Veena Das, "not whether we can completely obliterate the objectified character of social institutions, but rather whether it is at all possible to establish a relation of authenticity towards these institutions."[11] And finally, what can we say about the space from which the intellectual acts? Is this space "between Culture and System," in Edward Said's sense of the term?[12] Should this space carry names such as socialist, leftist, Marxist, democratic, etc., or should designations be avoided altogether (are these not ideological traps in the long run?) in a way that both Havel and Williams would approve? Analogously, how is the intellectual to carry his/her professional specificity in the context of a total constituency?

In a recent review of Raymond Williams entitled "Culture Heroes: Williams and Hall for the Opposition," in the *Voice Literary Supplement*, Rob Nixon sketches out a few significant characteristics of Williams that render him viable as an oppositional theorist of culture. First, there is Williams's "obsession with the practice of possibility [that] left him impatient with those critics of dominant culture who became grooved on an unimaginative cynicism empty of strategy or alternative ideals." Then, there is the Williams "who preferred the label 'revolutionary socialist' to 'Marxist' for similar reasons, believing that no tradition embracing millions of activists should be reduced to the name of any single figure, however grand." And finally, Williams was "a public intellectual, someone who spoke out in the conviction that knowledge was the shared property of cultures, in the most generous sense of that word, and could never be restricted to the little mounds of erudition kicked up by the archival moles tunneling beneath the lawns of his Cambridge surrounds."[13] The search for alternatives, a keen sense of the protean flows of experience that mock any single frame, a genuine populism that commits the intellectual to a general grass-roots constituency, and a consistently critical attitude toward modes of intellectual labor that turn hermetic in the name of professionalization: such was the nature of Williams's motivation as a cultural theorist; a sense of motivation that stayed with him till the very end.

In an essay written shortly before his death, we find Williams speculating strongly about the future of cultural studies and making a commitment to the future.

> Indeed, we should remind ourselves of that unpredictability, as a condition likely to apply also to any projections we might ourselves make, some of which will be certainly as blind. Yet we need to be robust rather than hesitant about this question of the future because our own input into it, our own sense of the directions in which it should go, will constitute a significant part of whatever is made. And moreover the clearing of our minds which might lead to some definition of the considerations that would apply in deciding a direction is both hard and necessary to achieve, *precisely because of that uncertainty*. (my emphasis)[14]

A number of themes emerge here. First, there is the confident assumption of an organic "we" as a collective agency. Secondly, there is the invocation of an intended future. In strong contrast to much poststructuralist thought that suspects collectivity from the point of view of "difference" and resists the project of willing an agential future for fear of repeating the history of the same, Williams takes a risk. In the face of unpredictability, not only does he make a choice, but he is also prepared to give that choice a name and an identity. Williams is aware that while progressive forces are absorbed in the task of infinite self-differentiation and protocols of pure self-reflexivity, right-wing forces, faced by no such identity crisis, march on, unmindful of their internal contradictions.[15] And thirdly, Williams is warning us that if we choose *not to will* a certain kind of future, we will all "be had" by a future that will not be of our making or choice. Unlike poststructuralism that privileges the notion of errancy, Williams's focus is on possibility. While acknowledging the fact that political agency can never fully pre-know its effect, Williams nevertheless insists that such an agency does make a difference. Here again, in opposition to the general trend of poststructuralism, Williams gives human intentionality an important, though not a unilateral, role in producing a directed and determinate history from uncertainty. The uncertainty (the indeterminacy, if you will) does not inhere structurally in the situation at some deep level that is impenetrable by human agency. To Williams, the historicity of uncertainty is the expression of a negotiable ratio of blindness to clarity; it is never a transcendent given. In a similar vein, Williams refuses to give in to the thesis of total objectification; his aim is to mobilize collective human intentionality by way of objective processes and formations. The theory of the collective subject is also a theory of intentional change. Very much in the tradition of Marxist cultural critics, Williams is interested in enabling historically specific changes; not for him those poststructuralist theories of subjectivity that provide explanations and rationalizations *apres coup*, or, produce accounts of a second-order determinism that rule out possibilities of determinate change.[16]

The envisioning of the future, Williams reminds us, is equally a matter of accounting for the present and how we got there. It is only on the basis of such a historical self-understanding that the future may be delineated. Recalling the origins and the historical development of Cultural Studies, Williams makes the point that "one cannot understand an intellectual or artistic project without also understanding its formation; that the relation between a project and a formation is always decisive; and that the emphasis of Cultural Studies is precisely that it engages with *both*, rather than specializing itself to one or the other." Rejecting a reductionist model, Williams argues that project and formation are "different ways of materializing—different ways, then, of describing—what is in fact a *common* disposition of energy and direction."[17]

The emphasis on commonality keeps alive a sense of constituency and within this constituency, the history of the project and that of the formation are rendered mutually accountable. It is indeed true that the *formation as such* inaugurates a secondary or self-conscious form of history, but this history of the formation cannot be evaluated except in terms of its relationship to the project. In other words, the project functions both as a mandate and as a ethico-political horizon for the formation. The formation as a mediated expression of the project does enjoy relative autonomy, but it should not be allowed to move away from the project: the common ground between the two must be maintained and nurtured. Thus, when Williams exhorts Cultural Studies to question and rehistoricize itself *as formation*, he is in effect calling for a rehistoricizing and a re-invention, in light of contemporary realities, of the project itself. He is also reminding the Cultural Studies experts and professionals of the original ethic of the formation. Williams wishes to keep alive an experiential space that is external to the morphology of the formation. His concern is that this experiential project

space not be structurally collapsed or made immanent within the secondary history of the formation. It is only in the name of the project
that changes can be announced and initiated. The intentionality that
drives the project requires the mediation of formations, but is not
rigidly or deterministically constituted by them. In a sense, to Williams,
human agency and intentionality are transcendent of the history of
structures and formations; if they were not, then all changes would
merely be structural or formational changes without a reference to the
world outside. Thus, though analytically distinct, the project and the
formation are part of a commonly experienced historical growth. Neither one is reduced to the other, although the project may be said to
be the driving force with the formation as its instrument.

Leaning more toward Gramsci than Foucault, Williams's cultural
theory is posited on the foundations of "constituency." The production
of knowledge in response to general community needs, the role played
by intellectuals in the organization as well as self-awareness of society,
the legitimation of professional/intellectual/specialized knowledge by
the felt needs and experiences of the people at large, and most significantly, the self-representation achieved by any community by and
through its "representative" intellectuals; these indeed are the
Gramscian themes that provide fuel to Williams's activist energy as a
public intellectual.[18] There is a certain tension in the very heart of
Williams's enterprise. Here is a sophisticated cultural theorist who in
many ways could be considered an example of the Foucauldian specific
intellectual, who is dedicated to the professional and specialized production of knowledge, and yet, refuses to make this specificity an end
in itself. For, to Williams, the term "representation" still retains a
political meaning; the relationship between the intellectuals and the
people is not done away with.

The institutionalization of Cultural Studies as an academic discipline
represents the reification of what once was a project into a mere
formation. Recalling the original intention of Literary Studies (and the
argument holds in the case of Cultural Studies too), Williams points
out that "in every case the innovations in literary studies occurred
outside the formal educational institutions." These innovations took
place "in adult education, where people who had been deprived of
any continuing educational opportunity were nevertheless readers, and
wanted to discuss what they were reading," and "among women who,
blocked from the process of higher education, educated themselves
repeatedly through reading, and especially through the reading of
'imaginative literature' as the phrase usually has it."[19] It is in response
to the demands of these powerless and disempowered groups that

literary studies was able to fashion itself as a project of social change. It is precisely because these disenfranchised groups constituted a powerful "outside" or *hors-texte* to the system that the system was able to change. Thanks to the questions raised by these groups, each discipline within the university was made to realize its own lack of touch with "the world." These people in their very powerlessness were in a position to demand of their teacher, "Well, if you tell me that question goes outside your discipline, then bring me someone whose discipline *will* cover it, or bloody well get outside of the discipline and answer it yourself."[20] The Open University and Cultural Studies, too, were formed in active response to such rebellious questioning from the outside.

Here perhaps is the space to articulate a poststructuralist critique of Williams's cultural politics. While it is quite appropriate that Williams is deeply solicitous of the need to maintain a sense of representative constituency (the kind of bloc sense that was important to Gramsci too), it still does not explain why he has such an unproblematic notion of representative politics in general and of the pedagogical situation in particular. Historians will of course point out that Williams's participation in the adult education program was extrainstitutional and that there was a larger macropolitics underlying that effort. As Williams himself explains autobiographically, it was "distinctly as a vocation rather than as a profession that people went into adult education— Edward Thompson, Hoggart, myself and many others whose names are not known."[21] I am also aware that Williams's own class position at that time makes him organic and internal to the adult education program; and yet, I believe that my criticism is valid, for, the poststructuralist problematization of representation is also an interrogation of organic political models.

Williams's analysis of the pedagogical situation would have us believe that there exists a relationship of organic solidarity between the dispossessed groups seeking answers and the teacher who is committed to finding the answers. The teacher, it is presumed, will come up with the answers that the groups "outside" are looking for. But I would argue that this situation is a lot more asymmetrical than Williams's explanation makes it out to be. First, we need to observe that more than one meaning of representation is involved here. In the exchange between the clamoring masses and the teacher, all moral and political authority rests with the masses, whereas epistemological authority resides with the teacher. It is indeed the questions that emerge from the dispossessed and the powerless that shake up and revolutionize the *status quo*, but the questioners at this stage are incapable of being the bearers of their own knowledge. They know enough to "ask" but not enough to produce their own answers in the form of an authentic and legitimate knowledge.

Let us examine this situation a little more diagnostically perhaps. The people who initiate the representational transaction challenge the teacher to somehow answer their question. This is construed by the teacher as the bestowal of representational sanction. He/she becomes the representative of the people. But unfortunately, this representational model works in contradictory ways. To begin with, the people make a demand: that a certain knowledge/answer be made available to them by the teacher. Such knowledge seems either not to lie within the discipline practiced by the teacher (in which case, break out of the disciplinary ghetto and seek interdisciplinary assistance), or it does not exist within the institution (in which case, "bloody well get out" and find the answer). Let us take up the scenario of "bloody well getting out," for that is what interests Williams most, and I agree that it should. Does the mere act of "getting out" (whatever that may mean) ensure that the "getting out" is in the name of the people? If indeed it is true that the answer to the people's question is already "there in the world," then the people are already there with the answer, but do not recognize it as "knowledge"; whereas the theorist is "elsewhere" but his/her expertise is required in finding and formalizing the answer into knowledge and bringing it to the people. In bringing it to the people, quite paradoxically, the teacher also brings it to the pedagogical scene which is within the university. In other words, the street scene as the site of knowledge has to be reproposed and transplanted as the pedagogical site before the answer to the question is apprehended as effective knowledge. This is a complicated and multi-leveled scenario. Is it a Gramscian scenario, where the historical reality that "all men are intellectuals" delegates the task of intellectuality to a select group of "professional intellectuals," or is it a Foucauldian scenario, that problematizes the very notion that representation is organic?

The contradiction deepens further. The people may be said to be the authentic holders of the knowledge, for it is their question asked from "without" that makes the production of the new knowledge. But whose knowledge is it? Though it would seem that the people are only demanding epistemological and theoretical representation of a knowledge that they do not have (except in the form of a perspectival question), what they are actually demanding is political representation. They are demanding that this knowledge be political, i.e., that this epistemological representation *be theirs*. Not only does this knowledge represent a certain "material" or "content," it also represents the people within the knowledge and as *agents of that knowledge.* A merely theoretical or cognitive representation of knowledge that would have us believe that knowledge can be "spoken for" by anybody for anybody, whereas the political model of representation, with its inalienably ideological sense of perspectivity, would insist on a distinction between "subject formation" and "agency formation."[22] To state this differently, the response to the people's question from outside the institutional walls may result in the formation of a new "subject," i.e., Cultural Studies, but the emergence of this subject may not carry with it a different subjectivity and the agency appropriate to it. It is undeniable that Cultural Studies has made a difference: but to whom? It is also undeniable that in responding to the question from without, the teacher has stepped out into the world, but it is not clear if it is the same world as the one from which the question was posed. I will mention in passing that there is another poststructuralist nuance that Williams's narrative overlooks, namely, that the creation of a new subjectivity is not entirely emancipatory; it is equally a matter of subjection and ideological interpellation.

Such a poststructuralist critique does not in any way belittle the radical significance of Williams's undertaking; it is only an attempt to illuminate certain blind spots that are inevitable to any affirmative politics. What is interesting is that the blindnesses are the flip side of the insights. For example, one of the chief strengths of Williams is that he preaches and practices the "pedagogy of the oppressed,"[23] and yet forgets that "speaking for the other," in spite of the best possible intentions, is a problematic venture. Similarly, Williams is quite brilliant in his assertion that the criteria for change have to come from the outside and not be produced narcissistically within the internal dynamics of any system or mediation.[24] But in doing so, he unwittingly repeats the very binary in/out split that he would wish to avoid and ends up privileging the "outside" as the pure preserve of experience and reality. Again, he argues for the nonspecialist's experience (for example, adults and women always "read" books though in an unprofessional way), but forgets that often the professionalization of common sense and experience may exceed or even falsify what seemed so self-evident in the experience.[25] Finally, his perennial questioning of the phenomenon of institutionalization, however necessary, oversimplifies the issue. For example, Williams is insensitive to the ambiguous and ambivalent politics of institutionality. I would contend that the institutionalization of any movement represents simultaneously a legitimation as well as a potential depoliticization. Thus, the setting up of Womens' Studies and Afro-American Studies disciplines within the university is enabling on one level and problematic on another. Academic and disciplinary enfranchisement raises the problem of deracination from grass-roots and constituency politics.[26] But Williams's perspective tends to be dismissive of subtleties that pertain to *institutionality as such*; in positing an absolute opposition between institutionality and politics, he denies the institution its own vital political dimension. This tendency in Williams makes him vulnerable to the charge that he is after all a romantic humanist who is still wedded to the idea of an authentic and universal human experience.

Williams's theoretical attitude to experience has a history too long to be discussed here. However, one notices a divide: the Williams of *The Long Revolution* still subscribes to the notion of unmediated experience,[27] but the later Williams admits to the inevitability of mediation. But even here, he has some misgivings about "mediation": "It is difficult to be sure how much is gained by substituting the metaphor of 'mediation' for the metaphor of reflection. On the one hand it goes beyond the passivity of reflection theory; it indicates an active process, of some kind. On the other hand, in almost all cases, it perpetuates a dualism. Art does not reflect social reality, the superstructure does not reflect the base, *directly*; culture is a mediation of society."[28] The thrust of Williams's argument is twofold: avoid simple base-superstructure reductionism, and not lose "experience" within the mere or sheer materiality of the mediation. A similar imperative may be seen at play in his formulation of "structures of feeling" where, too, the emphasis is on the fusion between thought and feeling, between form and content. It is important to understand the polemical trajectory behind Williams's abiding advocacy of "experience" as something rich, resistant, and transformative. In response to the team of interviewers from the *New Left Review*, Williams comments that from "the industrial revolution onwards, there has developed a society which is less and less interpretable from experience," and the result is that "we have become increasingly conscious of the positive powers of techniques of analysis, which at their maximum are capable of interpreting, let us say, the movements of an integrated world economy, and of the negative qualities of a naive observation which can never gain knowledge of realities like these." The privileging of such modes of analysis results in "a corresponding undervaluation of areas where there is some every day commerce between the available articulations and the general process that has been termed 'experience.' "[29] Here Williams is attacking the hyperrealization of theory, and he is also implicitly critiquing high structuralism that in focusing on systemic generalities had lost touch with the historically specific and circumstantial aspects of experience, i.e., the particular and the "concrete," which had become a predictable instantiation of the general systemic categories and laws. When asked by the NLR team if "the idea of an emergent experience beyond ideology" does not seem to "presuppose a kind of pristine contact between the subject and the reality," Williams makes it clear that his real quarrel is with a certain brand of formalists who "affect to doubt the very possibility of an 'external' referent." He declares that "we are in danger of reaching the opposite point in which the epistemological wholly absorbs the ontological: it is only in the ways of knowing that we exist at all."[30] The target of his criticism is a hypostatized theoretical consciousness that pretends to be its own material content. Williams, like Edward Said, is anxious that the "experiential" may get completely choked or denied by the formal densities of theoretical articulation. Experience to Williams is a powerful leverage to call into question the closure of systemic and theoretical orthodoxies. Williams's area of interest lies "between the articulated and the lived."[31]

The critical valence that Williams establishes for the phenomenon of experience is quite crucial. To Williams, "experience" functions as an independent principle of ethico-political legitimation, a principle that refuses to be reified or exhausted by the dogmatism of official systems and categories. It also works as a universal wavelength that cuts across situational and contextual barriers. This is particularly important when so much contemporary cultural theory, dedicated as it is to "difference," "heterogeneity," and "subject positionality," is unable to make global and general connections.[32] But this precisely is Williams's weakness: in his desire to give "experience" a strategically transcendent status, he fails to pay sufficient attention to its "constituted" nature, and, in his enthusiasm to envision a commonly shareable human experience,[33] he tends to oversimplify the disjunctures and asymmetries produced by the uneven histories of colonialism and imperialism. If in the earlier section I questioned Williams from a poststructuralist perspective (with its problematic attitude to the representational *episteme*), in this final part of my essay I shall be looking critically at Williams's theory from a postcolonial point of view. I will also try to demonstrate briefly that the poststructuralist project and the postcolonial project, despite basic differences in their geopolitical positioning, do enjoy great epistemological affinity. The articulation of poststructuralism with postcoloniality is both enabling and problematic.

In an impressive and moving conversation entitled, "Media, Margins and Modernity," Raymond Williams and Edward Said discuss ways in which theories travel, and their basic consensus is that theories and models are capable of being applied successfully in areas far removed from their initial spaces of origination: the human condition, despite locational variations, is indeed shared and shareable. During this dialogue, Williams makes a number of interesting and far-reaching claims: that "the analysis of representation is not a subject separate for history, but that the representations are part of the history," and that "people perceive situations, both from inside their own pressing realities and from outside them." Williams goes on to assert (a) that "a method of analysis, often initially of a strictly academic kind, can often find concrete embodiments which are more teachable and viewable and communicable beyond a narrow academic milieu," and (b) that "you can test the method of the analysis of representations historically, consciously, politically, in very different situations, and find that— subject always to argument about this detail and that—the method stands up."[34] To be fair to Williams, he does acknowledge that "there is an obvious distance between what is happening in the English countryside, or in the English inner cities, to the chaos of Lebanon," and yet, his basic faith in the method (and its ability to travel effectively) is unshakable. The two themes that Williams sounds here are very familiar to his admirers (myself included): the generalization of methods of analysis beyond their narrow disciplinary and academic provenance, and the opening up of a global space characterized by complementarity rather than by radical differences. I endorse these themes heartily; so, my criticism is not that Williams's claims are entirely wrong but rather that his approach is a little too felicitous and lacking in self-reflexivity. By way of offering a slightly different presentation of commonly shared experiences, I turn to Edward Said, who also cherishes the same possibilities as Williams, but with a difference. Said emphasizes a historical phenomenon that is dismissed to a mere epiphenomenal "detail" in Williams: the phenomenon of asymmetry that is so vitally constitutive of the postcolonial situation. (I am aware that my reading produces a difference between Said's and Williams's subject positions, whereas Said and Williams themselves, in their conversation, sound quite unaware of it.)

In an essay that has almost become a classic in the area of postcolonial studies, Said writes:

> The tragedy of this experience, and indeed of all post-colonial questions, lies in the constitutive limitation imposed on any attempt to deal with relationships that are polarized, *radically uneven, remembered differently* (emphasis mine). The spheres,

the sites of intensity, the agendas, the constituencies in the metropolitan and ex-colonized worlds overlap only partially. The small area that is common does not, at this point, provide for more than what I'd like to call *a politics of blame.*[35]

Unlike Williams, Said posits the asymmetry and the unevenness in their own terms before he begins to wish for something better than "a politics of blame." Surely, Said, too, would like theory to travel; we should not forget that it was Said who introduced this term to our critical vocabulary.

Like people and schools of criticism, ideas and theories travel—from person to person, from situation to situation, from one period to another. Cultural and intellectual life are usually nourished and often sustained by this circulation of ideas, and whether it takes the form of acknowledged or unconscious influence, creative borrowing, or wholesale appropriation, the movement of ideas and theories from one place to another is both a fact of life and a usefully enabling condition of intellectual activity. Having said that, however, one should go on to specify the kinds of movement that are possible, *in order to ask whether by virtue of having moved from one place and time to another an idea or a theory gains or loses in strength, and whether a theory in one historical period and national culture becomes altogether different for another period or situation.* (emphasis mine)[36]

Said proceeds to periodize and spatialize the travel in terms of a "point of origin," "the distance traversed," the conditions of reception, and the final transformation of the original idea in its new *habitus*. Within Said's model, there is plenty of room for the travel to go wrong, or be sabotaged, or found inapplicable or too aggressive in its new home. In contrast, Williams's confidence in traveling/comparatist method is entirely devoid of the kind of skepticism that comes out of serious self-reflexivity. This is particularly unfortunate since Williams's subject position is contradictory. For, it is both oppositional-marginal and dominant-central. As a Welsh "border" voice expressing revolutionary socialism, it is indubitably oppositional in a Thatcherite context, but at the same time, as a Western voice invested in English studies, it is a demonstrably metropolitan voice. I am aware that in a work like *The Country and the City*, Williams produces such telling insights: "Yet when we look at the power and impetus of the metropolitan drives, often indeed accelerated by their own internal crises, we cannot be in any doubt that a different direction, if it is to be found, will necessarily involve revolutionary change. The depth of the crisis, and the power of those who continue to dominate it, are too great for any easier or more congenial way."[37] But this insight, unaccompanied by a substantive awareness of *unevenness and asymmetry*, does not go far enough in deconstructing Eurocentrism or in raising the all important question of "who is speaking" rather than merely "what is being said." As a result, the politics of the margins are too easily and prematurely adjusted and accommodated within what Williams calls "a connecting process, in what has to be seen ultimately as a common history."[38] Said, too, and other postcolonial theorists, are interested in the "connecting process," but are more capable of articulating marginality *qua* marginality before the connecting process begins. The significant difference between Williams's vision and the postcolonial vision is that the latter is aware (a) that often "traveling theory" hides within it the agency of the dominant structure, (b) that the travel is mostly in one direction: postcolonial models hardly travel to the center, much less transform it, and (c) the connecting process itself is undertaken on terms set at and by the center.

The idea of a successfully transplanted method in the name of an international commonality is strongly called into question in a number of postcolonial theoretical texts, most notably, Partha Chatterjee's *Nationalist Thought and the Colonial World*. In direct opposition to Williams's claims, Chatterjee proves that both the political project of nationalism and the epistemological project of the Enlightenment have been enacted in the postcolonial context to the detriment of indigenous subaltern possibilities. The postcolonial nationalist project, underwritten by the rational philosophy of the Enlightenment, perpetrates an indigenous form of elitism and consequently, the nationalist narrative fails to speak for the people. Moreover, there is all manner of disjuncture between the political and the epistemological practices of nationalism. And besides, the transplantation of a Eurocentric nationalism in the postcolonial situation produces effects very different from those generated in Europe. The postcolonial people are often made to choose between being a nation and being themselves. Local and subaltern issues and themes do not figure in the nationalist equation precisely because the nationalist experiment is undertaken with a Western bias.[39] To Chatterjee and a host of other fellow subaltern theorists such as Ranajit Guha, Kumkum Sangari, Sudesh Vaid, Veena Das, Susie Tharu, and Dipesh Chakrabarty, the notion of "location" plays a very special and complex role in the adjudication of postcolonial/subaltern identity.

As postcolonial theorists, these writers exhibit and thematize a contradictory, fractal, and multivalent sense of "who they are": they are participants and citizens of multiple, uneven, overlapping and cross-hatched worlds and discourses. On the one hand, they are committed to the "insider" task of theorizing a truly hegemonic national identity representative of the many "sub-identities" that comprise it (an identity based not on essentialism), and on the other, in achieving an authentic transnational and global consciousness based not on the modernist imperative of deracination but on the concept of complex multiple rootedness. "Location," "position," and "travel" are so fundamental to postcolonial identity that we can perceive substantial variations among the postcolonial intellectuals: the resident theorist working through national and indigenous languages, the resident intellectual operating through Western discourses, and the diasporic, nonresident postcolonial intellectual who lives elsewhere but is abidingly committed to her/his nation. The differences among these types, although produced merely by varying subject-positional accents and inflections, often add up to a substantive disagreement about the nature of postcolonial politics and identity. There are debates about agendas and themes, about means and ends, about priorities, about insiders and outsiders, and about the conflict between, what Gayatri Chakravorty Spivak calls "subaltern material and elitist methodology."[40] These contestations that are typical of the postcolonial-nationalist conjuncture find no place in Raymond Williams's scenario, simply because Williams's notion of a transcontextual method is incapable of dealing with the subtle nuances of the politics of location.

Strange as it may sound, the travel of Williams's theory to postcolonial spaces would have been more successful with the help of a few poststructuralist indirections and *detours*. For, though the postcolonial predicament and poststructuralist politics are unevenly related, this relationship is potentially enabling and healthy, provided it is cultivated strategically. In other words, the last thing I am calling for is an easy travel of poststructuralist theory to postcolonial contexts; but I am suggesting that a few poststructuralist attitudes, if not themes, have the potential to assist postcolonial ventures. Poststructuralist "weak thought" (in this expression I am conflating a number of poststructuralist trajectories: the questioning of representation, the perennial deconstruction of identity, the sensitivity to difference and heterogeneity, the insistence on ongoing autocritique, and a noncoercive attitude to the production of knowledge) finds congenial soil in postcoloniality. For, in the postcolonial situation, identity is shot through and through with difference, and yet, identity is direly needed. Also, postcolonial reality demands multiple, nonsynchronous narratives, and not a single masterful story. The production of hegemonic subaltern historiographies requires the elaborate deconstruction of existing forms of dominant historiography. The attempt to forge a representative national identity is simultaneously an attempt to enfranchise the many differences that comprise it. Like deconstruction, postcoloniality is involved in the contradiction of a "double writing"[41]: on the one hand, it organizes itself as though nationalism were a desirable end, but on the other, it questions the very authority of the Eurocentrism inherent in nationalism. And like deconstruction, it looks for other and different options, but without the guarantee of an absolute break with the past. In deconstruction postcoloniality finds an ally across the asymmetrical divide, for poststructuralism (here I am using the two terms "poststructuralism" and "deconstruction" interchangeably in a limited sense) is an oppositional discourse within the metropolitan center. As opposition from "without," the semantics of postcolonial politics is bound to be different from that of poststructuralism, but syntactically, there is a complementary relationship between the two. The notion of a traveling or unfixed identity is yet another common feature, but the difference is that whereas poststructuralism (because it is of the First World) can afford to virtually "play" with identity, the postcolonial play with identity is much more serious: there is something at stake here. Gabriel Garcia Marquez and Salman Rushdie are but two examples of serious fictional and narrative play. One might even say that the daring and the risk-taking that remain merely playful, ludic, epistemological (i.e., disjuncted from real politics), and superstructural within poststructuralism, take on a sense of constituency and therefore became political in the postcolonial conjuncture. The need to find alternative political practices through an epistemological revolution and the desire to embody a historical significance for the language of the "post-" may be said to have found a concrete set of issues in postcoloniality that both uses and transforms poststructuralism.

I will conclude with a brief and selective look at a few postcolonial articulations that are perfectly compatible with Williams's cultural politics in a general sense, but are different in their self-awareness precisely because they have been touched by the poststructuralist attitude to "location." But, in these articulations, the attitude takes on the temporality of concrete, historical struggle and contestation.

In a powerful essay entitled "Multiple Mediations," Lata Mani confronts some of the difficulties that she has to face and theorize in her location as a Third World feminist residing in the U.S.A., who nevertheless presents her work in the U.S.A., Britain, and India.[42]

Drawing on Chandra Talpade Mohanty's definition of the politics of location as "the historical, geographic, cultural, psychic and imaginative boundaries for political definition and self definition," and enabled by Mohanty's description of location as a "temporality of struggle" characterized by nonsynchronous flows and by "a paradoxical continuity of self,"[43] Mani presents the reader with the narrative of how her own work on *Sati* is assimilated varyingly in the U.S.A., Britain, and India.[44] Mani is not suggesting for a moment that her project loses solidarity with itself because of these relativistic readings (she does not surrender intentional politics to the vagaries of a purely reception politics), but rather, she acknowledges and takes responsibility for the multi-accentual nature of her work. These different accents are constitutive of the work and are therefore not reducible to one dominant ideological valence. Nationalism, colonialism, First World feminism, Third World feminism: all these macropolitical discourses are imbricated in Mani's subject position, and her account moves among these spaces with a finely tuned sensitivity to the underlying asymmetries, tensions, and contradictions. Not only does she tell us how differently her work is received (as part of contemporary feminism in the U.S.A. and Britain, and as part of the critique of nationalism in India), but also how much it matters how she is perceived: as insider or as outsider to the indigenous politics of postcoloniality. It is only after a thorough and painstaking rehearsal of her crosshatched subject positionality that she makes the following recommendation: "The difficulties of straddling different temporalities of struggle cannot, however, always be resolved through listening for and talking about our specificities. There are political moments which pose limits to the possibility of conceiving of international feminist exchange as negotiated dialogues which, while they may alternately diverge and intersect, are ultimately benign and non-contradictory."[45] Unlike Williams's theoretical model, the politics of location sketched out by Lata Mani is laden with rich contradictions.

In a similar but differently inflected voice, Vivek Dhareshwar, in his essay, "Toward a Narrative Epistemology of the Postcolonial Predicament," maps out some of the incommensurabilities faced by the postcolonial intellectual when s/he tries to find his/her narrative/political identity within the theoretical/epistemological framework provided by the metropolis. The thesis here, too, is that "traveling theory" is full of pitfalls and detours. Dhareshwar observes that "the traveling problems of contemporary theory have a special significance for postcolonial intellectuals who have traveled in the metropolis to see how their part of the world gets mapped."[46] Unlike western or First World

293

theorists who tend to "privilege their subject positions unreflectively," "postcolonials cannot help noticing the condition of possibility of their theory." Dhareshwar is well aware that unreflective critical practice on the part of the postcolonial intellectual will only sell him/her to metropolitan interests. Emphasizing strongly the need for postcolonial intellectuals to be vigilant about their subject positionality (a theme inaugurated by Gayatri Chakravorty Spivak), Dhareshwar proposes that "instead of celebrating the pleasures of finding themselves in the tropics of metropolitan theory by theoretically recuperating the narratives of their detour, postcolonial theorists must narrativize the dissonance of that detour, and out of that dissonance, outline a new theory, a new practice of theory that would initiate a poetics of return, which will undoubtedly be as complex and ambiguous as the poetics of detour that postcolonials have been living, narrating, and theorizing."[47]

It would seem that the travel thought up by these postcolonial intellectuals is less natural, more deliberate and self-reflexive, and less self-assured than the resources of hope that stem from a metropolitan assumption of universal experience.

Notes

Series Editor's Introduction

1. Michael W. Apple, *Ideology and Curriculum,* 2d ed. (New York: Routledge, 1990); *Education and Power* (New York: Routledge, 1985); *Teachers and Texts* (New York: Routledge, 1988).
2. Robin Blackburn, "Introduction," Raymond Williams, *Resources of Hope* (New York: Verso, 1989), xii.
3. Ibid., ix.
4. Ibid.
5. Ibid., ix–x.
6. For discussion of the complicated meanings Marx associated with this position, ones that are often less reductive than some interpreters have claimed, see Jorge Larrain, *Marxism and Ideology* (Atlantic Highlands, NJ: Humanities Press, 1983).
7. For criticism of this developmental model, see Erik Olin Wright, "Capitalism's Futures," *Socialist Review* 13 (March–April, 1983), 77–126.
8. A clear description of Gramsci's position, one that can be usefully compared to that of Williams, can be found in Tony Bennett, "Introduction: Popular Culture and the Turn to Gramsci", in *Popular Culture and Social Relations,* ed. Tony Bennett, Colin Mercer, and Janet Woollacott (Philadelphia: Open University Press, 1986), xi–xix and Stuart Hall, "The Toad in the Garden: Thatcher Among the Theorists," in *Marxism*

and the Interpretation of Culture, ed. Cary Nelson and Lawrence Grossberg (Urbana: University of Illinois Press, 1988), 35–57.

9. Leslie Roman and Linda Christian-Smith, with Elizabeth Ellsworth, eds., *Becoming Feminine: The Politics of Popular Culture* (New York: Falmer Press, 1988).

10. For an insightful discussion of Williams's place within the cultural Marxist tradition, see Dennis L. Dworkin, *The Politics of Culture* (New York: Routledge, forthcoming).

11. Alan O'Connor, *Raymond Williams: Writing, Culture, Politics* (New York: Basil Blackwell, 1989), 110.

12. Raymond Williams, *Resources of Hope* (New York: Verso, 1989), 4.

13. Ibid., 5.

14. Allan Bloom, *The Closing of the American Mind* (New York: Simon and Schuster, 1987) and E.D. Hirsch, Jr., *Cultural Literacy* (New York: Houghton Mifflin, 1986).

15. Williams, *Resources of Hope*, 36.

16. Raymond Williams, *The Year 2000* (New York: Pantheon, 1983), 268.

17. Ibid., 268–269.

Introduction: The Cultural Politics of Location

1. Among tributes from the British Left are Terry Eagleton and Frank Kermode, *The Independent*, 28 January 1988; Francis Mulhern, *The Guardian*, 29 January 1988; Anthony Barnett, *The Listener*, 3 February 1988; Tony Benn, *The Morning Star*, 4 February 1988; Anthony Arblaster, *Tribune*, 5 February 1988; Stuart Hall, *The New Statesman*, 5 February 1988; Margot Heinemann, *Marxism Today*, March 1988. In April, 1988, *The Nation* in the United States published eulogies by Edward Thompson and Edward Said.

2. Edward W. Said, "Narrative, Geography and Interpretation," *New Left Review* 180 (March–April 1990), 82.

3. Raymond Williams, quoted in Raymond Williams and Edward Said, "Appendix: Media, Margins and Modernity," in Raymond Williams, *The Politics of Modernism: Against the New Conformists* (London: Verso, 1989), 178.

4. Larry Grossberg, "On Postmodernism and Articulation," an interview with Stuart Hall, *Journal of Communication Inquiry* 10 (Summer 1986), 60.

5. Nancy Fraser, "Introduction: Apologia for Academic Intellectuals," in

Unruly Practices: Power, Discourse, and Gender in Contemporary Social Theory (Minneapolis: University of Minnesota Press, 1989), 2.

6. Raymond Williams, *Marxism and Literature* (Oxford: Oxford University Press, 1977), 112.

7. We draw upon the recent work of Cameron McCarthy, who, following poststructuralist Emily Hicks, uses the term "nonsynchronous" to mean the ways in which the interests of class, race, and gender intersect in systematically contradictory ways in the institutional context and practice of the school. Nonsynchrony, according to McCarthy, refers to the "vast differences in interests, needs, desires and identity that separate different minority groups from each other and from majority whites in educational settings." See Cameron McCarthy, *Race and Curriculum* (Sussex: The Falmer Press, 1990), 9–10, and Emily Hicks, "Cultural Marxism: Nonsynchrony and Feminist Practice," in *Women and Revolution*, ed. Linda Sargant (Boston: South End Press, 1981), 219–38.

8. Williams, *The Long Revolution*, 145.

9. We are indebted to Forest Pyle for this phrase.

1   Autobiography and the "Structure of Feeling" in *Border Country*

1. Raymond Williams, *Border Country* (London: The Hogarth Press, 1988).

2. See the discussion in Alan O'Connor, *Raymond Williams: Writing, Culture, Politics* (Oxford: Blackwell, 1989), 83–85.

3. Raymond Williams, *Culture and Society* (Harmondsworth: Penguin Books, 1985), 248.

4. See what Williams himself says in the *New Left Review* interviews of 1979, reprinted as *Politics and Letters* (London: Verso, 1979), 271–286; and in "Region and Class in the Novel," in *The Uses of Fiction: Essays on the Modern Novel in Honour of Arnold Kettle*, ed. Douglas Jefferson and Graham Martin (Milton Keynes: The Open University, 1982), 60–63. See also what Dai Smith writes on this aspect of Williams's writing practice in his "Relating to Wales," in *Raymond Williams: Critical Perspectives*, ed. Terry Eagleton (London: Polity Press, 1989), 34–53, esp. 42.

5. Williams, *Border Country*, 12.

6. Ibid., 84–137.

7. Ibid., 13.

8. Ibid., 9.

9. Ibid.

10. Ibid., 14.

Notes

11. Ibid.

12. Ibid.

13. Ibid., 15.

14. Ibid.

15. Raymond Williams, *Politics and Letters*, 27, and "The Welsh Industrial Novel," in his *Problems in Materialism and Culture* (London: Verso, 1980), 213–29, esp. 222.

16. Raymond Williams, "The Social Significance of 1926," rpt. in Raymond Williams, *Resources of Hope* (London: Verso, 1989), 105–10, esp. 105–6.

17. Ibid., 6.

18. Chapter Four of *Border Country* explores the relation between loyalty to the working class and loyalty to the nation.

19. See Williams, "The Social Significance of 1926," 105–6.

20. Kiernan Ryan, "Socialist Fiction and the Education of Desire: Mervyn Jones, Raymond Williams and John Berger," in *The Socialist Novel in Britain*, ed. H. Gustav Klaus (Brighton: The Harvester Press, 1982), 166–84, esp. 173.

21. Ibid.

22. See Tony Pinkney, "Raymond Williams and the 'Two Faces of Modernism,' " in Eagleton, *Critical Perspectives*, 12–33, esp. 25–27.

23. Of course, I am referring here to Richard Hoggart, *The Uses of Literacy* (Harmondsworth: Penguin, 1968).

24. See Williams's chapter on "England Whose England?" in his *Orwell* (London: Fontana, 1971), 17.

25. Raymond Williams, "D. H. Lawrence," in *Culture and Society*, 209–12.

26. Raymond Williams, "Working-class, Proletarian, Socialist: Problems in Some Welsh Novels," in Klaus, 110–21, and *Country and City in the Modern Novel* (Swansea: University College of Swansea, 1987), 1–16, where the idea of a "knowable community"—already present in his *The English Novel from Dickens to Lawrence* (London: The Hogarth Press, 1984), 9–27—is further explored and developed.

27. On Welshness, see the rich and interesting book by Dai Smith, *Wales! Wales?* (London: G. Allen & Unwin, 1984) and Raymond Williams, *Politics and Letters*, 25–26.

28. J. P. Ward, *Raymond Williams* (Cardiff: University of Wales Press, 1981), 9.

29. Williams, *Politics and Letters*, 29–31.

30. Ibid., 40; and see what Stuart Hall writes on the similarity of his personal experience in his "Politics and Letters," in Eagleton, *Critical Perspectives*, 54–66, esp. 56–57.

31. Williams, *Border Country*, 265.

32. Ibid., 266.

33. Ibid.

34. Williams, *Politics and Letters*, 26.

35. I am referring to what Benedict Anderson has discussed in his *Imagined Communities* (London: Verso, 1983).

36. On the idea of nation and nationalisms, see Ernest Gellner, *Nations and Nationalism* (Oxford: Blackwell, 1983), Dai Smith, *Wales! Wales?* and *Formations of Nation and People* (London: Routledge & Kegan Paul, 1984).

37. Williams, *Border Country*, 290.

38. Ibid. 290–91.

39. Ibid., 292.

40. Ibid.

41. Raphael Samuel, " 'Philosophy Teaching by Example': Past and Present in Raymond Williams," *History Workshop* 27 (1989), 141–154, esp. 143.

42. Ibid.

43. Williams, *Border Country*, 292–93.

44. Ibid., 293.

45. See, for the many aspects dealt with, the essay by the "Popular Memory Group" of the Centre for Contemporary Cultural Study of Birmingham University: "Popular Memory: Theory, Politics, Method," in *Making Histories: Studies in History, Writing and Politics*, ed. Richard Johnson, Gregor McLennan, Bill Schwartz, and David Sutton (London: Hutchinson, 1982), 205–52; see also Christopher Shaw and Malcolm Chase, eds., *The Imagined Past: History and Nostalgia* (Manchester: Manchester University Press, 1989).

46. Williams, *Border Country*, 293.

47. Williams, *The Long Revolution* (Harmondsworth: Penguin Books, 1965), 64.

48. Ibid., 63.

49. Ibid., 64.

50. Ibid., 248.

51. Ibid., 254.

52. Ibid., 281.

53. Ibid., 281–82.

54. Ibid., 286.

55. Ibid., 287.

56. Ibid., 288.

57. Ibid., 289.

Notes

58. Ibid., 351.
59. Ibid.
60. Williams, *The Long Revolution*, 65

2 Cultural Studies and the Crisis in British Radical Thought

I would like to thank Arthur Knight, T.R. Quigley, and Leslie G. Roman for commenting on earlier drafts of this essay.

1. Raymond Williams, "The Future of Cultural Studies," in *The Politics of Modernism: Against the New Conformists* (London: Verso, 1989), 151–62.

2. Stuart Hall's analysis can be found in "Cultural Studies: Two Paradigms," *Media, Culture and Society* 2 (1980): 57–72. See also his introduction: "Cultural Studies and the Centre: Some Problematics and Problems," to *Culture, Media, Language: Working Papers in Cultural Studies, 1972–79*, ed. Stuart Hall, Dorothy Hobson, Andrew Lowe and Paul Willis, (London: Hutchinson, 1977), 15–47.

3. This is more fully argued in my dissertation, *The Politics of Culture: Critical and Historical Theory in Great Britain, 1946–79* (Ph.D. diss., University of Chicago, 1989). This larger work is an historical account of the dialogue between Marxist historiography and cultural studies in Britain which produced a cultural Marxist perspective.

4. Raymond Williams, *Culture and Society, 1780–1950* (New York: Harper and Row, 1966), 324.

5. Raymond Williams, *Communications*, 3rd ed. (Harmondsworth: Penguin, 1976), 115.

6. Raymond Williams, "Culture Is Ordinary," in his *Resources of Hope: Culture, Democracy, Socialism*, ed. Robin Gable (London: Verso, 1989), 3–18, esp. 13.

7. Williams, *Communications*, 115.

8. Quoted in Bill Schwarz, "The 'People' in History: The Communist Party Historians' Group, 1946–1956," in *Making Histories: Studies in History-Writing and Politics* (Minneapolis: University of Minnesota Press, 1982), 44–95, esp. 64.

9. Raymond Williams, "The New British Left," *Partisan Review* 27 (Spring 1960): 341–47, esp. 344.

10. Raymond Williams, *The Long Revolution* (1961; rpt., Westport, Conn: Greenwood Press, 1975), x.

11. See Terry Eagleton, *Criticism and Ideology: A Study in Marxist Literary Theory* (London: Verso, 1978), 39.

12. E. P. Thompson, "The Long Revolution II," *New Left Review* 6 (November-December 1960): 34–39, esp. 39.

13. Raymond Williams, "The New British Left," 341.

14. E. P. Thompson, "Commitment and Politics," *Universities and Left Review* 6 (Spring 1959), 50–55.

15. *Learning to Labour* was both an extension and critique of what might be termed "reproduction" theory: recent radical American and European work, predominantly structuralist in inspiration, which attacked the liberal idea that the schools were the principal means of achieving equal opportunity and a more democratic society. In this context, Willis's book was a critique of Samuel Bowles and Herbert Gintis's *Schooling in Capitalist America* which argued that the primary task of schools was to produce a compliant and obedient labor force, that is, to "reproduce" rather than obliterate unequal relations. Willis agreed with their interpretation of the result but put forward an alternative view of the process. See Michael Apple's review of *Learning to Labour*, "What Correspondence Theories of the Hidden Curriculum Miss," *The Review of Education* (Spring 1979): 101–112.

16. See Phil Cohen, "Subcultural Conflict and Working-Class Community," in *Culture, Media, Language*, ed. Hall et al., 78–87. This is an edited version of an article that originally appeared in the second issue of the Centre's journal *Working Papers in Cultural Studies*.

17. Paul Willis, *Profane Culture* (London: Routledge and Kegan Paul, 1978), 177, 182.

18. I have drawn on Leslie G. Roman and Linda K. Christian-Smith, introduction to *Becoming Feminine: The Politics of Popular Culture*, ed. Leslie G. Roman and Linda K. Christian-Smith (East Sussex: Falmer Press, 1988), 1–34.

19. Angela McRobbie, "Settling Accounts with Subcultures," *Screen Education* 34 (Spring 1980): 37–49, esp. 49.

20. Raymond Williams, *Marxism and Literature*, Marxist Introductions, ed. Raymond Williams and Steven Lukes (Oxford: Oxford University Press, 1977), 5.

21. Ibid., 110.

22. Ibid., 112.

23. See, for instance, Stuart Hall, "Notes on Deconstructing the Popular," in *People's History and Socialist Theory*, ed. Raphael Samuel (London: Routledge, 1981), 227–240, esp. 236.

24. Stuart Hall, "Cultural Studies: Two Paradigms," 69.

25. Dick Hebdige, *Subculture: The Meaning of Style* (London: Methuen, 1979), 121.
26. Patrick Brantlinger, *Crusoe's Footprints: Cultural Studies in Britain and America* (New York: Routledge, 1990), 52–53.
27. Jenny Bourne Taylor, "Raymond Williams: Gender and Generation," in *British Feminist Thought: A Reader*, ed. Terry Lovell (London: Basil Blackwell, 1990), 296–308, esp. 306.
28. Ibid., 307.
29. Raymond Williams and Edward Said, "Media, Margins, and Modernity," Raymond Williams, *The Politics of Modernism*, 177–98, esp. 179. The quotation marks have been retained, because they are in the original text.
30. Raymond Williams, "When Was Modernism," in *The Politics of Modernism*, 31–35, esp. 35.
31. Dick Hebdige, "Fax to the Future," *Marxism Today* (January 1990): 18–23, esp. 20.

3 Placing the Occasion: Raymond Williams and Performing Culture

1. Raymond Williams, "Culture is Ordinary," in Williams, *Resources of Hope: Culture, Democracy, Socialism*, ed. Robin Gable (London: Verso, 1989), 3–18, esp 4. All subsequent references are cited in text.
2. Raymond Williams, *The Long Revolution* (London: Chatto and Windus, 1961), 45. Hereafter cited in text as *LR*.
3. Stuart Hall and Richard Johnson demonstrate the practical and theoretical importance of understanding culture in terms of activities as well as products and their symbolic and evaluative implications. See Stuart Hall, "Cultural Studies: Two Paradigms," *Media, Culture and Society* 2 (1980): 57–72, and "Cultural Studies and the Centre; Some Problematics and Problems," in *Culture, Media, Language*, ed. Stuart Hall (London: Hutchinson, 1980), 15–47; Richard Johnson, "Histories of Culture/ Theories of Ideology," in *Ideology and Cultural Production*, ed. Michele Barrett (New York: St. Martin's Press, 1980), 49–77, and "What Is Cultural Studies Anyway?" *Social Text* 16 (1987): 38–80.
4. "Problematic" here follows Richard Johnson's inflection of Althusser: a "field of concepts, which organizes the field by making it possible to ask some kinds of questions and suppressing others." See Ben Brewster, trans., and Louis Althusser, Henri Balibar, and Jacques Rancière, eds., *Reading Capital* (London: New Left Books, 1970), 13–30, and Johnson, "Three Problematics: Elements of a Theory of Working Class Culture,"

in *Working-Class Culture*, ed. John Clarke, Richard Johnson and Chas. Crichter (London: Hutchinson, 1979), 201–37, esp. 206.

5. "Symbols . . . are strategies for handling situations." Kenneth Burke, *The Philosophy of Literary Form* (Berkeley: University of California Press, 1973), 1.

6. Raymond Williams, "The Idea of Common Culture," in *Resources of Hope*, 32–37, esp. 35. Hereafter cited in text as "Common Culture."

7. Johnson, "What Is Cultural Studies . . .?," 39.

8. F. R. Leavis, "Literary Criticism and Philosophy," in *The Common Pursuit* (London: Chatto and Windus, 1952), 202–28, esp. 213; T. S. Eliot, "The Function of Criticism," in *Selected Prose* (London: Faber, 1975), 68–76, esp. 69; Matthew Arnold, "The Function of Criticism at the Present Time," in *Selected Prose*, ed. P. J. Keating (Harmondsworth: Penguin, 1970), 130–56, esp. 146.

9. See *Annual Reports of the Arts Council of Great Britain*, 1946–1987, especially Secretaries General, W.E. Williams, *A Brighter Prospect, 17th Annual Report of the Arts Council of Great Britain (1961-62)*, 14, and Roy Shaw, *Patronage and Responsibility, 34th Annual Report of the Arts Council of Great Britain, 1978–79*, 6–7. For an analysis of the political and ideological dimensions of Arts Council aesthetics, see Robert Hutchison's *The Politics of the Arts Council* (London: Sinclair Brown, 1982).

10. The most trenchant analysis of Williams's habit of substituting "growth," "evolution," "compromise," etc., for the active agency of "revolution" and "[class] struggle" is E. P. Thompson's review of *The Long Revolution* in *New Left Review* 9/10 (July-October, 1961): 24–39. Williams later acknowledges that "behind the idea of social evolution was an . . . attachment to the development of a *single* form. . . . The real social and cultural variation of human history was thus reduced to a single model, familiar and predictable," *Modern Tragedy*, 2nd ed. (London: Verso, 1979), 70n.

11. *Hegemony*, in its *locus classicus*, refers to the " 'spontaneous' consent given by the great masses of the population to the general direction imposed on social life . . . by the dominant group" and the maintenance of that consent through this group's historical "prestige"; see Antonio Gramsci, *Selections from the Prison Notebooks*, ed. and trans. Quentin Hoare and G. N. Smith (London: Lawrence and Wishart, 1971), 12. My use of the term follows Williams in *Marxism and Literature* (New York: Oxford University Press, 1977): "[the ways in which] given forms of domination . . . are experienced and *in practice internalised*" as a "whole body of practices and expectations" (emphasis added). (110)

12. Legitimation is not just normal, "legal" aesthetic practice; it is also the dispute over what constitutes those norms. See Loren Kruger, "Staging

Boundaries: Institutional Limits to Legitimate Theatre," in *Proceedings of the 12th Congress of the International Comparative Literature Association*, Munich, 1988 (Munich: Iudicium Verlag, 1990) 4: 427–37.

13. John Caughie, "Popular Culture: Notes and Revisions," in *High Theory/ Low Culture: Analyzing Popular Television and Film*, ed. Colin McCabe (New York: St. Martin's Press, 1986), 156–71, esp. 161.

14. Williams' critical emphasis on activity is indeed often cited as the occasion of this break from the study of works to that of practices. See Literature and Society Group, "Literature and Society: Mapping the Field," in *Working Papers in Cultural Studies* 4 (Spring 1974): 21–44, esp. 29, and Hall, "Cultural Studies: Two Paradigms," 59. Hoggart's appeal, in "Contemporary Cultural Studies: Inaugural Lecture," *Contemporary Cultural Studies* 1 (1967): 7, for an immanent, rather than symptomatic, reading of popular phenomena forms the germ of the ethnographic studies of "lived (sub)culture," such as *Women Take Issue* (1978) and *Resistance through Ritual* (1977), published by the Centre.

15. Stuart Hall, "Notes on Deconstructing the Popular," in *People's History and Socialist Theory*, ed. Raphael Samuel (London: Routledge and Kegan Paul, 1981), 217–39, esp. 239.

16. Caughie, "Popular Culture," 161.

17. Johnson, in "Histories of Culture," 60–67, provides a systematic analysis of this tendency, in culturalist historiography in the tradition of *Culture and Society* and *The Making of the English Working Class*, to privilege "authentic experience" over any theoretical reflection. His most telling objection is that this stubborn resistance of abstraction makes it difficult to distinguish levels of particular instances and thus to make any general claims at all.

18. Williams, *Marxism and Literature*, 110.

19. See Gramsci, *Selections from the Prison Notebooks*, 57–59.

20. Williams develops the concepts of *dominant, residual*, and *emergent* social or cultural formations out of the argument that hegemony is never monolithic, but rather the result of successful hegemonic strategies; several formations and allegiances may be present, to a greater or lesser degree, at the same time and place, between or within the same social group or even individual. See *Marxism and Literature*, 121–27, and also Gramsci, *Selections from the Prison Notebooks*, 196–99, 324–43.

21. For an analysis of the role of occasion and place as "signals" for the identification of art, see Williams, *Culture* (London: Fontana, 1981), 130ff. Subsequent references cited in text.

22. See T. W. Adorno's analysis of the historical and epistemological interdependence of modern art and the culture industry, in *Aesthetische Theorie*

(Frankfurt: Suhrkamp, 1970), 168ff; trans. C. Lenhardt (London: Routledge, 1986).

23. "Cultivated classes" is the Victorian phrase; see Joseph Knight, *History of the Stage in the Victorian Era* (1901; rpt., New York: Garland, 1986) and, for a historical analysis of the "anti-theatrical" phenomenon, Jonas Barish, *The Anti-theatrical Prejudice* (Berkeley: University of California Press, 1981).

24. See Lawrence Levine, *Highbrow/Lowbrow: The Emergence of Cultural Hierarchy in America* (Cambridge: Harvard University Press, 1988), and Michael Booth, *Prefaces to Nineteenth Century Theatre* (Manchester; Manchester University Press, 1980) and "Shakespeare as Spectacle and History," *Theatre Research International* 1, no. 2 (1976): 99–113.

25. For a discussion of "majority theatre," more precise than "anti-apart-heid" or "political" theatre because it stresses the mixed tastes and contradictory experiences of its audiences, rather than an extractable political content or expectations of the intellectual few, see Robert Kava-nagh, *Theatre and Cultural Struggle in South Africa* (London: Zed Books, 1985). For an analysis of attempts to link town theatre and the majority, see David Graver and Loren Kruger, "The Market or the Street: South Africa's National Theatre?" *New Theatre Quarterly* 19 (1989): 272–81.

26. For an account of the Serpent Players, see Dennis Walder, *Athol Fugard* (New York: Grove, 1985), 30–31, 79–81, and Brian Astbury, "Fugard at the Space," in *Athol Fugard*, ed. Stephen Gray (Johannesburg: McGraw Hill, 1982), 57–63; for their work in the context of "town theatre" groups and the Black Consciousness movement, see Kavanagh, *Theatre and Cultural Struggle*, 54–57.

27. The critics in London and New York as well as South Africa routinely attribute the piece to Fugard; one notable exception is the review "Win-ston Ntshona and John Kani in New York," in the (largely) black arts magazine, *S'Ketsch* (Winter 1975), n.p.

28. Dennis Walder follows this tradition when he calls *The Island* a "power-ful tragedy, with universal implications for overseas audiences" (80). Fugard himself emphasizes the "heroic stance . . . of courageous pessi-mism" (the stance of Camus's rebel) rather than the enactment of solidar-ity (quoted by Walder, 81). John Kani makes the opposite claim, in "Art Is Life and Life Is Art: An Interview With John Kani and Winston Ntshona of the Serpent Players," *UFAHAMU* (Journal of the African Activist Association) 6, no. 2 (1976): 6–11, esp. 7.

29. "Sizwe Banzi is Dead," in *A Night at the Theatre*, ed. Ronald Harwood (London: Methuen, 1982), 21–33, esp 31–32.

30. The *locus classicus* for the term "public sphere" is Jürgen Habermas,

Strukturwandel der Öffentlichkeit [*Structural Transformation of the Public Sphere*, trans. Thomas Burger (Cambridge: MIT Press, 1989)] (Darmstadt: Luchterhand, 1962). In their *Öffentlichkeit und Erfahrung* (Public Sphere and Experience) (Frankfurt: Suhrkamp, 1972), Alexander Kluge and Oskar Negt critique the essentially bourgeois space of public opinion by proposing a counter public sphere located in the *experience* of those excluded from legitimate public opinion.

31. Even in the era of the portable camcorder, we should not forget that 90% of "public" airwaves belong to the 10 top broadcasting nations and that access to "private" channels is increasingly concentrated. See Armand Mattelart, Michèle Mattelart, and Xavier Delcourt, "International Image Markets," in *Global Television*, ed. Cynthia Schneider (Cambridge, Mass: MIT Press, 1984), 13–30, and Ben Bagdikian, "The Lords of the Global Village," *The Nation* 248, 23 (June 12, 1989): 800, 814–16.

32. As Victor Turner points out in "From Liminal to Liminoid," in *From Ritual to Theatre* (New York: Performing Arts Journal Publications, 1982), 20–60, esp. 30–37, the very notion of "leisure" as distinct from "work" is predicated on the rationalization of paid labor in industrial or technological societies.

33. Raymond Williams, "Brecht and Beyond," in *Politics and Letters: Interviews with the Editors of the New Left Review* (London: New Left Books, 1979), 214–34, 223–24. Hereafter cited in text as *Politics and Letters*.

34. For the problematic of watching, see Raymond Williams, "Drama in a Dramatized Society," in Williams, *Writing and Society* (London: Verso, 1984), 11–21, esp. 11–12, and Jane Feuer, "The Concept of Live Television: Ontology as Ideology," in *Regarding Television*, ed. E. Ann Kaplan (Frederick, MD: University Presses of America, 1983), 12–21; for the contradictions between critically inclined programs on television and the conditions of their reception—distracted viewing in the home—see Raymond Williams, *Television: Technology and Cultural Form* (New York: Schocken, 1975), 25–27, 86–96, and John McGrath, *A Good Night Out: Popular Theatre, Audience, Class and Form* (London: Methuen, 1981), 100–17.

35. McGrath provides an account of this production, as well as the conditions and challenges of popular theatre in Britain, in *A Good Night Out*, 18–80. McGrath and others working in community theatre show that this kind of work is at its best an attempt to combine forms familiar to a popular audience, from television to panto, with material that relates to daily life. See also Steve Gooch, *All Together Now* (London: Methuen, 1984) and Tony Coult and Baz Kershaw, eds., *Engineers of the Imagination: The Welfare State Handbook* (London: Methuen, 1983).

36. In "From Liminal to Liminoid," 41–54, Turner calls this space of enter-tainment *liminoid* as distinct from the liminal space of traditional ritual; while the latter is the site of community affirmation, the former outlines the terrain of experiment and social critique. Turner's assumption that advanced capitalist societies provide the best conditions for liminoid phenomena is, however, less convincing than his theoretical framework.

37. See "The Importance of Community" (1977) and "Decentralism and the Politics of Place" (1984), in *Resources of Hope*, 111–19 and 230–44, respectively.

38. Williams, "The Importance of Community," 117. Hereafter cited in text as "Importance of Community."

39. Sipho Sepamla, "Towards an African Theatre," *Rand Daily Mail*, 2 April 1982, p. 11.

40. For an account of the Women's Theatre Group in the context of British feminist theatre, see Michelene Wandor, *Carry on Understudies* (London: Methuen, 1986); for a detailed discussion of the formal and occasional features of *My Mother Says*, see Loren Kruger, "The Dis-Play's the Thing: Gender and Public Sphere in Contemporary British Theatre," *Theatre Journal* 42, 1 (1990): 27–47.

41. "My Mother Says I Never Should," in *Strike While the Iron Is Hot*, ed. Michelene Wandor (London: Journeyman Press, 1980), 1–5, esp. 3. Hereafter cited in text as "My Mother Says."

42. See Angela McRobbie, "Working Class Girls and the Culture of Feminin-ity," in *Women Take Issue*, ed. Womens Studies Group, Birmingham Centre for Contemporary Cultural Studies (London: Hutchinson, 1978), 96–108. As McRobbie notes, the girls' fierce defense of a "feminine" space defined by their interest in fashion, "boys," and marriage consti-tutes a contradictory response to the material limits of their horizons, since it articulates an ambivalent response to dominant gender relations. For a critique of the autonomy of a "culture of femininity," see Leslie Roman and Linda Christian-Smith, eds., *Becoming Feminine: The Poli-tics of Popular Culture* (London: Falmer Press, 1989).

43. Anonymous letter from a London teacher to the *Evening Standard*, 10 December 1978, p. 10, which complains that the play "incites underage *children* to break the law" (emphasis added).

4 Realisms and Modernisms: Raymond Williams and Popular Fiction

1. Raymond Williams, *Culture and Society 1780–1950* (Harmondsworth: Pelican, 1976).

Notes

2. Raymond Williams, *The Country and the City* (Oxford: Oxford University Press, 1973). Raymond Williams, *Marxism and Literature* (Oxford: Oxford University Press, 1977).

3. Raymond Williams, *The English Novel from Dickens to Lawrence* (London: Chatto and Windus, 1971).

4. Williams disliked the term "mass culture" because of its associations with tyranny, manipulation, and vulgarity. He preferred instead the term "popular culture" because of its emphasis on human agency. For more on this, see Stephen Heath and Gillian Skirrow, "An Interview with Raymond Williams," in *Studies in Entertaiment: Critical Approaches to Mass Culture*, ed. Tania Modleski (Bloomington: Indiana University Press, 1986), 3–17.

5. Williams, *Marxism and Literature*, 19.

6. Williams, *Culture and Society 1780–1950*, 289.

7. Hereafter, I will use "low" (or "popular" culture) and "high" culture as terms to designate the ways in which culture has traditionally been categorized. These terms, that is, should always be understood as being under quotation marks. My usage of these terms should not be taken as accepting these modes of valuation. These terms do not have any *ontological* meaning, but they do have a political significance inasmuch as they reveal the ideological values that permit the division of culture into different spheres.

8. Williams, *Marxism and Literature*, 121–127.

9. Raymond Williams, "The Metropolis and the Emergence of Modernism," in *Unreal City: Urban Experience in Modern European Literature and Art*, ed. Edward Timms and David Kelley (Manchester: Manchester University Press, 1985), 13–24, esp. 14.

10. Williams's approach to realism, and his critical appraisal of contemporary dismissal of realism is best summarized in *Keywords* (New York: Oxford University Press):

> More often, however, the argument [about realism] has been linked, in particular intellectual formations, with the idealist modes of **FORMALISM** and of **STRUCTURALISM** (qq,v), where the strength of attention to the detailed practice of composition, and especially to the basic forms and structures within which composition occurs, goes along with or can be used to justify an indifference to the forces other than literary and artistic and intellectual practice which it was the purpose of the broader **realism** (even at times naively) to take into radical account. The historical significance of **Realism** was to make social and physical **reality** (in a generally materialist sense) the basis of literature, art and thought (261).

11. In *Politics and Letters* (London: NLB, 1979), Williams notes:

    Now in the same period [in the last two decades of the nineteenth century], there had also been a very deep and successful reorganization of bourgeois cultural and educational institutions; the creation of the new public schools, the renovation of Oxford and Cambridge, the development of a fully extended bourgeois press, the modernization of publishing. Together with these changes went an increasing centralization in London, which now functioned much more as an imperial cultural capital. The result was an integrated and confident set of bourgeois cultural institutions such as had never existed in any previous period of English history. The social base of writers from 1880 to 1930 is much narrower and more standardized than 1830 to 1880. That is why I used the term insulated—the writers themselves had a much more limited experience. The characteristic change is from a George Eliot to a Forster. Now Forster proclaims the same aims as George Eliot, but there are areas of social experience to which he is no longer open (263).

12. See, for example, Williams's essays "The Metropolis and the Emergence of Modernism," 13–24, and "When Was Modernism?," *New Left Review* 175 (1989): 48–52.
13. Heath and Skirrow, "An Interview with Raymond Williams," 11.
14. Raymond Williams, *The Long Revolution* (New York: Columbia University Press, 1961), 279.
15. Ibid., 274–289.
16. Ibid., 278.
17. Roland Barthes, *Writing Degree Zero*, trans. Annette Lavers and Colin Smith (New York: Hill and Wang, 1968).
18. Williams, *The Long Revolution*, 288.
19. I have in mind *Marxism and the Philosophy of Language*, trans. L. Matejka and I.R. Titunik (New York: Seminar Press, 1973), *Freudianism: A Marxist Critique*, trans. I.R. Titunik (New York: Seminar Press, 1976), and M.M. Bakhtin's *The Dialogic Imagination*, ed. Michael Holquist and trans. Caryl Emerson and Michael Holquist (Austin: The University of Texas Press, 1981). The first two works appear in print in their English editions under the name of Volosinov, but there is a growing consensus that they were at least co-authored, if not in fact written, by M.M. Bakhtin. Due to this, and Bakhtin's emphasis that language is not owned by one writer or another but is accentuated by the intentions of other writers, it seems to make more sense to refer the co-authorship of the first two texts mentioned above.
20. V.N. Volosinov [and M.M. Bakhtin], *Freudianism: A Marxist Critique*, 100.

21. Andreas Huyssen, *After the Great Divide: Modernism, Mass Culture, Postmodernism* (Bloomington: Indiana University Press, 1986), ix.

22. I am echoing Terry Eagleton in *Literary Theory: An Introduction* (Minneapolis: The University of Minnesota Press, 1983): "As the philosophers might say, 'literature' and 'weed' are *functional* rather than *ontological* terms: they tell us about what we do, not about the fixed being of things" (9).

23. Tony Bennett, "Marxism and Popular Fiction, in *Popular Fictions: Essays in Literature and History*, ed. Peter Humm, Paul Stigant, and Peter Widdowson (London: Methuen, 1986), 237–265, esp. 244.

24. Michael Holquist uses the phrase "a horizon of expectations" to define what Bakhtin means by *genre* in his "Glossary" to *The Dialogic Imagination*, 423–434, esp. 428. For a more extensive treatment of this idea, see Mikael Bakhtin, "Discourse in the Novel," in *The Dialogic Imagination*, 259–422.

25. Ken Warpole, *Reading by Numbers: Contemporary Publishing and Popular Fiction* (London: Comedia Group, 1984), 20.

26. Raymond Chandler, "The Simple Art of Murder," in *The Art of the Mystery Story: A Collection of Critical Essays*, ed. Howard Haycraft (New York: Simon and Schuster, 1946), 222–237, esp. 234.

27. Raymond Williams explicitly theorizes the metropolis as the locus of modernism in "The Metropolis and the Emergence of Modernism."

28. For more on Hammett's tendency to see bourgeois norms as fictions, see Steven Marcus, "Introduction," *The Continental Op* (New York: Vintage, 1975), esp. xxiv.

29. Dashiell Hammett, *Five Complete Novels*, 102.

30. Marcus, "Introduction," xvii.

31. For more on this point, see Sinda Gregory, *Private Investigations: The Novels of Dashiell Hammett* (Carbondale: Southern Illinois University Press, 1985), 14.

32. Gregory, *Private Investigations,* 13.

33. Hammett, *Five Complete Novels,* 3.

34. Roland Barthes, *S/Z* (Paris: Seuil, 1970), esp. 9–12.

35. See Ken Warpole's essay "The American Connection: The Masculine Style in Popular Fiction," in his stimulating book *Dockers and Detectives* (London: Verso, 1983), 29–48, for more on the liberating effects of hard-boiled fiction on contemporary English fiction.

5 Rebuilding Hegemony: Education, Equality, and the New Right

I would like to thank the Friday Seminar at the University of Wisconsin, Dennis Dworkin, and Leslie G. Roman for their comments on the various drafts of this chapter. I am also especially indebted to Allen Hunter for his many insights on the issues I discuss here. His own work on this topic was of major importance in helping me think through these issues. A briefer articulation of my arguments in this chapter appears in Henry Giroux and Peter McClaren, eds., *Critical Pedagogy, The State, and Cultural Struggle* (Albany: State University of New York Press, 1989).

1. Alan O'Connor, *Raymond Williams: Writing, Culture, Politics* (New York: Basil Blackwell, 1989), 30.
2. Williams's discussion of the materiality of language is essential here. See Raymond Williams, *Marxism and Literature* (New York: Oxford University Press, 1977).
3. Stuart Hall, "The Toad in the Garden: Thatcherism Among the Theorists," in *Marxism and the Interpretation of Culture*, ed. Cary Nelson and Lawrence Grossberg (Urbana: University of Illinois Press, 1988), 35–57, esp. 42.
4. Ibid.
5. Michael W. Apple, *Teachers and Texts: A Political Economy of Class and Gender Relations in Education* (New York: Routledge, 1988).
6. Hall, "The Toad in the Garden," 35.
7. Ibid., 36. In many ways, Williams's own entire corpus of work embodies this commitment. See, for example, the volume of some of his collected essays, Raymond Williams, *Resources of Hope* (New York: Verso, 1989).
8. See the excellent discussion in Susan Rose, *Keeping Them Out of the Hands of Satan: Evangelical Schooling in America* (New York: Routledge, 1988).
9. Williams, *Resources of Hope*, 36.
10. Ibid., 38.
11. William J. Bennett, *Our Children and Our Country* (New York: Routledge, 1988), 9.
12. Ibid., 10.
13. See Apple, *Teachers and Texts*, and Henry Giroux, "Public Philosophy and the Crisis in Education," *Harvard Educational Review* 54 (May 1984): 186–94.
14. Michael W. Apple, *Education and Power* (New York: Routledge rev. ed., 1985), and Apple, *Teachers and Texts*.
15. Herbert Gintis, "Communication and Politics," *Socialist Review* 10 (March–June 1980), 189–232, esp. 193.
16. Ibid., 196.
17. Ibid., 197.
18. Ibid.
19. Ibid., 194. See also Samuel Bowles and Herbert Gintis, *Democracy and Capitalism* (New York: Basic Books, 1986).

Notes

20. National Commission on Excellence in Education, "A Nation at Risk," *Education Week*, 27 April 1983, 12–16.

21. Apple, *Teachers and Texts*.

22. Mary Anderson, "Teachers' Unions and Industrial Politics" (Ph.D. diss., Macquarie University, 1985), 6–8.

23. Ann Bastian, Norm Fruchter, Marilyn Gittell, Colin Greer, and Kenneth Haskins, *Choosing Equality: The Case for Democratic Schooling* (Philadelphia: Temple University Press, 1986), 14.

24. I wish to thank my colleague Walter Secada for this point.

25. Michael W. Apple, "National Reports and the Construction of Inequality," *British Journal of Sociology of Education* 7, no. 2 (1986): 171–90.

26. See Michael W. Apple, *Ideology and Curriculum*, second edition (New York: Routledge, 1990), and Jorge Larrain, *Marxism and Ideology* (Atlantic Highlands, N.J.: Humanities Press, 1983).

27. Stuart Hall, "Authoritarian Populism: A Reply," *New Left Review* 151 (May/June 1985), 115–27, esp. 122.

28. David Clark and Terry Astuto, "The Significance and Permanence of Changes in Federal Education Policy," *Educational Researcher* 15 (October 1986): 4–13; Frances Piven and Richard Cloward, *The New Class War* (New York: Pantheon, 1982); and Marcus Raskin, *The Common Good* (New York: Routledge, 1986). Clark and Astuto point out that during Reagan's term in office, the following initiatives characterized educational policies: reducing the federal role in education, stimulating competition among schools with the aim of "breaking the monopoly of the public school," fostering individual competition so that "excellence" is gained, increasing the reliance on performance standards for students and teachers, an emphasis on the "basics" in content, increasing parental choice "over what, where, and how their children learn," strengthening the teaching of "traditional values" in schools, and expanding the policy of transferring educational authority to the state and local levels (8).

29. Stuart Hall and Martin Jacques, "Introduction," in *The Politics of Thatcherism*, ed. Stuart Hall and Martin Jacques (London: Lawrence and Wishart, 1983), 9–16, esp.13.

30. Stuart Hall, "Popular Democratic vs. Authoritarian Populism: Two Ways of Taking Democracy Seriously," in *Marxism and Democracy*, ed. Alan Hunt (London: Lawrence and Wishart, 1980), 151–85, esp. 160–61.

31. Ibid., 161.

32. I realize that there is debate over the adequacy of this term. See Hall, "Authoritarian Populism: A Reply," and B. Jessop, K. Bennett, S. Bromley, and T. Ling, "Authoritarian Populism, Two Nations, and Thatcherism," *New Left Review* 147 (1984): 33–60. Authoritarian populism is,

of course, a term that denotes a central tendency of a broad and varied movement, as I shall show later on in my discussion.

33. Michael Omi and Howard Winant, *Racial Formation in the United States* (New York: Routledge, 1986), 214.

34. Walter Dean Burnham, "Post-conservative America," *Socialist Review* 13 (November-December 1983), 123–32, esp. 125.

35. Hall, "Authoritarian Populism: A Reply," 117.

36. Ibid., 112.

37. Hall, "Popular Democratic and Authoritarian Populism," 166.

38. Stuart Hall, "The Great Moving Right Show," in *The Politics of Thatcherism*, 19–39, esp. 31.

39. Apple, *Education and Power*.

40. Hall, "The Great Moving Right Show," 29–30.

41. Ibid., 36–37. For an illuminating picture of how these issues are manipulated by powerful groups, see Allen Hunter, "Virtue With a Vengeance: The Pro-Family Politics of the New Right" (Ph.D. diss. Brandeis University, 1984).

42. See Apple, *Teachers and Texts*.

43. Jessop, Bennett, Bromley, and Ling, "Authoritarian Populism, Two Nations, and Thatcherism," 49.

44. Hall, "The Great Moving Right Show," 21.

45. Allen Hunter, "The Politics of Resentment and the Construction of Middle America," unpublished paper, American Institutions Program, University of Wisconsin, Madison, 1987, 1–3.

46. Ibid., 9.

47. Samuel Bowles, "The Post-Keynesian Capital Labor Stalemate," *Socialist Review* 12 (September-October 1982): 45–72, esp. 51.

48. Hunter, "The Politics of Resentment and the Construction of Middle America," 12.

49. Omi and Winant, *Racial Formation in the United States*, 214–15.

50. Raskin, *The Common Good*.

51. Omi and Winant, *Racial Formation in the United States*, 215–16. See also Hunter, "Virtue With a Vengeance."

52. Omi and Winant, *Racial Formation in the United States*, 220. For a more complete discussion of how this has affected educational policy in particular, see Clark and Astuto, "The Significance and Permanence of Changes in Federal Education Policy," and Apple, *Teachers and Texts*.

53. Omi and Winant, *Racial Formation in the United States*, 220.

54. I have elsewhere claimed, and shall point out later, however, that some members of the new middle class—namely efficiency experts, evaluators and testers, and many of those with technical and management exper-

tise—will form part of the alliance with the New Right. This is simply because their own jobs and mobility depend on it. See Apple, *Teachers and Texts.*

55. Omi and Winant, *Racial Formation in the United States*, 227.
56. Ibid., 164.
57. Ibid. See also Samuel Bowles and Herbert Gintis, *Democracy and Capitalism* (New York: Basic Books, 1986). The discussion in Bowles and Gintis of the "transportability" of struggles over person rights from, say, politics to the economy is very useful here. I have extended and criticized some of their claims in Michael W. Apple, "Facing the Complexity of Power: For a Parallelist Position in Critical Educational Studies," in *Rethinking Bowles and Gintis*, ed. Mike Cole (Philadelphia: Falmer Press, 1988), 112–30.
58. See Apple, *Education and Power* and *Teachers and Texts.*
59. Omi and Winant, *Racial Formation in the United States*, 177–78.
60. Ibid.
61. Ibid., 180.
62. Ibid.
63. Ibid., 190.
64. Ibid.
65. Ibid.
66. Ibid., 252.
67. Ibid., 155.
68. Hunter, "The Politics of Resentment and the Construction of Middle America," 23.
69. Ibid., 30.
70. Ibid., 33.
71. Ibid., 34.
72. Ibid., 21.
73. Ibid., 37.
74. Apple, *Teachers and Texts* and "National Reports and the Construction of Inequality."
75. Stuart Hall, "Popular Culture and the State," in *Popular Culture and Social Relations*, ed. Tony Bennett, Colin Mercer, and Janet Woollacott (Milton Keynes, England: Open University Press, 1986), 22–49, esp. 35–56.
76. Omi and Winant, *Racial Formation in the United States*, 165.
77. Ibid.
78. I say "new" here, but the continuity of, say, African-American struggles for freedom and equality also needs to be stressed. See the powerful treatment of the history of such struggles in Vincent Harding, *There is a*

River: The Black Struggle for Freedom in the United States (New York: Vintage Books, 1981).

79. See also David Hogan, "Education and Class Formation," in *Cultural and Economic Reproduction in Education*, ed. Michael W. Apple (New York: Routledge, 1982), 32–78.

80. Omi and Winant, *Racial Formation in the United States*, 166.

81. See Williams, *Marxism and Literature*.

82. Apple, "National Reports and the Construction of Inequality."

83. See Apple, *Teachers and Texts*, and Martin Carnoy, Derek Shearer, and Russell Rumberger, *A New Social Contract* (New York: Harper and Row, 1984).

84. Apple, "National Reports and the Construction of Inequality." For a comprehensive analysis of the logic of capitalism, one that compares it with other political and economic traditions, see Andrew Levine, *Arguing for Socialism* (New York: Routledge, 1984).

85. See Apple, *Education and Power* and *Teachers and Texts*.

86. See Sara Freedman, Jane Jackson, and Katherine Boles, *The Effects of the Institutional Structure of Schools on Teachers* (Somerville: Boston Women's Teachers' Group, 1982).

87. For further discussion of this, see Apple, *Teachers and Texts*; Bastian, Fruchter, Gittell, Greer, and Haskins, *Choosing Equality*; and David Livingstone, ed., *Critical Pedagogy and Cultural Power* (South Hadley: Bergin and Garvey, 1987). "Substance" in Chicago and "Chalkdust" in New York City are other significant examples of such progressive groups.

88. Hall, "The Great Moving Right Show," 120.

89. Raymond Williams, *The Long Revolution* (London: Chatto and Windus, 1961).

90. Apple, *Ideology and Curriculum*.

91. I have discussed this in greater detail in Apple, *Education and Power*.

92. See, e.g., Margo Culley and Catherine Portuges, eds., *Gendered Subjects* (New York: Routledge, 1985).

93. For a clearer sense of what is occurring at the level of practice in some schools, see *Rethinking Schools*, the newspaper of the Rethinking Schools group in Milwaukee. It can be gotten by writing to Rethinking Schools, P.O. Box 93371, Milwaukee, WI 53203. See also Bastian, Fruchter, Gittell, Greer, and Haskins, *Choosing Equality*. The discussion of politically organized literacy programs in Colin Lankshear and Moira Lawler, *Literacy, Schooling and Revolution* (Philadelphia: Falmer Press, 1986) is helpful here as well. One of the most articulate discussions of an attempt at a more politically engaged pedagogy—one that is expressly counter-hegemonic—can be found in Elizabeth Ellsworth, "Why Doesn't

This Feel Empowering: Working Through the Repressive Myths of Critical Pedagogy," *Harvard Educational Review* 59 (August 1989), 297–324. For a history of past attempts at counter-hegemonic educational work, see Kenneth Teitelbaum, "Contestation and Curriculum: The Efforts of American Socialists, 1900–1920," in *The Curriculum: Problems, Politics and Possibilities* ed. Landon E. Beyer and Michael W. Apple (Albany: State University of New York Press, 1988), 32–55 and Clyde Barrow, "Pedagogy Politics and Social Reform: The Philosophy of the Workers Education Movement," *Strategies* 2 (Fall 1989), 45–66.

94. Raymond Williams, *The Year 2000* (New York: Pantheon, 1983), 268–69.

6 Raymond Williams, Affective Ideology, and Counter-Hegemonic Practices

1. See for example his trilogy of novels: *Border Country* (1960; rpt., London: Hogarth Press, 1988), *Second Generation* (1964; rpt., London: Hogarth Press, 1988), and *The Fight for Manod* (1979; rpt., London: Hogarth Press, 1988).
2. Erica Sherover-Marcuse argues, in *Emancipation and Consciousness* (London: Basil Blackwell, 1986), that this practice can serve an emancipatory role "as an ingredient in the political struggle for fundamental social change" (137).
3. Raymond Williams referred to the incorporation process in his work on hegemony. See, for example, *Marxism and Literature* (London: Oxford University Press, 1977).
4. Raymond Williams, *Towards 2000* (London: Chatto & Windus/Hogarth Press, 1983), 174.
5. Williams, *Towards 2000*, 3.
6. Feminism and ecology movements such as the "Greens" have provided necessary critiques of traditional Left politics. Williams learned from them. At the same time, he retained a radical economic critique that I believe is essential to any politics of the future.
7. Raymond Williams, *Problems in Materialism and Culture: Selected Essays* (London: Verso, 1980), 252.
8. Raymond Williams, *Resources of Hope: Culture, Democracy, Socialism*, ed. Robin Gable (London: Verso, 1989), 295.
9. Ibid.
10. Ibid., 255.
11. Ibid., 320.

12. Ibid., 75.

13. I think, for example, of Jean-Francois Lyotard's deconstruction of all metanarratives and his insistence on a "polytheism of values" that are equally privileged. See *The Postmodern Condition: A Report on Knowledge* (Minneapolis: University of Minnesota Press, 1984).

14. Ernesto Laclau and Chantal Mouffe, *Hegemony and Socialist Strategy: Toward a Radical Democratic Politics* (London: Verso, 1985), 178.

15. Throughout this text I use the term "working class," all the while recognizing that it is not a unitary construct; I know that class cuts differently across gender, race, region, ethnicity. This holds for the "middle class" as well.

16. It would have been difficult enough for my only brother to go to college if he had wanted. But to send a *girl* just didn't make economic sense. After all, the reasoning went, "she would just end up married anyway."

17. Valerie Walkerdine and Helen Lucey put it well: "Only through education could we avoid having to become like our parents, to carry in our bodies the pain of having to do that kind of work." *Democracy in the Kitchen* (London: Virago Press, 1989), 12.

18. See Williams's analysis of "selective traditions," developed in the work of Michael Apple, *Ideology and Curriculum* (London: Routledge & Kegan Paul, 1979); Henry Giroux, *Ideology, Culture and the Process of Schooling* (Philadelphia: Temple University Press, 1981); and Jean Anyon, "Social Class and School Knowledge," *Curriculum Inquiry* 11, no. 1 (1981): 3–42.

19. See Walkerdine and Lucey, 13.

20. Others have written about similar feelings. See, for example, Jake Ryan and Charles Sackrey, eds., *Strangers in Paradise: Academics from the Working Class* (Boston: South End Press, 1984).

21. A key theme in this essay is "internalized oppression." I believe that a great deal of damage done by oppression is done through its internalized forms—including self-invalidation and self-hatred, attacks upon each other by the members of an oppressed group, and attacks and competition *between* different oppressed groups. The self-invalidation results from a twofold process: believing the misinformation that circulates in a society about one's targeted group *and* emulating the attitudes and beliefs of the dominant classes in an effort to "become them." In no way do I want to suggest, however, that oppressed groups are responsible for their oppression. Nor do I want to diminish the devastating effects of materially oppressive conditions.

22. I am committed to eradicating all forms of oppression. In this paper, however, I will speak most directly to class oppression, knowing full well that the particular forms it takes are affected by gender, race, ethnicity,

and geographic region. By focusing on class, I am not suggesting that it has primacy over other forms of oppression.

23. See, for example, Chapter 9 of *Marxism and Literature*.
24. See, for example, the work of Michael Apple; Henry Giroux; Geoff Whitty, *Sociology and School Knowledge* (London: Methuen, 1985); and Paul Willis, *Learning to Labor* (Lexington, Mass.: D.C. Heath, 1977).
25. Williams, *Marxism and Literature*, 112.
26. The opening paragraph of *Second Generation* conveys the split: "If you stand, today, in Between Towns Road, you can see either way: west to the spires and towers of the cathedral and colleges; east to the yards and sheds of the motor works. You see different worlds, but there is no frontier between them; there is only the movement and traffic of a single city." (9).
27. Williams, *Border Country*, 82–83. Subsequent references cited in text as *BC*.
28. Williams, *Second Generation*, 252. Subsequent references cited in text as *SG*.
29. Williams, *Towards 2000*, 254.
30. Williams, *Marxism and Literature*, 110.
31. Ibid., emphasis mine.
32. Ibid., 111.
33. See, for example, Michael Apple's essay in this volume, p. 91.
34. Raymond Williams, *The Long Revolution* (New York: Columbia University Press, 1961), 50.
35. Ibid., 51
36. Ibid., 149.
37. Williams, *Marxism and Literature*, 132.
38. Quoted in Apple, *Ideology and Curriculum*, 6.
39. Ibid.
40. Williams, *Resources of Hope*, 76.
41. Williams, *The Long Revolution*, xi–xii.
42. Williams, *Resources of Hope*, 76. For more on Williams's analysis of "structures of feeling," see *Marxism and Literature*, Chapter 9.
43. Williams, *Marxism and Literature*, 132.
44. A great deal has been written about "internalized oppression" and the barriers *within* us. See, for example, Frantz Fanon, *The Wretched of the Earth* (New York: Grove Press, 1963); Paolo Friere, *Pedagogy of the Oppressed* (New York: Herder and Herder, 1972); Audre Lorde, *Sister Outsider* (New York: Crossing Press, 1984); Cherrie Moraga and Gloria Anzaldua, eds., *This Bridge Called My Back: Writings by Radical Women of Color* (Watertown, Mass.: Persephone Press, 1981); Jean Baker Miller, *Toward a New Psychology of Women* (Boston: Beacon Press, 1976).
45. Sherover-Marcuse, 5.
46. See Willis.

47. Williams, *Resources of Hope*, 76.

48. Herbert Marcuse once said: "The subjective side of the revolution is not only a matter of consciousness, and of action guided by knowledge; it is also a question of the emotions." Quoted in Sherover-Marcuse, 135.

49. Williams, *Resources of Hope*, 75, emphasis mine.

50. Ibid.

51. Reich, quoted in Sherover-Marcuse, 134.

52. Sherover-Marcuse, 134.

53. See, for example, Allison Jaggar, *Feminist Politics and Human Nature* (Sussex, England: Rowman and Allanheld/The Harvester Press, 1983); Nancy Harstock, "The Feminist Standpoint: Developing the Ground for a Specifically Feminist Historical Materialism," in *Feminism and Methodology*, ed. Sandra Harding (Bloomington: Indiana University Press, 1987), 157–180; and Teresa de Lauretis, ed., *Feminist Studies/ Critical Studies* (Bloomington: Indiana University Press, 1986).

54. When confronted by this criticism, Williams responds lamely: "I suppose I found it easier to explore that in more personal terms in my novels. That's no real excuse. I ought to have been doing this in my other work too; but by the time I came to understand it in that way it was already being done by a lot of good people who were no doubt making more sense of it than I could have done." *Resources of Hope*, 319.

55. Sherover-Marcuse, 133.

56. Williams, *Resources of Hope*, 75.

57. Sherover-Marcuse, 137.

58. The exception here, of course, is within most feminist circles.

59. See, for example, the work of Claude Steiner, Hogie Wyckoff, and Joy Marcus in *Readings in Radical Psychiatry*, ed. Claude Steiner (New York: Grove Press, 1974); or the writings of Harvey Jackins and others who are associated with theory and practice of Reevaluation Counseling; or Michael Lerner, Lee Shore, and others at the Institute for Labor and Mental Health, Oakland, California.

60. Sherover-Marcuse, 137.

61. Ibid., 141.

62. Ibid., 137.

63. Williams, *Resources of Hope*, 249.

64. Sherover-Marcuse, 135.

7 Williams on Democracy and the Governance of Education

1. Raymond Williams, *Towards 2000* (London: Chatto & Windus, 1983), 125.

2. Raymond Williams, *The Long Revolution* (London: Penguin, 1961), 334.

3. The notion of a rearticulation used here rests on the analysis developed by Stuart Hall, *The Hard Road to Renewal* (London: Verso, 1988).
4. Raymond Williams, *Keywords* (London: Fontana, 1976), 96.
5. Williams, *Towards 2000*, 103.
6. See, for example, Richard Norman, *Free and Equal* (London: Oxford University Press, 1988).
7. Williams, *Towards 2000*, 116.
8. Ibid., 117.
9. Ibid., 118.
10. Ibid., 119.
11. Ibid., 120.
12. Ibid., 122.
13. Raymond Williams, *Politics and Letters* (London: New Left Books, 1979), 426.
14. Alan O'Connor, *Raymond Williams: Writing, Culture, Politics* (Oxford: Basil Blackwell, 1989), 124.
15. Francis Mulhern, "Towards 2000, or News from You-Know-Where," *New Left Review*, 8 November 1984, 1–30.
16. Williams, *The Long Revolution*, 336.
17. Williams, *Towards 2000*, 123.
18. Ibid.
19. Ibid., 124.
20. Ibid.
21. Ibid., 125.
22. For a discussion of workplace and industrial democracy in a number of countries, both Western and Eastern, see Graeme Duncan, ed., *Democratic Theory and Practice* (Cambridge: Cambridge University Press, 1983).
23. For a comparative discussion of decentralization and devolution in educational administration in the U.S.A. and Australia, see William Boyd and Don Smart, eds., *Educational Policy in Australia and America: Comparative Perspectives* (London: Falmer, 1987).
24. Extracts from Kenneth Baker's House of Commons speech of 1 December 1987 are reprinted in Julien Haviland, ed., *Take Care, Mr. Baker!* (London: Fourth Estate, 1988), 2–6, esp. 2.
25. Ibid.
26. Many of ERA's operational principles have much in common with what in the U.S.A. has been referred to as the voucher system.
27. Brian Simon, *Bending the Rules* (London: Lawrence & Wishart, 1988), has been one of the most outspoken and influential public critics of ERA.
28. Extracts from the British Commission for Racial Equality's response to

the initial Discussion Paper outlining ERA proposals are reprinted in Haviland, *Take Care*, 17.

29. Reports of the Dewsbury case appeared in most national newspapers in Britain throughout August and September, 1988. For the most detailed account, see the September issues of the *Times Educational Supplement*.

30. Williams, *The Long Revolution*, 145.

31. Ibid., 174.

32. John Tomlinson, "Curriculum and Market: Are They Compatible?" in Haviland, *Take Care*, 9–13.

33. For a discussion of this issue, see Patricia White, "The New Right and Parental Choice," *Journal of Philosophy of Education* 22, no. 2 (1988): 195–99.

34. Samuel Bowles and Herbert Gintis, *Democracy and Capitalism* (New York: Basic Books, 1987), 123–25. It should be clear that Bowles and Gintis's analysis here is in fact a development of the traditional Marxist notion of ideology.

35. Lesley Johnson, "Raymond Williams: A Marxist View of Culture," in Diane J. Austin-Broos, ed., *Creating Cultures* (Sydney: Allen & Unwin, 1987), 163–77, esp. 170.

36. Raymond Williams, *Marxism and Literature* (London: Penguin, 1977).

37. Ibid., 122–25.

38. Williams, *The Long Revolution*, 68.

39. Ibid., 64.

40. Williams, *Marxism and Literature*, 129.

41. Ibid., 110.

42. Raymond Williams, *Resources of Hope: Culture, Democracy, Socialism*, ed. Robin Gable (London: Verso, 1989), 283.

43. Ibid.

44. Ibid., 285.

45. Ibid., 286.

46. Ibid., 285.

47. Raymond Williams, *Culture and Society, 1780–1950* (London: Chatto & Windus, 1958).

48. Williams, *Towards 2000*, 153–174.

49. Williams, *Resources of Hope*, 297.

50. Williams, *Keywords*, 75–76.

51. Frederick Tonnies, *Community and Association* (1887; rpt., London: Routledge & Kegan Paul, 1955).

52. Mulhern, 23.

53. Hall, 65.

54. Ibid., 66.

55. Williams, *Resources of Hope*, 301.

56. Mulhern, 23.

8 "On the Ground" with Antiracist Pedagogy and Raymond Williams's Unfinished Project to Articulate a Socially Transformative Critical Realism

I wrote this essay under much duress, not the least of which was produced by living and teaching in Louisiana. Shortly after rejoicing at having gotten a job elsewhere, my family was confronted with a devasting medical crisis. Many people were "sisters" or provided emotional and intellectual support through both ordeals. Livia Polanyi gave me the courage to nourish heretical unorthodox ideas through all stages of this writing. Marie Brennan, Ann Cvetkovich, Mimi Orner, Biodun Ignila, Wendy Kohli, Cameron McCarthy, JoAnne Pagano, Fazal Rizvi, and Ahmad Sultan provided sanity amidst the reactionary politics. Anthony Barthelemy, Pat McGee, and Prabhakara Jha know the meaning of camradeship in the academy. My partner, Mitchell J. Smith, provided unfailing support, critiquing my ideas in their formative stages and encouraging me to laugh more than I thought was possible in trying times. Michael W. Apple stood by me when I was most overwhelmed. He taught me long ago that *reality* claims must be subject to our critical analyses. Denise Bratton and Jayne Fargnoli have provided keen editorial insight. New colleagues in Vancouver or at the University of British Columbia, including David Beers, Deirdre Kelly, Josette McGregor, and Alan Segal have given me insightful comments in discussions of the essay. I also wish to acknowledge the students who took my critical ethnography course for teaching me more than this text could ever elaborate.

1. See Raymond Williams's essay "Media, Margins and Modernity" in *The Politics of Modernism: Against the New Conformists*, with a preface by Tony Pinckney (London: Verso, 1989), 177–195, esp. 177. Further references to the volume, abbreviated "PM," are cited in the text.

2. Raymond Williams, "A Defence of Realism," in his *What I Came to Say*, with a preface by Francis Mulhern (London: Hutchinson Radius, 1988), 226–239, esp. 239. Herein further references to this essay, abbreviated "DR," are cited in the text. This essay is transcribed from a version of the lecture first given by Williams at the SEFT/*Screen* weekend school on Realism held at the London International Film School on October 8–10, 1976. It also appears as "A Lecture on Realism," *Screen* 18 (Spring 1977): 61–74.

3. Raymond Williams, "Brecht," in *What I Came to Say*, 261–266, esp.

266. Further references to this essay, abbreviated "Brecht," are cited in the text.

4.   By feminist materialism, I do not mean abstract utopian principles. Nor do I mean that feminist materialism can be treated as an a priori set of theoretical and political ideas authorizing feminism. The value of a politicized conception of feminist materialism is its explanatory power to provide feminist struggles with the theoretical and practical resources of historical specificity, without denying that certain inequalities have a systematic basis over time. Feminist materialism, I believe, offers a compelling systematic explanatory account of the persistence as well as the transformations of existing social divisions and forms of oppression. I elaborate what I mean by feminist materialism not only in this essay but elsewhere as well. See, for example, my essay, "The Political Significance of Other Ways of Narrating Ethnography: A Feminist Materialist Approach," in *The Handbook of Qualitative Research in Education*, ed. Margaret LeCompte, Wendy Millroy, and Judith Preissle (San Diego, CA: Academic Press, 1991), 556–594, in which I reject the *subject-object dualism* as both epistemology and methodology and develop alternatives to both subjectivism and objectivism. Further references to this essay, abbreviated "Other," are cited in the text.

5.   The concept of "standpoint theory," or a feminist position based on "women's standpoint" critiques of the social world, remains a contested one which is still in the process of refinement by feminists whose definitions of it vary according to within which tradition of feminism they work. I use the concept as it is informed by feminist materialism to mean the political, theoretical, and methodological project of women, and other groups subordinated by class, race, national culture, sexual orientation, and/or age, collectively and democratically theorizing what is common and different in their experiences of oppression and privilege. Certainly, the aim would be to avoid *universalizing* such a standpoint from a prior specified position implicitly written as norm. My interest is in doing so without giving up on systematic explanations of the structural underpinnings of shifting power relations. Because increasingly I find the language of women's or feminist standpoint to be understood (whether justifiably or not) as underwriting a kind of universalism, I will further refine the concept's dialogical political commitments and its potential to recognize the inequalities of power that operate between and among women of differentially interested groups. I will propose what it means to be engaged in the contradictions of dialogical practice when *speaking with* others in order to find common ground from which we can systematically challenge prevailing inequalities. The works of Michelle Barrett, Alison Jaggar, Sandra Harding, and Dorothy Smith, to name a few, have

been important to me in the formulation of a provisional alternative to the idea of women being merely the objects of feminist or any other kind of analyses. See Jaggar's *Feminist Politics and Human Nature* (New Jersey: Rowman & Allenheld, 1983), esp. 370. But see also her elaboration of the problems facing women of different racial and class backgrounds working together to achieve more adequate representations of the social world on 369–371, 377–385, & 384–389. Further references to this volume, abbreviated *FPHN*, are cited in the text. See also, Sandra Harding's *Feminism and Methodology* (Bloomington: Indiana University Press, 1987), esp. 1–14 and her volume, *The Science Question in Feminism* (Ithaca: Cornell University Press, 1987). Further references to these volumes, abbreviated *FM* and *SQF*, are cited in the text. See Dorothy Smith's *The Everyday World as Problematic: A Feminist Sociology* (Milton Keynes: Open University Press, 1988). Further references to this volume, abbreviated *EWP*, are cited in the text. Among others doing work within this tradition, see Elizabeth Fee, "Is Feminism a Threat to Scientific Objectivity?" *International Journal of Women's Studies* 4 (1981): 378–392, Jane Flax, "Political Philosophy and the Patriarchal Unconscious: A Psychoanalytic Perspective on Epistemology and Metaphysics," in *Discovering Reality: Feminist Perspectives on Epistemology, Metaphysics, Methodology and the Philosophy of Science,* ed. Merrill Hintikka and Sandra Harding (Dordrecht: Reidel, 1983).

6. By arguing that postmodernism makes an a priori commitment to relativism, I join other critically minded poststructuralist and materialist scholars who also observe that postmodernism's and poststructuralism's laudable project to deconstruct the categories of the self, subject, identity, and voice, etc. "fails to ground historically its own capacity for this farsighted intervention," particularly when its analyses celebrate and reify what postcolonial poststructuralist R. Radhakrishan calls "indeterminacy-as-such" and thus lose sight of their actual constituencies "as though nothing were at stake." See Radhakrishan's essay, "Feminist Historiography and Poststructuralism," in *The Difference Within: Feminism and Critical Theory,* ed. Elizabeth Meese and Alice Parker (Amsterdam/Philadelphia: John Benjamins, 1989), 189–203, esp. 190.

7. I shall consider the paradoxical impasse posed by postmodernism for feminism later in the paper. But my argument benefits from the analysis of feminist literary critic Toril Moi, who similarly assesses the relativism impasse for postmodernist feminism; see her article, "Feminism, Postmodernism and Style: Recent Feminist Criticism in the United States," *Cultural Critique,* 9 (Spring: 1988): 3–22. Moi argues compellingly that theories of the post-Enlightenment variety, such as postfeminism, postmodernism, and poststructuralism, all avoid taking sides by treating

the historical specificities of women's oppression as equatable with the abstract category of ontological Otherness. On the other hand, she, like me, is open to the possibility of feminists drawing upon the critical insights of recent postmodernist and poststructuralist theory without resorting to relativism or agnosticism. Moi cites Gayatri Chakravorty Spivak's important collection of essays, *In Other Worlds: Essays in Cultural Politics* (New York: Methuen, 1987), as her model for the kind of bold and committed poststructural textual and political project to which her own feminist materialism aspires. Spivak herself recommends the textual and political strategy of making different discourses "critically interrupt each other [in order to] bring each other to crisis." See esp., 47. My essay similarly aims to interrupt relativistic varieties of postmodernism, as well as to challenge other more critical postmodernists to show how their epistemological and ontological assumptions and methodologies inform a *critically evaluative basis* for ruling out unacceptable claims to be members of particular oppressed groups.

8. Stuart Hall, "Politics and Letters," in *Raymond Williams: Critical Perspectives*, ed. Terry Eagleton (Boston: Northeastern University Press, 1989), 54–66, esp. 62. Further references to this essay, abbreviated "Politics," are cited in the text.

9. Jenny Bourne Taylor, "Raymond Williams: Gender and Generation," in *British Feminist Thought: A Reader*, ed. Terry Lovell (London: Basil Blackwell, 1990), 296–308, esp. 298. Further references to this essay, abbreviated "GG," are in the text.

10. One recent example of this position is articulated by Carolyn Knowles and Sharmila Mercer, who argue that because "there is no general relationship between race and gender," antiracist and feminist political coalitions can only be formed on a case-by-case basis. In their view, the lack of "fixity" to the subject positions of race, gender, and class means that coalitions between antiracist and feminist movements can only be understood to "indicate a temporary association between individuals and a potential set of political demands which may counter or reinforce the manner in which individuals are located in positions by the agencies with which they deal." They clearly reject the idea of theorizing the contradictory interests of race, gender, and class in terms of specifying how longer-term or broader coalitions between differentially oppressed groups can be built when they state: "There is no need to construct a broader constituency for the purposes of mounting a campaign." See their chapter, "Feminism and Antiracism: An Exploration of the Political Possibilities," in *Antiracist Strategies*, ed. Alrick X. Cambridge and Stephen Feuchtwang (Aldershot: Avebury, 1990), 61–87, esp. 61, 83–84. This position, however, seems to rely on voluntarist notions of alliance

as well as oppression. It appears to underestimate how oppression is constituted systematically and institutionally rather than in any voluntary or short-term way. The involuntary nature of oppression thus may dictate, with little individual choice, how people identify with particular struggles against specific forms of oppression. But that does not mean we can combat systematic forms of oppression through a less than systematic approach to coalition politics.

11. Linda Alcoff, "The Problem of Speaking for Others" (paper presented at The Second Biennial New Feminist Scholarship Conference, Buffalo, New York, 1990), esp. 1–4. Further references to this paper, abbreviated "SFO," are in the text.

12. See Michelle Barrett, "Some Different Meanings for the Concept of 'Difference': Feminist Theory and the Concept of Ideology," in *The Difference Within: Feminism and Critical Theory*, Elizabeth Meese and Alice Parker, ed. (Amsterdam/Philadelphia: John Benjamins, 1989), 37–48. Further references to this essay, abbreviated "Difference," are cited in the text.

13. This critique by now has its standard referents, including Fredric Jameson, "The Politics of Theory: Ideological Positions in the Postmodernism Debate," *New German Critique* 33 (1984): 53–65, Jean-François Lyotard, *The Postmodern Condition: A Report on Knowledge* (Minneapolis: University of Minnesota Press, 1984); Jane Flax, "Postmodernism and Gender Relations in Feminist Theory," *Signs* 12, no. 4 (1987): 621–643.

14. Nancy Fraser and Linda Nicholson, "Social Criticism without Philosophy: An Encounter Between Feminism and Postmodernism," in *Universal Abandon?: The Politics of Postmodernism*, ed. Andrew Ross (Minneapolis: University of Minnesota Press, 1988), 83–104, esp. 84.

15. Diana Fuss makes this point well when she argues to other poststructuralists that their critiques of essentialism may have forgotten that " '[e]ssentially speaking,' we need both to theorize essentialist spaces from which to speak and, simultaneously, to deconstruct those spaces to keep them from solidifying" as universals (118). See her chapter "Essentialism in the Classroom," in her volume *Essentially Speaking* (New York/London: Routledge, 1989), esp. 113–119. Further references to the volume, abbreviated *ES*, are cited in the text.

16. See for example, Alison Jaggar's *FPHN* and Sandra Harding's *SQF*.

17. Carol Nicholson, "Postmodernism, Feminism and Education: The Need for Solidarity," *Educational Theory* 39, no. 3 (1989): 197–205, esp. 203. Further references to this article, abbreviated "PFE," are cited in the text.

18. Nicholson's description of "postmodernism's apologies for the status quo" reminds me of Alison Jaggar's important discussion of just such an example vested in the legal case of *Gilbert v. the General Electric Com-*

pany, which reached the U.S. Supreme Court in 1976 (*FPHN*, 47). In this case, the Court ruled against the charge of the female employees that exclusion of pregnancy-related disabilities from their employer's disability plan constituted sex discrimination. Using an argument that anticipates the relativism of postmodernist discourses, the Supreme Court ruled that this was not the case. Pregnancy, in the Court's view, was merely one physical condition exempt from disability coverage. The Court overlooked the fact that it was a biological reality to which only women are subject! Thus, on the face of it, the Court's relativism and "gender-blind" ideology held as equally valid the employer's claim that it had not discriminated against the women employees. Yet its ruling, far from being neutral, actually served as an apology for a gender-based discrimination by favoring the interests of male employers and corporate capital. This case is but one example of the unequal consequences of relativism for differentially located groups. It begins to suggest the dimensions of the problem of accepting postmodernist relativism under a priori or absolutist conditions. This decision, according to Jaggar, was later reversed by Congress, and the Disability Amendment went into effect in October of 1978; see *FPHN*, esp. 50.

19. I am indebted to philosopher of education James A. (Tony) Whitson for this insightful critique of willful voluntarism, which he applies to the work of Stanley Aronowitz, but which I believe is apropos for some postmodernist feminists as well. See his "Post-structuralist Pedagogy as Counter-hegemonic Praxis (Can We Find the Baby in the Bathwater?)," *Education and Society* 9, no. 1 (1991): 73–86. Further references to this article, abbreviated "PP," are cited in the text.

20. Patti Lather, *Getting Smart: Feminist Pedagogy with/in the Postmodern* (New York: Routledge, 1991). Further references, abbreviated *GS*, are cited in the text.

21. The statistics on Duke's broad class support are by now well-known, but see Leonard Zeskind, "For Duke, Just a Start?," *New York Times*, 9 October 1990, sec. A, p. 25 as well as Peter Applebome, "Louisiana Tally Is Seen as a Sign of Voter Unrest," *New York Times* 8 October 1990, sec. A, pp. 1, 12, which anticipated Duke's increasing political legitimation.

22. Colin MacCabe, "Realism and the Cinema: Notes on Some Brechtian Theses," in his *Theoretical Essays: Film, Linguistics, Literature* (Manchester: Manchester University Press, 1985), esp. 34. This essay was first published by MacCabe in 1974, but a revised version written in 1976 also appears in *Theoretical Essays*, 58–81. I refer to his earlier essay as a theoretical rejection of realism that was characteristic of a particular stance he and others have taken, and not necessarily as his present position.

Notes

23. See Edward Said's trenchant criticism of the retreat into formalist aesthetics and literary theory on the parts of some anthropologists in his essay, "Representing the Colonized: Anthropology's Interlocutors," *Critical Inquiry* 15, no. 2 (Winter, 1989): 205–225, esp. 211, 220. Further references, abbreviated "RC," are cited in the text.

24. Raymond Williams, *Drama from Ibsen to Brecht* (London: Chatto and Windus, 1968), 277–290. Further references to this volume, abbreviated *DIB*, are cited in the text.

25. Raymond Williams, "The Achievement of Brecht," *Critical Quarterly* 3 (1961): 153–162, esp. 155, 157. Further references to this article, abbreviated "AB," are cited in the text.

26. Raymond Williams, *The Politics of Modernism: Against the New Conformists,* with a preface by Tony Pinkney (London: Verso, 1987), esp. p. 90. Further references, abbreviated as *PM*, are cited in the text.

27. Raymond Williams, "Brecht and Beyond," in *Politics and Letters: Interviews with New Left Review* (London: Verso and New Left Books, 1979), 214–234, esp. 214. Further references to the volume in which this essay appears are abbreviated *PL* and cited in the text.

28. See note five.

29. See, for example, Williams's argument that the mediation of critically realist drama occurs through a conscious development of a shared politicizing reality. Williams argues against the notion of the isolated individual confronting social problems, favoring instead the idea that such problems are best articulated widely among feminist materialists, who aspire to democratize the production of theory, in collectively organized consciousness-raising groups and issue-specific coalitions. See note five for examples of this argument.

30. Maria Lagones and Elizabeth V. Spelman, "Have We Got a Theory for You! Feminist Theory, Cultural Imperialism, and the Woman's Voice" (paper delivered at the Tenth Anniversary Conference of the Eastern Division of the Society for Women in Philosophy, Northampton, October 1982) 7, 20, and published in *Hypatia*: *Women's Studies International Forum* 6, no. 6 (1983): 578–581.

31. See Sandra Harding, *SQF* and her *FM*, esp. 181–190.

32. Lesley Johnson makes a similar point when she argues that Williams does not analyze the formation of social movements such as the women's movement. By describing such movements in vague terms as "resources in a journey of hope," Johnson argues that Williams avoids showing how the women's movement will transform socialist politics and analysis. See her excellent essay, "Raymond Williams: A Marxist View of Culture," in *Creating Culture: Profiles in the Study of Culture*, ed. Diane J. Austin-Broos (Sydney: Allen & Unwin, 1987), 163–177, esp. 176.

33. The New Left interviewers and members of its editorial board include Perry Anderson, Anthony Barnett, and Francis Mulhern.

34. Lisa Jardine and Julia Swindells, "Homage to Orwell: The Dream of a Common Culture, and Other Minefields," in *Raymond Williams: Critical Perspectives*, ed. Terry Eagleton (Boston: Northeastern University Press, 1989), 108–129.

35. Among others, Stuart Hall and Ernesto LaClau have developed a more Gramscian understanding of the positioning of social subjects through conflicting discourses and ideologies. See, for example, Hall's "The Toad in the Garden: Thatcherism Among the Theorists," in *Marxism and the Interpretation of Culture*, ed. Cary Nelson and Lawrence Grossberg (Urbana: University of Illinois Press, 1988), 35–57, and LaClau's *Politics and Ideology in Marxist Theory* (London: New Left Books, 1977).

36. See, for example, Paul Willis's *Learning to Labour: How Working Class Kids Get Working Class Jobs* (Westmead: Saxony Press, 1977), a now well-known ethnography that erroneously generalized its understanding of working-class interests and subjectivity from the experiences of twelve nonconforming "lads" to those of nonconforming working-class young men, while it largely ignored and misunderstood the gender interests of working-class young women. For a critique of the ways in which masculinist and class essentialist terms circumscribed the terms of debate with which feminists had to contend, see Leslie G. Roman and Linda Christian-Smith's "Introduction" to our co-edited volume with Elizabeth Ellsworth, *Becoming Feminine: The Politics of Popular Culture* (Sussex: Falmer Press, 1988), 1–34.

37. This illogic of pseudo-neutrality and disinterest renews a McCarthyist atmosphere of intellectual and cultural politics. The fervor to reshape issues of academic and intellectual freedom in the interests of the Right is part of a recent attack on the Left through the discourse of "politically correct" criticism. See one notable example, George Jonas, *Politically Incorrect: Notes on Liberty, Censorship, Social Engineering, Feminism, Apologists and Other Topics of Our Times* (Toronto: Lester, 1991).

38. My argument concerning the importance of teachers developing with students the practice of becoming critically aware subjects and objects of their own epistemic standpoints, and of the claims they and others make to know and represent reality, follows Alison Jaggar's logic concerning the role of feminist theorizing in enabling women to participate as subjects and objects in their different experiences of oppression and privilege. See her *FPHN*.

39. Thomas McCarthy, "The Politics of the Ineffable: Derrida's Deconstructionism," *Philosophical Forum* 21, nos. 1–2 (Fall/Winter 1989–1990): 146–168.

Notes

40. See Leslie G. Roman, *A Tenuous Sisterhood: Women in an American Punk Subculture* (New York: Routledge, in press) or my essays, "Double Exposure: The Politics of Feminist Materialist Ethnography" (paper presented to the Second Annual *New Feminist Scholars Conference*, Buffalo: State University of New York, 31 March–1 April, 1990), also solicited and in revision for *Harvard Educational Review*, and Leslie G. Roman and Michael W. Apple, "Is Naturalism a Move Away from Positivism?: Materialist and Feminist Approaches to Subjectivity in Ethnographic Research," in *Qualitative Inquiry in Education*, ed. Elliot Eisner and Alan Peshkin (New York: Teachers College Press, 1990), 38–73.

41. See references cited in note 37 for specific applications of these concepts in my fieldwork with young Punk women. Although these are exaggerated "ideal types," I use the terms to define the dominant conventions prescribing the field roles and narrative authorial voices for ethnographers. The concept of *intellectual tourist* refers to the discursive codes and cultural practices to which an ethnographer consents when she or he conducts research as a brief excursion, foray, or sightseeing tour into "other" people's lives. The *intellectual tourist* may become deeply involved in the lives of the research subjects so as to achieve *cultural immersion* or the status of the *participant observer*. Even though the intellectual tourist has worked quite hard to establish rapport with the research subjects, she or he strains to write an account in which she or he appears as distant and disengaged. She or he recalls copious field notes as *snapshot* descriptions taken on the scene of the research subjects' cultural practices. In the final account, though, the researcher draws upon dense theoretical language recognizable to those in her or his field but possibly obscure to those studied. Such language often has the effect of mystifying to the research subjects the very conditions of their lives about which the researcher theoretically aims to develop critical understanding. By *voyeurism*, I mean the discursive and cultural practices to which an ethnographer consents when she or he accepts a privileged vantage point from which she or he discloses minimally the prior theory she or he uses to describe, view, or interpret, and frame questions in the process of representing the knowledge and meanings of the research subjects. A subject position of ethnographic *voyeurism* occurs both when the use-value of the research subjects' knowledge is transformed into the reified or objectified pleasure (sexual or economic) of the researcher and when the groups under study feel intruded upon. Unlike the *intellectual tourist*, the *voyeur's* rapport may be short-lived, having been premised on the idea that the ethnographer extracts the common sense knowledge of the research subjects and then withdraws from the intimacy established when the research is completed. Research subjects may find that in either case (*intellectual*

330

tourism or *voyeurism*), the ethnographic researcher's accounts are of little use to grasping or transforming various inequalities they may experience in their daily lives.

42. Specific revisions of my field work strategies are discussed in Roman, "Double Exposure."

43. Throughout, I use pseudonyms for the students to protect their confidentiality. Whenever possible, the pseudonyms were approved of or chosen by the students. I did not give pseudonyms for institutions because their actual names were obvious.

44. Nancy A. Hewitt makes this point well in her essay, "Beyond the Search for Sisterhood: Women's History in the 1980s," in *Unequal Sisters: A Multicultural Reader in U.S. Women's History*, ed. Carol Dubois and Vicki Ruiz (New York: Routledge, 1990), esp. 1–14.

45. It is well known that Southern educational institutions, such as Louisiana State University, failed to comply expeditiously when the Supreme Court's decision of 1955 in *Brown v. Board of Education (II)* (Topeka, Kansas) required them by law to desegregate with "all deliberate speed." Less commonplace, however, are ethnographic analyses of residual institutional racism on the inter-generational consciousness of African-American and white students and their consequent social relations in classrooms of the 1990s. *Brown (II)* was the remedy that followed the Court's previous ruling in 1954, which found that separate but equal education was invalid. See this opinion in *Brown v. Board of Education (Brown II)*, 349 U.S. 294 (1955).

46. Four students commuted together from New Orleans out of convenience, and of these only two previously knew one another on personal and professional terms. The other commuted from a small town west of Baton Rouge and was unfamiliar with the other African-American students at the outset of the course.

47. Two of the white students knew each other well before enrolling in the class.

48. On at least two occasions—one being the end of the last class, admittedly, a tension-filled confrontation—all of the eight students who were eligible to receive credit for a second term reaffirmed their commitment to remain for that term. In fact, most of the students acknowledged endorsement of the rationale for the course being a two-semester sequence. They expressed on a number of occasions their interest in the plan to follow the first semester's survey of traditions of ethnography and brief field forays with a second semester's focus on an ethnographic project of their own design, for which they could receive collective feedback from others, including myself.

49. Even though I designed the course as a sequence of two three-credit

courses, students were not obligated and would certainly not be penalized for discontinuing after the first term. It is important to note, though, that the department had a six-credit requirement for research methodology courses, which could have been fullfilled by taking this sequence.

50. Revisions of curricular aims and pedagogical strategies on the parts of educators in relation to specific classroom needs and dynamics are not unusual. But rarely, and with good reason in the post-Reagan climate of teacher-bashing, do educators feel inclined to engage in public self-criticism about their own implication in the need for pedagogical and curriculum revision.

51. After the conclusion of the second term, I was unsuccessful at reaching Ruby, one of the African-American students who took the first semester course and was ineligible to pursue it in the second term because she had completed her methodology course requirements. I was, however, able to include her observations of the first term of the course in my attempts to understand and assess the classroom interactions.

52. Whenever possible, I discussed my emerging hypotheses concerning classroom dynamics with the students. While their thoughtful feedback sharpened my analysis, in-depth exploration of its implications for my work as well as for dialogical research praxis in general must be left for a subsequent essay.

53. Among the assigned and recommended texts with which the African-American students identified were Edward Said's *Orientalism* (New York: Vintage Books, 1979) and two of his essays, "RC" and "Orientalism Reconsidered," *Race and Class* (1985): 1–15, and Lois Weis, *Between Two Worlds* (New York and London: Routledge and Kegan Paul, 1987).

54. See Trihn T. Minh-ha, *Women, Native, Other* (Bloomington: Indiana University Press, 1989), which informed one of my lectures as well as references in note 47.

55. See examples of this argument in Elizabeth Ellsworth's article, "Why Doesn't this Feel Empowering? Working Through the Repressive Myths of Critical Pedagogy," *Harvard Educational Review* 59, no. 3 (1989): 297–324 and Lather's *GS*. It was Gayatri Chakravorty Spivak who reminded me that "in taking the responsibility of saying that there *is* a relationship between feminism and critical theory, we graduate ourselves into the responsibility of having to become self-critical in our subject position as academics, teachers, students in a capitalist country. If Marxism is our enemy, perhaps we want to knock Marxism because we happen to be American. We are written in the narrative of the United States that, in trying to find something better (inevitably conflating the history of Marxism with Marx), we go back to ethnicity and "my folk." We are

written by a narrative which is bigger than we are; that is our subject position and there is no loss in accepting that." See her essay, "Feminism and Critical Theory," in *The Difference Within: Feminism and Critical Theory*, ed. Elizabeth Meese and Alice Parker (Amsterdam/Philadelphia: John Benjamins, 1989), 207–220, esp. 217–218.

56. See Anne Oakley, "Interviewing Women: A Contradiction in Terms," in *Doing Feminist Research*, ed. Helen Roberts (London: Routledge & Kegan Paul, 1981), 30–61; Judith Stacey, "Can There be a Feminist Ethnography?" *Women's Studies International Forum* 11, no. 1 (1988), 21–27; and my work cited in notes 4, 37, and 38.

57. Telling differences arose in the nature of the projects students chose. In the interest of economy, I shall only mention these differences in general terms. Generally speaking, all of the African-American students chose projects that self-consciously explored some aspect of racial oppression or the social construction of racial identities among African-Americans, while only one of the white women chose a comparable project to research the construction of white racial privilege or identities. This becomes especially significant when one considers the fact that, with the exception of Dana, the white students chose predominately white groups to investigate and yet did not consider white racial interests as significant enough to analyze explicitly. For example, as the director of media technology and resources for a large parish, Coretta, an African-American, chose to study the social construction of African-Americans in AIDS education films and to research how African-American students of different class backgrounds received their ideologies of racial identity. She discussed in class how she found it necessary to reject naturalism's assumption of the passive observer role or else collude in the use of the racially stereotypic films on AIDS. Coretta shared with the class her attempts to work collectively with teachers, who also found the films problematic. Ceciley, an African-American who worked as a dean at a public commuter university with an open admissions policy, predominantly attended by African-Americans, chose to conduct life histories with a group of academically successful African-American students. Ceciley hoped her choice of topic would challenge the mainstream educational ideological assumptions underlying the labeling of racially subordinate groups as being "at risk" for dropping out, teen pregnancy, and academic failure. She debated with the class the ethical methodological issues entailed in conducting life history work with students whose lives intersected with her conflicting roles as a researcher, dean, mentor, and friend. Ruby, an administrator of a program for so-called underachieving African-American high school students, studied the social construction of racial identity within the policies of a reading program designed to offer "remedial" reading ser-

vices to these students.

In contrast, the white students did not make such conscious choices to focus on the social construction of racial groups or of their own interestedness as racial subjects in the conduct of their research. For example, Susan did not focus on the fact that the all-white women's aerobics class she chose to study was significantly composed in homogeneous racial terms, even though the class was part of a private club. Nor did Marsha make any connection to the fact that the white teachers she studied as part of the "Gifted and Talented Program" were racial subjects. Karina, a white exchange student from Germany, chose to study the controversial ethnographic practices of Gunter Wallraff, who has been known to take the "going native" approach to fieldwork to new extremes by surgically altering his facial features so he could pretend to live as a Turkish immigrant worker in Germany and document the racially exploitative employment practices of German corporate employers. Even though she bravely took on this topic that raised racial oppression as an issue, she did not then locate herself in relation to her ethical stances and racial privileges as a reader of the text.

58. These instances included KKK hoods being left at the work stations of the LSU custodians; Nazi flags appearing on the front yards of Jewish homes; a rise in the number of bomb threats and militant actions being taken against women attempting to enter abortion clinics; and a greater legitimacy being given in the local media to David Duke's pro-racist campaign platforms and group, the National Association for the Advancement of White People.

59. This is a lesson many feminists have begun to draw within the women's movement.

60. bell hooks (Gloria Watkins) similarly identifies a divisive veneer of Southern politeness that she argues has been problematic for the women's movement. She observes that "[o]ften the nice, nice behavior privileged white women had rebelled against in their relations with white men was transposed onto relations between white women and women of color." See her chapter, "Third World Diva Girls: Politics of Feminist Solidarity," in her volume *Yearning: Race, Gender, and Cultural Politics* (Boston: South End Press, 1990), 89–102, esp. 89.

61. SUNO, a relatively small open-admissions public commuter university predominately attended by African-Americans, was created in 1959 as part of the separate but equal ideology that discouraged African-American students from attending the former branch campus of LSU at New Orleans, now the University of New Orleans (UNO). UNO has become a private university attended predominately by white, middle-class students.

62. See Figure I, p. 209 for excerpt from map of New Orleans pertaining to the *Desire Housing Project*.

63. This was a point driven home to me by Amy Gordon's analysis of the differential "double-edged" political stakes effected by white feminists' fascinated identifications with slave narratives. She argues that white women's utilization of the slave woman as a figure or metaphor for woman's oppression often obliterates the particularities of African-American women's experiences of oppression, while it expresses the desire to be included in the accountability of the public and historical record of slavery. See her unpublished dissertation, "Ghost Stories" (Boston College, 1990), 240.

64. Because thus far I have been unable to locate any court records of residents of Orleans parish initiating a lawsuit against the U.S. Army Corps of Engineers for negligence in the alleged decision to divert the Mississippi in the manner described in my class, I have not been able to verify what appears to be popular history on the parts of African-American and white residents of the area concerning these events. This, however, does not mean the story as told is untrue, because the lack of a lawsuit may only mean that residents could not afford to pursue such a case. I was, however, able to confirm by way of an interview with the editor for *The Louisiana Weekly* (the oldest African-American newspaper in New Orleans) that several disputes with city officials and the Army Corps of Engineers occurred regarding the decision to divert the Mississippi River, the lack of timely warning systems, and the slowness of efforts to pump water out of the flooded areas (Interview, Norbert Davidson, December 6, 1991). To say the least, the historical record is contested on these issues, both in terms of which news sources record particular victims' stories and allegations and the ways people remember the events. Although conventional news sources show that the death toll eventually rose to fifty-eight, early reports documented lower figures in their description of the devastation to the residents of Orleans parish, St. Bernard, and Carolyn Park. Among them are Roy Reed, "New Orleans Loss In Storm Heavy; 23 Dead in Three States," *New York Times*, 11 September 1965, sec. 1, p. 10; "Hurricane Flood Raises Death Toll to 50; Crews Still Finding Bodies in Louisiana—Storm Is Ebbing in Arkansas," *New York Times*, 12 September 1965, sec. 1, p. 1, late edition, describes onrushing waters burying people who failed "to scramble fast enough to rooftops and trees"; "Pumping Started by New Orleans: Police Rope Off 300 Block Section to Drain It," *New York Times*, 16 September 1965, sec. 1, p. 32; David Snyder, "Betsy Veterans Stay Put Despite Bad Memories," *Times-Picayune* (New Orleans), 9 September 1988, sec. AA, p. 1, first edition; John C. Hill, "$6.7 Million Levee Bill Could Break St. Bernard,"

Times-Picayune (New Orleans), 17 March 1990, sec. AA, p. A1, recalls the dispute over St. Bernard paying the Army Corps of Engineers six million dollars for the Mississippi River Gulf Outlet, whom St. Bernard officials alleged allowed the "tidal surge to flood parish homes and businesses near the Industrial Canal during *Hurricane Betsy*."

65. The occasion for this comment was Alexa's recent experience of her family expecting her to manage all the funeral arrangements upon the death of her father.

66. I am reminded of Fuss's argument that the tendency to psychologize and personalize issues of oppression often has the undesirable effect of depoliticizing the structural and institutional bases of racism. See *ES*, esp. 117.

67. Joanna Frueh and Arlene Raven, "Feminist Art Criticism: Its Demise and Resurrection," *Art Journal* 50, no. 21 (Summer 1991): 9.

9 Raymond Williams and British Colonialism: The Limits of Metropolitan Cultural Theory

1. Brian Doyle, *English and Englishness* (London and New York: Routledge and Kegan Paul, 1989); Alan Sinfield, *Literature, Politics, and Culture in Postwar Britain* (Berkeley: University of California Press, 1989); Robert Colls and Philip Dodd, *Englishness: Politics and Culture, 1880–1920* (London: Croom Helm, 1986).

2. Doyle, *op. cit.*, 12.

3. Sinfield, *op. cit.*, 130.

4. Some of these questions are implied in several recent critiques of Williams. See Edward W. Said, "Intellectuals in the Post-Colonial World," *Salmagundi* 70–71 (Spring/Summer 1986): 44–64; Benita Parry, "Problems in Current Theories of Colonial Discourse," *Oxford Literary Review* 7, nos. 1–2 (1987): 27–58.

5. Raymond Williams, *The Country and the City* (London: Chatto and Windus, 1973), 278.

6. See *The Long Revolution* (New York: Columbia University Press, 1961), 66–67, for Williams's all-too-abbreviated account of the Empire as a place of emigration to solve working-class problems at home. In *Culture and Society* (1958; rpt., New York: Columbia University Press, 1986) Williams discusses Gaskell's *Mary Barton* more closely to show that the emigration to Canada with which the book closes is a feeble solution proposed by its author, a "cancelling of the actual difficulties and the removal of the persons pitied to the uncompromised New World" (91).

In reading emigration as a form of negation, Williams reinforces the insubstantiality of territories abroad.

7. It is true that in *The Sociology of Culture* (New York: Schocken Books, 1982) Williams attempts to account for the contribution of twentieth-century immigrants to metropolitan formations, but his indecisiveness about the status of these contributions is unsettling: do new groups from peripheral regions cause ruptures in "national tradition" or do their intellectual and creative activities become identified with the dominant culture? His difficulty in answering this question must surely be related to his framing it within the context of a "single national social order."

8. Williams, *The Country and the City*, 281.

9. Ibid.

10. Edward W. Said, *Problems in Materialism and Culture* (London: Verso, 1980), 21; also cited in Edward W. Said, *The World, the Text, and the Critic* (Cambridge, Mass.: Harvard University Press, 1983), 239.

11. Said, *The World, the Text, and the Critic*, 239.

12. Raymond Williams, "Base and Superstructure in Marxist Cultural Theory," *New Left Review* 82 (1973): 3–16, esp. 7.

13. Williams, *Culture and Society*, ix.

14. Raymond Williams, "Base and Superstructure in Marxist Cultural Theory," 7.

15. Raymond Williams, *Marxism and Literature* (Oxford: Oxford University Press, 1977), 113.

16. See Edward Said, "Traveling Theory," in *The World, the Text, and the Critic*, 226–47, esp. 241, for an illuminating discussion of Williams's critical recognition of the answerability of theory to historical and social situations. See also "Media, Margins, and Modernity: Raymond Williams and Edward Said," in *The Politics of Modernism*, ed. Tony Pinkney (London: Verso, 1989), 177–98, for further elaboration of this theme in relation to alternative cultural analyses; and Edward W. Said, "Jane Austen and Empire," in *Raymond Williams: Critical Perspectives*, ed. Terry Eagleton (Cambridge: Polity Press, 1989) 150–64, for a refilling of those spaces left empty by Williams.

17. Williams, *Culture and Society*, 280.

18. For a recent reassessment of the recovery of value in Marxist critical theory, see Frank Kermode, *History and Value* (Oxford: Clarendon Press, 1988). Kermode points out that though Marxist literary theory attempts to repudiate transcendental notions of value in art, the archeological activity it endorses implicitly locates value in the hidden or suppressed quality of literature's material relation to historical process. Kermode hastens to say that there is nothing wrong in considering value in terms that render art a document in the class war. But why, he asks, do even

the most uncompromising of Marxist critics, like Terry Eagleton, find it so difficult to get away from the idea that there is something in art that makes it art and *not* a mere document in the class war? Kermode demonstrates how Marxist and liberal humanist theories of art converge on this point. He suggests that Marxist literary theory is no less essentialist, no less able to escape history's mediation of value in its assumption that there is a "real history" that is covered over by false ideological versions of it. By insisting that value lies in the historical conditioning that is concealed by aesthetic expression, Marxist theories of art paradoxically save the value of past art. For art produced even under "old abhorrent dispensations" now superseded can legitimately claim value because of its usefulness in uncovering a suppressed history. Even Marx and Engels were susceptible to this current of thought, as the great esteem in which they held Balzac proves.

19. Williams, *Culture and Society*, 274.
20. Ibid.
21. Ibid., 95.
22. Engels, letter to J. Bloch, 21 September 1890, quoted in Williams, *Culture and Society*, 267.
23. Williams, *Culture and Society*, 200.
24. Alan O'Connor, *Raymond Williams: Writing, Culture, Politics* (Oxford: Basil Blackwell, 1989), p. 58.
25. In "Culture is Ordinary," in *Resources of Hope: Culture, Democracy, Socialism*, ed. Robin Gable (London: Verso, 1989), 3–18, Williams personalizes the idea of culture as encompassed by a "whole way of life" to distinguish between cultural and educational institutions, which as bastions of privilege are the purveyors of a single culture, and "English" or lived culture, which is possessed by working classes and upper classes alike, though expressed in different ways (7).
26. Williams, *Culture and Society*, 61–63.
27. Williams, *The Long Revolution*, 137.
28. A plaque honoring Andrew Bell's contribution to English education hangs in Westminster Abbey, describing Bell as "the eminent founder of the Madras system of education who discovered and reduced the successful practice of mutual instruction founded upon the multiplication of power and division of labour on the moral and intellectual world which has been adopted within the British empire as the rational system of education of the children of the poor." For further illustration of the crossover of educational theory and practice from the colonies to England, see my *Masks of Conquest: Literary Study and British Rule in India* (New York: Columbia University Press, 1989).
29. Joseph Lancaster, *Improvements in Education as It Respects the Indus-*

trial Class of the Community, 1803 (2d edition); excerpted in *Education and Democracy*, ed. A.E. Dyson and Julian Lovelock (London: Routledge and Kegan Paul, 1975), 40–43, esp. 40. See also J. Stuart Maclure, ed. *Educational Documents: England and Wales 1816–1963* (London: Chapman and Hall, 1965), for extracts of commission reports on popular education alluding to the success of the Lancaster and Bell system.

30. Patrick Parrinder, in *The Failure of Theory* (Sussex, Harvester Press, 1987), has accused Williams of narrowly national concerns, and though his language is strong, I think there is merit in asking why Williams was more intent on discovering the possibilities of "commonness" and "solidarity" rather than affirming hybrid cultures in a multicultural society. Williams's historical interest may have been in the sources of fragmentation and dissolution of identity, but that interest metamorphoses into a project for recovering and reuniting identity. His eagerness to achieve a common culture may partly explain Williams' inability to take a structurally disjunctive view of cultural formation. Parrinder interprets Williams's increasing emphasis on national culture as evidence that he is more interested in addressing the historical experience of a nation accustomed to the rigors of war than to one experiencing insulation from military aggression (323).

10 Country and City in a Postcolonial Landscape: Double Discourse and the Geo-Politics of Truth in Latin America

Research for this essay was supported by the Michigan Society of Fellows and the Spencer Foundation. We were affiliated in Venezuela with the Centro de Estudios Latinoamericanos Rómulo Gallegos (CELARG). This analysis draws on interviews with followers and political colleagues of Rómulo Gallegos as well as with a wide range of people involved in the Amparo massacre, including the survivors and relatives of the victims, clergy, political leaders, media figures, and human rights activists. We would like to thank these institutions and individuals for their support and cooperation. We are grateful to Roger Rouse for his comments on an early version of this paper, particularly as regards the centrality of mediation in the articulation of populist projects; to Valerie Kivelson and David Scobie for their constructive suggestions; and to Rafael Sánchez for his observations concerning the situational logic of political culture in Venezuela.

1. For an analysis of populist ideology and political violence in Venezuela, see Fernando Coronil and Julie Skurski, "Dismembering and Remember-

ing the Nation: The Semantics of Political Violence in Venezuela," *Comparative Studies in Society and History* 33, no. 2 (April 1991): 288–337.

2. W.E.B. DuBois, *The Souls of Black Folk* (New York: Fawcett World Library, 1961); Frantz Fanon, *Black Skin, White Masks* (New York: Grove Press, 1967). For further discussion of double consciousness, see Lauren Berlant, "Race, Gender, and Nation in *The Color Purple*," *Critical Inquiry* 14 (Summer 1988): 831–59; and "The Female Complaint," *Social Text* 19/20 (Fall 1988): 237–59. For "double voiced discourse," see Henry Louis Gates, Jr., *The Signifying Monkey* (New York: Oxford University Press, 1988); and for the "double and split time" of national representation, see Homi K. Bhabha, "DissemiNation: Time, Narrative, and the Margins of the Modern Nation," in *Nation and Narration*, ed. Homi K. Bhabha (New York: Routledge, 1990), 291–322.

3. Raymond Williams, *The Country and the City* (New York: Oxford University Press, 1973).

4. See Raymond Williams, *Politics and Letters* (London: NLB, 1979), Chap. 4, for a discussion of representation and historical reality in *The Country and the City*.

5. Williams, *The Country and the City*, 279.

6. Ibid., 284.

7. Ibid.

8. Ibid., 286.

9. This argument is developed in Julie Skurski, "The Civilizing Mission: Representing 'the People' in Venezuelan Nationalism" (Ph.D. diss., University of Chicago, 1992).

10. Anthony Pagden, *Spanish Imperialism and the Political Imagination* (New Haven: Yale University Press, 1990), Chap. 6.

11. Venezuela was a neglected outpost of the Spanish empire whose economy rested on the export of cattle hides and of cacao. Escaped slaves and peons lived as cattle hunters and contrabandists on the vast cattle savannas (llanos) which formed its social and geographic frontier. They became the troops for the War of Independence (1811–21) and for the continuing caudillo-led rebellions of the nineteenth century. For an insightful analysis of cattle frontiers and violence, see Silvio R. Duncan Baretta and John Markoff, "Civilization and Barbarism: Cattle Frontiers in Latin America," *Comparative Studies in Society and History* 20, no. 4 (October 1978): 587–620.

12. Rómulo Gallegos, *Doña Bárbara*, in *Obras Completas*, vol. 1 (Madrid: Aguilar, 1962), 493–803. All further references cited in text.

13. For the relationship between the petroleum state and Venezuelan political and economic culture, see Fernando Coronil and Julie Skurski, "Reproducing Dependency: Auto Industry Policy and Petrodollar Circulation in

Venezuela," *International Organization* 36, no. 1 (Winter 1982): 61–94; and Fernando Coronil, *The Magical State: Oil Money, Democracy, and Capitalism in Venezuela* (Chicago: University of Chicago Press, forthcoming).

14. William Roseberry, "Images of the Peasant in the Consciousness of the Venezuelan Proletariat," in *Proletarians and Protest*, ed. Michael Hanagan and Charles Stephenson (Westport, Connecticut: Greenwood Press, 1986), 149–69, esp. 160. Roseberry analyzes the historical bases for the contradictory images attached to country and city in Venezuela, disputing the tendency of moral economy analysts to treat the peasant past in romantic and unambiguous terms.

15. Rómulo Gallegos, *Una posición en la vida* (Mexico City: Ediciones Humanismo, 1954), 84.

16. For the ideological bases of the Gómez regime, see Arturo Sosa, *Ensayos sobre el pensamiento politico positivista venezolano* (Caracas: Ediciones Centauro, 1985); Elías Pino Iturrieta, ed., *Juan Vicente Gómez y su epoca* (Caracas: Monte Avila, 1985); and Ramón Velásquez, ed., *Juan Vicente Gómez ante la historia* (San Cristobal: Biblioteca de autores y temas Tachirenses, 1986).

17. Gallegos, *Una posicion en la vida*, 101–2. For the reconfiguration of Latin American identity in relation to the "discourse of authenticity" and metaphysical notions of racial synthesis during the 1920s, see Julie Skurski, "Ambiguous Authenticity: *Doña Bárbara* and the Construction of National Identity," *Poetics Today* 14, no. 2 (Fall 1992): forthcoming.

18. See Mario Torrealba Lossi, *Los años de la ira* (Caracas: Editorial Ateneo de Caracas, 1979), on the political context of the novel and its reception; and Ricardo Montilla, ed., *En las bodas de plata de "Doña Bárbara": Homenaje continental a Rómulo Gallegos* (Caracas: Ediciones del Congreso de la Republica, 1985), for a discussion of the novel's impact on continental political thought.

19. The central characters' names call attention to their allegorical status. Santos Luzardo's name is Holy Light, Doña Bárbara means Lady Barbarian, Marisela is a version of the name Maria, and the predatory U.S. adventurer who covets Marisela and symbolizes petroleum investors is named Mister Danger. The hacienda owned by Doña Bárbara is named "El Miedo" (Fear), and Luzardo's hacienda is "Altamira" (View From Above).

20. This depiction of Doña Bárbara as a person who wields primitive powers and rules despotically was read as a reference to Gómez. Doña Bárbara is labeled a "cacique," an Indian term for a local strong man (or, exceptionally, woman). The term "caudillo" refers to a personalistic leader who commands a regional following and has political functions.

21. On the formation of the bourgeois subject through the differentiation of

high and low and the instruction in manners, see Norbert Elias, *The History of Manners* (New York: Pantheon Books, 1978); and Peter Stallybrass and Allon White, *The Politics and Poetics of Transgression* (Ithaca: Cornell University Press, 1986).

22. For Sommer's analysis of the relationship between romances and the construction of Latin American nationalisms, see "Irresistible Romance: The Foundational Fictions of Latin America," in *Nation and Narration,* ed. Homi K. Bhabha (New York: Routledge, 1990), 71–98; and *Foundational Fictions: The National Romances of Latin America* (Berkeley: University of California Press, 1991).

23. For a discussion of nationalism and the novel that has oriented much subsequent analysis, see Benedict Anderson, *Imagined Communities* (London: Verso Books, 1983).

24. Concerning his analysis of the representations of country houses in *The City and the Country,* Williams notes, "The tendency in some recent criticism on the left has been to exclude these conditions (of the means of production), dismissing any concern with them as historicism and sociologism. Against that, my intention was to dramatize the tension between the houses and the poems. . . . The emphasis of the book is certainly not on literary texts as records, but as representations of history." See Williams, *Politics and Letters* (London: NLB, 1979), 304.

25. Roberto González Echevarría, *The Voice of the Masters* (Austin: University of Texas, 1985), 54. See also Carlos J. Alonso, " 'Otra sería mi historia': Allegorical Exhaustion in *Doña Bárbara,*" *MLN* 104, no. 2 (March 1989): 418–38.

26. Our analysis of literary configurations of national identity has benefitted from Lauren Berlant's work on national fantasy in the construction of the citizen-subject, "America, post-Utopia: Body, Landscape, and National Fantasy in Hawthorne's Native Land," *Arizona Quarterly* 44, no. 4 (Winter 1989): 14–54; and *The Anatomy of National Fantasy: Hawthorne, Utopia, and Everyday Life* (Chicago: University of Chicago Press, 1991).

27. Critics canonized Doña Bárbara as a "novel of the land" and only recently have located it in relation to nationalist discourse. See Instituto Internacional de Literatura Iberoamericána, *Relectura de Rómulo Gallegos* (Caracas: Ediciones del Centro de Estudios Latinoamericanos Rómulo Gallegos, 1980); Harrison Sabin Howard, *Rómulo Gallegos y la revolución burguesa de Venezuela* (Caracas: Ediciones del Centro de Estudios Latinoamericanos Rómulo Gallegos, 1976); Maya Scharer-Nussberger, *Rómulo Gallegos: el mundo inconcluso* (Caracas: Monte Avila Editores, 1979); Skurski, "The Civilizing Mission"; Sommer, *Foundational Fictions.*

28. Edward Dudley, "The Wild Man Goes Baroque," in *The Wild Man Within*, ed. Edward Dudley and Maximillian E. Novak (Pittsburgh: University of Pittsburgh, 1972), 126–32.

29. González Echevarría reads Barquero as having "the final authority in the novel," 54–55.

30. Gallegos's first novel, *Reinaldo Solar* (1920), in *Obras Completas*, 5–229, examines the failed ventures of idealistic young men of the Caracas elite who ally with caudillo leaders.

31. Luzardo's grandfather "snatched from the Indians their property under natural law, and as they tried to defend it, he bloodily exterminated them; but when the cacique saw his huts turned to ashes, he cursed the palm grove, so that the invader and his descendants would only find disaster and disgrace there." (570).

32. If it suited her to be erotic, "she was so more as a man who takes, than as a woman who gives" (523–24).

33. To these factors of "lawlessness" with which the state of Apure is identified may be added the history of violent assaults on the remaining indigenous groups by landowners and the encroachment by large landowners on peasant smallholdings. For a discussion of a recent massacre of indigenous inhabitants of this region, see Walter Coppens, *Los Cuiva de San Estéban de Capanaparo* (Caracas: Fundación La Salle de Ciencias Naturales, 1975), 80–84.

34. The CEJAP, "Comando Específico 'General en Jefe José Antonio Páez' " (named after the llanero independence leader) was granted considerable autonomy under the Border Law. It was to coordinate the activities of the army, the PTJ (Policia Técnica Judicial), and the DISIP (Dirección de los Servicios de Inteligencia y Prevención). The latter is a heavily armed intelligence police, trained to combat guerrillas and criminals, which operates under presidential command via the Interior Ministry.

35. General Camejo Arias, who was close to the president, has ties to the conservative economic elite in the Andean city of San Cristobal where he was based. Henry López Sisco, trained in counterintelligence at Israeli facilities and the chief of operations of the DISIP, was the leader of the CEJAP.

36. Amnesty International's report on police and military abuses, "Human Rights in Venezuela" (London: Amnesty International Publications, 1988), found systematic violations of the human rights of criminals as well as of political critics. The government, which has long presented itself as exemplary in the human rights field, dismissed the report as false.

37. Pérez was president from 1974–79 during the oil boom period, and he continued subsequently to be a popular and powerful leader. Since Lusinchi could not run for re-election, he had lobbied for his own nomi-

nee, whom Pérez defeated in the party primary. Fearing his faction's loss of power after the election, Lusinchi maneuvered for advantage during the campaign.

38. Ibáñez, whose official post was secretary to the president, figured prominently as a distributor of favors to the poor, reportedly modeling herself on Eva Perón. She was rumored to be the power behind the president, a notion ratified for many by his unheard-of attempt to divorce his wife while in office. In political circles it was said that Ibáñez was instrumental in naming directors of the DISIP, including her son and the CEJAP director, Henry López Sisco, and had used the agency against government critics. For a discussion of Ibáñez, see Agustín Beroes, *RECADI: La gran estafa* (Caracas: Editorial Planeta, 1990).

39. A long-standing border dispute with Colombia, involving rights to underwater oil, was a major campaign issue, with Pérez, who was raised near the Colombian border, accused by conservatives of making secret deals with its government.

40. After the attack the DISIP officer "Hipólito," who was well-known to townspeople, bragged to police chief Adan Tovar that he had killed a group of guerrillas and would catch the two who had escaped.

41. Pinilla, 28, is a fisherman, and Arias, 35, is an employee of a surveying company and godson of the deceased boat owner. Arias and police chief Tovar served in the army together.

42. Márquez is a political independent, elected on the slate of the socialist party Movimiento al Socialismo, MAS. A historian and activist from an Andean border town, he has defended peasants in cases of land disputes and military abuse.

43. *El Nacional*, 5 November 1988. Lusinchi participated in AD's 1950s clandestine opposition to the dictator Gen. Pérez Jiménez. When AD held the presidency in the 1960s, it was opposed by a leftist guerrilla movement.

44. *SIC* (December 1988): 440.

45. Certain army officials objected to the attack because the DISIP, a police agency, directed the CEJAP, thus involving army officers in actions outside military control. The director of the military intelligence agency (DIM), General Citraro, threatened to take the case to an international court. He was forced to resign by President Lusinchi.

46. República de Venezuela, *Gaceta del Congreso* 18, 1 (March 1988–January 1989), 458–59.

47. Aside from death threats, right-wing groups attempted to intimidate the survivors and Márquez through a defamatory ad campaign whose financing came in part from a branch of Lyndon Larouche's extreme

Right party in the United States. The campaign portrayed the Gnostic church, to which Marquez belongs, as being satanic and a guerrilla front. See *El Nacional*, 28 January through 3 February 1989.

48. Pérez Gutiérrez, the military judge assigned to the case, was a former member of AD and an ally of General Camejo Arias. He was hostile to the survivors throughout, and his actions were later censured by the Congressional Commission.

49. *El Nacional*, 3 November 1988.

50. The Commission, which held extensive hearings, delivered a report to Congress on January 18, 1989 that was approved unanimously. It challenged the official version of events, concluded that a clash with guerrillas had not occurred, and called for a judicial investigation. See Republica de Venezuela, *Gaceta del Congreso* 18, no. 1 (March 1988–January 1989): 448–67.

51. *El Nacional*, *El Diario de Caracas*, and *Ultimas Noticias* led the reporting, as well as the Jesuit-run magazine *SIC*. Television was notably absent from investigation and debate of the case. A talk show where it was discussed encountered serious pressures.

52. Argument often underlined the opposition of "truths." Congressman José Vicente Rangel, a former presidential candidate (MAS), wrote, "The official truth, the truth of power . . . has nothing to do with the true truth . . . that the people who died . . . were simply massacred." *El Diario de Caracas*, 26 December 1989.

53. The military court refused to release the results of the autopsy, but members of the Congressional Commission made statements to the press. The newspaper *El Nacional* later wrote that eleven people had been shot from the back, seven were tortured and badly beaten, one was castrated, and the faces and tattoos of several men were defaced with acid. *El Nacional*, 24 March and 25 March, 1989.

54. He called attention to the parallels between the Amparo case and four previous CEJAP massacres occurring in 1988, all of which involved Gen. Camejo Arias, the DISIP's Lopez Sisco, and military judge Pérez Gutiérrez. *El Nacional*, 1 February 1989; *El Diario de Caracas*, 18 March 1989; personal interviews, April–July, 1989. On the use of torture and terror by the CEJAP, see the investigative reports by Ralph Schusler, *El Diario de Caracas*, 22 and 23 December 1988, and *El Nacional*, 1 and 3 May 1989. Congressman Raul Esté stated in personal interviews that these attacks parallel DISIP massacres against purported leftists in Cantaura and Yumare. See Raul Esté, *La masacre de Yumare* (Caracas: Fondo Editorial Carlos Aponte, 1987).

55. Some theorized that the DISIP promoted the outing, promising the boat

owner a chance to carry contraband. Congressman Esté suggested a link between the drug trade and the massacre. *El Diario de Caracas*, 29 November 1988.

56. *El Diario de Caracas*, 30 November 1988.

57. As a result of the Amparo massacre, activist clergy obtained the creation of a Human Rights Vicarate, and a new human rights organization, PROVEA, established a newsletter and initiated the evaluation of legal codes and police practices.

58. Congressman Márquez secretly helped them reach the embassy, and clergy aided them during their month of asylum.

59. Both the survivors and their assailants were jailed for brief periods. When the CEJAP members were freed on a technicality, Arias and Pinilla took sanctuary, in April–May 1989, in a church in a Caracas barrio. In April 1990 the Martial Court ruled that a confrontation with guerrillas had occurred, and that the survivors were in fact imposters. The Supreme Court in September 1990 overturned this decision and reopened the case against the CEJAP.

60. Upon taking office, Carlos Andrés Pérez applied an IMF austerity program which provoked massive urban rioting beginning February 27, 1989, as a result of which an estimated eight hundred people were killed, largely by the military. For the place of the Amparo massacre in the development of mass protest, see Coronil and Skurski, "Dismembering and Remembering the Nation: The Semantics of Political Violence in Venezuela."

61. Michel de Certeau, *The Practice of Everyday Life* (Berkeley: University of California Press, 1988), 201.

62. According to Walter Benjamin, modern mass technologies create "information" as a "new form of communication" in which events are already "shot through with explanation." See *Illuminations* (New York: Schocken Books, 1969), 83–89.

63. De Certeau, 178–201.

64. For a discussion of Noelle Bisseret Moreau's argument, see Mary Louis Pratt, "Toward a Linguistics of Contact," in *The Linguistics of Writing: Arguments Between Language and Literature*, ed. Nigel Fabb, Derek Attridge, Alan Durant, and Colin MacCabe (New York: Methuen, 1987), 48–66.

65. On the figure of the mediator in Latin America, see Roberto Da Matta, *Carnival, Rogues and Heroes* (South Bend, Indiana: Notre Dame University Press, 1991).

66. Tom Nairn, *The Breakup of Britain* (London: Verso, 1981), 339–50. For Lenin's analysis of Russian populist politics as "Janus-faced," see

Andrej Walicki, "Russia," in *Populism*, ed. Ghita Ionescu and Ernest Gellner (London: Macmillan, 1969), 62–96.

11   Raymond Williams and the Inhuman Limits of Culture

1. Walter Benjamin, "Karl Krauss," in *One Way Street and Other Writings*, trans. E. Jephcott and K. Shorter (London: Verso, 1979), esp. 297.
2. Walter Benjamin, "Theses on the Philosophy of History," in *Illumina-tions*, trans. Harry Zohn (New York: Schocken Books, 1969), 253–64, esp. 257.
3. See in particular Williams's "Base and Superstructure in Marxist Cultural Theory," in *Problems in Materialism and Culture* (London: Verso, 1980), 31–49; and *Marxism and Literature* (Oxford: Oxford University Press, 1977). Further references to this book, abbreviated *ML*, are included in text.
4. See, for instance, Williams's treatment of the terms "base" and "super-structure" in his reading of Marx's 1859 preface to *A Contribution to the Critique of Political Economy* in *Marxism and Literature*, 75–82. In "Base and Superstructure in Marxist Cultural Theory," Williams asserts the need to recover Marx's understanding of "the dynamic variation of these forces" or "processes," a recovery which demands a critical "revaluation" of the fundamental terms of Marxist cultural analysis (34).
5. *Politics and Letters: Interviews with New Left Review* (London: Verso, 1981), 109.
6. The extent to which this historicism may be taken is evident from the work of a literary critic such as Stephen Greenblatt who has described his own critical project as a "poetics of culture." In the recent and pedagogically important volume of *Critical Terms for Literary Studies*, Greenblatt—the Renaissance critic whose name is most directly associ-ated with the appearance in literary studies of the "New Historicism"—has taken on the assignment of defining the term "culture"; and his account makes explicit the historicism of culture and cultural studies. Greenblatt's vision of a "full cultural analysis" which can "push beyond the boundaries of the text to establish links between the text and values, institutions, and practices elsewhere in the culture" displays its deep affinities to Raymond Williams and is organized on an even deeper faith in the capacity of historical reconstruction: "To recover the meaning of such texts, to make any sense of them at all, we need to reconstruct the

situation in which they were produced." There is very little "new" about the epistemological assumptions of this historicism, one which ignores here the powerful theoretical challenges—from Nietzsche to Benjamin to Derrida—to this form of historical knowledge. See Stephen Greenblatt, "Culture," in *Critical Terms for Literary Study*, ed. Frank Lentricchia and Thomas McLaughlin (Chicago: University of Chicago Press, 1990), 226–27.

This is not meant to deny the importance or the subtlety of Greenblatt's own readings of Renaissance culture and literature; but I would argue that the considerable insights of his work are achieved in spite of the assumptions of his historicism. Greenblatt's pioneering work remains *Renaissance Self-Fashioning* (Chicago: University of Chicago Press, 1980). *The New Historicism*, ed. H. Arom Veeser (London: Routledge, 1989), is to date the most important critical anthology of the debates in and around the recent reconsideration of history within literary and cultural studies.

7. *Culture and Society: 1780–1950* (New York: Columbia University Press, 1983), xvii.

8. Williams produces such a reading in his indispensable discussion of Matthew Arnold in *Culture and Society*, 110–29. See also Williams's brief 1970 essay on "A Hundred Years of Culture and Anarchy," collected in *Problems in Materialism and Culture*, 3–10. Reminding us of the demonstration in Hyde Park that spurs the writing of *Culture and Anarchy*, this essay stresses the deeply reactionary tendencies of Arnold's politics, and is thus an important supplement to Williams's earlier interpretations.

9. *The Sociology of Culture* (New York: Schocken Books, 1982), 12. Further references to this book, abbreviated *SC*, are included in text.

10. It is worth noting the decisive distance between this formulation of Williams's "cultural materialism" and the considerably more "empiricist" disposition of the social historian E. P. Thompson. The most polemical version of Thompson's position is represented by his vituperative attack on the developments of a "structuralist" Marxism in *The Poverty of Theory* (New York: Monthly Review Press, 1978).

11. *The Country and the City* (New York: Oxford University Press, 1973), 165. Further references to this book, abbreviated *CC*, are included in text.

12. Two recent important essays which read for the textual nature of these divisions in George Eliot and which pursue the implications such irreconcilable divisions pose for the possibilities of narrative "knowledge" are: Cynthia Chase, "The Decomposition of the Elephants: Double-Reading

Daniel Deronda," in *Decomposing Figures* (Baltimore: Johns Hopkins University Press, 1986), 157–74; and Jacqueline Rose, "George Eliot and the Spectacle of the Woman," in *Sexuality in the Field of Vision* (London: Verso, 1986), 104–22.

13. Tony Pinkney, ed., *The Politics of Modernism: Against the New Conformists* (London: Verso, 1989). Pinkney's introductory essay is an important contribution to the study of Williams's work, and most directly on the issues of modernism and the status of culture that are of concern to me here.

14. Paul de Man, "The Task of the Translator," in *The Resistance to Theory* (Minneapolis: University of Minnesota Press, 1986), 73–105, esp. 101. Further references to this book, abbreviated *RT*, are included in text.

15. Paul de Man, "Phenomenality and Materiality in Kant," in *Hermeneutics: Prospects and Questions*, ed. Gary Shapiro and Alan Sica (Amherst: University of Massachusetts Press, 1984), 144.

16. Edward Said, "Jane Austen and Empire," in *Raymond Williams: Critical Perspectives*, ed. Terry Eagleton (Boston: Northeastern University Press, 1989), 150–64. Further references to this essay, abbreviated "JAE," are included in text.

17. See in particular, "The Analysis Extended," in *The Year 2000* (New York: Pantheon, 1983), 175–240.

18. The most concise account of this critical morphology is to be found in the opening pages of "The Rhetoric of Blindness," de Man's essay on Jacques Derrida's reading of Rousseau, in *Blindness and Insight*, second rev. ed. (Minneapolis: University of Minnesota Press, 1983), 102–9.

19. Roberto Fernandez Retamar, "Caliban: Notes Toward a Discussion of Culture in Our America," in *Caliban and Other Essays*, trans. Edward Baker (Minneapolis: University of Minnesota Press, 1989), 3–45. Further references to this book, abbreviated *C*, are included in text.

20. William Shakespeare, *The Tempest*, ed. Robert Langbaum (New York: Signet, 1964), act 1, scene 2, 363–365. For two recent readings of the play which pursue its colonial and imperial inscriptions and the dramatic instabilities they generate, see Francis Barker and Peter Hulme, "Nymphs and reapers heavily vanish: The Discursive Con-texts of *The Tempest*," in *Alternative Shakespeares*, ed. John Drakkis (London: Methuen, 1985), 191–205; and see Terence Hawkes, *That Shakespherian Rag* (London: Methuen, 1986). Stephen Greenblatt's account of the concept of "culture" in *Critical Terms for Literary Study* concludes with a brief treatment of the play's colonial thematics.

21. See in particular Fernandez Retamar's essay, "Some Theoretical Problems of Spanish-American Literature," in *Caliban and Other Essays*, 74–99.

Notes

12 Cultural Theory and the Politics of Location

1. For a thorough discussion of the problems faced by the subaltern subject in its attempt to produce its own history, see Ranajit Guha, "Dominance without Hegemony and its Historiography," in *Subaltern Studies VI: Writings on South Asian History and Society*, ed. Ranajit Guha (Delhi: Oxford University Press, 1989), 210–309.

2. For a clear and thought-provoking analysis of some of the political perils of a philosophical relativism, see Satya Mohanty, "Us and Them: On the Philosophical Bases of Political Criticism," *Yale Journal of Criticism* 2, no. 2 (Spring 1989): 1–31.

3. For sustained analyses of the Eastern European situation in the context of Marxist history, see issues of *The Nation*, 29 January, 26 February, and 19 March 1990.

4. The thoroughly researched work done by the Subaltern Studies Group demonstrates with telling clarity the complicity of nationalism with elitist and dominant historiographies. See Ranajit Guha and Gayatri Chakravorty Spivak, eds., *Selected Subaltern Studies* (Oxford: Oxford University Press, 1988).

5. Samir Amin's *Eurocentrism* (New York: Monthly Review Press, 1989) is brilliant in its simultaneous and conjunctural critique both of capitalism and Eurocentrism.

6. Drawing on the work of Jacques Lacan, Chantal Mouffe and Ernesto Laclau posit their critique of a total reality, but nevertheless keep alive possibilities of articulating coalitional and democratic connections among different subject positions. See their *Hegemony and Socialist Strategy: Towards a Radical Democratic Politics*, trans. Winston Moore and Paul Cammack (London: Verso, 1985).

7. Michel Foucault develops this notion of the subject position as "assigned" in *The Archaeology of Knowledge*, trans. A. M. Sheridan (New York: Pantheon, 1972). For a politically specific application of the assigned subject position, see Gayatri Chakravorty Spivak, "A Literary Representation of the Subaltern: A Woman's Text from the Third World," in her *In Other Worlds: Essays in Cultural Politics* (London and New York: Methuen, 1987), 241–68.

8. I am referring here to the theory of language developed by Jacques Lacan that has been so influential in the development of poststructuralist attitudes to cultural politics. Simply stated, to Lacan, meaning is constitutively implicated in the possibility of errancy. Also, meaning is represented through the network of signifiers where every word finds its semantic

charge through a perennial process of syntactic transfer and displacement. See Jacques Lacan, *Ecrits: A Selection*, trans. Alan Sheridan (New York: W. W. Norton, 1977).

9. See Michel Foucault, "Intellectuals and Power," in *Language, Counter-memory, Practice*, trans. Donald F. Bouchard and Sherry Simon (Ithaca: Cornell University Press, 1977), 205–17. For a substantive subaltern critique of the position held by Foucault and Deleuze, see Gayatri Chakravorty Spivak, "Can the Subaltern Speak?" in *Marxism and the Interpretation of Culture*, ed. Cary Nelson and Lawrence Grossberg (Urbana: University of Illinois Press, 1988), 271–311.

10. For a critical positioning of the postcolonial subject in the context of Foucault's and Gramsci's politics, see my essay, "Toward an Effective Intellectual: Foucault or Gramsci?" in *Intellectuals: Aesthetics, Politics, Academics*, ed. Bruce Robbins (Minneapolis: University of Minnesota Press, 1990), 57–99.

11. Veena Das, "Subaltern as Perspective," in *Subaltern Studies VI*, ed. Ranajit Guha, 310–24, esp. 312.

12. Edward Said, "Criticism Between Culture and System," in Said, *The World, the Text, the Critic* (Cambridge: Harvard University Press, 1983), 178–225.

13. Rob Nixon, "Culture Heroes: Williams and Hall for the Opposition," *Voice Literary Supplement* 79 (October 1989): 15.

14. Raymond Williams, "The Future of Cultural Studies," in *The Politics of Modernism* (London: Verso, 1989), 151–62, esp. 151.

15. I have in mind here passages in Marx's *Grundrisse* (Harmondsworth: Penguin, 1973), for example 408–10 and 539–40, where Marx demonstrates the ability of capital to conceal its own internal contradictions and crises while continuing to perform its "universalizing" function.

16. See R. Radhakrishnan, "The Changing Subject and the Politics of Theory," *Differences* 2 (Summer 1990): 126–52 for a detailed analysis of poststructuralist possibilities for the "changing subject."

17. Williams, "The Future of Cultural Studies," 151.

18. Antonio Gramsci's contribution to the cause of political pedagogy is of vital importance. See the pieces in "Part Two: Gramsci in Prison, 1926–1937," in *Modern Prince and Other Writings*, trans. Louis Marks (New York: International Publishers, 1957), 58–132. For a contemporary application of Gramsci's cultural politics, see Stuart Hall, "Gramsci and Us," in his *The Hard Road to Renewal* (London: Verso, 1989), 161–73.

19. Williams, "The Future of Cultural Studies," 152.

20. Ibid., 157.

21. Ibid., 154.

22. Gayatri Chakravorty Spivak's essay, "Reading *The Satanic Verses*," *Public Culture* 2, no. 1 (Fall 1989): 79–99, deals with some of the differences between "subject formation" and "agency formation."

23. My reference here is to Paulo Freire, *Pedagogy of the Oppressed* (New York: Continuum, 1986).

24. See Tony Pinkney, "Editor's Introduction: Modernism and Cultural Theory," in *The Politics of Modernism*, 1–29, for a vigorous summary of Williams's attitude to the self-consciousness of high modernism. It is in the same spirit that Williams, in his review of Edward Said's *The World, the Text, the Critic* in *The Guardian*, praises Said as "someone who not only has studied and thought so carefully but is also beginning to substantiate, as distinct from announcing, a genuinely emergent way of thinking" (quoted on back cover). Here again, Williams valorizes "substance" over a self-conscious "form" that pretends to be its own substance.

25. There are two debates involved here. One concerns the issues of knowledge and experience. Is experience the raw material that is produced into knowledge, or, does experience have its own direct epistemological status? For a discussion of this issue in terms of common sense versus professional knowledge, see Antonio Gramsci, *The Modern Prince* and *Selections from the Prison Notebooks*, trans. Quintin Hoare and Geoffrey Nowell Smith (New York: International Publishers, 1971). The second debate, within social psychology, pits the principle of ecological validity against the experimental validity achieved within the context of scientific study. For a provocative position paper on this issue, see Mahzarin R. Banaji and Robert G. Crowder, "The Bankruptcy of Everyday Memory," *American Psychologist* 44, no. 9 (September 1989): 1185–93.

26. For a significant discussion of the predicament of the black intellectual *vis-à-vis* her/his constituency, see Cornel West, "The Dilemma of the Black Intellectual," *Cultural Critique* no. 1 (Fall 1985): 109–24.

27. Raymond Williams, *The Long Revolution* (London: Chatto and Windus, 1961), 63–65. See the question posed to Williams, *Politics and Letters*, 166–67.

28. Raymond Williams, *Marxism and Literature* (Oxford: Oxford University Press, 1977), 99.

29. Raymond Williams, *Politics and Letters* (London: Verso, 1979), 172.

30. Ibid., 167.

31. Ibid., 168.

32. For a coalitional application of poststructuralism to the theory of ethnicity, see my essay, "Ethnic Identity and Post-structuralist Difference," *Cultural Critique* no. 6 (Spring 1987): 199–220.

33. See R. Radhakrishnan, "Culture as Common Ground: Ethnicity and Beyond," *MELUS* 14, no. 2 (Summer 1987): 5–19.

34. Williams, *The Politics of Modernism*, 179.

35. Edward Said, "Intellectuals in the Post-Colonial World," *Salmagundi* nos. 70–71 (Spring–Summer 1986), 44–81, esp. 45.

36. Edward Said, "Traveling Theory," in Said, *The World, the Text, the Critic* 226–47, esp. 226. For other and equally stimulating notions of geopolitical cultural travel, see the special issue of *Inscriptions* entitled "Traveling Theories, Traveling Theorists" 5 (1989); Arjun Appadurai, "Disjuncture and Difference in the Global Cultural Economy," *Public Culture* 2, no. 2 (Spring 1990): 1–24; and Adrienne Rich, "Notes Towards a Politics of Location," in *Blood, Bread and Poetry*, Selected Prose 1979–85 (New York: W. W. Norton, 1986), 210–31.

37. Raymond Williams, *The Country and the City* (Oxford: Oxford University Press, 1973), 288.

38. Ibid.

39. See Partha Chatterjee, *Nationalist Thought and the Colonial World* (Delhi: Oxford University Press, 1986), 1–53.

40. See Spivak, "A Literary Representation of the Subaltern: Deconstructing Historiography," in *In Other Worlds*, 197–221.

41. The reference here is to the Derridean notion of "double writing" as developed in Jacques Derrida, *Dissemination*, trans. Barbara Johnson (Chicago: University of Chicago Press, 1981).

42. Lata Mani, "Multiple Mediations: Feminist Scholarship in the Age of Multinational Reception," *Inscriptions* 5 (1989): 1–23.

43. Chandra Talpade Mohanty, "Feminist Encounters, Locating the Politics of Experience," *Copyright* no. 1 (Fall 1987), esp. 42.

44. The reference here is to Lata Mani, "Contentious Traditions: The Debate on Sati in Colonial India, 1780–1833" (Ph.D. diss., University of California, 1989).

45. Mani, "Multiple Mediations," 14.

46. Vivek Dhareshwar, "Toward a Narrative Epistemology of the Postcolonial Predicament," *Inscriptions* 5 (1989): 135–57, esp. 144.

47. Ibid., 156.

Notes on Contributors

Michael W. Apple is the John Bascom Professor of Education at the University of Wisconsin-Madison. An activist and former president of a teachers' union, he has written extensively on the relationship between culture and power in education. Among his many books are *Ideology and Curriculum* (Routledge, 1979; second edition, 1990), *Education and Power* (Routledge, 1985), *Teachers and Texts* (Routledge, 1988). He is also the series editor of Critical Social Thought for Routledge.

Fernando Coronil teaches in the Anthropology and History Departments at the University of Michigan in Ann Arbor. His work focuses on state formation and popular culture in Latin America. His forthcoming book, *The Magical State: Money, Fetishism, Democracy and Capitalism in Venezuela*, is forthcoming from The University of Chicago Press. Presently, he is examining the relationship between political violence and the historical imagination in Venezuela.

Laura Di Michele is a Professor of English at the Instituto Universitario Orientale in Naples, Italy. Her publications include *L'Educazione del sentimento: La crisi del romanzo inglese fra gotico e sentimentale (1750–1800)* (1977), *La scena dei potenti: Teatro politica spettacolo nell'età di Shakespeare* (1988) and various essays on eighteenth-century literature, science fiction of the late twentieth century, and cultural

354

studies. She is currently working on a book on the poetry of James Thomson.

Dennis L. Dworkin is an Assistant Professor of History at the University of Nevada, Reno, where he teaches European intellectual history. His essay is part of a larger project which traces the development of British Marxist historiography and cultural studies, *The Politics of Culture* (forthcoming, from Routledge, Chapman and Hall).

Wendy Kohli, Assistant Professor of Education at the State University of New York at Binghamton, teaches courses in educational foundations and critical reflective practice. Kohli's research interests include Marxist theory, femininst pedagogy, teacher empowerment, and democratic schooling. Her work has appeared in *The Harvard Educational Review, Education and Society, Studies in Philosophy and Education, The International Journal of Qualitative Studies in Education*, and *Philosophy of Education*. She currently serves on the editorial board of *Educational Theory* and is involved in scholarly pursuits in Eastern Europe and the former Soviet Union.

Loren Kruger teaches drama and cultural theory at the University of Chicago. She is the author of *The National Stage* (University of Chicago Press) and translator of *The Institutions of Art: Essays by Peter and Christa Bürger* (University of Nebraska Press).

Forest Pyle teaches English and Humanities at the University of Oregon in Eugene. He has written on the topics of Romantic poetry, Victorian narrative, contemporary culture, and critical theory. He has completed a book, *The Ideology of Imagination*, under contract with Stanford University Press. His essay on Raymond Williams is part of an ongoing book-length study entitled "The Limits of Culture: 'From Which One Turns Away.' "

Fazal Rizvi, Associate Professor of Education at the University of Queensland in Brisbane, Australia, is a philosopher of education interested in democracy and social justice in education. He has conducted a number of projects researching problems of democratic reform in educational administration. Among his many research interests are contemporary expressions of racism, multiculturalism, theories of the state, educational policy and reform.

Notes on Contributors

R. Radhakrishnan, Associate Professor of English at the University of Massachusetts at Amherst, is finishing a volume, *Theory in an Uneven World* (Basil Blackwell, forthcoming). He has written widely on the politics of identity, diaspora, and ethnicity in journals such as *Cultural Critique, Transition, Differences,* and *Boundary 2*.

Leslie G. Roman is an Assistant Professor of Social and Educational Studies and Women's Studies at the University of British Columbia-Vancouver. Currently, she is completing an ethnography, *A Tenuous Sisterhood: Women in an American Punk Subculture* (Routledge, Chapman and Hall, forthcoming). She is co-editor with Linda Christian-Smith and Elizabeth Ellsworth of *Becoming Feminine: The Politics of Popular Culture* (Falmer Press, 1988).

Julie Skurski teaches at the University of Michigan in Ann Arbor. Her work focuses on the social and cultural foundations of nationalist ideology. Presently, she is engaged in anthropological research on gender and concepts of power in Venezuela.

Jon Thompson, Assistant Professor of English at North Carolina State University in Raleigh, received his B.A. and M.A. from the University College of Dublin in Ireland and his Ph.D. from Louisiana State University. He pursues, among other research interests, twentieth-century literature, critical theory, cultural studies, British and postcolonial literature, and popular fiction. He has contributed articles to *Literature and History* and *Works and Days*. His essay on Raymond Williams is part of a larger project, tentatively entitled *Fictions of Crime: Clues to Modernity and (Post)Modernism* (forthcoming, University of Illinois Press).

Gauri Viswanathan teaches English and comparative literature at Columbia University. She is the author of *Masks of Conquest: Literary Study and British Rule in India* (New York: Columbia University Press, 1989). A Guggenheim Fellow (1990–1991), she is currently at work on a study of conversion and cultural change in British colonialism.

356

Index

Index

Index

Index

Index